THE NOTORIOUS MRS. CLEM

THE NOTORIOUS
MRS. CLEM
MURDER AND MONEY IN THE GILDED AGE

Wendy Gamber

Johns Hopkins University Press   *Baltimore*

2 4 6 8 9 7 5 3 1

Johns Hopkins University Press
2715 North Charles Street
Baltimore, Maryland 21218-4363
www.press.jhu.edu

Library of Congress Cataloging-in-Publication Data

Names: Gamber, Wendy, 1958– author.
Title: The notorious Mrs. Clem : murder and money in the Gilded Age /
   Wendy Gamber.
Description: Baltimore, Maryland : Johns Hopkins University Press, 2016. |
   Includes bibliographical references and index.
Identifiers: LCCN 2015036004 | ISBN 9781421420202 (hardcover : alk. paper) |
   ISBN 9781421420219 (electronic) | ISBN 1421420201 (hardcover : alk. paper) |
   ISBN 142142021X (electronic)
Subjects: LCSH: Clem, Nancy E. | Women murderers—Indiana—Biography. |
   Murder—Indiana—Case studies. | Crime—Indiana—History—19th century. |
   Indiana—History—19th century.
Classification: LCC HV6248.C468 G36 2016 | DDC 364.152/3092—dc23
   LC record available at http://lccn.loc.gov/2015036004

A catalog record for this book is available from the British Library.

Special discounts are available for bulk purchases of this book.
For more information, please contact Special Sales at 410-516-6936
or specialsales@press.jhu.edu.

Johns Hopkins University Press uses environmentally friendly book
materials, including recycled text paper that is composed of at least
30 percent post-consumer waste, whenever possible.

For Ian

CONTENTS

Nancy Clem has been with me for a long time. In the process of researching and writing her story, I've incurred many debts. Stephanie Bower, James H. Madison, and Jocelyn Wills each read an early draft of the entire manuscript. Each, albeit in very different ways, offered just the right mix of encouragement and sharp-edged criticism. I'm also indebted to Alecia P. Long, the reader for Johns Hopkins University Press, whose excellent advice vastly improved the final product.

Numerous friends and colleagues read portions of the manuscript, responded to presentations, or mulled over the mystery of Mrs. Clem with me—some did all three. I thank Judith Allen, Robert Barrows, Darrel Bigham, Mary Blewett, John Bodnar, Ann Carmichael, Claude Clegg, Daniel A. Cohen, the late William B. Cohen, Will Cooley, Thomas Dublin, Ellen Dwyer, Susan Ferentinos, Tamara Gaskell, Richard Godbeer, Michael Grossberg, Hendrik Hartog, Morton Keller, Pamela Walker Laird, Bonnie Laughlin-Schultz, Alan Lessoff, Ed Linenthal, Phyllis Martin, Michael McGerr, Thomas Pegram, Jeanne Peterson, Elyce Rotella, Scott Sandage, Andrew Sandoval-Strausz, Eric Sandweiss, Tara Saunders, Philip Scranton, Kathryn Kish Sklar, Paula Tarankow, Michael Ayers Trotti, Leigh Ann Wheeler, and Mary Yeager. I bumped into Dallett Hemphill at the 2013 Organization of American Historians (OAH) meeting, never realizing it would be the last time I'd see her. I'm glad I had the chance to talk with her about this project—and much else. I'm grateful to audiences at Binghamton University and to those who attended presentations at meetings of the Indiana Association of Historians, the Social Science History Association, and the OAH. Here at Indiana University I've benefited from the wisdom of colleagues at various venues—the Criminal Justice Brownbag seminar, the Gender Studies Colloquium, the Committee of Historians for Intellectual Culture, and the U.S. History Workshop.

I owe considerable gratitude to two indefatigable research assistants. Peter Rowley diligently searched predigital versions of various Indianapolis newspapers. Susan Ferentinos devoted her characteristic energy and persistence to the task of locating trial transcripts, deeds, and lawsuits.

This book could never have been completed without the able assistance of librarians and archivists. I thank the staffs of the Indiana Office of Supreme Court Records, the Marion County Courts, and the Indiana State Library, especially former newspaper librarian John Selch, whose enthusiasm sustained my early interest in Mrs. Clem, and Indiana Division librarians Monique Howell and Justin Davis, who cheerfully tracked down hard-to-find newspaper articles and illustrations. Anyone who researches the history of the Midwest knows that the Indiana Historical Society is a marvelous place to work. I owe particular thanks to Leigh Darbee, former curator of the IHS's printed collections, who generously shared her notes on the Young murders with me, and Nadia Kousari, who provided last-minute help with images. Current and former staff at the Indiana State Archives, including Stephen Towne and Michael Vetman, unearthed prison records, legal appeals, and military rosters. Jennifer Capps, Vice President of Curatorship and Exhibition at the Benjamin Harrison Presidential Site, offered expert advice on photographs and a wealth of research materials. Tom Davis, Crown Hill Cemetery tour developer, arranged access to Nancy Clem's death and burial records. Thomas Hamm, Curator of the Quaker Collection and Director of Special Collections, Earlham College, answered my questions about Albert Patton's short-lived academic career. Indiana University librarians, as always, proved indispensable. I'm especially appreciative of the much-needed help of GIS librarian Theresa Quill and digital imaging specialist Caitlyn Smallwood.

A Director's Grant from the Indiana Historical Society supported this project in its earliest stages. I thank former History Department chair Peter Guardino and Larry Singell, Dean of Indiana University's College of Arts and Sciences, for providing more recent research support through the Robert F. Byrnes Endowment.

The professionalism, efficiency, and artistry of the people who constitute the village of Johns Hopkins University Press continue to amaze me. Special thanks are due to Robert J. Brugger for his longtime encouragement of this project and to Elizabeth Demers for enthusiastically taking it on. Catherine Goldstead, Isla Hamilton-Short, Kimberly Johnson, Kathryn Marguy, and Juliana McCarthy shepherded this book through its various stages as if it were their own.

Glenn Perkins's virtuoso copyediting improved my prose, and his eagle eye saved me from numerous errors. I'm thrilled once again to be working with Jim O'Brien, the best indexer on the planet.

I'm grateful to my family—Michael Gamber, Claudia August, Margaret and Gordon Byers—for their love and encouragement. I thank Ian Byers-Gamber for taking photographs, making the maps, and for so much more. And, of course, nothing would be possible without Tim Byers.

Portions of this book appeared in slightly different form in "The Notorious Mrs. Clem: Class, Gender, and Criminality in Gilded Age America," *Journal of the Gilded Age and Progressive Era* 11, no. 3 (July 2012): 313–343, and "The Cold Spring Tragedy: Murder, Money, and 'Women's Business' in the Gilded Age," in *American Public Life and the Historical Imagination*, ed. Wendy Gamber, Michael Grossberg, and Hendrick Hartog (Notre Dame, Ind.: University of Notre Dame Press, 2003), 113–138.

THE NOTORIOUS MRS. CLEM

Prologue

Saturday, September 12, 1868, was a beautiful day in central Indiana. Apart from a brief afternoon shower, the weather was sunny and the temperature "unusually warm"—the sort of day that encouraged city dwellers to make country excursions. Cold Spring, on the west bank of the White River just a few miles northwest of Indianapolis, was a logical destination. Thirteen-year-old Millie Locke and her eleven-year-old brother, Seymour, went fishing there that afternoon with their father, Major Erie Locke. (The senior Locke was a wealthy Indianapolis paper manufacturer, but like all men who had served in the recently concluded Civil War, he retained his military title even though he had long mustered out of the army.) The fish weren't biting, and the children grew bored. They asked their father if they might go wading. Locke checked his watch and decided that since it was only four o'clock, there was time enough for a swim before they headed back to the city.[1]

From their vantage point in the water, just downriver from their father, Millie and Seymour could see a man and a woman on the nearby shore resting in the shade of a willow tree. Because wisps of smoke rose above the reclining woman, they assumed that she was smoking a pipe. Millie and Seymour—hardly the sheltered children of nostalgic imagination—thus concluded that the pair constituted a "lewd" couple, a reasonable assumption even in the absence of a pipe-smoking female, since prostitutes and their clients as well as respectable people like the Lockes frequented Cold Spring. A little later, Andrew Locklear, an African American farm laborer, observed the couple, still reclining, as he passed by. So, too, did young Robert Bowman, who was rounding up his family's cows on the other side of the river. Neither thought anything of it; Bowman supposed he saw a fisherman napping beside his fire. But early the next morning, he noticed that the smoke remained and that the man had not moved. He crossed the river and found two dead bodies. He alerted his father and brother, who rushed to the city to inform the authorities.[2]

Word spread rapidly; a crowd of curious Indianapolis residents accompanied the Marion County coroner to the scene. There they confronted a gruesome sight. Once again, the Civil War provided a frame of reference. A reporter for the *Indianapolis Sentinel* described "a picture of grisly horror

JACOB YOUNG,   NANCY JANE YOUNG.

The victims, Jacob and Nancy Jane Young. This image, probably based on a photograph, appeared in a trial pamphlet. Publications of this sort typically featured gruesome illustrations of female murder victims, who were often prostitutes. Nancy Jane Young's reputation as a "pure [C]hristian woman" probably discouraged lurid visual depictions of her disfigured corpse. *The Cold Spring Tragedy* (Indianapolis: A. C. Roach, 1869), following p. 20, courtesy of the Herman B Wells Library, Indiana University.

seldom seen except upon the battle field."[3] A good part of the man's face had been blown off, apparently by the shotgun that lay a few feet away. Flies buzzed around his body, spiders and black beetles crawled about his wound. Even those who had grown accustomed to the numerous "grisly horrors" that accompanied the nation's first modern war found the second discovery disturbing. The smoke came not from a pipe or a fisherman's fire but from the smoldering body of a "small, delicate woman." She had been badly burned from the chest down, so badly that her intestines were exposed, the flesh on her thighs burned away, and the bones partially reduced to powder. ("**BURNED TO A CRISP**," the *Indianapolis Journal* would bluntly put it.)[4]

A member of the crowd that gathered on the sandbar identified the pair as Mr. Jacob Young and his wife, Nancy Jane, "highly respectable residents of Indianapolis." The local press quickly heaped praise on the deceased. The Republican *Journal* described Jacob Young as "an honest, industrious, thrifty citizen, respected among business men for his uprightness, and honored among his neighbors for his exemplary social qualities." The Democratic *Sentinel* called him a "sober, industrious, shrewd, and responsible business man." Eyewitnesses supposed that they had stumbled onto a tragic instance of murder-suicide, a case of a jealous, enraged, or otherwise unhappy husband who had killed his wife and then himself. Testimony before a hastily convened coroner's jury cast doubt on that theory. According to Lizzie Henry, the Youngs' domestic servant, the couple "lived together peaceably and contentedly," an opinion with which their twelve-year-old niece, Mary Belle, concurred. More convincingly, the position of Jacob Young's body relative to the shotgun argued against suicide. So, too, did the discovery during her autopsy that Nancy Young had been shot with a different weapon—a pistol—and dealt a blow to the head with a blunt instrument.[5] The jury quickly concluded that both husband and wife were victims of foul play.

An additional revelation further inflamed a public reeling from the news that two "harmless and respected people" had been murdered. Returning to the crime scene a day later, investigators discovered a key piece of evidence, miraculously preserved given the general pandemonium that had prevailed—a footprint that did not match the shoes of the victims, "the print of a neat little lady's gaiter in the yielding soil." "A woman in such a crime," the *Journal* lamented. "Who *could* she be?"[6]

CHAPTER ONE

New Year's Day

New Year's was a time for reflection, a day to settle one's debts, an opportunity to begin anew. Like their counterparts elsewhere, Indianapolitans marked January 1, 1868, with celebrations large and small. Churches hosted "holiday festivals." The city's African American citizens commemorated the fifth anniversary of Emancipation with orations and a parade. Newsboys, as was their custom, recited speeches to subscribers, hoping that "heavy pockets" would be their reward. A German immigrant "got slightly elated with '65 wine." The owner of a wheel-making factory gave his workmen "some very fatherly and heartfelt advice," urging them "to avoid intoxication" and—given the hazards posed by newly acquired machinery—purchase life insurance. And William and Margaret Abrams held a party.[1]

Bill and Maggie, as family and friends knew them, had much to celebrate. Only months earlier they had been poor, barely scraping by on a carpenter's wages. Now they lived comfortably, the proud owners of a home in a respectable neighborhood on Indianapolis's near northeast side. The gathering they convened seems to have been an intimate one, uniting people connected by long-standing communal and familial ties. Like their hosts, the assembled guests were "Kentuckians," the colloquial term Indianapolis residents applied to upland southerners regardless of their state of origin. Like their hosts, almost all had come of age in Pike Township, a rural community some 20 miles northwest of the city.[2]

Those in attendance included Matthew Hartman, his wife, Rebecca, and his sister, Nancy. Matthew's and Nancy's younger brother, Silas, was probably there as well, for Syke, as he was known, was one of Bill's oldest friends. Also present were Jacob and Nancy Jane Young. On New Year's Day in 1868, at Bill and Maggie Abrams's house at 419 N. East Street, the Youngs first encountered the woman who would become known as the notorious Mrs. Clem.[3]

■ ■ ■

There was nothing notorious about Nancy Clem that winter's day. To the contrary, she was charming—"a beautiful, fascinating, and clever woman" possessed of a "winning personality." Blue-eyed, fair-skinned with auburn hair, the thirty-five-year-old Clem was vivacious and sociable, her good looks marred only by a "somewhat sunken" mouth (like most nineteenth-century Americans who had reached middle age, she had lost teeth).[4]

Apart from her conviviality and beauty Clem was utterly ordinary, a typical resident of the Hoosier state, her life a typical Indianapolis story. Born in the North Carolina Piedmont, she had moved to Indiana as a child, along with her parents, three sisters, and four brothers, part of a larger migration of upcountry southerners in search of fertile land and richer prospects. Clem's father, a "plain farmer" named John Hartman, was among the earliest white settlers of Pike Township, territory only recently ceded to the United States by Delaware, Miami, and Potawatomi peoples. Despite being "one of the best known and most highly respected of Central Indiana's pioneers," he was, like many early-nineteenth-century Hoosiers, illiterate, a man who signed his will with "his mark."[5]

Nancy, too, possessed only minimal literacy, but book learning counted for little in rural Indiana, especially among the white Kentuckians who dominated Pike Township. Labor did, and in this respect wives and daughters were as valuable as sons. Women cultivated gardens that fed their families; they preserved fruits, vegetables, and meats; they cooked, cleaned, and sewed. They sheared sheep, processed their wool, and spun it into yarn. They milked cows and tended chickens; they churned the butter and collected the eggs that purchased the things Indiana farmers could not grow—coffee and tea, needles and nails, hammers and hoes. This was the life and livelihood that Nancy's three older sisters, each of whom married a prosperous farmer, opted to pursue. Nancy did not follow in their footsteps. But if she rejected a life of rural drudgery, she would retain a keen sense of her economic worth.[6]

In 1849, at the age of nineteen (some would say she was only fifteen), Nancy Hartman married twenty-four-year-old William Patton. "An excellent man," Patton was a plasterer, part-time schoolteacher, and almost certainly a friend of her brother Matthew, a fellow plasterer.[7] Marrying William, Nancy must have realized, meant leaving Pike Township, for her brother and her soon-to-be husband had already acquired property in Indianapolis. The city was a logical destination for men who made their livings in the building trades. "Houses are going up in every direction," the editor of the *Rushville (Ind.) Republican* exclaimed—or, rather, supposedly exclaimed; the *Indianapolis Journal* reprinted his remarks "in nearly his own words": "Almost everywhere we saw improvements in progress, or preparation for improvement hereafter." The same improvements that bedazzled a small-town editor encouraged men such as Patton and Hartman to seek their fortunes in the state's fledgling capital. And so they did, contributing to the city's progress by erecting nearly identical houses on the lot they had purchased on North Alabama Street, situated just inside the mile square that marked Indianapolis's original boundaries. William and Nancy Patton settled into one; Matthew and his new wife Rebecca, into the other.[8]

Like most booster accounts, the *Republican* and its *Journal*-istic collaborators exaggerated. Indianapolis, to be sure, was growing by leaps and bounds, a fact contemporaries attributed to the recently completed Madison-Indianapolis Railroad. Still, the city the Hartmans and the Pattons encountered was nothing more than a good-sized town, numbering only a little more than eight thousand souls. Designed by architect Alexander Ralston, who had assisted Pierre L'Enfant in planning Washington, D.C., "the City of Indiana," a name one local historian termed "unique, dignified, prophetic," was attractively platted, with a central circle and diagonal avenues that overlay a basic grid. In the early 1850s, however, it had yet to realize its potential. Practical-minded early residents had chopped down centuries-old trees, divesting the scenery of any natural beauty. Pigs, cows, and sheep ambled through the carefully delineated, albeit muddy, streets; only Washington Street, the main commercial thoroughfare, had been graded and graveled. The fate of "Governor's Circle," the site of a never-occupied governor's mansion razed in 1857, was indicative.[9]

In other respects, "Nopolis," as upland southerners pronounced it, left much to be desired. It had only recently adopted "something like a regular city government of a mayor and Council" and was only just acquiring the sorts of institutions that befitted a state capital and "civilized" city. A courthouse, a two-story structure built in the "southern style," had been erected in 1824, replacing the log cabin that housed previous proceedings. A Female Collegiate Academy had been founded in 1843; insane, blind, and widows and orphans asylums and a "Deaf and Dumb School" followed soon after. Other amenities would have to wait. A public school system waited until 1853; yet another year elapsed before Indianapolis established a police force. Not until 1859 did a professional fire department replace a series of competing volunteer fire companies (among them the Invincibles, the Rovers, the Union Company, the O.K. Bucket Company, and the Young America Company). Streetcars began operation only in 1860. Until then, residents who lacked horses and carriages had to hire conveyances or brave the "aboriginal mud."[10]

If they often waded through city mud, the Hartmans and the Pattons had shaken much of the country dust from their feet. For people raised in log cabins, they lived in considerable style. Their houses, built on a variation of the Greek Revival design, featured large plate-glass windows, sitting rooms, and parlors; the Hartmans (and, perhaps too, the Pattons) eventually acquired a piano. The two couples apparently practiced the sexual self-control that was fast becoming synonymous with urban middle-class identity. Nancy and Matthew came from a family of eleven children; *their* children had no siblings. And their children would be literate. Albert Patton, unlike his mother, received the rough equivalent of a high school education; Mary Hartman, known as "Pet," was at the very least a grammar-school graduate. Both families joined the North Street Methodist Episcopal Church, a brick and steepled structure that bore little resemblance to the log cabin meeting houses of Pike Township.[11]

By the late nineteenth century, Indianapolis's New England elite would consider people like the Hartmans and Pattons "white trash" and condemn the "relics of barbarism"—belief in witchcraft, adherence to superstitions, and use of folk remedies—white southerners brought with them. Such opinions would eventually push many "old settlers" of upland southern origins to the social margins. But in the 1850s and 1860s these sorts of disparagements were more a matter of wishful thinking; little besides speech patterns distinguished middling Kentuckians from their Yankee neighbors. North Alabama Street was a case in point. A remarkably cosmopolitan, if entirely white, neighborhood, it accommodated New Englanders, New Yorkers, southerners, Ohioans, Germans, lace-curtain Irish, and native Hoosiers. Tradespeople rubbed elbows with professionals; a carpenter, a cooper, a teacher, a minister, and a lawyer all lived within shouting distance of the Pattons and Hartmans. In 1861 up-and-coming attorney and future president of the United States Benjamin Harrison would take up residence just a few houses down and across the street. As Harrison's presence suggests, the Hartman-Patton homes stood in firmly respectable territory, literally and figuratively removed from the city's south-of-Washington-Street slums—Irish Hill, Vinegar Hill, Vinegar Slip, and Dumptown.[12]

In time, education, literacy, and genteel refinement would trump craft training and skilled housewifery. But even into the 1860s, distinctions that would later carry great weight meant little. What mattered most was not so much whether one performed "head work" or "hand work," wore a white collar or leather apron, but whether one was "respectable." Respectability, in turn, was an elastic social category, equal parts comportment, economic success, and residential stability. Homeowners and churchgoers, industrious men and women of steady habits, the Pattons and Hartmans were undeniably respectable. As the years passed, their claim to middle-class membership only deepened. Matthew Hartman, one observer would note in 1868, "has resided in this city for seventeen years" and enjoyed a "reputation . . . without spot or blemish." His sister Nancy "mov[ed] in respectable society." Some people even described her as "very prominent."[13]

■ ■ ■

William Patton died in late September 1857, at the age of thirty-six, leaving behind Nancy and six-year-old Albert. We have no means of learning the cause of his demise. If the "fall sickness" (the vernacular term for malaria) were to blame, such occurrences were far too common to be noted in the city's newspapers. If his death resulted from accident—a fall from a ladder, a careless dash across a busy street—the incident must not have been spectacular enough to merit mention. Neither was the predicament Nancy Hartman Patton faced in his absence. Widowhood was common, even expected, in nineteenth-century America. Nancy was luckier than many women forced to don widow's weeds, for William seems to have been a man of foresight. He left behind two properties, the house on North Alabama, in which she and her son continued to reside, and a second dwelling that generated an annual rent of a couple hundred dollars.[14]

Still, $200 did not amount to much, even in the 1850s. William Patton's earnings were bound to have been diminished during his final months of life in 1857, a depression year. Understandably, Nancy sought additional income. She did what most women in her circumstances would have done: she took in boarders. "Think she had four at one time," Matthew would recall. Like most such women, she did not describe her dwelling as a "boarding-house"; to do so potentially placed her in the same socially suspect category as servants, washerwomen, and prostitutes. Patton was not the sort of person to risk her reputation. Her neighbors in all likelihood considered her a good Christian woman.[15]

According to some accounts, Patton found an additional way to make ends meet, loaning out money William left her and charging interest. At any rate, she fared well during her widowhood, acquiring a reputation for "industry and frugality." She did not remain a widow long. Simple demographics were in her favor; although Indianapolis had long passed its "pioneer" period, men still outnumbered women. Patton, moreover, had many charms. She was a careful manager of household finances, an asset that surpassed beauty in many men's eyes. She was also attractive and exceedingly personable. Twenty-eight years old at the time of her second marriage, she passed for a woman several years younger. The man she married on January 11, 1859, was a twenty-nine-year-old bachelor, William Franklin Clem. It is likely they first met across the counter at Clem & Brother's grocery, only a short walk from her Alabama Street home.[16]

We do not know why Nancy Patton, a woman likely to have many suitors, chose Franklin Clem. Perhaps Frank was charming; perhaps he was handsome (he was tall and had a black beard); perhaps he was kind. A Virginian by birth, he presumably spoke in the same "peculiar drawl" that distinguished his brother Aaron's manner of speaking—"peculiar," that is, to the ears of the displaced New Englanders who would later chronicle the city's history. As far as money was concerned, Frank Clem had all the makings of an ideal husband. Like his brother, whose reputation for fair dealing earned him the nickname "Honest Aaron," Frank was a "careful trader" and "enterprising young man" who "attend[ed] closely to [his] business." A correspondent for the credit-reporting firm R. G. Dun & Co. described him as a man of "gd habits," standard shorthand for a range of characteristics—punctuality, thrift, and sobriety—nineteenth-century analysts associated with business success. While the reporter cautioned that "they do not have much property out[side] of the business," all evidence indicates that the Clem brothers earned perfectly respectable, if not astronomical, profits, in the 1860s reporting annual incomes between $400 and nearly $500 apiece (nearly $100,000 in 2014 dollars).[17]

Nancy Patton undoubtedly knew that good habits carried a person only so far in the volatile economy of the mid-nineteenth century. That line of reasoning may explain the ante-nuptial contract that gave her "control of . . . her own business affairs." People would later argue over whose idea the agreement had been, whether it furnished evidence of Frank's "manly" consideration or Nancy's grasping avarice. Nancy certainly exercised no more than her legal right. Married women's property acts passed by the Indiana legislature in 1852 and 1853 granted her control over any property she possessed prior to her marriage, but continuing to do business on her own account required a special arrangement. Certainly this was a sensible decision for an enterprising widow to make; without it, anything she earned belonged to Frank. If, as evidence suggests, she was already experimenting with investment schemes, she probably decided her "business affairs" were worth protecting. Perhaps Nancy had already become, as she would later be described, "a monomaniac on the question of money."[18]

■ ■ ■

Nancy Clem's father, John Hartman, was a respected member of his community, so devout a Methodist that strangers mistook him for a preacher. Nor did he neglect his earthly estate. He acquired 140 acres, holdings that placed him in the middle ranks of Pike Township society and provided his family a comfortable sufficiency. But if Hartman fulfilled his role as provider, he failed a second test of upcountry manhood, for he died before he was able to settle his six sons, two of them born after the move to Indiana, on neighboring homesteads of their own. Thus, Silas Hartman, his youngest child, would become a carpenter, not a farmer. He would grow up in the "Hollingsworth neighborhood," not one that bore his name.[19]

Syke came of age a somewhat aimless young man, one who evidently lacked the ambition that inspired his older brother's move to Indianapolis. Still he found plenty of work. The township was growing in the late 1850s and early 1860s albeit far more slowly than the city. So too was the demand for barns, outbuildings, houses, and furniture.[20] Syke had other reasons to stay put. The greater Hollingsworth neighborhood was home, home to his mother, several of his siblings, and numerous aunts, uncles, and cousins. It was home to friends, many of them brother and sister Methodists. The latter included the Abramses, another middling farming family with whom the Hartmans were particularly "intimate." John Abrams—literally a Kentuckian, for he hailed from the Bluegrass State—was one of the "fair and judicious neighbors" called on to appraise John Hartman's personal property when the family patriarch died, in 1841. Abrams's son William was one of Syke's closest friends. Schoolmates and later workmates, they apprenticed together, learning the carpenter's trade. It was a vocation that suited them. Both men were "strongly built"; both sported sandy whiskers. Indeed they looked so much alike that people sometimes mistook them for each other.[21]

■ ■ ■

Jacob Young made his way to Pike Township around 1853, nearly four years
tthew Hartman and Nancy Patton left for Nopolis. His life had al-
n marked by tragedy, for he came from a family plagued by physi-
ental illness. A journalist described his father, a native Virginian,

as a "hopeless lunatic," a fact two successive census takers confirmed by decisively writing "insane" in the column that asked enumerators to note "whether deaf and dumb, blind, insane, idiotic, pauper, or convict." By the late 1860s, all four of his brothers would be dead of consumption. Jacob, too, suffered from poor health. Why he left Lost Creek, Ohio, at the relatively young age of fifteen is not entirely certain, but a mentally unstable parent would have been incentive enough. Why he chose Pike Township is the better question. Americans on the move often selected their destinations with family in mind, but the available evidence suggests that Jacob had few if any Hoosier relations. A sister eventually joined him in Indiana, and one of his brothers lived for a time in Marion County—whether he preceded Jacob or followed him is unknown. There remains the distinct possibility that the tall, sickly adolescent traveled alone, settling in a community of strangers.[22]

Young may have been without family, but he was not long without friends. He soon fell in with Syke Hartman and Bill Abrams. He, too, became a carpenter's apprentice. "I have always been on intimate terms with Mr. Young," Abrams would recall. "We learned our trade together." Proud of his accomplishments and confident in his skills, Young told a census taker in the summer of 1860 that he was a "master carpenter." Here he revealed a penchant for deception or perhaps wishful thinking. The propertyless twenty-three-year-old, who boarded with a poor farming family, was master of nothing—not even his own household.[23]

Perhaps it is understandable that Young stretched the truth, for only a few months later he would be a married man. His bride, Nancy Jane Case, was also a relative newcomer. Born and raised nearby, in Hendricks County just to the west, "Janey," like her future spouse, evidently arrived in Pike Township unaccompanied by kin. Orphaned at the age of ten, she came to Pike to live with Jonas Case. Twenty-five years her senior, Jonas was Janey's uncle or cousin (available evidence does not allow us to discern which). He was *old* enough to be her father, but the various writers who later identified him thus seem to have been mistaken—at least in the literal biological sense. Whatever paternal affection he felt for his poor relation, he expected her to make her own way. At age nineteen, Nancy Jane was lodging with another Pike Township family, described by a census enumerator as "serving." It was while serving at farmer James Raveal's that she met her future husband. Fragmentary and not altogether reliable evidence suggests that Jonas Case disapproved of the match.[24]

Bill Abrams had also gone a-courting. His intended was Margaret Jones, the daughter of a landless farmer from Kentucky. Bill had known Maggie most of his life; she had been brought up by Syke Hartman's older sister, Anna McCurdy, who had taken her in after her parents moved to an adjoining township. By 1860, at age twenty-two, Maggie, like Janey Case, was a live-in servant, employed by one of the ubiquitous Hollingsworths. She married Bill Abrams on the same day, September 18, 1860, as Nancy Jane Case married Jacob Young in a ceremony that affirmed the bonds of friendship.[25]

Whether they wed against their families' wishes or with their families' blessings—a determination surviving evidence does not allow us to make—the two couples snubbed tradition. In an era when most rural Americans married at home, joined in wedlock by a local preacher, William and Margaret and Jacob and Nancy Jane selected a more stylish and secular venue, the Spencer House hotel in Indianapolis—their excursion made possible by the newly graded Lafayette road. It was a choice, perhaps, that foreshadowed their future aspirations.[26]

■ ■ ■

War disrupted any plans the newlyweds and their bachelor friend, Syke Hartman, might have made. Bill Abrams deposited his savings with two township farmers, loaning them the money "on interest." Then, in 1862, he enlisted in the Union army, moved his wife to the city, and joined the Seventy-Ninth Indiana Infantry. He saw action, among other places, at the bloody Battle of Stone's River in Murfreesboro, Tennessee, and the siege of Atlanta. Though he never advanced beyond the rank of private, his performance under fire earned him a commendation for distinguished service—a record that would serve him well in later years.

Jacob Young tried to enlist alongside his friend but was rejected, probably on medical grounds. He and Janey settled near Zionsville, just to the north of Pike Township in a neighboring county. He gave up carpentering to become a traveling salesman who peddled "Buckeye reapers and mowers" to farmers in the surrounding hinterlands. This career change, almost certainly a concession to his declining health, suited Young, a man who possessed "exemplary social qualities." He knew a good opportunity when he saw one. Reapers and mowers were quickly replacing men—the fathers, sons, and hired hands who left their farms for the battlefield.[27]

Silas Hartman left, but not for soldiering. Drafted in 1864, he chose to "skedaddle" rather than serve, fleeing to Canada for the duration of the conflict. Perhaps, as his detractors later claimed, he was a coward; perhaps as the son of North Carolinians, he was too much of a Confederate sympathizer to fight for the Union. If Bill Abrams's wartime bravery later worked to his benefit, Syke Hartman's decision to dodge the draft helped to seal his eventual fate.[28]

Matthew Hartman and Frank Clem, both eligible for conscription, had the good fortune not to be called up. Neither did they volunteer. If they harbored feelings of disloyalty, as some southerners did, they kept their opinions to themselves; the enumerator who compiled the city's enlistment rolls failed to write "Secesh" beside their names—as he did for known Confederate sympathizers. Apart from participants in a foiled plot to liberate Confederate prisoners, true "Secesh" were few and far between in a heavily Republican city. But as the war wore on, plenty of Indianapolitans, most of them Democrats, opposed what they saw as government tyranny at both federal and state levels. They opposed as well the Lincoln administration's shifting goals—from a war to save the Union to a war to end slavery.[29]

Matthew Hartman, a Democrat, presumably hewed to his party's line. No evidence survives, however, to tell us where Frank Clem stood, whether he was a Republican like his brother or a Democrat like his brother-in-law. No letters, diaries, or newspaper accounts reveal whether he proudly wore butternut pins or copper pennies—symbols of opposition to the war—or whether he was a dyed-in-the-wool Unionist who simply preferred to avoid military service. Whatever their sectional loyalties, it seems safe to say that neither Frank Clem nor Matthew Hartman was eager to shed his blood for the Union.[30]

Hartman and Clem escaped the battlefield, but the war nevertheless wrought changes in their lives. Tensions between Republicans and Democrats, abolitionists and proslavery zealots, war enthusiasts and peace proponents, volunteers and shirkers infused public commentary and private conversations, "sever[ing] old friendships and social relations." We cannot know if the residents of North Alabama Street exchanged angry words or hostile glances. But if actions speak louder than words, the neighborhood, like the larger city, was divided. Commissioned a second lieutenant, Benjamin Harrison marched off to war while his neighbors stayed behind.[31]

War transformed the City of Indiana. A newly erected federal arsenal employed nearly seven hundred workers, among them one hundred women and girls who made cartridges. Other sorts of manufactories multiplied— woolen mills, meat-packing plants, railroad shops, rolling mills, foundries.

Indianapolis was the recruitment and training center for the majority of the state's 169 regiments; already a railroad hub, it also served as a major transport center for Union troops. Soldiers filled the city. At one point more than twelve thousand occupied the twenty-four training camps located in Indianapolis and its vicinity; others passed through as they made their ways to battlefields and returned for furloughs. "Saloons and evil resorts," as well as more legitimate businesses, profited from their presence. As in New York, Philadelphia, Cincinnati, and elsewhere, reports of crime and disorder increased. In Indianapolis the impression that "the streets were not safe" prompted a ban on the sale of alcohol to soldiers, one undoubtedly honored in the breach.[32]

The unsettling presence of a multitude of strangers, not all of them military men, added to Indianapolitans' general sense of chaos and confusion. Many of the people who flocked to the city to join the army, bid farewell to menfolk, or seek employment were transients, people whose sojourns could be measured in days, weeks, or months. But a good proportion of them came to stay. As one local historian observed, by the end of the Civil War "much more than half the population were new-comers." He did not exaggerate; population more than doubled during the war decade, from just under nineteen thousand in 1860 to over forty-eight thousand in 1870. "The quiet town with its simple life was gone forever," he noted somewhat wistfully, "and in its place was the bustling city with new ideas, new aspirations, new ways."[33]

■ ■ ■

Bill Abrams was one of the bustling city's many "new-comers." Mustered out of the army in August 1865, he chose to remain in Indianapolis instead of returning to his country home. Maggie was already there, one of the many soldiers' wives who had moved to the city in search of work. Perhaps she had relied on assistance from the various benevolent associations organized to aid destitute and "friendless" women. Probably not, for Bill maintained that she "kept herself during the war." Able-bodied veterans expected no such charity. "Brought up, as our young men of the North are, to industry and self-exertion, you will find it no inconvenience or hardship to exchange the discomforts of camp and the vicissitudes of military life for the peaceful avocations of the citizen," read the departing order issued by Major General D. S. Stanley, the commander of the Fourth Army Corps, in which Bill Abrams served.[34]

Abrams had survived a brutal war physically unscathed, although he would attribute the rheumatism that later afflicted him to the hardships induced by military service.[35] Now, like countless others, he faced the uncertain transition to civilian life. Whatever "industry and self-exertion" he possessed did not bring him prosperity. For the time being he stuck to his trade, city directories alternately listing him as a "carpenter" and a "journeyman carpenter." The latter designation proved more accurate, for in carpentry at least, Bill Abrams never became his own boss. While there was plenty of work to be had in a rapidly growing city, men like Abrams faced plenty of competition from fellow "new-comers" and from subcontractors who disrupted the traditional pathways by which journeymen became masters. Nor did Abrams—universally described as "poor"—have the capital with which to outfit his own shop. He worked for a time at a window-sash factory and then for Henry W. Hildebrand, a Prussian-born master carpenter, who would later become the proprietor of a successful lumberyard. Bill, Maggie, and their daughter, Cora (born in 1866), lived in two rented rooms.[36]

"Affable" in manner, persuasive in conversation, Abrams would soon exchange manual labor for a job that offered greater rewards. Much the same could be said of his old friend Jacob Young. Young, too, decided to relocate to Indianapolis, taking a job as the driver of a delivery wagon for the hardware store run by Robert Dorsey, the man for whom he had sold reapers and mowers. Perhaps because his health had worsened, perhaps because he displayed a talent for numbers, Young was promoted to clerk during his final year in Dorsey's employ. But in 1867 he quit the store, though he continued to do business with his former boss. "That fellow made me six thousand dollars the last year," Dorsey marveled to an acquaintance.[37]

Syke Hartman returned to Pike Township when the war ended, but not for long. In the late summer or early fall of 1867, when he was around twenty-nine or thirty, he joined a larger exodus of rural folk who left the surrounding townships of Marion County for Indianapolis. His sister Nancy and brother Matthew were by now "old residents" of the city. Even his mother, "Grandmother Hartman," spent a considerable portion of the year in Nopolis, dividing her time between her children's two houses on North Alabama Street.[38] Syke settled in at Nancy's, where she let him board "free of charge." He stopped working; rumor had it that his occupation was "watching the corners." According to his older brother his health was poor. Syke, Matthew explained, had developed "a sort of a cough." Less sympathetic observers believed him an able-bodied loafer rather than a tubercular semi-invalid. An apparently confirmed bachelor, he freely partook of the pastimes postwar Indianapolis had to offer. He spent his money "in ways not at all reputable," frequenting saloons, beer gardens, dance halls, and, by some accounts, brothels.[39]

■ ■ ■

The 1868 New Year's party reunited old friends—Bill and Maggie Abrams, Jacob and Janey Young, and (in all likelihood) Syke Hartman. Matthew Hartman and his sister, Nancy Clem, renewed their acquaintance with their hosts, who in turn introduced them to the Youngs.

It must have been comforting to reconstitute the old Hollingsworth neighborhood in a city remade by war. Yet if the people who congregated at the Abramses' shared a common background, their wartime experiences potentially divided them. Sparks might fly at a gathering that included a courageous Union veteran, a would-be volunteer, a draft dodger, and a man who had chosen not to fight. Evidently they did not; by all accounts the get-together was a pleasant and congenial affair. In its own small way, then, the Abramses' party issued a challenge to the Emancipation celebrants who paraded only a few blocks away. New Year's at Bill and Maggie's might be catalogued among the innumerable instances in which white Union supporters and Confederate sympathizers buried the proverbial hatchet, albeit at freedpeople's expense.[40] Chances are the Abramses and their guests rejected lofty symbolism. If Bill Abrams had ulterior motives, they probably had to do with money not politics. Quite possibly, he saw the occasion as an opportunity to do a little business. On New Year's Day his prospects looked bright.

CHAPTER TWO

Business

Jacob Young and Nancy Clem were kindred spirits. Both were charming, outgoing, smart, and persuasive. Contemporary descriptions of Young— a possessor of "exemplary social qualities," a "sober, industrious, [and] shrewd . . . business man"—could just as easily describe Clem, once allowances were made for gender. But in her telling, Clem was especially drawn to Jacob's wife, Nancy Jane. "I got quite intimate with Mrs. Young, as I thought her a very clever woman," she recalled. Clem's tale represents one highly contested version of how her financial transactions with Jacob Young began. If it is true that she did not meet him until January 1868, she was a latecomer to the "ring" she supposedly orchestrated and the scheme she supposedly invented.[1]

Jacob Young had come a long way from Pike Township. He was a man of substance, an upstanding citizen of the City of Indiana. He owned a two-story frame house on East St. Clair Street, where, in the front room, Janey displayed the "parlor ornaments" she fashioned from fossil shells.[2] He hired a domestic servant; now Janey, a former serving girl, had a girl of her own. He purchased a buggy and a fast horse—the nineteenth-century equivalent of a sports car. He took daily afternoon drives in hopes of improving his health. He invested in real estate and the city's "new rolling mill," the White River Iron Works. Economic prosperity and bourgeois respectability translated into modest political success; in the fall of 1867 Young was elected deputy constable, charged with the task of collecting bills from delinquent debtors. He gave every impression of being a "sober, industrious, shrewd, and responsible business man," a "highly respectable resident of Indianapolis."[3]

Not all of Young's recently acquired wealth went to luxuries. He took in his niece, Mary Belle, the daughter of his deceased older brother. He and Janey sought treatment for their own son, Ophir Homer, who had been stricken with "brain fever" and rendered "insane"—or as a census taker later put it, "idiotic." What exactly this meant is not clear. Brain fever was a blanket term that described any number of maladies, ranging from nervousness to mental instability to fever-induced delirium. For some patients the effects were temporary, for others, permanent. Ophir might have inherited his grandfather's disorder; "insanity," like "brain fever," was at best a vague descriptor. Or he might have suffered the consequences of bacterial infection; meningitis and encephalitis, because they cause inflammation of the brain, can lead to mental retardation, cerebral palsy, or both in young children. At some point in 1868 the Youngs sent six-year-old Ophir to an asylum in Philadelphia, possibly the Pennsylvania Training School for Feeble-Minded Children. If so, they chose an institution that promised more specialized treatment than local facilities offered. Whatever the nature of Ophir's affliction, his parents hoped for a cure.[4]

Both his son's condition and his own ill health cast a shadow on Young's good fortune. At the ripe old age of twenty-nine he was making plans for retirement. In the summer of 1868, with "a purpose to abandon . . . business," he made arrangements to buy a 150-acre farm back in Pike Township, enlisting the help of his wife's former employer, James Raveal, who negotiated the terms of sale: $100 per acre. The purchase would have been a fitting capstone to Young's career; owning $15,000 worth of land would have placed the formerly penniless carpenter securely in the upper echelons of township society. Young never got the chance to play gentleman farmer. He failed to complete the transaction.[5]

Sometime in 1867—about the same time that Jacob Young quit Dorsey & Layman's hardware store—Bill Abrams left carpentry and his rented rooms behind. He purchased the house on East Street, only a block or so from Jacob Young's, and "several other pieces of real estate" as well. The residence itself was relatively modest—a one-and-a-half-story frame structure on a long narrow lot with a stable at the rear, but it was a significant improvement over his previous digs. Abrams kept up with the Youngs by becoming the proud owner of a fancy new top buggy and two horses, in addition to other, unnamed "conveniences." He, too, hired a domestic servant, a German girl named Flora Ellerhardt.[6]

Acquaintances remarked that Abrams lived "in style," "extravagantly," and "in leisure and luxury." Some estimated his overall worth at between $25,000 and $30,000, the equivalent of approximately $3 million in today's currency. Yet, one observer marveled, Abrams "did no work." His old friends and neighbors back in Pike Township wondered how he made his living; many "thought he was making money too fast to be engaged in any honest occupation." Frank Clem, "a patient, plodding honest man," also grew suspicious. He and his wife stopped visiting the Abramses, he explained, because "we were afraid he was making money too fast." Little did Frank realize that he spoke for himself.[7]

■ ■ ■

Even if Jacob Young had not possessed "exemplary social qualities," it was only natural that he and his wife would renew their longstanding friendship with Bill and Maggie Abrams and add Frank and Nancy Clem and Matthew and Rebecca Hartman to their social circle. All lived within blocks of each other. All attended Trinity Methodist, which had replaced the old North Street Church. All save Frank and Rebecca were from Pike Township. It was not in the least surprising that people with so much in common should visit each other frequently. They did.[8]

Many of these visits combined business with pleasure. And, indisputably, Jacob Young, William J. Abrams, and Nancy Clem were engaged in business. During the summer of 1867, Young and Abrams had abandoned their previous callings to become street brokers, people who trafficked in stocks, mortgages, and, especially, promissory notes without undertaking the burden of keeping a brick-and-mortar establishment.[9] They left behind a world premised on making and selling *things* to inhabit a world of abstractions, a shadowy economic universe defined by the dubious promise of easy money. They initiated a series of complex and mysterious transactions, dealings that reportedly explained their newfound prosperity. Prosecutors would later term Nancy Clem the "mastermind" of the financial scheme. But unless she'd met the Youngs before the New Year's party, the business, which seems to have begun with Young borrowing substantial sums from his former boss, Robert Dorsey, predated her involvement. Clem would later claim that shortly after their initial meeting, Nancy Jane Young "came to me and said she understood I managed my own affairs, and had some money; that her husband was engaged in a business in which he could make a good deal of money, and would pay me a high rate of interest for the use of mine."[10]

While there is reason to doubt that events transpired in quite this way, one fact seems indisputable: Nancy Clem joined Young and Abrams's virtual firm that spring. Soon she was a regular caller at the Young house, usually arriving in the company of her sister-in-law. From the beginning, this business differed from the informal lending in which she supposedly had previously participated. Most important in this respect was its clandestine nature. Clem cautioned Rebecca to keep the visits secret—especially from Frank Clem and Matthew Hartman. Even the path the sisters-in-law trod suggested they did not wish to be seen. The quickest way for Rebecca

1. **266 N. Alabama Street**
   Nancy E. & William Franklin Clem
   William Albert Patton
   Silas Hartman
   Nancy "Grandmother" Hartman*
   Jane Sizemore

2. **262 N. Alabama Street**
   Mathew & Rebecca Hartman
   Mary Alice "Pet" Hartman
   Julia McCarty

3. **299 N. Alabama Street**
   Benjamin & Caroline Scott Harrison
   Russell Harrison
   Mary Harrison
   two servants and four boarders

4. **419 N. East Street**
   William J. & Margaret Abrams
   Cora Abrams
   Flora Ellerhardt

5. **290 E. St. Clair Street**
   Jacob & Nancy Jane Young
   Ophir Homer Young**
   Mary Belle Young
   Lizzie Henry

* divided her time between the Clem and Hartman households
** institutionalized in Pennsylvania at the time of his parents' murder

Nancy Clem's neighborhood, Indianapolis, 1868. The key players in what would become known as "the Cold Spring Tragedy" all lived in close proximity. Clem's future prosecutor, Benjamin Harrison, lived across the street from her, just a few doors down. Map by Ian Byers-Gamber, adapted from *Insurance Maps of Indianapolis* (Sanborn Maps & Publishing Co., 1887) and *Logan's Indianapolis Directory . . . for the Year Commencing July 1, 1868* (Indianapolis: Logan & Co., 1868).

and Nancy to reach the Youngs' would have been to exit through Nancy's front door, turn left and walk the three blocks down North Alabama Street to East St. Clair Street—a route that incidentally would have taken them past Benjamin Harrison's house at the corner of Alabama and North Streets. Instead, they habitually walked out Rebecca's *back* door and through the alley that ran behind their houses, an itinerary that added an extra block to their journey.[11]

The visits themselves assumed the form, but not quite the substance, of conventional social calls. Rebecca chatted with Janey in the front room while Jacob and Nancy briefly consulted behind closed doors. During one such encounter, Ophir—not yet an inmate of the Pennsylvania asylum and perhaps not yet afflicted—fetched paper, pen, and ink from his father's desk. Visits to the Abramses—which continued long after Frank thought they had ended—followed a similar pattern. Rebecca talked with Maggie; Nancy met with Bill for five or ten minutes in another room. And Jacob Young made several calls on Nancy Clem, though he always did so when Frank—renowned for his close attention to business—was away at work.[12]

Secrecy enveloped Clem's business in every detail. Able to read but not to write, she enlisted the help of a neighbor, Madeline Everson, who recorded her transactions in an account book. On these occasions, the two women closeted themselves in Clem's locked parlor, where Clem warned Everson against mentioning their dealings to either Frank Clem or Matthew Hartman. Once Everson suggested that Clem—in her estimation a woman of means and ability—lend money to another neighbor, a grocer named Levi Wright. Clem refused. Wright could not be trusted to keep a secret. "His tongue . . . [is] so long he would blab it before night," she told Everson. "[He] would tell Frank Clem before the sun went down."[13]

■ ■ ■

A lot was going on behind Frank's back. What exactly it entailed—despite the gallons of ink that newspapers would later spill on the subject—remains uncertain. What can be said is that Nancy Clem joined Jacob Young and William Abrams in an enterprise that relied on a frenetic cycle of borrowing and lending. Those who agreed to loan their money were promised, and in many cases realized, high rates of interest. Investors included Young's old boss, Robert Dorsey; William Duzan, Clem's family physician; Arthur L. Wright, the Marion County treasurer; and Stephen Keyes Fletcher, son of one of Indianapolis's first families and another of Dorsey's former employees, now a wealthy farmer. They also included Clem's dressmaker, Ann Hottle, who invested her life savings of $925. Rumors abounded that the venture included some of the city's most prominent businessmen, and indeed it did. With real and personal property valued at over $50,000, Wright was the genuine article; so, too was Fletcher, worth almost three times as much. Yet some of the unnamed bigwigs who supposedly participated probably were

figments of the principals' imaginations, intended to entice potential investors. As Dr. Duzan explained, Clem "represented herself as being engaged in business transactions with a body of responsible gentlemen, by
which she made large profits."[14]

Contemporary commentators never quite understood what this business
aimed to accomplish, but in retrospect it seems clear that it was not exactly
on the up-and-up. Nor, one suspects, was it particularly unique. Schemes of
this sort, large and small, flourished in the post–Civil War years, a time
when it was not always clear which financial practices constituted good
business behavior and which a notorious lack of business ethics. While the
great scandals of the period—Crédit Mobilier, the Whiskey Ring, Tammany
Hall—lay in the future, variations on the Clem-Young-Abrams enterprise
invested the "Gilded Age," the term Mark Twain and Charles Dudley Warner later coined to describe the era, with much of its explanatory power.
Possibly, as some observers hinted, Clem and her associates were counterfeiters. The recent adoption of a uniform national currency renders this
scenario unlikely. No longer could bogus notes supposedly issued by distant
state banks be passed off as legal tender; while Indianapolis had only recently been the site of a major counterfeiting operation, creating realistic fac-
similes of government-issued greenbacks required skills and equipment that
none of the partners possessed.[15] Newspaper reports sometimes described the
Clem-Young-Abrams relationship as a "ring," an expression that in the years
after the Civil War often connoted political corruption. One correspondent
would later term Clem a "female Tweed," likening her to the infamous boss of
the Tammany machine. It proved a faulty comparison. Indianapolis had its
share of corrupt officials, and, indeed, accusations of misconduct would dog
both prosecution and defense in the trials to come. Yet apart from the participation of the county treasurer (who seems not to have abused his official position), Clem, Young, and Abrams's business was political only in the broader
sense that prominent people were rumored to be involved.[16]

Faced with the task of explaining what Clem, Young, and Abrams were
up to, most observers opted for a vaguer label: "confidence game," a catchall
term that described any number of ways that naïve and greedy people might
be separated from their money. "Games" were nothing new; both antebellum and postbellum newspapers in Indianapolis and elsewhere were rife
with reports of swindles confidence men and women perpetrated on trusting individuals. The typical scam involved a transaction between strangers,
the typical perpetrator a city slicker who preyed on a credulous "countryman."

In January 1868, for example, an "old gentleman" from Springfield, Ohio, waiting for a train at Indianapolis's Union Depot met a man who desperately needed money to pay a freight bill. The "sharper" promised a U.S. government bond as collateral, but he vanished before producing it, leaving his victim $150 poorer.[17]

Clem, Young, and Abrams played a somewhat less typical game, for they rarely relied on the credulity of strangers. They occasionally took out loans from banks, with which they repaid investors and each other. For the most part, however, they borrowed from people who knew and trusted them. Duzan had known Clem since she was a child; he had treated her father during his "final illness" and had been the late William Patton's close friend. Hottle's position as Clem's dressmaker placed her on terms of intimacy with her client. Dorsey was Jacob Young's good friend and former boss. Yet the three brokers took care to conceal their relationships to each other, a circumstance made possible in part by the divergent chronological pathways various participants trod from countryside to city and in part by explosive urban growth. By the late 1860s, when its population reached nearly fifty thousand (up from eighteen thousand at the beginning of the decade), Indianapolis was on its way to becoming a city of strangers. Hence, Duzan dealt with Clem but did not know Abrams and was acquainted with Young only as a patient who had visited his office some years earlier. Dorsey did business with Young and knew Abrams but had never met Mrs. Clem. Wright knew Young but neither Abrams nor Clem (despite the fact that he, too, lived on North Alabama Street, only a block away from the Clems).[18]

Such assertions, extracted from reluctant witnesses, should be taken with a grain of salt; many people soon would be eager to distance themselves from Young and his associates. Yet they ring true precisely because they describe an entirely plausible arrangement, one that allowed Clem, Young, and Abrams to hide the fact that each was playing with the same pot of money—most of it Dorsey's and Duzan's. Even as they insisted on secrecy—a strategy that no doubt only enhanced their scheme's allure—they assured wary customers that they were working with people they knew. Clem "represented the persons she was dealing with to be honorable men of my acquaintance, but would not name them," Duzan explained. In short, Clem, Young, and Abrams depended on longstanding personal ties rather than far-flung regional or national networks. At a time when both legitimate and illegitimate business was becoming increasingly centralized, the Clem-Young-Abrams "ring" for the short while it lasted remained a neighborhood affair.[19]

Most likely, the trio carried out what would later become known as a Ponzi scheme, named for Carlo Ponzi, an early-twentieth-century Italian immigrant who bilked hundreds of gullible investors out of millions of dollars. The basic scenario, one more recently employed by Bernard Madoff and Kenneth I. Starr, involved persuading people to lend money in exchange for spectacularly high rates of interest. Sometime perpetrators returned the promised interest but not their clients' principal; in this case the supposed "interest"—unbeknownst to the lender—consisted of a portion of his principal. Sometimes they paid back both principal and interest to initial investors, a ploy intended to establish their credibility and to persuade others—who would not be so fortunate—to join the game. In this rendition, they used newer players' investments to repay their original sponsors. Dr. Duzan, for example, realized a handsome profit in only four months, more than $9,000 (well over $100,000 in today's currency). Ann Hottle, on the other hand, lost everything. Yet it is entirely possible that Duzan's fortunes also were in danger. Sometimes schemers borrowed successively higher amounts from the *same* investor, absconding with his or her money when their profits reached what they judged to be the maximum the investor was willing to lend. Duzan's outlays increased rapidly during the brief period that elapsed between early April and late July. He lent Clem first $500, then $2,000, then $8,000, then $15,000, then $20,000. Had he been able to give her the $22,000 she asked for in September, he might never have seen his money again.[20] Or, as one observer noted, he might have been taken for a buggy ride from which he would never return.[21]

Smooth talkers all, Young, Abrams, and Clem were well suited to their newfound profession. Young made ample use of his "exemplary social qualities." Abrams was "affable" in manner, with a "modulation of . . . voice in conversation" that bespoke "the cultivation so well adapted to sharp trading." Clem was pretty, vivacious—and persuasive. She was already renowned for her business acumen and careful management of her money. Long before she began doing business with Jacob Young, she reportedly turned small profits by loaning out money left her by her first husband. "A woman of brain and of power," a woman supposedly capable of "twirl[ing]" men "around her fingers like ribbons," she had discovered her calling.[22]

The business flourished not only due to collective force of personality but also as a result of the period's general mania for speculation combined with a largely unregulated economy. Indeed, the financial mystery that would come to enthrall residents of Indianapolis and elsewhere had its origins in more innocuous transactions. In an era when banks—especially the un-regulated "private" establishments recent federal legislation ignored—could be less than solidly reliable, friends, relatives, neighbors, and strang-ers routinely lent money to each other and just as routinely charged interest.[23] Ann Hottle complained that before she lent her money to Clem she "was only getting eight per cent"—a rate of interest she received not from a bank but from her brother-in-law. Dissatisfied with his investment strategy, she turned her money over to a Dr. Carter but then quickly trans-ferred her assets to Clem, who promised returns of "ten, fifteen or twenty per cent."[24]

The instrument borrowers and lenders typically employed was the prom-issory note, or IOU. Numerous Indianapolitans bought and sold notes, whether as casual speculators or professional street brokers. "I wish to buy a few thousand dollars' worth of secured notes," the Reverend T. A. Goodwin informed the readers of the *Journal*'s classifieds on Christmas Day in 1868. "Some good notes wanted," read an ad in the *Sentinel*.[25] Notes functioned as an alternative currency, serving the needs of borrowers who did not have cash on hand. The bearer of a note could wait until it came due and seek payment from its original signer, collecting any interest previously speci-fied. Or he could sell it to a third party (a bank, a firm, or an individual) at a "discount," accepting an amount less than its face value in exchange for ready cash. Buyers could realize tidy profits—albeit by assuming significant risk—by "shaving notes," purchasing them at a discount and redeeming them in full—with interest—at a later date. Some condemned the practice, claim-ing with considerable justification that it exploited "needy sellers." "While there *may* be such a thing as honorable and humane note shaving," Henry Ward Beecher would contend in 1871, "there very seldom *is* any such thing." Others invoked longstanding hostilities toward nonproductive labor, pit-ting honest farmers and mechanics against economic parasites who pro-duced nothing of tangible value. According to this philosophy, note shavers, like all breeds of speculators "earned little or nothing by personal labor or exertion." Still others simply denounced speculation in any form as inher-ently exploitative and immoral; references to "the robbers and swindlers of Wall Street" filled nineteenth-century newspaper and magazines. These criticisms did little to disrupt flourishing national and local markets, a fact that made Clem's, Young's, and Abrams's propositions all the more persua-sive, their assurances all the more plausible. "[I am] shaving notes in as hon-orable as way as any bank in the city," Jacob Young told an initially skeptical

Robert Dorsey. It is entirely possible that at this juncture, Young was telling the truth.[26]

■ ■ ■

Terms such as "confidence game," "Cassie Chadwick system" (one local historian's description of the venture), and "Ponzi scheme" denote a degree of intentionality that may—or may not—have been present from the start. We do not know whether Clem, Young, and Abrams deliberately formed a "conspiracy" with the goal of fleecing friends and acquaintances, whether legitimate transactions gradually devolved into fraudulent practices, or whether any of the three principal players intended to cheat each other. Were they co-conspirators? Did one serve as mastermind, the others, subordinates? Was one the innocent dupe of the others? Did they realize the money they borrowed had to be repaid? What does seem clear is that they lent each other the funds from which they dispensed interest to their investors. Subsequent examination of their accounts would reveal a "singular correspondence between the loans obtained of one and the payments made to another."[27]

Still, like much else that would ensue, the mechanics of the game remained a mystery. Ponzi schemes by definition are unsustainable; a successful schemer skipped town before his creditors realized anything was amiss. But Clem and Abrams did not seem to be going anywhere. Young's planned return to Pike Township, had it materialized, would have put very little distance between himself and the people he defrauded. Perhaps the three business partners planned to rely on the power of embarrassment, guessing that gullible empty-handed investors would be too ashamed to demand their money. Or perhaps they were so caught up in the day-to-day frenzy of borrowing and lending other people's money that they yet to consider what would happen when their lenders insisted on being repaid in full. Still, none of the brokers planned to remain in business indefinitely. Young had "a purpose to abandon . . . business." "I may soon Close bisness in the Money line," Abrams wrote in May 1868. Clem, too, seems to have been thinking ahead. In August 1868 she told Duzan that "by the middle of October . . . this business would terminate." She did not say how.[28]

Clem did not purchase a fancy buggy or a fast horse. These were men's playthings. Instead she paid her son's, her mother's, and her late sister's medical bills. She also chose to "repair and refurnish my home." She arranged to have the interior of her Alabama Street house painted and freshly wallpapered. Her own German girl having left her employ the previous spring, she hired a "colored girl" in the late summer of 1868; for a white daughter of a "plain farmer," this perhaps was her crowning social achievement.[29]

Clem's paramount desire, or so she claimed, was "to give my son a collegiate education." Frank thought his stepson should learn a trade, but Nancy had higher ambitions for now sixteen-year-old Albert. Like many midcentury Hoosiers, Frank may have had little use for book learning beyond the practical training—usually acquired on the job—on which tradespeople relied to balance their accounts. To be sure, Frank expressed his opinion on Albert's future somewhat later, after circumstances had changed considerably. But his recommendation was entirely in character for, whatever his merits, Frank seems to have been a bit of a cheapskate. At the very least, he was content to let his wife shoulder financial burdens a husband might have been expected to assume. His assent to the ante-nuptial contract allowing her to "manage . . . her own business affairs" may have signaled admiration for his bride's "great business tact," an "honorable" intention to "marry the woman, not the money," or, quite possibly, both.[30] The arrangement had benefits for Frank as well. It freed him from any obligation to support sick in-laws, bankroll a stepson's postsecondary schooling, or even finance home improvements—266 North Alabama Street, was, in fact, Nancy's house, not his. Any attempt to pin down Nancy's motives—Why would a respectable housewife who lived in relative comfort risk so much by transacting shady business deals?—is destined to end in frustration. Nancy Clem was a woman about whom much would be written but little explained. Frank's possible tightfistedness is as good a theory as any.

Nancy's wishes prevailed. She asked Dr. Duzan to write a letter of reference, attesting to Albert's "satisfactory moral character," to accompany his application to Earlham College, a Quaker institution in eastern Indiana that had recently begun to admit non-Quaker students. College ledgers credit "W. F. Clem" for paying Albert's tuition ($115 per biannual session), although he likely did so with Nancy's money. Possibly wearing new shoes she purchased for the occasion, Nancy escorted Albert to college, boarding the train for Richmond on the morning of September 9, 1868, and returning that very evening.[31] Three days later, Jacob and Nancy Jane Young were dead.

CHAPTER THREE

Cold Spring

ometime during the summer of 1868, Jacob Young had begun to fear for his safety. He paid his taxes under a false name, albeit one that scarcely concealed his identity: Jacob Youngerman. Asked why, he explained that "there were certain persons about town whom he did not want to know that he was making so much money." From whom Young feared harm is not clear. His habit of showing off large packets of cash around town was bound to attract attention. As it turned out, his concern was well founded.[1]

On Friday, September 11, Young withdrew more than $7,500 from Merchants' Bank. That afternoon and the following morning, numerous Indianapolitans encountered him as he flashed his usual wad of cash. Young's Saturday morning errands included a visit to Matthew and Rebecca Hartman's house, where he talked with Nancy Clem. He returned home for dinner, but before he sat down to eat, his servant, Lizzie Henry, observed him put "a roll of money about as thick as my wrist" into his vest pocket. Around 1:30 or 1:45 in the afternoon Young decided to take one of his customary Saturday afternoon buggy drives. His wife asked if she might come along. Jacob replied, "Yes, get ready." Nancy Jane said "she would dress and get ready as soon as she could." She donned a brown checked gingham dress fastened with pearl buttons, worn over a crinoline hoopskirt. A brooch, a straw hat with a veil, a small handbag, and a parasol completed her ensemble. As he hitched his horse to his carriage, Jacob glanced up at the sky and noticed that the weather looked "showery." He called to his niece, Mary Belle, and asked for an umbrella. She fetched it and watched as her aunt and uncle drove away. She never saw them alive again.[2]

■ ■ ■

Bill Abrams recalled his activities that Saturday with "almost painful minuteness." In the morning he put on a straw hat and drove his horse and buggy to the Clem grocery to buy peaches and molasses. When he arrived home, Maggie complained that she had no vinegar. Although Aaron Clem would later testify that his store generally kept vinegar in stock, Bill drove out of his way, "across the canal" to the Fruit House in the western part of the city to procure it, returning around 10:00 a.m. Then he helped Maggie peel and sort the bushel and a half of peaches he had purchased earlier. Donning a "long linen coat" designed to protect his clothing, he next commenced a weekend ritual that would later occupy the owners of horseless carriages: he began washing his buggy, a task interrupted by the news that dinner was on the table. After finishing the job and checking to see how the painters working on his house were coming along, he decided to take a bath, a process that required fetching several bucketsful of water from an outdoor pump. The unnamed "conveniences" the Abramses enjoyed did not include indoor plumbing.

Afterward, Abrams put on clean clothes and declared his intention of going downtown. He stopped to visit Matthew Hartman, but finding him away from home, conversed with Rebecca instead. He chatted with James Brown and his son William, who were hanging wallpaper next door at Mrs. Clem's, and listened to a political debate between the Browns and Julia McCarty (sometimes given as McCarthy), the Hartmans' servant. The Browns were Democrats, he explained, McCarty, a Republican. (Though he had the sort of forehead—"exceedingly full above the eyebrows"—that phrenologically minded nineteenth-century Americans associated with a good memory, Abrams got it backward; the two paper hangers would later write a letter to the *Journal* insisting they were "staunch Republicans.")[3]

At the Clem house, Abrams found Grandmother Hartman and Jane Sizemore, her daughter's "colored girl," peeling peaches; "they remarked that I had come just in time to help them peel, and I sat down and peeled a good many peaches." He chatted again with Rebecca Hartman, who had come over from next door. He eventually made his way back over to the Hartmans. "[Mrs.] Clem then came in and we sat and talked together a little bit, and she went home." Then he listened to fifteen-year-old Pet Hartman play the piano. "I told Pet to play a few good tunes and sing." After "three or four tunes," Abrams left to go downtown, promising Rebecca that he would look for a "definition book" for Pet—a favor he was unable to fulfill since none were to be had in the city until the following week. He paid a butcher's, grocer's, and clothing merchant's bills, then returned home for supper. Afterward he went downtown again to hear a speech at the Masonic Hall.[4]

Or so Bill Abrams told the *Journal*. A reporter for the *Sentinel* lampooned the published account, "which is full of the most startling facts. . . . From all this we infer that Mr. Abrams was somewhat in the peach business," he quipped.[5] But if the other "facts"—startling or otherwise—are hazy, one seems indisputable: on the morning of September 12, 1868, Bill Abrams—or someone who looked very much like him—bought a gun.

■ ■ ■

Apart from rising early, Silas Hartman spent Saturday in a manner befitting his loafer status. He breakfasted with the Clem family. After Frank departed for the grocery and Nancy for various errands, he read the newspaper. Sometime around nine o'clock he went downtown, stopping on the veranda of the Spencer House hotel for about half an hour to chat with his cousin, Cravens Hartman, who was visiting from Missouri. From there he returned home on the street cars, as was his habit, though his sister's house was only a twenty-minute walk away. When he crossed her threshold he found the house abuzz with activity. Paper hangers were working in the front hall, and Nancy was busily stripping the old paper off the sitting room walls. Syke lent a hand, helping with wallpaper removal in one of the upstairs bedrooms. Everyone, including the workmen, broke for dinner, the latter adjourning to their nearby house. Frank Clem, who had arrived home at noon, ate hastily—Saturday was a busy day at the grocery—and left fifteen or twenty minutes later.

With fewer pressing tasks to accomplish, Silas Hartman did not rise from the table until one o'clock, when he decided (this time) to walk downtown. His itinerary included a cigar store, a saloon where he "had a drink with the bartender," and a second visit with his cousin. He returned home in time for the evening meal, carrying a beefsteak he had purchased at a butcher's shop on Massachusetts Avenue. (Syke paid no board but often bought meat for his sister's family as a means of showing appreciation for their hospitality.) As he walked into Nancy Clem's front hall, his brother Matthew, who had just quit work for the day, called him over and asked him to supper. Silas accepted the invitation. At the table Syke was his usual "funny and jovial" self, laughing and joking with his niece Pet. Afterward, he went downtown for a third time. He loitered at "John Hank's store on Wash. Street" for about an hour, then met a friend, a fiddler named Ben Gresh, who suggested they head to "Captain Jacob's dance house on Kentucky Avenue." Syke's aimless comings and goings flouted the purposeful time-conscious behavior of upwardly mobile strivers like his brother and brother-in-law, for whom Saturday was a workday. His choice of pastimes confirmed his "reputation of being rather 'fast.'" Nevertheless, he returned home to the Clem house at the relatively early hour of ten o'clock and went to bed. It had, after all, been a long day.[6]

Sometime on that Saturday afternoon, Silas Hartman decided that he, too, wanted to go for a ride. Having no conveyance of his own, he walked to Drew and Sullivan's livery stable on Pearl Street and rented a horse and buggy. He stopped by the Spencer House to pick up Cousin Cravens and they went for a country drive. They intended to visit Frank Clem's brother-in-law, Chris Lout, but Syke did not know the way, so they settled on an excursion to Lanesville, heading northeast on the Pendleton road. Or so Syke claimed. Other witnesses placed his hired rig moving in the opposite direction, on the road to Pike Township—and Cold Spring.[7]

Never one to be idle, Nancy Clem bustled about that Saturday. Indeed, observers would later contrast her "busy brain" and "keen lively eye" with her younger brother's general listlessness.[8] Before breakfast she walked the two and half blocks to the house of paper hangers James and William Brown to engage their services. She continued on to William H. Roll's carpet, oilcloth, and paper store downtown on Illinois Street to purchase new wallpaper, leaving without making a selection. She returned with her sister-in-law, to be sure she purchased the same pattern as Rebecca's. At home she remained busy. In addition to accomplishing her "general housework," she tore away old wallpaper, oversaw the paper hangers, and supervised her mother and her servant as they canned peaches. She put down carpet in preparation for the coming winter.[9]

After dinner, she prepared to go out. She asked Jane Sizemore to put out a "buff colored" dress and requested her help in "arranging the skirt." She shopped downtown for stockings. She stopped at the post office to collect Albert's first letter home from college, calling at the gentleman's delivery window because Albert had addressed his letter to his stepfather. That evening she read it aloud to her mother, who could not read—at least, as Grandmother Hartman put it, "not to do any good."[10]

The paper hangers found Clem's absence that afternoon puzzling—and frustrating, for they had intended to complete the job at 266 North Alabama Street that day. Clem had insisted on having her house "done up quick," and she repeatedly checked on them during the morning to ensure that work was proceeding. The Browns finished papering the parlor shortly after their return from dinner and turned their attention to the next room, where Nancy and Syke had not quite finished removing all of the old paper. Wondering if they should paper over imperfectly prepared walls, they called for Mrs. Clem. They received no answer. They asked Jane Sizemore and Grandmother Hartman if they knew when their employer would return, and failed to receive a definitive answer. They waited around for half an hour or so, William standing at the back door eating peaches while the women peeled them. At about quarter to three, they gave up and went home.[11]

Lucy Brouse saw her neighbor standing on her porch that evening chatting with her brother Syke. Noting that Clem's face was flushed, she remarked that she must have been working over a hot stove. Clem replied that indeed she had; she had been canning grapes a friend had brought her from the country.[12]

Jane Sizemore would later testify that no grapes had been canned that day.[13]

■ ■ ■

Much of what happened that afternoon at Cold Spring remains a mystery. The sandbar on the riverbank was familiar territory to Jacob and Nancy Jane Young; they had been there many times during their spring and summer of leisure and affluence. Because the day was unusually warm, Jacob doffed his coat, hat, and vest and hung them on a willow branch. Janey strolled on higher ground while her husband walked near the water's edge.[14]

As they sat futilely waiting for the fish to bite, Millie and Seymour Locke saw two women and a man walking on the bluff above them. Shortly thereafter, around four o'clock, their father checked his watch to see if his children had time for a swim before they all headed home. Just a few minutes later, all three Lockes heard a "very loud report," a shot, Seymour recalled, that sounded like a cannon. Since hunters frequented the surrounding woods they thought little of it. Another witness would later testify that at about the same moment she heard a shot and a woman's scream. At the time she did not find either noise sufficiently alarming to inform the authorities.[15]

In fact, no one bothered to inform the authorities until the following morning, when Robert Bowman noticed that the man he supposed was a sleeping fisherman had not moved since the previous day and discovered the bodies of Jacob and Nancy Jane Young. If the question of *who* killed the Youngs had yet to be decisively settled, how they died quickly became clear once police had investigated the crime scene, the coroner had conducted his autopsy, and the coroner's jury heard its testimony. Jacob Young was shot as he gathered shells at the river's edge, apparently by someone hidden in the bushes behind him. Nancy Jane Young screamed when she saw her husband fall and immediately confronted a second assailant, this one armed with a pistol, a weapon never recovered. Small and delicate though she was, Young struggled with her foe—her hat and veil had been knocked off, her care-fully braided auburn hair was in disarray, her "false upper teeth" lay on the ground.[16] The shot fired into her temple, the coroner claimed, was not im-mediately fatal. Her murderer resorted to a blunt instrument, possibly a rock or the butt of the pistol.

Rumors would surface a decade later claiming that Nancy Young had been pregnant at the time of her death.[17] If this allegation had any basis, no one—not the coroner, not the physicians who autopsied her, not the prosecutors—mentioned it. Perhaps the omission (if indeed it was one) stemmed from delicacy, various authorities believing public mentions of pregnancy improper. Or perhaps any evidence of a fetus had burned away. No one ever definitively accounted for the grotesque condition of Nancy Young's body. Some speculated that the murderers deliberately set her corpse alight to disguise its identity (a turn-of-the-century newspaper account claimed they purposely brought coal oil to the crime scene). The doctors who performed her postmortem, however, failed to detect an accelerant. Others suggested that the gunpowder from the pistol shot ignited her crino-line petticoat. This was far from idle speculation; crinoline had acquired a well-deserved reputation as a fire hazard. Newspapers and popular maga-zines on both sides of the Atlantic warned of the dangers of the highly flam-mable stiffened fabric. *Godey's Lady's Book* offered helpful hints for "extin-guishing burning clothes" in its September 1868 issue, instructing victims to forego "the first impulse . . . to rush about shrieking for help" in favor of roll-ing on the ground. (We don't know if Janey Young read *Godey's*, though it would have been exactly the sort of publication to which an upwardly mobile housewife would have subscribed.) Whatever caused it to ignite, Young's crin-oline fulfilled the dire warnings that cautionary tales like "A Funereal Fash-ion," "Dangerous Dresses," and "A Coroner on Crinoline" promised. Those who discovered Young's body noted that her shoes and stockings were rela-tively well preserved. But apart from a few scraps of brown gingham and the "fringed edges of a white chemise," all that remained of the rest of her clothing were the metal hoops of her petticoat, the "cage" that supported the crinoline.[18]

■ ■ ■

The Youngs' funeral inevitably became a public spectacle and an occasion for spiritual and secular soul-searching. Two hearses conveyed their bodies from their house on St. Clair Street to Trinity Methodist, at the corner of

North and Alabama Streets, only a block from Nancy Clem's and Matthew Hartman's houses. A "large procession, in carriages and on foot" accompanied the Youngs' caskets to their church. There the aisles and gallery overflowed "with a mournful audience" that included not only the "large circle of family and friends," whose presence the *Journal* dutifully noted, but also many curious onlookers. Three ministers, the Reverend Burgner of nearby Strange Chapel, a hotbed of "old fashioned Methodism," the Reverend Stillwell of the Cincinnati Conference, and Trinity's Reverend D. D. Robinson, presided over the service. Burgner offered the opening prayer.[19] Then Robinson preached a sermon "of more than ordinary feeling and power," taking as his text First Chronicles 28:9: "And thou, Solomon, my son, know thou the God of thy Father, and serve him with a perfect heart and with a willing mind, for the Lord searcheth all hearts and understandeth all the imagination of the thoughts. If thou seek him, he will be found of thee; but if thou forsake him he will cast thee off forever."

The meaning of Robinson's sermon—or at least of the *Journal*'s explication of it—was unambiguous. "The first position taken," its reporter explained, "was that sin strengthens in the soul in proportion as we voluntarily depart from the truth, and the counsel and the love of God." Robinson compared "the growth and effect of sin" to a poisonous snake. "When a viper is small a school boy may take it in his hand, lay it in his bosom, allow it to crawl on his face, or around his neck, but the same viper when grown may fasten its venomous bite on him who made it but a toy for play, and sudden death ensures. So it is to depart from the living God. The powers of the soul becomes [*sic*] poisoned and perverted until, like the first murderer of the race of mankind, a brother may take the life of a brother." Poisoned and perverted by sin, presumably—given reports that Young had been robbed—the sin of greed, the Youngs' assailants had resorted to murder. Robinson's choice of texts suggested that authorities already suspected that someone close to Jacob Young—almost a "brother"—had killed him.

By the time of his funeral, local publicity had made clear that Jacob Young's business dealings were somewhat shady. For his minister to suggest that he was anything other than the innocent victim of a horrible crime, however, would have been in poor taste; in any case, the violent circumstances of his death temporarily trumped any misgivings about the activities he pursued while alive. And to voice such doubts would have deprived the assembled mourners of "fervent words of Christian consolation." The godly, Robinson assured his listeners, would be rewarded. "That to seek to know the truth of God, to obey the wise counsel of God, to serve God with a perfect heart and with a willing mind, would secure the Divine favor, develop moral character, afford happiness in time, and give a readiness for death, even at the hand of the assassin." Those in attendance sang a hymn, which implicitly promised salvation to the Youngs and eternal damnation to their murderers.

> In expectation sweet,
>   We'll wait, and sing, and pray,
> Till Christ's triumphal car we meet,
>   And see an endless day.
>
> He comes! the Conqueror comes!
>   Death falls beneath his sword;
> The joyful prisoners burst the tombs,
>   And rise to meet their Lord.
>
> The trumpet sounds, "Awake!
>   Ye dead, to judgment come!"
> The pillars of creation shake,
>   While man receives his doom.
>
> Thrice happy morn for those
>   Who love the ways of peace;
> No night of sorrow e'er shall close,
>   Or shade their perfect bliss.[20]

After Stillwell's closing prayer, the Youngs' bodies were carried back to Pike Township and buried in the cemetery behind North Liberty Christian Church, the congregation to which Nancy Jane's relative and former guardian, Jonas Case, belonged. A limestone obelisk marked their grave. Despite its simplicity, it was literally the height of sepulchral fashion.[21] Pike Township was no longer the frontier.

Jacob Young's status as an outsider followed him in death. No one knew his exact date of birth. "Born—1839; [died] Sept. 12, 1868, aged—about 29 years," his inscription read. Nancy Jane's statistics were recorded with greater precision. "Born—July 24, 1840; [died] Sept. 12, 1868, aged—28 yr. 1. mo. 18 da." But these discrepancies would not have been the first thing a visitor to the tiny cemetery would have noticed. Between each Young's birth and death dates, the stone carver inscribed, "MURDERED AT COLD SPRINGS."[22]

Detail of Jacob and Nancy Jane Young's gravestone, North Liberty Cemetery, Pike
Township, Indianapolis, Indiana. A single monument marks the Youngs' graves;
Jacob's inscription is on one side, Nancy Jane's on the other. Both include "Murdered
at Cold Springs," a notation that suggests the public outrage the crime inspired.
Photograph by Ian Byers-Gamber.

Positioned directly below the *Journal*'s coverage of the Youngs' funeral
was a description of "a singular phenomenon . . . observed in the heavens"
the previous evening. "Two black bands, about three degrees in breadth,
spanned the entire arch from east to west." The *Journal* drew no explicit
connection between the "black bands" that appeared in the skies above Indianapolis and the Youngs' untimely and unnatural deaths. To readers, the
meaning of the juxtaposition would have been clear. The black bands were
an emblem of mourning, commemorating the violent deaths of two out-

wardly respectable people. They represented the loss of civic innocence as well. Cold Spring was a fascinating mystery but also a blot on the city's reputation. The gruesome event had taken place against a backdrop of explosive urban growth, increasing crime, and local political corruption, further diminishing boosters' hopes of portraying Indianapolis as a "moral city." In more ways than one, the "singular phenomenon" did not bode well.[23]

■ ■ ■

Nancy Clem stood at her gate and watched the Youngs' funeral procession go by. Asked by a neighbor why she did not attend their services, she replied that she did not know them.[24]

CHAPTER FOUR

Detection

The pistol ball changed everything. Jacob Young owned two pistols but took neither with him to Cold Spring. Even had he possessed a third, it was difficult to imagine him shooting his wife with one weapon, speedily disposing of it, and shooting himself with another. Witnesses, moreover, testified that the "report" of a shotgun preceded the sound of the pistol, and that the two "reports were as close together as could be."[1] And Young had been shot in the *back* of the head. He could have maneuvered himself into position to do so only with great difficulty. Had he managed this improbable feat—one worthy of a circus contortionist—the shot he fired would have traveled upward. His autopsy indicated that its path followed a downward trajectory. If the examination of Young's body cast doubt on the murder-suicide theory, the pistol ball extracted from Nancy Jane Young's skull indicated decisively that the Youngs had been murdered—either by more than one assailant or (less probably) by a single assailant who wielded two different weapons. An explicable, if tragic, instance of domestic violence ("the common solution of the mystery") became "one of the most horrible tragedies that history ever recorded."[2]

This was hyperbole and the *Journal* knew it. Murder made for good copy; what the local press dubbed "the Cold Spring Tragedy" was a boon to circulation. Both the *Journal* and the *Sentinel* would devote hundreds of pages to the case. To local boosters and enterprising reporters, Cold Spring, an "atrocity . . . committed . . . within sound of . . . church bells," sadly confirmed that Indianapolis was no longer a "moral" city, if indeed it had ever been. At the same time, however, it put Indianapolis on the map. Appropriating the sensational style and lurid themes that characterized crime reporting in other parts of the nation, Indianapolis papers rose to the occasion, the Republican *Journal* initially taking fullest advantage of the opportunities the killings provided. "It would be hard to find a more gloomy, more sequestered spot," read its description of the crime scene. "It is just the place of all places for a deed of blood like this, the very thought of which, as we stood on the spot marked by the blood and ashes of the victims, sent a succession of chills from head to foot that kept us in a perfect shiver. To the natural gloominess of the spot seems now to attach a chilling stillness similar to that which one feels creeping over him while passing alone, in the night, some lonely spot associated in his memory with stories of spectres, shrouded skeletons and unearthly sounds."[3]

Despite their theatricality, these sorts of observations captured the public mood. Indianapolis had never witnessed anything quite like this. To be sure, there had been other killings. In 1819, George Pogue, one of the vicinity's first white settlers, became, in the words of nineteenth-century local historian W. R. Holloway, "its first martyr" when he disappeared after going off in search of horses stolen by a Shawnee band. The newly incorporated town's "first murder" took place more than a decade later when a ferryman drowned his wife's reputed lover by literally rocking the boat as they crossed the White River. By midcentury, fatal encounters reflected social problems as likely to afflict eastern cities as pioneer settlements. Drunken revelers killed each other in barroom brawls. Gamblers lashed out—sometimes fatally— against fellow players who cheated them. And in the heat of anger, men sometimes killed their wives.[4]

The Cold Spring case, however, represented the city's first "cold-blooded" (premeditated) murder. More to the point, it featured unlikely victims. Even if Jacob Young's business methods were not quite legitimate, he seemed to have been both "industrious" and "sober." He comported himself respectably; how else could he have persuaded upright, God-fearing citizens to invest in his dubious schemes? He was a church member, his wife "a pure [C]hristian woman."[5] The Youngs, in short, were not the sorts of people Indianapolitans expected to find on a sand bar, brutally murdered by persons unknown.

City residents responded to this mystery with a predictable a mix of fascination and horror. They crowded outside Charles Weaver's undertaking "shop," where a hastily assembled coroner's jury, which included an attorney, a letter carrier, a lighting-rod salesman, and two policemen, heard evidence. They took repeated trips to the "gloomy spot" where the Youngs had met their untimely deaths; neither city nor county officials made any attempt to secure the crime scene. Nor did they limit access to the bodies or the evidence. "Didn't hear who those people were that were murdered until Monday," Silas Hartman recounted matter-of-factly. "Didn't go to see the dead bodies." The coroner later testified that someone made off with the balls removed from the shotgun, though the powder remained.[6]

Apart from these gaffes, authorities proceeded with a fair degree of professionalism. The *Journal*, too, for all its talk of chills and specters, embraced the art of modern detection. "A murder, in this age, can rarely remain involved in mystery," it confidently asserted.[7] The coroner's jury immediately began to interview witnesses. It began with Robert Bowman, who explained how he had discovered the bodies. Major Erie Locke testified to hearing the "report" of a shotgun; asked to view the bodies through the undertaker's window, thirteen-year-old Millie Locke confirmed that the dead man was the same person she had seen walking with two women along the sand bar. Lizzie Henry, the Youngs' "servant girl," told of seeing Jacob Young with a thick roll of money and explained her employer's "habit of taking rides in the afternoon and in the evening." She corroborated what the pistol ball in Nancy Jane's skull already suggested: the Youngs had been happily married, a fact that cast further doubt on the initial hypothesis of murder-suicide. Mary Belle Young repeated much of Henry said; as the *Journal* put it, "Nothing was elicited additional to that shown by the testimony of Lizzie Henry."[8]

Neither the *Journal* nor the *Sentinel* commented on the propriety of exposing Jacob Young's twelve-year-old niece (the *Journal* thought she was "about eleven") or, for that matter, the two Locke children, to two horribly mutilated corpses. Nineteenth-century children were no strangers to death, which by today's standards visited relatively often. Bodies were laid out in home parlors, and open caskets were the norm. Jacob and Nancy Young were on display in their own front room for an hour or so before their funeral, whether in open or closed caskets we do not know. Still, as the papers made abundantly clear, the Youngs' bodies presented especially gruesome spectacles. Their effect on a child who had already lost both her parents could only have been disturbing.

The autopsy completed and cause of death determined, the coroner's jury moved the next day to a more congenial location, the office of attorney James Sweetser, who had been appointed foreman. As the jury continued to interview witnesses, Coroner Garrison W. Allred issued a plea requesting "all persons who may have seen or conversed with Mr. Young at any time immediately preceding his murder; all who may have seen him in his buggy on the day of the fatal occurrence; all persons who know aught in the least concerning the matter or who have heard of any others who may know anything of it" to call at his office. "It is only by the shrewdest handling of smallest facts, facts that in themselves appear unimportant, even worthless, that this awful mystery will ever be unraveled," the *Journal* solemnly proclaimed, "and we trust that our citizens will lend the Coroner all the assistance in their power."[9]

Meanwhile investigators and curious citizens returned to Cold Spring, reporters in tow. "Our party found nothing save the print of a neat little lady's gaiter in the yielding soil," the *Journal* reported, neglecting to note that "our party" included a policeman and one of the physicians who had conducted the postmortem. As the *Journal* well knew, the discovery hardly amounted to "nothing," for several witnesses, including Millie Locke, had seen Jacob Young walking on the sandbar in the company of *two* women. Locke thought Nancy Jane Young's female companion wore a "lead colored dress"; another witness described the fabric as "very light with a large flower." The footprint confirmed her presence and suggested that whoever she was, she had taken part in the murder. "Who is the third woman?" the headline for Tuesday, September 15, asked.[10]

Authorities quickly answered the question—too quickly, it turned out. Lizzie Henry, the domestic servant who admitted to seeing Young's thick roll of money, was the first to be arrested, taken into custody the very day after the murder. European authorities and American police in some localities were already taking plaster casts of perpetrators' footprints, a practice that would become increasingly common in the late nineteenth century.[11] But in 1868 Indianapolis investigators at the crime scene relied solely on observation, which revealed the sharply defined impression of a relatively new shoe, and measurements—taken with a green papaw stick. In a case that would more than once evoke the tale of Cinderella, Henry had the good fortune to be an ugly stepsister, her foot too large to fit the imperfectly documented prints discovered at Cold Spring. She "was accordingly discharged." Police also detained "two bad characters," both of whom "came into town from the North very muddy, and looking like they had been concerned in some bad business or other." No evidence of murder could be mustered against them, but the authorities nevertheless managed to find charges that would stick. One "was successfully prosecuted on the charge of having in his possession a full assortment of nearly every kind of burglar's implements," the other charged with "professional gambling."[12]

■ ■ ■

In the end, shrewd handling of facts proved more profitable than familiar linkages between class, "character," and propensity to criminal behavior. Even before the advent of modern ballistics testing, the shotgun that lay at Jacob Young's side provided important clues. It was old and rusty and it had a broken thimble—a poor choice of weapon for anyone who wished to conceal his crime. Through a remarkable—and, for the perpetrators, extraordinarily unfortunate—coincidence it was identified almost immediately. The man who recognized it was none other than Indianapolis's chief of police, Thomas S. Wilson, who had recently been shopping for a gun for one of his sons. He had considered buying this very weapon but decided against it because it was too heavy for "his boy."

Wilson took the shotgun to the place where he had first seen it, the Solomon Brothers' pawnbrokers shop on Illinois Street. Described in a near contemporaneous account as "belong[ing] to that highly respectable class of citizens known as Hebrews, which Gentiles call Jews," Joseph and Morris Solomon, originally from England, had begun their Indianapolis careers as tobacconists but had recently switched pursuits, becoming the first licensed pawnbrokers in both the city and the state. Successful enough to be included favorably, if condescendingly, in a series of "short biographical sketches of a few" of Indianapolis's "prominent business men," their entry emphasized their "accountability to the police" and the "social qualities [that] make them ever welcome at our firesides." While the latter assertion is questionable, the former proved correct. Presented with the gun, Joseph Solomon readily agreed that it had been purchased at his store the morning of the murder. So did Isaac Sweede, his "negro clerk." Sweede and Solomon described a man who looked very much like Bill Abrams.[13]

A city of nearly forty-eight thousand people included many men who bore a general resemblance to Abrams: tall, broad-chested, sandy-haired, and—like nearly all men at the time—bearded. But authorities soon learned through testimony before the coroners' jury that Abrams had "been a particular friend of Young" and that the two had "business connections" as well.[14]

Abrams's behavior, moreover, aroused suspicion. Elisha Kise, the man who identified the bodies on the sandbar, wanted to be sure he had not been mistaken. "I was the only person who had identified them, and I wanted to be certain in my own mind . . . before I told any one of the fact," he explained. Only hours after the discovery of the bodies, Kise, along with another man, William Coleman, drove to Abrams's house. When they arrived, Kise asked Abrams if he knew whether the Youngs were at home. Bill replied that he did not know. Kise and Coleman next called at the Youngs and found them absent. They returned to the Abramses, where Kise announced that he "thought Young and his wife had committed suicide, or had been murdered." Maggie screamed and threw her arms around her husband's neck, but Bill pushed her away and told her to be quiet. He said he believed that the victims must be someone else, for he thought he'd seen Mrs. Young that morning.[15]

Kise asked Abrams to accompany him and Coleman to the undertaker's to view the bodies. As they drove downtown, Abrams talked about everything except the subject at hand. When Coleman brought up "the manner in which Young was shot," Abrams responded that Young "had the fastest horse in town. . . . When any allusion was made to the murder of Young, he would try to change the conversation," Coleman recalled. Kise agreed. "Whenever the murder was spoken of by either Mr. Coleman or myself, he would mention some other subject; and did not speak of the murder, or ask a single question about it; I though he acted in a very singular manner during the whole ride." Once there was no longer any question regarding the identities of the deceased, Abrams became a vocal proponent of the murder-suicide theory, even following one visitor "to the gate and talking about it."[16]

Abrams's appearance, relationship to the victims, and "singular manner" convinced authorities to take action. They lured him downtown to the Palmer House Hotel, next door to the Solomon Brothers pawnshop, where the county sheriff pointed him out to Joseph Solomon and Isaac Sweede. Both thought "he looked very much like the man buying the gun," although neither professed absolute certainty. "The impression gained from Mr. Solomon," the *Journal* explained, "was, that he was nearly sure that Abrams was the man." Near certainty was enough, and Sheriff Parker easily convinced a judge to issue a warrant. The identities of the officials who "repaired to Abrams' residence," which included the sheriff, deputy sheriff, Chief Wilson, and an additional city police officer, indicated the serious nature of the crime and the importance placed on solving it. The party arrived at the house on East Street at five o'clock on the afternoon of Tuesday, September 15, just three days after the murder, and placed Abrams under arrest.[17]

■ ■ ■

When the Youngs' funeral commenced the next morning, Abrams, fortified with a bible and other religious reading material, was securely housed in the Marion County Jail, a stone building that stood behind the county courthouse, only eight blocks from his house. Abrams's cell was a fourteen-by-nine-foot chamber made "entirely of boiler iron." Intended to prevent conflagrations and breakouts (the previous jail had been destroyed when inmates attempted to escape by setting it on fire), "iron cells" offered protection to prisoners as well. Protection might well have been necessary. On the morning after Abrams's arrest, the day his trial was scheduled to begin, people congregated outside the judge's office. A "strong current of indignation" rippled through the crowd when it became clear that the proceedings would be postponed. "Indignant" citizens believed that Abrams planned to bribe his way out, that "having money, the lawyers were undertaking to cheat justice of her dues." Lawyers would indeed be paid plenty, but there was reason for delay: the coroner's jury was continuing to gather evidence, "mostly of such a character," the *Journal* explained, "as it would not be proper to publish." It did let slip that the evidence suggested that Abrams was part of a "ring" involving "many who stand to-day, in the eyes of the community, above suspicion." "We regret to see such a state of feeling," the *Journal* noted in reference to the surly crowd, failing to acknowledge its own role in creating a potential "flood of fury."[18]

Abrams vehemently protested his innocence. "The news of [Jacob Young's] murder," he insisted, "shocked me as much, I believe, as would the news of my brother's death in a similar way." He agreed to an interview with the *Journal*, providing a thorough and largely accurate account of his whereabouts on the Saturday of the murder. If the narrative subsequently pieced together by prosecutors was correct, Abrams's recitation of peach peeling and vinegar purchasing, bathing and buggy washing, music appreciation and definition-book shopping omitted four crucial details. First, he bought a shotgun at Solomon Brothers but not before rejecting the wares offered by Aaron Hunt's auction room and the Exchange Store. Second, he met up with Nancy Clem when she ventured downtown to Roll's wallpaper store, directly across the street from Solomon Brothers pawnshop. Third, he rendezvoused with Silas Hartman at the Fruit House early that afternoon (not at ten in the morning) to let him know that the Youngs were heading off for a drive and to hand over the gun. Fourth, during their brief late-afternoon conversation in the hallway of the Hartman house, Clem gave him a $500 bill.[19]

■ ■ ■

Another set of footprints left their marks in Cold Spring's "yielding soil." They may have belonged to Pet—not Pet Hartman, but a bobtail sorrel mare that Syke Hartman, a regular customer of Sullivan & Drew's livery stable, rented along with a buggy on the day of the murder. Pet was a "good traveler—a four minute nag," meaning that she could cover a mile in four minutes. She was a distinctive animal; as her owner John Drew described her: "blaze in her face, which can be seen some distance; hind legs white nearly to her knees; small white spots all over her body." Pet, it turned out, also wore "preventive" or "interfering" shoes, the same sort of equine foot-wear that left the impressions found at the crime scene. While she was the only inhabitant of Sullivan & Drew's stable so shod, many Indianapolis horses wore such shoes. "Interference," the tendency of a horse's foot to strike the opposite leg while it trotted or galloped, was a common problem. "Interfering feet are not unusual," Drew explained, "all shoes of that kind are similar."[20]

Pet's condition when Hartman returned her that Saturday evening *was* unusual. "She had been driven hard," Drew recalled. "She was so exhausted thought she was sick." Rather than lead her back into her stall, he tied her outside to cool down "and watched to see what effect that hard driving would have on her." Happily she recovered.[21] Pet represented Drew's liveli-hood; hence his concern for her health and ability to describe her distin-guishing features in precise detail. Yet he also comes across as a man who knew and loved horses (and, given her name, perhaps this particular horse), indignant that she had been so poorly used.

Hartman remained mum on the speed with which he drove, but he read-ily admitted renting the mare and buggy. *Where* he went was the issue. In an interview with the *Journal* he claimed that he and his cousin Cravens Hartman drove northeast on the Pendleton Pike, the opposite direction from Cold Spring. Unfortunately, Hartman explained, Crave was not around to vouch for him. He had left for Missouri the Saturday of the mur-der on the midnight train.[22]

On the afternoon of September 12, sixteen-year-old Pike Township res-ident John P. Wiley was driving into the city, a traditional Saturday habit for farmers, with his father on the Lafayette road. Around 2:30 the Wileys' open-spring wagon passed a "top carriage" occupied by a man and two women "driving along at a fast trot." His father, John H. Wiley, spoke to the man and to one of the women. Though he was "close enough to see the wrinkles in their faces," the younger Wiley did not know any of the three occupants. But he recognized the man following "about sixty rods" behind them. "There comes Sike Hartman," he remarked to his father. John H. agreed that the man driving the chestnut sorrel was Silas Hartman, a man he had known "ever since he was a little boy." But the man turned away and stared down at his wheels as if they were the most interesting things in the world. John P. Wiley later learned that the man and the woman his father had greeted were Jacob and Nancy Jane Young.[23]

Like all good citizens who had seen the Youngs on the day of their murder, both Wileys voluntarily testified before the coroner's jury. "Some man," possibly Coroner Allred, possibly Foreman Sweetser, told John P. "that there was a woman" in the room whom "he wanted me to look at." Asked if she might have been the woman riding in the Youngs' carriage, he thought she "fill[ed] the bill . . . but don't know that I can be positive, sure, and certain." The woman in the jury room was Nancy Clem.[24]

■ ■ ■

When Silas Hartman was arrested on September 21, the *Journal* explained that "the evidence . . . was considered quite ample to warrant that step[,] though what it is in detail we are requested not to publish." The suppressed evidence, as subsequent proceedings would show, was that he had been seen driving behind the Youngs' carriage on the road to Cold Spring. The *Journal* combined prudence with indiscretion. While it dutifully declined to publish the nature of the evidence against him, it took care to explain that Silas Hartman was the brother of Mrs. Nancy Clem, the wife of William F. Clem, the grocer. Rumors that Mrs. Clem had been arrested, the *Journal* insisted, were false.[25]

Even before her name appeared in the papers, Clem knew she was under suspicion. She was subpoenaed to testify before the coroner's jury (where she was pointed out to John P. Wiley) on the same day her brother was arrested. She swore that she was either at home or next door at her brother Matthew's house the entire afternoon of the murder. Rebecca and Pet Hartman, also called to testify, swore the same. Shortly thereafter, Clem appeared before the grand jury that had been summoned to hear the evidence against William Abrams and Silas Hartman. There she reiterated her claim that she had been home all afternoon.[26]

Like Abrams, Clem behaved strangely in the aftermath of the murders. She denied knowing the Youngs, an assertion numerous people would have disputed, and did not attend their funeral. As did Abrams, she voiced the belief that Jacob Young had killed his wife and then himself. She asked Madeline Everson, the neighbor who recorded her accounts, about prevailing public opinion regarding the murders. When Everson replied that it was "thought there is a gang whose operations, when developed, will astonish the public," Clem exclaimed, "My God! I know nothing of the murder!" When she learned of Abrams's arrest she gave Rebecca Hartman a packet of money "concealed in an old boot, and asked her to hide it for her." "Put it anywhere, for God's sake," Clem exclaimed, "for they will search my house for it tonight!"[27]

Bill Abrams inadvertently brought Nancy Clem to the authorities' attention. He needed money—money for a lawyer, money for his family's support—and money for Silas Pollard, a wealthy Pike Township farmer. Pollard visited Abrams in jail "frequently," less concerned about his friend's predicament than the fate of his cash. Besides having loaned Abrams a few thousand dollars outright, he had endorsed one of his promissory notes; if Abrams failed to pay it off, Pollard would be held liable. Abrams sent for his brother Benjamin and asked him to get money from Nancy Clem. Ben Abrams did not realize that he was being watched. When he left the jail, police detectives followed him.

Bill had had the presence of mind to tell Ben not to knock on Clem's door but to go to the Hartmans' and ask Rebecca to call her sister-in-law. There, Ben spoke with Clem privately. "You know my brother wouldn't hurt a hair of Young's head. My brother was raised with Janey Young, and wouldn't hurt a hair of her head," he reportedly told her. Later he would insist that "my memory is poor as to the recollection of details in conversation." He did remember asking Clem for four thousand dollars on his brother's behalf. She asked Ben to return half an hour later. When he did, she drew a packet from her bosom that she said contained four or five thousand dollars. The exact amount, counted in the back room of attorneys Hanna & Knefler's law office, turned out to be $4,915—enough to pay off the note Pollard had endorsed, retain counsel, and temporarily sustain Abrams' wife and child—but not enough to pay back Pollard's loan. Ben returned twice for more money, both times knocking at the Hartmans' back door, as Clem had instructed him. By the third visit, she was exasperated. "She told me to go back and tell Bill she could not get the money, and for him to tell Pollard to shut his mouth about the money. She told me to tell Bill that if he didn't quit sending there for money it would create a suspicion." "Don't mention my name under the high heavens!" she implored him.

Ben was not Clem's only visitor in the aftermath of the murders. Dressmaker Ann Hottle was also worried about her money. Bill Abrams had cosigned the promissory note Clem had given her; Hottle understandably "felt uneasy" when she learned of his arrest. Clem initially promised to repay her money "soon," then "in a day or two." Suspicious, Hottle "talked independently," threatening to sue. Clem in turn threatened Hottle with bodily harm. "She did not say *she* would kill me," Hottle explained, "but that some of a company would." Hottle lived to tell the tale, but she never saw her money again. Neither evidently did Silas Pollard.[28]

■ ■ ■

Clem's warnings to Ann Hottle were empty threats. She was already under surveillance. From September 21 (the day Syke was taken into custody) onward, police detectives stood watch outside the house on Alabama Street to prevent her from leaving town until they had accumulated sufficient evidence against her. On the afternoon of Wednesday, October 7, the county sheriff asked her to accompany him to the courthouse. She assumed that she would be asked for further testimony. Not until they reached their destination did Clem realize that she, too, was under arrest. She joined her brother and her surviving business associate in the county jail. She "gave way to her feelings," the *Journal* reported, "in outbursts of grief that were frequently repeated during the afternoon." The story, "The Cold Spring Tragedy: Another Arrest," smugly noted that "Mrs. Clem, it will be remembered, has been suspected ever since a few days after the murder."

The *Journal* proceeded to give its readers their first introduction to the woman who would become known as "the notorious Mrs. Clem." She "is about thirty-five years of age, rather under the medium size, with a pleasant and intelligent countenance, of lady-like deportment and previous good character."[29] In other words, an unlikely murderess whose appearance and demeanor signaled the beginning rather than the ending of a puzzling case. As the *Sentinel* would put it on the opening day of her trial, "the Cold Springs tragedy is . . . as great a mystery as it was when the mutilated corpses of Jacob Young and his wife were first found lying upon the ground."[30]

Two days after Clem's arrest, Jacob Young's property was sold at auction, bringing "almost fabulous prices, far beyond its real value." "Some people will submit to almost any thing to secure an inch of the rope with which some graceless scamp is hung," the *Journal* grumbled. The house on East St. Clair Street remained an object of local children's fascination for years to come. Timid youngsters ran past quickly; their bolder companions hung on the gate. The settlement of the estate revealed that Young was far from the rich man he represented himself to be; he died $40,000 in debt. The biggest living loser, Robert Dorsey, to whom Young had lately been paying only "interest," was out $10,500. "He is reaping the bitter fruits of those who make haste to get rich," prosecuting attorney John T. Dye would solemnly declare. Others who had trusted their money to Young found themselves in similar straits.[31]

The Cold Spring tragedy inflicted emotional as well as material damage. Jonas Case was appointed Ophir Young's guardian; by 1870, probably earlier, he had removed him from the Philadelphia asylum and brought him to Pike Township. The much anticipated cure had not materialized; in that year the census taker noted that "Ofer H. Young" was "idiotic." For reasons at which we can only guess, the now eight-year-old child resided not with Case but with his minister's son, a township farmer. We know nothing more of "Ofer's" brief life except that he died in 1878, aged fifteen or sixteen, of unknown causes.[32]

Nancy Clem lived on. On October 10, the day after the auction on St. Clair Street, the coroner's jury announced its verdict, pinning probable guilt on William Abrams, Silas Hartman, Nancy Clem, and "two other persons." Though various guesses would be ventured, the identities of the two others were never determined; the grand jury returned indictments only against Abrams, Hartman, and Clem. Clem was and would remain the center of attention. When the members of the trio entered their respective pleas of "not guilty" on October 23, Indianapolis residents, including "several ladies," crowded into "the little Criminal Court room." They "seemed to feel a great anxiety," the *Sentinel* explained, "to see Mrs. Clem."[33] The "anxiety" seldom abated. Clem would remain in the public eye, her various exploits documented by both local and national newspapers, for the next thirty years.

■ ■ ■

The records of the coroner's and grand juries have been lost; what we know about the alleged sequence of events comes from the subsequent trials of the accused. No one will know for certain what happened on the afternoon of Saturday, September 12, 1868, but this is the prosecution's version: William Abrams purchased the shotgun that lay on the sand near Jacob Young's body. Silas Hartman rented the buggy and mare that transported him to the scene of the crime. There his sister, Nancy Clem, having accompanied the Youngs on their Saturday excursion, joined him in committing "cold-blooded atrocity." Hartman killed Jacob Young with the shotgun. Clem shot Nancy Young with a pistol that was never found, striking her with a rock or the pistol itself when the bullet failed to effect Young's immediate demise.[34]

Prosecutors offered two possible motives for the crime. Robbery was the most obvious; the roll of bills thick as Lizzie Henry's wrist was missing from the murdered man's pocket. That very evening Bill Abrams repaid an overdue note at 25 percent interest with a $500 bill. Abrams owed Young money and so did Clem, who had recently failed to secure a $22,000 loan from Dr. Duzan. Prosecuting attorneys also alleged that Jacob Young had threatened to tell Frank about his wife's business dealings if she did not pay up.[35] Business, broadly defined, would form the crux of the state's case. Nancy Clem's insistence on retaining control over her own business affairs, her failure to reveal her transactions to her husband, and the fact that she transacted at all would provide prosecutors with ample ammunition. Her trial would amount to more than a simple determination of innocence or guilt. It would serve as a social referendum—as prosecution and defense offered competing definitions of gender, economy, and the myriad obligations of faithful wives.

■ ■ ■

Many facts about Nancy Clem reached the newspapers during the fall of 1868, but one would not be noted until later: when she was arrested, she was wearing her "colored servant girl's" shoes.[36]

CHAPTER FIVE

Trial

During the early days of December 1868, newspapers across the nation leaked previews of disgraced President Andrew Johnson's self-congratulatory and self-serving farewell address and reported commanding general and president-elect Ulysses S. Grant's "terse but conclusive remark . . . on a very important question": "Troops are still needed in the Southern States." The drama about to ensue in an Indianapolis courtroom seemed far removed from national events. Yet many of the "important questions" that underlay Reconstruction—disagreements regarding the authority and scope of government, debates concerning the incorporation of African Americans into the body politic, and differences between and within political parties—would surface in the Cold Spring case as well. For the moment, however, the local, the particular, and, in the most literal sense, the spectacular took precedent. Indianapolis papers continued to carry national news, on which the *Journal* and *Sentinel* took predictably partisan positions. But in the coming weeks both papers would devote enormous portions of their limited space to the trial of Nancy Clem.[1]

Clem dressed carefully for opening day. She made her appearance on December 1 attired in a "Bismarck brown merino dress" ornamented with tasteful accessories. A "plain gold brooch" adorned her "neat collar." "Earrings," the *Journal* noted, as if captioning a fashion plate, "were worn of the same pattern." Clem wore a waterproof cloak with a fur collar over her dress, "a jaunty back velvet hat, with brown grenadine veil," on her head. Not to be outdone, the *Sentinel* provided its readers with their own vicarious fashion show. Clem's hands were sheathed in "neatly fitting kid gloves." Her hair was "neatly arranged" in the current fashion, "in coils upon the back of her head." Although no one mentioned it, she must have been wearing new shoes.[2]

Clem knew that people would be looking at her. On that day and in the weeks to come, curious crowds filled the Marion County Courthouse. The building, which had been designed to accommodate one hundred people, had been spacious by the standards of the 1820s. Now it threatened to collapse under the weight of curious onlookers—"every neck . . . stretched to catch a glimpse of the woman about whom so much has been said,"

The frontispiece of *The Cold Spring Tragedy* (Indianapolis: A. C. Roach, 1869) depicted Clem in the clothing she wore during her first trial. It was published, however, after her second trial and first conviction. The artist Henry C. Chandler captured the subject described in the text as a woman with a "dangerous expression" on her face, a "sinister turn of her eye," and a "resolute set of her jaws." Courtesy of Herman B Wells Library, Indiana University.

claimed the *Sentinel*. "The defendant is not a wild beast to be stared at as in a menagerie," the *Journal* noted indignantly—and somewhat disingenuously, for its own coverage, it proclaimed, "should satisfy the public fully and completely." Both the *Journal* and the *Sentinel* made a point of noting the presence of women among the spectators. Among them was Indianapolis teenager Sarah Hill Fletcher, who attended the proceedings with her mother and aunt having "had the good luck to get in a back window." Speaking for many, Fletcher remarked that "it was all intensely interesting."[3]

Indianapolitans found Clem "intensely interesting" because of the sensational nature of her alleged crime but mostly because of her gender. As the *Journal* had so succinctly put it, "A woman in such a crime!" Pairing women with murder, a powerful—and, for publishers, lucrative—combination, was nothing new. Since the late eighteenth century, women had figured prominently in lurid narratives of violent crime, providing fodder for broadsides, trial pamphlets, and newspapers. But the women featured in these sensational tales were almost always victims, often of explicitly sexual crimes.[4] Murderesses, on the other hand, were rare. When they surfaced they appeared as sexual predators who lured unsuspecting men to their untimely deaths or as perpetrators of typically "female" transgressions: killing unwanted infants, sexual rivals, tyrannical husbands, or faithless lovers. By dubbing it a "tragedy"—a term often invoked to describe sensational crimes— Indianapolis newspapers tried to assimilate Cold Spring into predictable scenarios. But the case was an oddity. It had its female victim to be sure—but also apparently a female perpetrator. And she neither looked the type nor acted according to script.[5]

Journalists marveled at Clem's behavior. The *Journal* found her "firmness of demeanor absolutely astonishing." Its reporter discerned "no perceptible change of feature" as the prosecution's opening statement detailed the evidence against her. The *Sentinel* largely agreed: "While betraying some little agitation, her manner was calm and self-possessed, and during the whole day she sat quietly in her chair, looking on at the proceedings apparently with as much interest and as coolly, as any spectator." In the late 1860s, "the defendant showed no emotion" was a freshly minted cliché; nineteenth-century Americans expected criminals to look and act guilty. Yet, as the *Journal* explained, Clem's "bearing . . . [was] such as to baffle all the usual tests of guilt."[6]

Even had she betrayed more than a "little agitation," Clem was an unlikely murderess. Her alleged offense was not a woman's crime. She had purportedly conspired to kill a business partner, not a lover or husband. And she was not the *kind* of woman nineteenth-century Americans typically envisioned when they thought of murderesses. Had she been, Indianapolis residents would have been interested, but not "intensely" so. Like many Hoosiers, Clem was poorly educated; she had been reared in an atmosphere of rustic simplicity, not urban refinement. She was an upland southerner, yet many of the Indianapolis's "best people," including the majority of the lawyers involved in the case, were southern men or sons of southern men. And by the standards of her day—standards that, to be sure, were in flux—Clem was respectable, not disreputable. She was not, in nineteenth-century parlance, a woman of "ill fame." Rather, she was the wife of a "worthy tradesman" of unquestioned character, a man who sat at her side for the duration of her trial, testament to his belief in her innocence. Clem dressed in "very appropriate and unobtrusive" attire, not the ostentatious finery of a prostitute or a servant aping her betters. "Her manners were those of a well bred lady."[7]

Had Clem confessed to the crime, had there been eyewitnesses to the actual event, appearance and demeanor would have counted for little. As it was, however, the evidence prosecuting attorneys assembled was entirely circumstantial. Hence they confronted a difficult assignment: to convince twelve jurors that a middle-class, married woman of "lady-like deportment" was capable of cold-blooded murder.

■ ■ ■

Clem's trial would reveal numerous examples of less-than-professional conduct, but in at least one respect it was an exercise in legal modernity. The proceedings took place in the Marion County Criminal Court, an institution that had come into existence only recently, the result of an act passed by the state legislature in the waning months of 1865. Intended to ensure speedier prosecutions, the new law mandated the establishment of separate courts to try criminal cases in counties whose population included at least ten thousand voters; as the location of the state's largest city, Marion County was the site of the first such experiment. Challenges to its constitutionality delayed its implementation, but in late December 1867, little more than a year before Clem's first appearance, the criminal court opened for business on the second floor of the county courthouse, with George H. Chapman its first presiding judge.[8]

A New Englander by birth, the bespectacled Chapman, who a decade later would become a founding member of the Indianapolis Literary Club (an organization devoted to "social, literary, and aesthetic culture"), had little in common with the barely literate defendant. His father, Jacob Page Chapman, had been a prominent Democrat and newspaperman, one of the editors of the *State Sentinel*. The younger Chapman rejected this partisan heritage with a vengeance, becoming "as strong a Republican as his father had been a Democrat." He rejected his father's occupational legacy as well, turning to the law after only a brief career in journalism. By the time of his judicial appointment, he was a prominent local attorney. Like nearly all of the attorneys who appeared before him, the former commander of Indiana's Third Cavalry was as renowned for his military service as for his legal career.[9]

This is not to say that the lawyers in question were less than distinguished; far from it. As was typical of notorious murder cases, both prosecution and defense commanded impressive arrays of legal talent.[10] As was also typical, private attorneys for all practical purposes tried the case. Burdened with heavy caseloads and rewarded with only the paltry salaries states and localities were willing to provide, public prosecutors tended to be young, inexperienced, and not especially qualified to try important or complex cases. The Marion County prosecuting attorney proved no exception to this rule. A graduate of Harvard Law School, twenty-one-year-old John Duncan possessed impressive credentials but little experience. Three established practitioners lent him what would turn out to be much-needed assistance. One of them was Clem's neighbor, future president Benjamin Harrison. Thirty-five years old, he had already held the positions of city attorney and reporter for the state supreme court (the latter post temporarily interrupted by his wartime service as colonel of the Seventieth Indiana Infantry and eventually a brigadier general) before returning to private practice barely a year before the murders. Busy with other cases, he played at best a supporting role. For the time being, it was Harrison's law partner, William Pinckney Fishback, a former county prosecutor, a rising star in local Republican circles, *and* also a future Literary Club founder, who would most impress the spectators who gathered in the crowded courtroom. Fishback's friend and future partner, John T. Dye—soon to become one of the city's "distinguished legal lights"—completed the state's team.[11]

The defense assembled an equally qualified roster, one that senior counsel John Hanna, a former U.S. district attorney and a childhood friend of Frank Clem, probably organized. Joining Hanna were his law partner General Frederick Knefler, a Civil War hero who claimed the distinction of being the highest ranking Jewish officer in the US Army, and William Wallace Leathers, who would be remembered as "perhaps the best criminal lawyer at the [Indianapolis] bar." Knefler remained largely in the background, rounding up witnesses and planning strategy. Hanna and Leathers would be the public faces of Clem's defense.[12]

Attorneys for both prosecution and defense, all Republicans of various persuasions, were members of a tightly knit professional community. Over the next few decades they sometimes worked together, sometimes on opposing sides. However earnestly they argued their cases, they knew that trials were spectator sports, that not only jurors but members of the general public would be watching. So, too, would their colleagues.[13] Hence they sought not only to convict or acquit defendants as the occasion demanded but to outperform and outwit each other. Success in the courtroom depended on the ability to marshal evidence into a convincing story, to convey that narrative with compelling oratory, and to anticipate the maneuvers of one's opponents. Harrison, Dye, Fishback, Hanna, Leathers, and Knefler were known quantities, unquestionably capable of taking on the city's (and, indeed, the state's) hitherto most important case. But in 1868 they were men whose reputations, by and large, had yet to be made. Clem would provide them with the opportunity.

Both sides would make the most of their legal expertise, the prosecution citing precedent that endorsed the value of circumstantial evidence, the defense invoking authorities who declared its fallibility.[14] Both would call expert witnesses, shoemakers and blacksmiths who offered competing professional opinions concerning the human and equine footprints pressed into the crime scene's "yielding soil."[15] But given the paucity of hard evidence linking the defendant to her alleged crime, both sides would also have to construct stories about Clem herself. As the historian Ann Jones has observed, "Where issues are blurred, attention centers on personality, or to use the nineteenth-century term, character. The question becomes: Is the accused the sort of person who could have committed the crimes charged?"[16]

The defense, it turned out, had attempted to answer that question even before the trial began. Seeking to place an appropriate murderess at the scene of the crime, Clem's lawyers—sometime in late October or early November—conducted a Cinderella search for a disreputable villainess whose shoe size matched the incriminating foot prints at Cold Spring. They arranged for ("hired" is a word they would have deliberately disavowed) a detective to seize three likely suspects, illegally confine them in a room above a piano factory—and measure their feet. Then they enlisted local officials in a heavy-handed campaign to convince potential witnesses that Cal Prather, a prostitute who wore size 3 gaiters, not the respectable Mrs. Clem, was the woman they had seen riding in the Youngs' carriage on the day of the murder. The full story would not come out until later, but in the coming weeks, jurors, spectators, and readers of city newspapers would learn that a former deputy sheriff and the current deputy city marshal had driven to at least two men's homes with Prather seated beside them. At the beginning of the trial, however, listeners must have been puzzled when Dye's opening statement declared emphatically that "No woman from a house of ill fame could have been in the buggy with Jacob Young and his wife."[17]

Dye's speech would have to wait until a jury was impaneled in what everyone expected would be a long and cumbersome process given the substantial publicity the case had received. Yet the panel was assembled with surprising speed—in less than two hours, after attorneys had questioned barely half of the eighty-person pool. None of the twelve chosen lived in

Indianapolis or its surrounding environs. All came from the southeastern corner of the county, as far removed as possible from Pike Township, where impartial jurors were least likely to be found. The eleven who left behind traces in the historical record were farmers. As was typical of the men who served on nineteenth-century juries, they were prosperous, with land holdings ranging from nearly $4,000 to almost $20,000 in value; only one owned no real estate. All save two were married. Jury service embodied both the rights and obligations of citizenship; hence jurors, especially those who decided important cases, were expected to be men of standing. "Are you a householder?" was one of the standard questions potential jurors were asked. Most of those selected were southern by birth or heritage (Kentucky being the most common point of origin), a reflection of township demographics rather than deliberate design, but nevertheless potentially helpful to the defense. By law, all twelve jurors were men. All were white.[18] Judge Chapman was indeed a "strong Republican," one who leaned toward Radicalism. According to a local history, the first African American juror in Marion County served in Chapman's court.[19] In 1868, however, this first lay in the future. Gender aside, Clem would tried by a jury of her peers.

Very likely, the twelve men selected settled into the jury box with mixed feelings. On one hand, they had secured front-row seats to the city's hitherto most sensational trial, a trial in which they would be participants, not mere spectators. On the other hand, they must have known that the duties they were about to undertake were not for the faint of heart, for they faced the real possibility of condemning an outwardly respectable middle-class woman to death. Moreover, they would be sequestered for the duration of the trial—a "confinement" that in some ways mirrored the defendant's— subject to the constant surveillance of the bailiff appointed to supervise them. Too embarrassed to explain why he wished to "evade the imprisonment of the jury box," William Colley, a fifty-six-year-old widower, had to postpone his wedding. One of Colley's married colleagues, similarly reticent, failed to mention his wife's advanced state of pregnancy; she would give birth to twins while he was sequestered. ("He is not a very happy father as yet, and is probably the uneasiest man in town," the *Sentinel* would report on December 11. "He wants to go home to see the things, you know.")[20]

■ ■ ■

On December 1, 1868, at five minutes to three o'clock, John T. Dye began his opening statement for the prosecution. A Kentuckian who had distinguished himself as the only voter in his home town to cast his ballot for Abraham Lincoln, he was a relative newcomer to Indianapolis, having arrived in 1861. Renowned for his learnedness, his graceful speech and "most beautiful" diction, and his ability "to take a complicated case [and] reduce it to its fundamentals," Dye was well suited to the task at hand.[21] It would, indeed, be easy for jurors to lose sight of "the fundamentals." The state would call 101 witnesses, the defense, 54. The trial would take nearly three weeks—a duration unprecedented in Indianapolis, the state of Indiana, and much of the nation.

Dye outlined the state's largely circumstantial argument in a carefully crafted statement designed to preserve clarity even as it engendered suspense. "The murder was the result of concert and conspiracy . . . between parties known to the deceased," he declared. Young had not killed his wife; rather, the physical evidence "pointed to two persons as being the murderers, one killing Mr. Young and the other Mrs. Young." The testimony would show, Dye claimed, that on the morning of the murder, William J. Abrams purchased a gun; "he had no money that morning; but after the murder he was in possession of a large amount." On the day of his death Jacob Young "had in his possession a large sum—several thousand dollar bills and several five hundred dollar bills."

Next Dye noted that the "track of a woman [led] . . . from the body of Jacob Young to the back of a tree where the coat of the deceased . . . was found." That Young's handkerchief lay on the ground indicated that "the pocket of the coat had been searched in a great hurry." Dye acknowledged that the "murder was . . . well planned, and the directing mind of the plot possessed more than ordinary executive ability." In vivid language he suggested the means by which the mystery of the Young murder would be solved: "The gun, the very gun Abrams bought shall yet tell its tale, and the money missing from Young's pocket will speak in crushing tones against the real actors in this dreadful drama. It will be proven that some woman was in the habit of coming to Young's house in the night time, that at those times Young would go to the door with papers and pen and ink, and some mysterious business would be transacted."

Dye deliberately constructed his own "dreadful drama." Without revealing the identity of that woman (although only the most distracted or simple-minded spectator could have failed to guess who she was), Dye introduced the third participant in the conspiracy: Clem's brother, Silas Hartman, who had been seen driving on the Lafayette road, following just behind Jacob and Nancy Jane Young's carriage. Hartman's conduct, Dye explained, was suspicious in other respects; he put the buggy top up on a warm day and "turned his head" to "examin[e] the wheels of his vehicle" when he encountered people he knew. If no one saw him at Cold Spring, the various pieces of evidence he and his alleged accomplice left behind told *their* tales. Horse and carriage tracks were discovered in the woods near the crime scene, as well as the footprints of a man and a woman who appeared to have run from the spot where Jacob Young fell. And the horse left behind prints "of a peculiar character, made with 'interfering shoes.'" These were the shoes worn by the mare Hartman had rented from Sullivan & Drew's livery stable that afternoon, Dye insisted. "No other shoes of any other horse will fit those tracks, nor shoes from the same horse put upon his feet since that time. . . . It is clear then, that Hartman was a party. Abrams had bought the gun and Hartman had used it."

Dye waited until the last possible moment to mention Clem by name. "But who was the woman? That was the great mystery. . . . No woman from a house of ill fame could have been in the buggy with Jacob Young and his wife; for Mrs. Young was a pure, christian woman." The woman who rode with the Youngs "laughed and chatted gaily"; she could have been no stranger. But, Dye maintained, "God has so arranged that crime can never go unpunished." A few days after the murder Mary Belle Young quite by accident had pointed out Clem's house "as the residence of the strange woman who had secret transactions" with her uncle, a "strange woman" who possessed "more than ordinary executive ability." Dye's use of a nineteenth-century term typically employed to describe a prostitute, "strange woman," was no accident. To the contrary it anticipated the rhetorical strategy the prosecution would employ, suggesting a moral equivalency between "executive ability" and illicit sexuality.[22]

As befitting a woman of "more than ordinary executive ability," Clem had taken measures to avoid detection. She had asked her servant for help as she put on a buff-colored dress but had then secretly changed into darker clothing, climbed over the Hartmans' back fence, and intercepted the Youngs' carriage as it passed by. "Who was that second woman seen in Young's buggy just before the murder?" Dye asked. "It must have been a woman possessed of the means, the ability, with the preparation and having the opportunity. Mrs. Clem was gone from home that afternoon just long enough to have done the job."

Dye then catalogued Clem's various "falsehoods." She had denied doing business with Young and Abrams. She had persuaded her sister-in-law to falsely swear before the coroner's jury that she had been home the entire afternoon of September 12. Worse, "she has suborned others of Mrs. Hartman's family, one of them a little girl, the details of which can not be given now." She had persuaded others "outside the family" to lie as well. And on the very day that Abrams was arrested, Clem had given her sister-in-law "a package of money corresponding in every respect to that in Young's pocket . . . and asked her to hide it." The very next day, when he needed funds for his defense, Abrams sent his brother to Mrs. Clem, who readily dispensed a sizeable sum.

Dye concluded with an eloquent flourish. Members of the prosecution, he insisted, bore no "ill will" toward Clem. Rather, their sole concerns were the "vindication of justice, and . . . the protection of the lives of the public."[23]

■ ■ ■

Before the trial could proceed further, another drama ensued—dreadful in its own way for those who cherished the First Amendment. John Hanna made a motion on behalf of the defense, asking Judge Chapman to suppress publication of the testimony in the city's newspapers. Hanna and his partners had also been engaged to represent Silas Hartman and William J. Abrams. He argued that publishing the evidence presented during the current proceedings would make it more difficult for Clem's alleged accomplices to receive fair trials, and might necessitate future (and expensive) changes of venue. The judge, a former newspaperman himself, agreed.

The press was outraged. The *Journal* published a lengthy letter to the editor accusing Chapman of a "judicial coup d'état." Fiery editorials in the *Journal*, *Sentinel*, and the upstart *Evening Mirror* (which published its first issue in November 1868) championed freedom of the press. "Having been in the cavalry," Chapman "is disposed to ride, roughshod, over the popular will," the *Mirror* complained. Reporters remained in the courtroom, busily scribbling away; the *Journal* and the *Sentinel* defied the court order and published their accounts. Chapman retaliated by fining each of the participating reporters $25, having the managing editors of each paper arrested, and barring journalists from his courtroom. It was the *Journal*'s and *Sentinel*'s finest hour. Of course, the editors of both papers were keenly aware that more than principle was at stake, as a notice published in the *Journal* made clear: "The Young murder trial, now in progress in the city and which is reported in full in the JOURNAL each day, is creating a profound sensation in all parts of the country. Our agents outside of this city have been unable to supply the demands for papers. Hereafter they should send their orders in advance. The most interesting part of the testimony is yet to come. . . . Send in your orders."[24] Others found means to capitalize on the newspapers' predicament. "The evidence in the Young murder trial is being suppressed," read one ad, "but Porter & Vance still sell the best oysters in the market."[25]

Chapman's decision created difficulties that Hanna and his colleagues had not anticipated. If it promised greater fairness in subsequent trials, in the short run it was a public relations disaster. Indianapolis residents were angered by the decision because they, too, supported freedom of the press but also because those without Sarah Fletcher's "good luck" were eager to hear news of the case. And to at least some observers, defense attorneys' insistence on secrecy was tantamount to admitting their client's guilt, suggesting an equally problematic "determination to use improper influences in the procurement of a verdict of acquittal." On the third day Clem's trial, Hanna withdrew the request. The "rights of citizens," the *Sentinel* proclaimed, had been restored.[26]

Meanwhile, the trial was under way. Chapman's orders had done little to suppress the flow of information; ordinary citizens had stepped in to fill the places of the banished correspondents and shared their notes with the city's newspapers. The defense, these amateur journalists reported, decided against an opening argument. "They are proceeding with extreme caution, evidently determined to make no mistakes, and as though feeling their way," the *Cincinnati Daily Gazette* observed.[27] The weight of the evidence confirmed the wisdom of this strategy. No one saw Clem shoot Nancy Jane Young; no one affirmed beyond the shadow of a doubt that Clem was the woman seen riding in the Youngs' carriage. Still the cumulative effect of the testimony was damaging—most especially the various and telling differences between witnesses' previous statements before the coroner's and grand juries and their subsequent testimony at the trial itself. The prosecution carefully choreographed its case, calling witnesses in a logical sequence that began with the discovery of the bodies and ended with a detailed examination of Clem's, Abrams's, and Young's transactions. Dye did most of the questioning, the wet-behind-the-ears county prosecutor John Duncan "giving the lead to older heads."[28]

Luther D. Waterman, one of the physicians who conducted the postmortem examination, was the first to take the stand. Establishing that a double homicide (rather than a murder-suicide) had occurred was essential to the prosecution's case. In an era that preceded the use of autopsy photographs,

Waterman's description also served to convey righteous horror, to fix the gruesome image of the Youngs' mutilated remains in jurors' minds. A succession of witnesses followed, ascertaining to hearing two successive "reports" in the vicinity of Cold Spring sometime between 3:30 and shortly after 4:00 p.m. on the afternoon of September 12. Millie and Seymour Locke told their story of seeing a man ("I think it was the same man I saw at the Coroner's inquest," eleven-year-old Seymour testified) and two women walking along the river bank and, sometime later, what they thought was a reclining "lewd couple."[29] As their father acknowledged when he testified the next day, Cold Spring was a "favorite locality for all manner of people."[30]

On that second day of the trial, prosecutors asked the jailer to bring William J. Abrams into the courtroom. Joseph Solomon and his clerk, Isaac Sweede, identified Abrams as the probable purchaser of the rusty double-barreled shotgun with the broken thimble. Aaron Hunt, Rebecca Marot, and twelve-year-old Josephine Stevens agreed that he was probably the man who had visited their various establishments on the morning of the murder hoping to buy a gun. Another clerk testified that Nancy Clem had called at Roll's wallpaper and carpet store between eight and nine o'clock in the morning, nearly the same time as the man who looked very much like Abrams was buying a shotgun at the pawnshop directly across the street.[31]

The state next moved to place Silas Hartman at the crime scene. John Drew testified that early on Saturday afternoon Hartman rented a buggy and the mare named Pet from his stable. Drew's testimony, moreover, suggested that whoever killed the Youngs could have made the round trip between Indianapolis and Cold Spring in only a little over an hour: "Thirty minutes would be sufficient to reach the spot where the murderers' horse was tied," and another ten to walk to the scene of the crime. This was more than mere conjecture; Drew and Pet had taken a test drive at the prosecution's request. Now he reported the results, which fit the state's timeline nicely. Blacksmith Thomas Mansfield and his employer, the aptly named John G. Smith, each affirmed that the horseshoe prints discovered at the crime scene in all probability belonged to Pet. John Culp, the sheriff of nearby Hendricks County, reported seeing two men in a buggy near Cold Spring the day *before* the murder. One of them, he maintained, was Syke Hartman.[32]

Prosecutors waited until day four to introduce evidence that directly concerned the defendant. Madeline Everson admitted to recording her neighbor's accounts and reluctantly recalled that Clem had threatened "in a

1. Nancy E. & William Franklin Clem
2. Mathew & Rebecca Hartman
3. James D. Brown, paper hanger
4. William J. & Margaret Abrams
5. Jacob & Nancy Jane Young
6. Clem & Bro. grocery
7. W. H. Roll's wallpaper store
8. Aaron Hunt, auction room
9. J. R. (& Rebecca) Marot, second-hand store
10. Mrs. Hattie Stevens, Exchange Store
11. J. & M. Solomon's pawnshop
12. Sullivan & Drew's livery stable
13. Post Office
14. New York Store
15. Marion County Jail
16. Marion County Courthouse

E. ST. CLAIR ST.
N. EAST ST.
E. WALNUT ST.
E. NORTH ST.
MASSACHUSETTS AVE.
E. MICHIGAN ST.
N. NEW JERSEY ST.
E. VERMONT ST.
N. MERIDIAN ST.
N. ALABAMA ST.
E. NEW YORK ST.
N. PENNSYLVANIA ST.
E. OHIO ST.
← COLD SPRING
← Fruit House
E. MARKET ST.
N. DELAWARE ST.
E. WASHINGTON ST.
S. ILLINOIS ST.
E. MARYLAND ST.
N

On the morning of September 12, 1868, Nancy Clem walked to paper hanger James D. Brown's house, then to W. H. Roll's wallpaper store. William J. Abrams patronized Clem & Bro. Grocery at about the same time. Prosecutors claimed he made four additional visits—to Hunt's auction room, Marot's second-hand store, the Exchange Store, and Solomon's pawnshop—in search of a gun. In the afternoon, Abrams drove to the Fruit House and Silas Hartman rented a horse and buggy from Sullivan & Drew's livery stable. Prosecutors believed Hartman drove it to Cold Spring, following closely behind a carriage that held Jacob and Nancy Jane Young and a female passenger. After first swearing that she was at home all afternoon, Clem later insisted she had been at the post office and the New York Store. Both the county jail and the courthouse were just blocks from her home in the compact city of 1868. Map by Ian Byers-Gamber, adapted from *Insurance Maps of Indianapolis* (Sanborn Maps & Publishing Co., 1887) and *Logan's Indianapolis Directory . . . for the Year Commencing July 1, 1868* (Indianapolis: Logan & Co., 1868).

joking way . . . to cut my throat" if she mentioned her business dealings to Frank. Jacob Young's sister, Mary Server, testified that Clem had visited her brother's house and that "the two took pen, ink and paper, went into a room together, and were there fifteen or twenty minutes." Mary Belle Young testified to having seen the woman she now knew as Mrs. Clem at her uncle's house often. She corroborated her aunt's description of Clem and Young's business meetings and added a small, but telling, detail. "When the neighbor women" came to visit, Mary Belle explained, they "did not go into the back room." Clem, however, did.[33]

Ann Hottle temporarily interrupted the prosecution's winning streak. Clem's dressmaker told her sad story of losing her life savings. She recounted Clem's threat to have "a company" kill her if she continued to ask for her money back. At this point, reporters noticed, Clem lost some of her usual composure. But not for long: cross-examination revealed that Hottle had twice contacted Frank Clem offering to be "absent herself from the trial" if he paid her off.[34]

Added to these more or less straightforward accounts was the all-too-ample evidence that the defense had attempted to unduly influence witnesses. Wayne Township farmer Perry Todd had "the impression" that Clem was one of the two women riding in Young's carriage on that fateful Saturday afternoon. He also testified that "since the murder" former Deputy Sheriff William Robinson and current Deputy City Marshall Michael Scudder had driven past his house "with a lady in his buggy." (The "lady" was none other than the prostitute Cal Prather.) Robinson "said the woman he had with him he knew to be connected with the murder." Todd demurred: "I told him the woman looked too big and sat up too high in the buggy." "Very well, Mr. Todd," Robinson replied. "We know this is the woman, whether you do or not." Sixteen-year-old John P. Wiley recounted much the same experience. "When Robinson and Scudder brought out the woman to our house, Robinson said . . . 'John, this is the woman that was in the buggy.' . . . He told me if I swore positive as to any woman, to swear that it was this one."[35]

Then there were witnesses who could recount improper conduct on the part of the defendant herself. Seamstress Louisa Merchant stated that Clem had offered her $500 (twice what a sewing woman might earn in a year) if she would swear in court that she saw her sitting on the Hartmans' porch the afternoon of the murder. Prosecutors hoped to repeat their success by calling Clem's neighbor, Viola Pierson, to the stand. In her statement to the grand jury the previous fall, Pierson swore to having seen Nancy Clem at home shortly before four o'clock on Saturday, September 12. Dye and Fishback had reason to believe that she had told something other than the truth; now they expected her to retract her previous testimony. But to their visible surprise and dismay, twelve-year-old Pierson stood her ground: Clem was in her hallway around 4:00 p.m. with a broom in her hand. "Have talked with no person since I have been before the Grand Jury," Pierson insisted, "neither to father, mother, or any one. Have not mentioned it to any one. Have not talked with any of the lawyers in this case."[36]

■ ■ ■

Those who attended the trial created their own rituals. Chapman did what he could to maintain decorum, threatening to bar spectators from the courtroom when witnesses' statements provoked laughter from the audience. He could do little, however, to deter the masses of people who jammed hallways and antechambers, forcing the defendant and bailiff to walk a gauntlet of curious onlookers. Courtroom spectators included "our best citizens"— among them women who peered at Clem through opera glasses—as well as the usual "idlers." Regulars brought their dinners with them and ate them in the courtroom during the brief half-hour noon recess—a time-saving departure from the customary two-hour break. They followed Clem as she was escorted back to her jail cell when court adjourned for the day. They congregated on Alabama Street to gawk at her house, their numbers increasing on Sundays, when court was not in session.[37]

If some showed up at the courthouse door day after day, eager to gain admittance, others crossed its threshold more reluctantly. A trial inevitably requires the presence of unwilling participants—most obviously the defendant, but also jurors who prefer to avoid the financial and emotional demands of service and witnesses who for various reasons would rather not take the stand. The proceedings of December 1868 proved no exception; some of the people closest to Nancy Clem were compelled to testify against her. The law exempted Frank Clem, for it could not force husbands to testify against wives. Clem's sister-in-law Rebecca Hartman had no such recourse. She acknowledged having accompanied her sister-in-law on four or five visits "in the evening" to the Youngs' house. On each such occasion, she explained, "Mrs. Clem went into the adjoining room with Mr. Young"— that is, the back room into which ordinary visitors never stepped. "The interviews would last five or ten minutes generally; after they were over we went home."[38]

Benjamin Abrams was another reluctant witness. For the moment, Clem's—not William J. Abrams's—life and liberty were at stake, but Ben must have known that his words would have bearing on his brother's fate and that he would be called to testify at Bill's upcoming trial as well. He must also have known that taking the stand was likely to jeopardize the longstanding "intimacy" between the Abrams and Hartman families. Little wonder then that his testimony, detailing his three visits to Clem in the wake of his brother's arrest, was equal parts confusion and evasion. He responded to Dye's questions thus: "Don't recollect." "Don't remember." "Can't say whether I told [Frederick Knefler] where I got the money." "Can't tell when I first went up to Mrs. Clem's." "Don't recollect whether I saw [Bill Abrams] more than once that day." Described by the *Cincinnati Daily Gazette* as "a plain, laboring man, with not an inordinate amount of intelligence," he evidently lacked his older brother's capacity for "sharp trading." In fact, he apparently couldn't tell the difference between one hundred and one thousand dollars. "I saw some figures on it and supposed it was a $1,000 bill," he explained. But the note in question—part of the packet Clem drew from her bosom—turned out to be worth only $100—or so Ben said.[39] Here, perhaps, was evidence that he was smarter than he seemed—or evidence that he had been coached. The defense intended to suggest that Clem had had a relatively modest sum of cash on hand; therefore she could not have had Jacob Young's stolen wad of money in her possession. $100 served this purpose better than $1,000.

If Ben Abrams's testimony left jurors confused about the origins and amount of Clem's money, his description of their interactions did not bode well for the defendant—or for his brother. Bill, Ben explained, had expressly instructed him *not* to knock on Clem's front door but to "go into Hartman's and get Mrs. Hartman to call in Mrs. Clem." Ben did as he was told. Once he had the roll of money that contained what he thought was a $1,000 bill, he "went out the back way." He went *in* the back way the next time he called. If the surreptitious nature of these visits failed to arouse jurors' suspicions, Ben's recollections of his conversations with Clem surely strengthened the prosecution's case. "She told me to tell Bill that if he didn't quit sending here for money it would create a suspicion. She told me not to mention her name in this matter," Ben Abrams stated. "Her language was: 'Don't mention my name under the high heavens.'" "Don't remember anything else she said about mentioning her name," he added.[40]

The burden of testimony also fell heavily on Julia McCarty, who described herself as "almost one of the family." Unlike many of the supposed facts jurors would hear, this one rang true. Nineteen-year-old McCarty, the daughter of illiterate and impoverished Irish immigrants, had lived with Matthew and Rebecca Hartman since the age of thirteen—an extraordinarily stable career at a time when domestic servants rarely stayed any one place for long. Now she was in the unenviable position of testifying against one of her almost kin. A day after Abrams's arrest, Clem had given her mistress a packet of money to hide. Before the grand jury, McCarty had stated she had overheard Clem tell Rebecca Hartman that the cash amounted to $21,000. Now, some two months later and "exceedingly ill at ease," she backpedalled, explaining that "since . . . she studied over the matter," she was no longer certain that the package had contained "large bills. . . . Can't be positive now on that subject. I cannot be positive now; think there were hardly none there. When I first saw the roll, just looked over it, and thought the bills were large. I thought I saw two or three $1,000 bills; thought so, when I testified before the Grand Jury." Asked why she had changed her testimony, she replied, "Don't know what has happened since to change my opinion." Few found McCarty convincing; "gave indications of having been tampered with," one reporter noted. Recalled to the witness stand two days later, McCarty had another change of heart. "Mrs. Clem had a package of money in Mrs. Hartman's house on the morning of the murder, which she said she got at Mr. Young's. Think she said there were $21,000." Cross-examined by the defense, she once more claimed not to be certain whether the package contained "$21,000 or $2,100." Questioned again by prosecuting attorney John Dye, she once again wavered: "Think Mrs. Clem said it was $21,000."[41]

McCarty's testimony did not quite accomplish everything prosecutors hoped. On one hand, her attempts to minimize the amount of money in the roll fooled no one. On the other, she stated that Clem acquired it from Jacob Young *before* his murder, casting doubt on the state's version of events, which had Clem taking the money from the dead man's pocket. Still, McCarty, like Rebecca Hartman and Mary Server, had confirmed Clem's and Young's business relationship. She also confirmed that Clem had behaved suspiciously after the murders. Asked by Dye what Clem said when she handed over the packet that contained either $2,100 or $21,000, McCarty answered, "Her words were, 'Julia, don't say anything about the money.'" Equally damning, Clem had also instructed McCarty "to say nothing about her being away that afternoon."[42]

On Wednesday, December 9, Jane Sizemore, the prosecution's eighty-third witness, took the stand. Nancy Clem's "colored girl" proved one of the state's most important informants. Prosecutors might well have wished she were an Irish or German "girl," for judges, lawyers, and juries matter-of-factly questioned the credibility of African American witnesses. Even after the passage of the federal Civil Rights Act of 1866, some Hoosiers continued to believe that their state constitution prohibited African Americans from testifying against whites. Prosecutors were fortunate to try Clem in a court in which a Radical presided.

Despite her significance to the proceedings, we know little about Sizemore other than her race. We do not know, for instance, how old she was. In nineteenth-century parlance, "girl" might describe any servant regardless of age; defense attorney John Hanna's subsequent characterization of Sizemore as "more . . . a fiend than a woman" suggests that she was not, in fact, a "girl." Nor do we know if Sizemore was married, widowed, or single, whether she had been born free or whether she was a recently emancipated slave who had come north to Indiana. (The presence of now-former slaveholders named Sizemore in Alabama and Virginia—and the absence of people named Sizemore in Indiana—suggests the latter.) And we do not know Sizemore's whereabouts after the winter of 1869. What we do know is this: while she had been hired only a little more than a month before the Youngs' deaths, Sizemore was still the Clems' live-in servant at the time of the trial. Testifying put her livelihood and possibly her life at stake. If Clem had threatened to hire "a company" to kill a white dressmaker, what threats might she have uttered to an African American domestic?

Under the circumstances, then, Sizemore's testimony was nothing short of courageous. For the state, it was nothing short of essential. Sizemore could not say whether or not Clem had *purchased* new shoes shortly before September 12, but she remembered *seeing* a pair of new shoes on her bed the Tuesday before the murders. (It was Clem's habit to keep her shoes under the bureau in Sizemore's room.) She did not "remember seeing the shoes since the Sunday after the murder." Recalled to the stand two days later, Sizemore testified that the "new shoes that lay on my bed were laced gaiters, No. 3"—precisely the size and style that left behind the footprints at Cold Spring.[43]

On December 10, the ninth day of the trial, a group of "ladies" who had been trying without success for the past week to gain admittance to the courtroom finally triumphed. When at last they laid eyes on Nancy Clem, they were surprised, "finding nothing peculiarly bloodthirsty or brutal in her appearance." Much to their disappointment, "she was not the horrible looking creature their imaginations had conjured up."[44] They might well have been disappointed by the proceedings themselves. The testimony that followed Sizemore was in some respects anticlimactic. It was also confusing, as Robert Dorsey, William Duzan, and a multitude of bank cashiers and bankers detailed Clem's, Young's, and Abrams's various transactions. Dr. Duzan would be remembered less for his meticulous recounting of money lent, money repaid, and interest accrued than for his appraisal of Clem's character. After consulting his bank book and describing several profitable deals, Duzan offered a passionate defense of his longtime friend and patient. "I trusted her freely and without reserve. Free her from these suspicions and I will trust her again." "She is a wonderful woman," Duzan insisted as he left the witness stand, "strong-minded, self-reliant, and inflexible in the pursuit of her purposes."[45]

On Friday, December 11, after ten days of testimony and 101 witnesses, the prosecution rested its case.

■ ■ ■

Evidently still feeling its way, the defense declined to deliver an opening statement but proceeded directly to its examination of witnesses. In the main, its strategy was simple: to suggest that Clem's money came from a source other than a dead man's pocket, that someone other than Bill Abrams purchased the murder weapon, and that Nancy Clem and Silas Hartman had been anywhere *but* the vicinity of Cold Spring on the afternoon of the murder. A surprising number of witnesses offered evidence to support these claims. A motley assortment with varying personal, familial, and financial relationships to the defendant, they did not prove the most reliable informants. Their sworn statements revealed something else as well: in the immediate aftermath of the murders, Frank Clem had been doing his part to turn up evidence that might exonerate his brother-in-law and his wife. Clem's attorneys hoped, however, that their witnesses would prove credible enough to raise reasonable doubts in jurors' minds.

Defense attorneys called their most credible witness early on. Matthew Hartman's integrity rested less on the substance of his testimony than on his character. A longtime resident of the city—itself a quality that conferred respect—he enjoyed a "reputation . . . without spot or blemish." This "honest mechanic" swore to seeing his younger brother Silas at his sister Nancy's house shortly before five o'clock and inviting him to supper, which they ate at 5:30. "I carried a watch that day," he insisted. "Keep the time correct always." Nor did Hartman think it possible that Syke had eaten supper before returning to the livery stable. "Saw no buggy about. If one had been hitched in front I should have seen it."[46]

Next Hanna called witnesses whose testimony positioned Silas Hartman driving northeast toward Lanesville rather than northwest toward Cold Spring on the day of the murder. William Dowden, a farmer who had known Hartman for "six or seven years," claimed to have met him on the Pendleton road in the late afternoon. "Am not related to him, or Mrs. Clem, or Abrams," Dowden insisted. Martin J. Marshall, who lived near Lanesville, likewise testified to having seen someone driving a horse that looked like Pet sometime "past the middle of the afternoon." So far, so good. But Marshall admitted during cross-examination that Frank Clem "has been to see me twice since the murder." Both times Clem had driven a bobtailed mare with a blazed face.[47]

Then, on the second day of defense testimony, Hanna took a considerable risk: he called Silas Hartman to the stand. Syke offered a detailed account of his activities on September 12, 1868. He told of meeting his cousin Cravens in the early afternoon, of renting the horse and buggy from Sullivan & Drew's livery stable while Cravens purchased tobacco. And, of course, he reiterated his previous statement that they took the Pendleton Pike toward Lanesville but turned back before they reached the town. He had been to Cold Spring only twice, he explained—"at a Sunday School celebration" the previous year and at a picnic in mid-August. Consistent with Sheriff Culp's testimony, Hartman claimed he had passed by the area while driving with his cousin on the Lafayette road on *Friday* but had been nowhere near there on Saturday. On the whole, Syke's testimony was surprisingly convincing, conforming for the most part to the statement he had given to the *Journal* shortly after his arrest. "He told his story but with little variation, and as though it had actually occurred as related," the *Cincinnati Daily Gazette* observed.

"[O]r he had given it much thought," it added.[48]

Cravens Hartman posed a problem that would continue to plague the defense. Syke was a "fast" young man known for his conviviality and sense of humor, but he had introduced none of his friends, acquaintances, and drinking buddies to Cousin Crave during the latter's brief visit to Indianapolis. He had refrained from bringing Cravens home to Alabama Street because "there is not a good feeling between the families." Hard feelings, if Syke were to be believed, ran deep; it would soon become clear that Cravens would make no appearance in court. The one person who could have provided

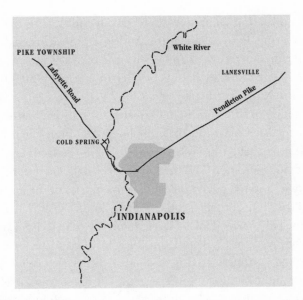

Silas Hartman's direction of travel, September 12, 1868. Witnesses for the prosecution placed Hartman on the Lafayette road heading toward Cold Spring. Hartman maintained that he drove his rented horse and buggy in the opposite direction, on the Pendleton Pike, toward Lanesville. Map by Ian Byers-Gamber.

his cousin Silas with a reliable alibi—and hence potentially exonerate his cousin Nancy as well—was nowhere to be found.[49]

Nevertheless, additional testimony supported Syke's version of events. Aaron and Mary Ann Fee, the keepers of a tollgate on the Pendleton road, swore on the witness stand that two men passed through between one and two o'clock that Saturday afternoon—and that one of them was Syke Hartman. "Nearer two o'clock than one," sixty-one-year-old Aaron Fee recalled, for "we took dinner at one o'clock," and his wife was "washing up the dishes" when the men arrived. The men were driving a "sorrel horse" with a "blazed face" and "short tail . . . with either three or four white feet." One dismounted to get a drink of water from Fee's well, stopping in his kitchen to light his pipe. Fee thought that man was Hartman. Mary Ann Fee substantiated her husband's account. The men, she testified, drove "a sorrel horse, blazed face, short tail and white hind feet; it had white spots; the buggy was red with black top." Indeed, Mrs. Fee expressed greater certainty: she had "no doubt" that the man who lit his pipe on her kitchen stove was Silas Hartman.[50]

Cross-examination suggested these recollections bore the imprint of witness tampering. Frank Clem, jurors and spectators learned, had called at the Fees' tollgate shortly after rumors surfaced of Syke's impending arrest—seated in the same carriage that his brother-in-law had rented from Drew's livery stable, a buggy predictably driven by Pet. "Mr. Clem told me there was a probability of some one being arrested for murder, and wanted to get some clew to clear them, and that this horse and buggy had been driven through there on that Saturday," Aaron Fee acknowledged. Fee's admission raised an obvious question: Did the toll keepers' detailed descriptions of the men, the horse, and the buggy reflect their memories of the day of the murder? Or did they reflect their recollections of Frank's visit?[51]

Noah Mock also placed Silas Hartman on the road to Lanesville. Mock, a farmer who lived on the Pendleton Pike, testified to seeing a horse and buggy carrying two men driving east shortly after two o'clock, returning between four and five the same afternoon. "The horse was sorrel, with light face and white hind feet. The running gears of the buggy were red and black. The top of the buggy was black." The pair drove at "a moderate like gait," an assertion that cast doubt on John Drew's description of Pet's condition on her return.

Once again, cross-examination undermined testimony favorable to the defense. Asked by Dye if he had seen the sorrel horse since, Mock admitted he had: "Franklin Clem had it." Nevertheless Mock insisted that "he recognized the horse before my attention was called to it." "I noticed the buggy because my mother had a buggy something like it, and she traded it to two men in town here, and in a manner got cheated out of it. That was the reason I noticed it." Mock admitted under further questioning that "the horse might have looked a little sweaty," but otherwise he did not budge. Pet, he claimed, was trotting at "a moderate road gait."[52]

If defense attorneys hoped to distance Silas Hartman from the crime scene, they also managed to produce a witness whose testimony suggested authorities had arrested the wrong man—and the wrong woman. A peddler named Hampton Clark testified to having seen a man and a woman in a buggy driving down Indiana Avenue "very fast" in the direction of Cold Spring. "The woman had hold of a gun. . . . Think the gun was an old rusty looking shot gun." In a moment engineered for maximum drama, William Leathers asked Nancy Clem to stand. "That is not the lady," Clark declared.[53]

■ ■ ■

Hanna, Leathers, and Knefler's next move was to construct an alibi for Bill Abrams. For if jurors could be convinced that the purchaser of the rusty secondhand shotgun was someone other than a good friend of Silas Hartman and Nancy Clem, the prosecution's theory of conspiracy would collapse. Flora Ellerhardt, the Abramses' "German girl," corroborated the account her employer had given shortly after his arrest. Her memory was not as helpful as defense attorneys might have hoped. Abrams, Ellerhardt testified, left home between seven and eight o'clock in the morning and returned with a bushel and a half of peaches between nine and ten. Interpreted strictly, this timeline gave Abrams only an hour in which to visit four stores in search of a gun *and* buy fruit at the Clem grocery, a near impossible feat by the standards of nineteenth-century commerce. Interpreted liberally, it gave him plenty of time—nearly three hours—in which to accomplish these errands. Aaron Clem confirmed that Abrams purchased peaches at his store between 7:30 and 8:00. He could not, however, explain why Abrams had needed to go elsewhere that afternoon in search of vinegar: "We generally aim to keep it."[54]

Albert McLain, an agricultural implements dealer, offered a mix of behavioral observation and useful detail. McLain recalled meeting Bill Abrams at a Republican meeting at the Masonic Hall on the evening of Saturday, September 12. Abrams did not act like a man who had just participated in a murder. "His manner was not peculiar," McLain explained. McLain also recalled several encounters with Jacob Young. Young had "exhibited money" on either the morning of the murder or the previous day—McLain could not remember which. Nor could he say just how much Young had stashed in his "large morocco leather pocket book," but "there was a considerable roll of it." When he saw Young again in the early afternoon of September 12, the soon-to-be-murdered man "exhibited no money." Young was driving a buggy and had "but one lady with him."[55]

Defense attorneys saved witnesses who provided information regarding the whereabouts of Clem herself for last, a tactic meant to ensure that exculpatory evidence bearing the most direct relationship to their client would remain fresh in jurors' minds. Lumber dealer Charles Donnelan claimed to have seen her not once but twice on the afternoon of the murder—and nowhere near Cold Spring. At approximately half past two, he saw (and heard) her "hallooing" to a neighbor from the Hartman's upstairs window; about an hour later, he bumped into her—literally—at the post office. "I begged the pardon of the lady; the lady passed me on the left side; my left eye is totally blind; had a bayonet run into it in the service; at the time I thought it was the same lady I saw in the window halloo." Henry Reed, an out-of-work painter who had "been engaged somewhat in buying lumber" but who was "not doing anything now," also swore to having seen Clem at the post office "between three and half past three o'clock." Dye's pointed questions during cross-examination revealed his suspicion that Reed had been tampered with and that the shenanigans had been carried out by the usual suspects. "Don't know that I know Colonel Robinson," Reed explained. ("Colonel Robinson" was none other than ex-deputy sheriff William Robinson.) "Think I do now. Don't remember of ever talking with him about my evidence in this case. . . ." Questioned once again by Clem's attorneys, Reed insisted that the same had "never intimated to me that I should ever receive one cent for my testimony." Levi Pierson, twelve-year-old Viola's father, testified that he had been the person to whom Clem had "hallooed" at 2:30 p.m. "Saw her up-stairs in Mathew Hartman's front window. She hallooed at me, and I hallooed back at her."[56]

Additional testimony supported the defense's claim that, on Saturday, September 12, Clem had never strayed more than a few blocks from home. Eva Bright and her mother, Frederica (sometimes Christina) Ginther, met her in the hosiery department of the New York Store on Washington Street sometime between three and four; Marion C. Wilson, a Pike Township farmer, saw her there as well. Frank Clem's brother-in-law Chris Lout (sometimes Louts or Loucks) personally delivered a sack of flour to the defendant at four o'clock.[57] Hanna and his colleagues thus constructed a sequence of events that rendered a murderous buggy ride on the afternoon of September 12 impossible: Clem had gone to the post office sometime after 2:30; from there, she had briefly visited the New York Store. At the very moment the murders were said to have been committed, Clem was once again at home gratefully acknowledging her brother-in-law's gift of 45 pounds of flour.

Defense attorneys called their own expert witnesses, who cast doubt on the state's interpretation of physical evidence. John J. Gates, a blacksmith with twenty-seven years' experience, testified that the horseshoes presented by the prosecution could not have been worn by Pet; they were too narrow and would have rendered her lame. Ladies shoe dealer David Cady, who had also appeared for the state, admitted that number 3 was the most common size of women's shoes.[58] Any number of women, the defense intended jurors to conclude, could have left behind the clearly delineated footprints, made by a barely worn new gaiter, at the crime scene.

It remained for seventeen-year-old Albert Patton to show that his mother could not have been one of them. Clem, he testified, "wore old gaiters" during their trip to Earlham College two days before the murders. Having been "about the house all summer," he had "no knowledge of my mother having any new pair of shoes within four weeks before I went away." Cross-examination revealed that Patton, like most teenage boys, paid little attention to his mother's wardrobe. No, he could not remember what kind of dress she had worn to Richmond, though he did recall that she on a waterproof cloak. No, he was "not familiar with mother's shoes. Did not know where she kept them." How, then, could he be certain whether the shoes she wore on the train were old or new? "Know the gaiters she had on were old," he answered, "because she remarked to me about them." Here prosecutors had to tread carefully to avoid the appearance of badgering the witness. The defense's strategy was in part pragmatic. Old shoes bolstered its case; new shoes did not. Yet the decision to call Albert Patton had as much to do with generating sympathy for the defendant as with eliciting facts in support of her defense. Patton, a correspondent for the *Chicago Tribune* reported, was "an intelligent and honest appearing boy" who "left a favorable impression." So, too, did Clem's "quiet manifestation of . . . maternal affection."[59]

On Tuesday, December 15, after thirteen days of testimony (nine for the prosecution, four for the defense), the defense rested its case. Its witnesses were a mixed bag—a few "honest farmers," a pair of elderly toll keepers, family members with obvious loyalties, a half-blind veteran, a Pike Township man who had known Nancy Clem "all his life" but had only "the impression" that she was the woman he had seen in the New York Store, a huckster who offered a dubious account of a woman who was *not* Mrs. Clem riding through the streets of the city with a shotgun in her hands. At least four had received visits from Frank Clem and a four-minute nag named Pet.[60]

Rebutting testimony cast further doubt on the defense's witnesses and its case. A grocer testified that the already suspect Henry Reed was working in his store at the very hour he claimed to have seen Clem at the post office. Overruling Hanna's strenuous objections, Judge Chapman allowed Clem's statement before the coroner's jury to be admitted as evidence. "I was at my own house or at my brother's next door, all the afternoon of the murder," it read. Next prosecutors produced a new witness, a neighbor named Lucy Brouse, who reported seeing a flushed and excited looking Mrs. Clem sitting on her front porch at approximately 6:00 p.m. on the day of the murder.

Asked if she'd been working over a hot stove, Clem replied that indeed she had: she had been canning grapes all afternoon. Recalled once again to the stand, Jane Sizemore testified that no grapes had been canned that day.[61]

That was the least of the damage. This time Sizemore admitted that she *had* seen the new gaiters again—"on the morning after the murder, by the back kitchen door." Moreover "they had been recently worn." After Clem "passed out by them," Sizemore "saw them no more."[62]

Then the state called William Pray, the proprietor of a different livery stable from the one Syke Hartman had patronized on Saturday, September 12. According to Pray, Hartman had hired a sorrel mare from *his* establishment on the previous day.[63] Pray's testimony all but dismantled the version of events defense attorneys had hoped to plant in jurors' minds. It enabled prosecutors to advance an utterly plausible alternative: Those who testified to having seen Hartman driving toward Lanesville were telling the truth. But they had encountered him on Friday, September 11, *not* Saturday, September 12. On Friday, Hartman had deliberately chosen a horse that resembled the one he planned to drive on Saturday. In short, Dye and Fishback would claim, Hartman spent Friday afternoon establishing an alibi that would depend on witnesses mistaking one day's occurrences for another.

Save for a soldier who confirmed the hour at which the arsenal gun sounded—an indicator by which several witnesses marked time—the last person to testify was Clem's niece, Mary Alice Hartman. The fact that she was the penultimate witness was no accident; rather, it was part and parcel of prosecutors' careful—some said "brilliant"—strategy. If they hoped to leave a lasting impression on impressionable jurors, there were few better means of doing so than calling Hartman to the stand for the very first time. At fifteen, *this* "Pet" was not quite "the little girl" those who attended closely to John Dye's opening statement might have expected. (Clem, Dye had claimed, "has suborned others of Mrs. Hartman's family, one of them a little girl.") Nevertheless she was an only child, sickly, and, as her nickname implied, cherished. Pet suited Dye's tale of innocence corrupted nicely. Contemporary accounts failed to record her demeanor; whether she was poised or timid, whether she spoke haltingly or with confident assurance no one bothered to say. *What* she said was more important. As Dye had predicted, she testified that Clem had asked her to tell the grand jury that "she was at home all the afternoon of September 12," a fact she knew to be untrue. And between one and two in the afternoon Pet had seen her aunt wearing—not the light-colored "buff" dress—but a dark brown calico.[64]

■ ■ ■

On Wednesday, December 16, the parade of witnesses finally came to an end. Although their testimony was confusing and contradictory, on the whole it did not favor Clem. Much of the evidence that did had been discredited. Given ample indications of witness tampering and attempted bribery, was there reason to believe *anyone* called by the defense? And then there was the mysterious Cravens Hartman, whom no one but Syke seemed to have seen. Numerous observers wondered why the defense did not call him as a witness; prosecutors would allege that Cravens did not exist. One reporter suggested that the man witnesses saw riding with Syke Hartman was none other than Nancy Clem dressed in men's clothing. Others would later suggest that Bill Abrams "personated" Cravens Hartman.[65]

Still, local and regional press coverage suggests that the defense succeeded in casting doubt on the state's version of events. "Thus far, instead of unraveling the mystery, the investigation seems to increase it," the *Cincinnati Daily Gazette* observed.[66]

Whether closing arguments could unravel the mystery remained to be seen. What the *Gazette* implied but did not say was that Clem's appearance, demeanor, and social respectability provided its own kind of evidence. Indeed, for courtroom spectators, journalists, and perhaps for jurors, the mystery was Clem herself.

CHAPTER SIX

Self-Reliant and God Defiant!

Trials are narratives. Both prosecution and defense arrange testimony in carefully ordered sequences; both use opening and closing statements to construct plausible scenarios. Findings of guilt or innocence depend a good deal on which side tells the more convincing story. The stories that lawyers tell need to make sense in two respects. They allow jurors to make sense of inconclusive and often contradictory evidence. If they are to persuade, they also need to make cultural sense. They help their audiences—jurors, spectators, and members of the reading public—grapple with larger social issues; they may even suggest new problems—and new solutions.[1] Nancy Clem posed such a problem. Despite the considerable mass of circumstantial evidence accumulated against her, the "facts" of her case made little sense in light of preexisting interpretations of women and crime. Faced with a novel dilemma, prosecution and defense fashioned new narratives of female guilt and innocence, narratives that offered competing interpretations of women's rightful place in the economic world.

On the morning of Thursday, December 17, lead prosecuting attorney John Dye rose to make his closing statement. He began by appealing to the "majesty of the law," upon which "depend[ed] the security of society from the repletion of such atrocities." Acknowledging that the prosecution based its case on evidence at which "the defense affect to sneer," he insisted that "without circumstantial evidence but few criminals would be convicted in our courts." He presented what was on the surface an airtight case. First he argued that placing Clem at the crime scene was not necessary to convict her, since she had conspired with Hartman and Abrams, whom he declared undeniably guilty. Then he proceeded to "destroy" her alibis, arguing that she *had* indeed been at Cold Spring. After all, John H. and John P. Wiley, "honest, open-faced, candid sturdy farmers," testified that Clem was "the woman who was in the carriage with Mr. Young and his wife."

Dye proceeded to offer an elaborately detailed explanation of the financial transactions between Jacob Young, Williams Abrams, and Nancy Clem, "showing how the money passed between Young, Abrams, and Mrs. Clem; how the transactions of each dovetailed into the other." Here his reputation for clarity foundered. "We have not the space and it would too intricate to attempt to follow this part of the argument in detail," the *Journal* explained. In various conversations as well as in her testimony before the coroner's and grand juries, Clem had denied her business relationships with Abrams and Young, "denials," Dye maintained, that "could only strengthen suspicion." Equally suspicious, Clem's defense refused to lift the veil of secrecy that shrouded these transactions. Defense attorneys could have called William J. Abrams as a witness and asked him explain the nature of the business, but they did not do so. They might even have asked their client to take the stand, but they did not. "They ask if a woman on trial must go into the details of her private business transactions, and we answer that if that business is murder[,] society has a right to inquire into it and to demand an explanation."

Still, Dye faced the difficult task of convincing jurors that the tastefully dressed, respectable woman who occupied the defendant's chair was a murderess. He began by repeating his previous assertion: "No woman from a house of ill-fame" had killed Nancy Jane Young. But the woman who did, he asserted, behaved in ways that were less than reputable. "Mrs. Clem goes to Mr. Young's house . . . at night. . . . No other woman visited Young in that clandestine way."

However much it resonated with social expectations, illicit sexuality provided an inadequate explanation—and Dye knew it. Both prosecution and defense would revisit this particular cultural script, but it was clear that money, not sex, was at the heart of the case. Despite her "clandestine" visits with Jacob Young, Clem's virtue appeared above suspicion. After all, Nancy Young and Rebecca Hartman had been present during these not-so-social calls. More to the point, tarring Clem too heavily with the brush of immorality risked creating sympathy for the defendant; indeed, her attorneys would term her a "a poor persecuted woman." Consciously or not, prosecutors cast about for another means of tarnishing her character. They opted for a rhetorical strategy predicated on gender deviance, but one that departed from familiar scenarios that distinguished passionless ladies from degraded prostitutes. Clem, in Dye's words, was "a woman of brain and of power." This was hardly a compliment; rather it was evidence that an apparently ordinary woman had dangerously seized masculine prerogatives. Clem, as Dye saw it, wielded a particular kind of power, not a sexual power, the sort identified with the villainesses of antebellum crime literature. Clem's power, rather, was a "calculating" power, one that explained her ability to commit premeditated murder. She was, after all, a woman who possessed "more than ordinary executive ability." In Dye's refashioning of criminal femininity, a likely murderess was not a "strange woman." She was a woman of business.

A story that featured a powerful female "executive" called for proportionately powerless men. The more unwomanly Clem waxed in Dye's pronouncements, the more unmanly he rendered her alleged partners in crime. "Can the guilt of Abrams and Hartman be compared with the guilt of this woman?" Dye asked. The answer, of course, was no, for they were "not self-reliant men" but weaklings manipulated by "a woman who has twirled these men around her fingers like ribbons."

Unlike her feeble co-conspirators, Clem *was* self-reliant. Here Dye shrewdly exploited the opportunity Dr. Duzan had unwittingly provided. In testimony Dye considered "absolutely startling," Duzan declared his willingness to do business with Clem again. "She is a wonderful woman," Duzan had claimed, "strong-minded, self-reliant, and inflexible in the pursuit of her purposes." Dye did not find Clem quite so wonderful—at least not in the favorable sense of the term. Rather, he pronounced her "self-reliant and God-defiant."[2]

Dye explained Clem's unnatural and ungodly self-reliance by telling a story, or rather his version of Clem's story, advancing a particular interpretation of her personal economic history. The deprivations she had faced in the years after William Patton's death had embittered her, fueling an obsession with money that "turned her mother's milk to gall" and rendered her capable of murder. By extending her pecuniary concerns beyond mere subsistence, Clem had overstepped the boundaries of virtuous widowhood.[3] She had overstepped the boundaries of virtuous womanhood as well. Dye's summation implicitly invoked his belief that respectable women belonged in the home, not the marketplace, a social configuration, as Dye's memorable rhyme suggested, established by divine as well as human authority. "Is there any more such women? For the honor of the sex, and for the credit of our city and of humanity, God forbid that there should be one other such woman on the continent."[4] Whether he meant a "self-reliant woman," a murderess, or both was not entirely clear. If female self-reliance explained murder, it also threatened to become a crime itself.

■ ■ ■

Dye finished his six-hour oration around 4:00 p.m., and the court adjourned for supper. All parties reassembled at seven o'clock to hear the twenty-one-

year old Marion County prosecuting attorney "win his spurs" with a relatively brief two-and-a-half-hour closing argument. John S. Duncan, the
Journal reported, went "over the same ground to a considerable extent, as
did Mr. Dye, but he handled the facts and the points of testimony in such a
manner as to secure the utmost attention of the jury." Expectations were
low, for Duncan's speech "agreeably surprise[d] his friends." It was not,
however, sufficiently eloquent or entertaining to merit reproduction in the
city's newspapers.[5]

One small portion of Duncan's statement would become familiar even to
those who had not been present in the courtroom. It would be repeated several times over the course of the next few days. At some point during his
brief address, the inexperienced prosecutor committed a serious blunder,
apparently making a disparaging remark about Clem doing "her own
work"—that is, managing without a servant—for the duration of her widowhood. Duncan's statement struck many as elitist. It was an especially
foolish thing to say to a jury of farmers. Only one headed a household that
included a woman who *might* have been construed as a servant, although,
importantly, she was not identified as such. In other words, all of the jurors,
save for the two bachelors and, possibly, the one who escaped the census
taker's scrutiny, were married to women who "did their own work." They
might easily take Duncan's statement as an insult. His opponents would
make the most of his mistake.[6]

■ ■ ■

Defense attorney William Wallace Leathers began his closing statement but
spoke only for an hour before the court adjourned. He continued speaking
for much of the following day. A physically imposing figure—"large and
towering above the average height"—Leathers had a gift for oratory, and
he would soon acquire a reputation as a formidable criminal lawyer. As the
Cincinnati Daily Gazette would later put it, for a defendant " 'not to have
Leathers on his side' was paramount to conviction." At the time of Clem's
first trial, however, the thirty-one-year-old attorney had practiced law for
only eight years, most recently in the capacity as county prosecutor. Like his
legal opponents, Leathers was a Republican, but he had come to the Grand
Old Party via the Democrats, not the Whigs. The arguments he would make
in Clem's defense reflected this partisan heritage.[7]

Whether or not he had yet perfected his trademark technique of "pound-
ing the jury," Leathers, like virtually all of the attorneys involved, knew that

the Cold Spring case represented a career-making opportunity. He did not disappoint. Admirable thoroughness—he offered a rebuttal to virtually every one of the prosecution's claims—characterized his "masterful" summation. Little wonder that his closing statement took seven hours—confirming and perhaps originating his reputation for endurance.[8]

Apart from an archaic appeal to legal tradition—Duncan's explanation for the trajectory of the footprints was faulty, he claimed, because "history gives no instances of murderers returning to their victims when the work of death is done"—Leathers relied on ruthless logic. He seized on inconsistent testimony and faulty memories, taking advantage of the inevitable confusion witnesses, most of whom never imagined they'd be called to testify about seemingly mundane events, inevitably displayed. He embellished his version of the events of September 12, 1868, with phrases such as "beyond all question" and "beyond controversy," emphases intended to imbue with absolute confidence witnesses the state considered unreliable and to cast doubt on testimony prosecutors considered unimpeachable.

The two John Wileys, Leathers argued, were mistaken, for three other witnesses placed Silas Hartman on the Lanesville road, "at least seven miles away in a diametrically opposite direction," at the very time the Wileys claimed to have seen him following the Youngs' carriage to Cold Spring. "If there has been anything proved beyond a reasonable doubt," Leathers claimed, "it is that Syke Hartman took that trip to Lanesville on the afternoon of the murder. That point is settled beyond controversy": "Old man Fee and his wife," keepers of the toll gate on the Lanesville road, saw Hartman at two o'clock that Saturday. Noah Mock, "an honest and intelligent farmer" plowing his field, also testified to seeing a man who closely resembled Hartman drive by on the Lanesville road in the early afternoon. Leathers desired "to treat Mr. Drew fairly" but contrasted his uncertainty about the exact time Hartman rented the horse and buggy ("between one and two and a half o'clock") with his precise recollection of the time of return. "[N]otice how definite he is at one time, and how indefinite at others." Drew testified that Hartman paid for the rental in advance but then said that Hartman "paid his bill" when he returned with poor overheated Pet. "If Hartman paid the hire when he took out the mare what is the meaning of the statement that when he got back he 'paid his bill?' The mare was in a very bad condition, and yet there were no questions asked! That is the first time I ever heard of a horse being returned to a livery stable in this city in a bad condition, returned to the proprietor and yet not a single question asked, not a word of censure; no inquiry made, not a syllable of reproof!"

If Hartman had not returned Pet until after seven, how was it that his brother Matthew had seen him at Nancy Clem's house before five o'clock? And given that the murder had indisputably been committed around four in the afternoon, how could Silas Hartman have arrived back home by five, or even earlier? To do so he would have to have driven "twenty-five miles within an hour"—"a physical impossibility." (Here Leathers pointedly ignored the results of John Drew's experiment, which suggested that returning from Cold Spring in little more than half an hour lay well within the realm of physical possibility.) Leathers pounced on the prosecution for doubting Matthew Hartman's testimony, for implying that his "relationship with Syke and Mrs. Clem" made him "necessarily a perjured witness": "Matthew Hartman has resided in this city for seventeen years and never a breath raised against his character." Hartman was "an honest mechanic . . . whose reputation is without spot or blemish," who told his "story simply and artlessly, in an honest and straightforward manner." If Matthew Hartman could not be trusted, no matter. Mrs. Brouse, "an honest, truthful Christian woman," had seen Nancy Clem and Silas Hartman sitting on Clem's porch shortly before six o'clock. Leathers took special delight in using Brouse, the newly discovered witness for the state, for the purposes of his client's defense. True, Brouse had testified that Clem had said she had "been putting up grapes over a hot stove," a statement everyone agreed had been false. But an "error" of this sort, Leathers assured the jury, was easy to make. More to the point, Brouse placed Silas Hartman on Nancy Clem's porch more than an hour before the time that Drew claimed he returned the horse. And if Brouse had encountered Clem *after* Pet's supposed return to the stable, it would have been too dark to discern a flush on a neighbor's face. In any case, "the flush could not have been the result of the ride to Cold Spring, for it was two hours after the commission of the murder." Nor, Leathers claimed, could it have been attributed to "excitement, for the State's own witnesses prove that the conduct and appearance was in no wise different from what it had generally been." If Syke had made "incoherent and inconsistent statements" to the press, that was understandable for he had been set upon by reporters "*one minute* after his arrest." Naturally, he had been flustered. Any geographic inconsistencies on Hartman's part reflected his incomplete knowledge of the "locality" through which he and Cravens drove.

Leathers did the best he could to account for the puzzling absence of Cravens Hartman. Cravens, he insisted, was no mere figment of the imagination. The register of the Spencer House showed that "C. L. Hartman" slept there on September 7, although not on subsequent nights. Undaunted by this evidentiary gap, Leathers briskly carried on: "There is no evidence to show that he did not continue to take his meals there and lodge elsewhere." Recognizing that Cravens presented a problem that needed to be speedily dealt with and just as quickly discarded, Leathers argued that his testimony was in any case utterly superfluous. "The counsel for the State ask why has Cravens Hartman not been brought into court to corroborate the statement of Syke Hartman? It is a sufficient reply to that inquiry to say, that if old Mr. Fee and wife, Mr. Mock, Mr. Marshall and Mr. Jones, witnesses of unimpeachable character, whose testimony fully corroborates the statements of Syke Hartman are not regarded as sufficient, of what avail would be the testimony of Cravens Hartman?"

Leathers cast doubt on his opponents' interpretation of the physical evidence as well as the accounts provided by their witnesses. Nothing, he maintained, proved that Pet and her interfering shoes had been anywhere near Cold Spring on that fateful Saturday afternoon. Given the absence of witnesses who saw Pet—or any horse—at the crime scene, there was no means of telling when the impressions on which the prosecution's case relied had been made. Besides, Leathers claimed, it was doubtful that the prints belonged to Pet. Blacksmith John Gates had testified that "the shoe taken off the front foot would not fit the track." As for Clem's alleged footprints, several people had measured them and there were "discrepancies in the results, amounting to ¼ to ½ of an inch." No. 3, moreover, was an extremely common size, and Clem's "naked foot" was shorter than most women who wore that size. Nor was the shoe salesman questioned certain he sold Clem a pair of no. 3 gaiters. "The boy at Cady's says he *thinks* he sold a pair of shoes a short time before the murder, but is this the sort of evidence upon which the State hopes to convict the defendant?" Similarly, Leathers continued, Jane Sizemore "thinks she saw a new pair of gaiters." She also had given conflicting—and therefore unconvincing—accounts as to when the imagined footwear disappeared from the premises.

As for Clem's whereabouts, she could not, Leathers insisted, have gone out to Cold Spring and returned with Syke Hartman because, first, *he* had been seen on the Lanesville Road and, second, *she* had been seen downtown in the early afternoon and at home at the time of the murder—a fact "proven beyond all question." Eva Bright and Mrs. Ginther greeted her at the New York Store. Charles Donnellan and Henry Reed met her at the post office earlier that afternoon—at the very time that the prosecution insisted she was riding in Jacob and Nancy Young's carriage. Chris Lout had seen Clem when he delivered a sack of flour to her house shortly after four; Viola Pierson had seen her at home sweeping her front hall about the same time.

Then, Leathers explained, there was the problem of Nancy Jane Young's demise. The prosecution claimed the perpetrators planned on killing her. Mrs. Young knew Clem did business with her husband, so its reasoning went, and she would have immediately suspected Clem's involvement in his death. But Mary Belle Young had testified that her aunt had decided to accompany her uncle to Cold Spring only at the last minute.

Finally, there was the issue of motive, which Leathers shrewdly sought to deflect. "Haven't scores of persons in this city who had business with Mr. Young in the past year or so . . . the same motive? . . . If having business relations with Young establishes a motive for his murder, these scores of persons are as worthy of accusation as the defendant." Clem was an unlikely perpetrator, for as tradition held, "men are more given to deeds of violence for the acquisition of money than women." Leathers had one particular man in mind: Robert Dorsey. Though he disingenuously claimed, "I do not say that the parties with whom Mr. Dorsey was connected had anything to do with the murder of Mr. Young," Leathers not-too-subtly suggested that Jacob Young's former employer was an excellent candidate for perpetrator (implications that would prompt Dorsey to write a letter to the editor of the *Journal* denying his involvement). "Mr. Dye asks what was done with the money Mrs. Clem got of Dr. Duzan, and why ask this question? May I not ask, with equal propriety, what Dorsey did with the $60,000 he borrowed at different times, and used in connection with Jacob Young . . . ?"[9]

Here Leathers paused to make his own argument about the gender of business. By shifting suspicion from Clem to Dorsey, Leathers suggested that jurors focus their attention not on female self-reliance but on the more general practices of street brokerage and speculation. In the moral economy that Leathers constructed, Clem was the victim of unscrupulous businessmen. She was a lender, not a borrower; Young "was using money that she controlled, and making thereby for her, more money than she could make out of it herself." But then she had been unjustly "hunted down and prosecuted in place of others." If Dye insinuated that women's business was necessarily illegitimate business, Leathers raised the question of what men's business should be. This did not, however, mean that prosecution and defense agreed on the proper business of women. Rather than lament Clem's entry into the marketplace or bemoan her avariciousness, Leathers praised her reputation for "economy" and "industry," qualities that rendered her a "faithful wife" and "model woman."[10]

■ ■ ■

William Pinckney "Pink" Fishback spoke next—for the prosecution. He gave what was, by all accounts, a brilliant performance, one that the *Journal* pronounced "both elegant and masterly." Even the *Sentinel*, which only a few months earlier had condemned his support for "Negro suffrage" and sarcastically likened a previous speech to a funeral sermon, complimented Fishback for making "a clear, logical convincing argument, covering the whole ground, embracing the slightest points, and delivered with great force and earnestness."[11]

Fishback repeated many of the same points that Dye and Duncan had already covered but skillfully expanded them to paint a portrait of a calculating murderess and—in a pointed rejoinder to Leathers—*faithless* wife. Like Dye, Fishback emphasized gender reversals, but he extended them to the murder itself. According to Fishback's reconstruction, Clem had exhibited unwomanly courage; Silas Hartman, unmanly cowardice. Clem had coolly stopped to rob Young's coat pocket after his murder and calmly disposed of the pistol that she handled with "dexterity and precision"; the spineless Hartman had panicked, leaving his weapon at the crime scene. Clem, Fishback explained, "brought off her artillery from the field, while her blundering male accomplice fled, leaving his gun lying on the ground." Clem had approached her victim openly, even struggling with her; Hartman "skulked in ambush," concealed in a clump of bushes. To a post–Civil War audience, the implications would have been clear: Clem played the part of soldier; Hartman, of "bushwhacker"—an ambusher and unmanly coward. (As Indianapolitans would subsequently learn, Hartman had indeed "skedaddled" to Canada to avoid military service.)[12]

Like Dye, Fishback counted "avaricious[ness]" among Clem's crimes.[13] As his colleague had done, he turned to Clem's past for an explanation. Once again, however, Fishback extended his rhetorical reach, turning Dye's denunciation of sheer greed into a discourse on the political economy of marriage. "Upon her marriage with her present husband," Fishback explained, "she by arrangement with him, took control of and managed her own business affairs." Fishback imbued Clem's ante-nuptial arrangement with sinister meaning, insisting that "such a woman was well qualified to act a part in this tragedy."[14] That Clem had chosen money over love, economic autonomy over male protection, was evidence of a cold heart, a calculating disposition—and guilt.

Clem's business exceeded the requirements of financial necessity or even prudent foresight. "It is well enough to lay up in time of health and prosperity for a rainy day," Fishback maintained, "and in so far as she exhibited the commendable virtue of economy . . . praise is merited. But that cursed passion of avarice stepped in the moment she stepped out from the plain, straightforward path of duty as a faithful wife, to enter upon the dangerous paths of financial speculation." Clem, in his estimation, had crossed an imaginary line between "industry" and "avarice," between "faithful wife" and dangerous speculator.

The problem as Fishback presented it was not Clem's avarice per se but that her alleged greed sundered her from the moorings of an idealized family economy. To a certain extent, the Cold Spring case was about sex after all, for both prosecution and defense defined marital fidelity in economic terms. If Leathers believed that "economy" and "industry" were the hallmarks of "model women" and "faithful wives," for Fishback, the faithless wife was not an adulteress but one who ventured boldly into the marketplace. Clem's financial dealings violated her marriage contract, thereby rendering her capable of the worst of acts. "It is one of the happiest of the pleasures of married life," he regretfully explained, "to be able to impart to the wife the secrets of the day's transactions, and to exchange congratulations in the success of a venture; but Frank Clem knew nothing of what was transpiring between his wife and Jacob Young and William Abrams. He never knew that these business relations existed until that final settlement at Cold Spring."[15]

No one commented on the confusion Fishback's statement embodied; perhaps this apparent blunder (in contrast to his younger colleague's actual mistake) was part of his "masterly" strategy. Wittingly or unwittingly he reversed the sexes, noting that a husband was supposed to "impart to the wife the secrets of the day's transactions." In short, he killed two birds with one stone, condemning Clem both for keeping secrets from her spouse—rather than "imparting" them—and for transacting at all. Such arguments had the added advantage of deflecting the questions that Leathers had raised about the character of Jacob Young's business. In Fishback's view, women's business, not "speculation," was illegitimate.

As Fishback's reference to the "final settlement at Cold Spring" suggested, business provided him with a metaphor for understanding Clem's actions and a mechanism by which to prove her guilt. He constructed a scenario that not only stressed Clem's economic deviance and her failure to act the part of wifely dependent but also emphasized her "managerial" power, her ability to orchestrate the business of murder. As Fishback explained, "In commercial enterprises we find proprietors, book-keepers, salesmen, and porters. So, in this criminal enterprise, we find confederates and each one plays an appropriate part."[16] Clem's part was that of proprietor, the most unlikely position for a woman to hold, even in a criminal enterprise.

Like his colleague, Fishback made much of Clem's alleged self-reliance. Dr. Duzan's intended compliment backfired, Fishback explained. "The shaft aimed at us struck the prisoner." Changing the arrow's course required careful reinterpretation of a time-honored concept. Normally a term that had positive connotations, self-reliance conjured up visions of breadwinning, entrepreneurial independence, and individual responsibility. But it was also a gendered notion, one that, as the prosecution's rhetorical strategy implied, was meant to describe masculine self-making, not feminine initiative. Applied to Clem, self-reliance became a sort of distorted Emersonianism, supplying additional evidence of her ability to plan and commit murder. "Ah! how strong-minded and self-reliant, how inflexible in the pursuit of her purpose must that woman who rode out with the Young and his wife that Saturday afternoon," Fishback proclaimed.[17]

Clem, in Fishback's view, had exchanged wifely dependence for managerial power. If the prosecution's case served on one level to vilify an unlikely villainess, it also validated an idealized model of gender relations, one in which men whispered business secrets to wives who, for their part, carefully observed the fictive boundaries between home and marketplace.

■ ■ ■

Fishback had one additional weapon in his prosecutorial arsenal, a comparison that would have resonated with local memories of Indiana's "pioneer" period. Clem, he argued in closing, was not only a faithless wife but a "savage." Her alleged actions on the day of the murder recalled "the cruelty of the savage who mutilated the body of his victims." Not satisfied with homegrown analogies, Fishback next likened Clem to the murderous "Thugs" of India. Thugs figured prominently in novels and in both religious and secular periodicals. Thugs, as presented in these literary venues (recent scholars have argued that they were an invention of the colonial imagination), were renowned for tricking their hapless victims, gaining their trust before strangling them. If Thugs had terrorized India until "the bible and the British army exterminated [them]," worse had befallen the City of Indiana. As Fishback put it, "the comparison is favorable to the Thugs. . . . Here in Marion county—in Indianapolis—the Capital and pride of a noble Christian State. Here under the very shadow of the church spires which on every corner point the sinner to his God—we have a murder which in its cold-blooded atrocity, its avarice and cruelty, in its hypocrisy, puts Thuggery to the blush."[18] Calling into question her sexual morality, feminine propriety, marital fidelity, Christian piety, and implicitly even her whiteness, Fishback left little doubt to his opinion of Clem's character. She was a faithless wife, a self-reliant murderess, a "Thuggish" hypocrite—an outwardly respectable woman who, blinded by greed, had resorted to "heathen" savagery.

"Gentlemen," Fishback eloquently concluded, "the case is now with you. We who represent the State do not ask that you shall deal with this woman in any spirit of vindictiveness. Deal with her mercifully, if you choose, but with that measure of justice that bloody-minded men shall pause and forsake their guilty purposes."[19]

■ ■ ■

John Hanna, closing for the defense, had the last word—or rather words, nearly six hours of them. Lacking his colleague's endurance, he delivered the final two hours of his speech sitting down. The forty-one-year-old lawyer stood five feet eight inches tall, "with a heavy, square frame, though not inclined to corpulency." In the eyes of one observer he resembled "an early Indiana circuit rider." An undated photograph shows a man with piercing eyes, dressed in a jacket and white shirt without tie or collar—a portrait that personified his "plain and unassuming manner."[20]

Born in Warren Township, where he made the early acquaintance of Frank Clem, Hanna was the kind of self-made man Americans loved to celebrate. An 1885 local history termed his life story "a great incentive to other poor young men to go and do likewise." His father, a farmer born in South Carolina but raised in frontier Indiana, died when he was twelve, his mother five years later. At the age of nineteen, "determined to acquire an education," he walked the nearly 70 miles to Asbury College (now DePauw University) in Greencastle, "with only $4 in his pocket." He supported himself by working as the college's janitor and graduated with honors. He read law with a local attorney, became a partner, and served as mayor of Greencastle before heading to "Bleeding Kansas," albeit not until 1858, after the worst violence was over. Hanna left the Democratic Party about the same time he left for Kansas. Elected to the territorial legislature as a member of the recently formed Republicans, he introduced the law that ended slavery in the territory. He returned to Greencastle in 1860 and in 1861 Abraham Lincoln appointed him the United States attorney for Indiana, a position that entailed prosecuting draft dodgers and Confederate sympathizers. A "decided, outspoken Republican," Hanna lost his job five years later, after publicly criticizing Andrew Johnson. After suffering a second political defeat, this time at the polls, when he lost a campaign for the state legislature in the fall of 1868, he decided to focus his efforts on private practice (he would briefly return to political life in the 1880s when he served a term in Congress). The law firm he formed with Frederick Knefler was based in Indianapolis, where prospects were plentiful, but Hanna continued to live in Greencastle, commuting to the capital when legal duties required his presence.[21]

Clem's case, his first murder defense, could not have come at a better time. Hanna knew a good opportunity when he saw it; his performance on his client's behalf would cement his reputation as a defense attorney. Nearly twenty years later, the anonymous author of *The History of Hendricks County* described his practice as "remunerative." "A stranger upon entering our court could at once single him out as one of the leading spirits of the Indianapolis bar," the *History* smugly proclaimed. David McDonald, an Indianapolis judge best remembered for his curmudgeonly diary, offered a less flattering assessment: "destitute of legal learning and intellectual strength."[22]

Hanna knew that Fishback would be a hard act to follow, but he shrewdly deployed his opponent's eloquence to his own advantage. He stated his intention of "talk[ing] to the jury frankly and seriously, as man to man, rather than in the language of a professional attorney." "I don't profess to be a popular speaker," he admitted, a maneuver meant to cast doubt on the motives of "popular speakers." "I am not here bidding for applause as before a popular assemblage. I am only talking to a jury of twelve men solemnly impressed with their deepest responsibility, and not to the outside—not to a town meeting. I am not here to endeavor to please your ear with skill in rhetoric or ingenuity in the construction of sentences."

These disclaimers notwithstanding, Hanna's performance was every bit as skillful, as he donned the mantle of folksy lawyer and played the part for all that it was worth. No quotations from Shakespeare, no references to barbaric inhabitants of foreign shores graced his closing argument. Instead he opted for an unpretentious style, punctuated with occasional humor. "My God," he declared at one moment, "I've heard more about ladies' shoes in this trial than I ever heard in all the balance of my natural life." (A subsequent "facetious reference to shoes in connection with his home affairs . . . provoked demonstrations of merriment from the spectators.") Hanna's simple, unaffected language was probably genuine, in keeping with the dialect of a self-made man, but it was also strategic. He knew that his audience— the members of the "jury of twelve men solemnly impressed with their deepest responsibility"—consisted of men whose origins were very much like his own.

Realizing that he needed to do more than merely charm the jury, Hanna devoted a good part of his closing oration to dismantling the "cluster of suppositions, perhapses, supposes, guesses, and may be sos" that—in his view—characterized the state's case. Aware of the necessity of refuting the prosecution's conspiracy theory as well as its claims regarding Clem's whereabouts on the day of the murders, he endeavored to uncouple the chain of evidence the prosecution had forged. There was no proof, he insisted, that the money stolen from Jacob Young's pocket was the same money that Clem retrieved from her sister-in-law's basement. None of the merchants and clerks who encountered the purchaser of the old rusty shotgun with the broken thimble was absolutely certain that man was Bill Abrams. "Abrams is not an unknown man here, but possesses a very large and general acquaintance. The Jury is asked to believe the remarkable story that Abrams, liable to be recognized in every part of the city, would in broad daylight, with murder in his heart, go about the city saying 'trot out your guns.' . . . This is the baldest kind of nonsense." Several witnesses, including Mr. and Mrs. Fee ("honest people"), who ran the tollgate, testified to seeing Silas Hartman on the Lanesville road, at the very time the prosecution claimed he was heading to Cold Spring. If the man driving the buggy "sixty rods" behind the Youngs' carriage was staring down at his wheels, John P. Wiley could not have seen his face. How then could he be sure that the man was Syke Hartman? The shoes supposedly worn by Pet, retrieved from a pile of discarded horseshoes at a blacksmith's shop, did not match her hind feet. Wiley and Perry Todd had only the "impression" that the woman riding with Jacob and Nancy Jane Young was Nancy Clem. Hanna's rejoinder demonstrated that he, too, had his moments of eloquence: "Gentlemen, if human life rests on so flimsy a thread burn your Court Houses. Farewell public justice!"

Hanna emphasized testimony that placed Clem anywhere that Saturday afternoon *but* at the scene of the crime. He recited the sequence his colleague had already enumerated: a trip to the post office sometime after two o'clock, a brief stop at the New York Store, then home again. If Clem's own previous recounting of her whereabouts contradicted the various alibis presented at her trial that, Hanna explained, was entirely understandable. The "poor and persecuted woman" had been "hunted and hounded." Besides, he maintained, testimony before the coroner's jury "amount[ed] to nothing" because that body had been "irregularly and irresponsibly constituted."

Hanna, like Leathers, faced the problem of defending a client who refused to explain the nature of her business. First, he claimed that none of the evidence presented constituted proof that Clem had engaged in transactions with Jacob Young. Second, he appealed to pecuniary logic. If, as the prosecution maintained, "Mrs. Clem was making money by letting Young have money . . . would she have wanted to kill the man that was making money for her?" Rather than invoke feminine delicacy, as had Leathers, Hanna suggested that Clem remained silent to protect unnamed others. "Her tongue is tied," he explained. "If the padlock were taken from her mouth, she could tell a simple, businesslike story." Absent this story, he resorted, as had his colleague, to innuendo. Could S. K. Fletcher or Robert Dorsey explain *their* business with Young? "How would [Dorsey] explain his reasons for indorsing for a man who had been his indigent porter, and whose business was a mystery to him?" Hanna alluded to the "far greater suspicions surrounding certain other parties now at large . . . about the excessive haste to have letters of administration taken out for Young's estate." Everyone present knew that Dorsey was the "party" who had been anxious to gain access to Young's assets.[23]

■ ■ ■

At the heart of Hanna's closing argument was a populist defense of working people in general and of "self-reliant" working women in particular. He, too, capitalized on Duncan's remark that Clem's had "done her own work." By incorporating his client and those who testified on her behalf into a pantheon of virtuous working people, he painted attorneys for the prosecution as elitists who scorned "the middle and lower classes." "During her widowhood" Clem had been "thrown upon her own resources. She took boarders, did her own work, sewed for those she boarded, and proved herself a self-reliant woman. Nothing whatever could be produced against her virtue." Dye, Fishback, and most especially John Duncan disdained manual labor. They harbored little sympathy for women "thrown upon their own resources."

As for Clem's economic activities since her second marriage, Hanna appealed to listeners who viewed women's participation in family economies as both expected and essential. He acknowledged that she had been "foolish" to conceal her dealings from her husband but otherwise approved her diligence and savvy. Far from condemning Clem's self-reliance, he praised her "great business tact." "Trumpet-tongued" prosecutors, Hanna implied, had little respect for working people, not even for the honest farmers who sat on the jury. Not so John Hanna. "I honor the men and women who work: I honor and respect the laborer." The members of the prosecution, on the other hand, "sneered" at the evidence various "laborers" provided. They used the "poverty" of Mrs. Ginther, "an old German lady," as a "ground of suspicion against her integrity," Hanna complained. "Why these insinuations against the purity of witnesses because of their poverty[?] . . . Work don't impeach them for truth and veracity. . . . If all the honesty in this land, gentlemen, is confined to the rich, God pity humanity. The solid reliable worth of this country is found in the working classes. If you want virtue, industry and solid worth, go among the women who work. Go to the women who stand before the wash tub," Hanna thundered.[24]

And in the story Hanna told to the jury, Clem was one of those virtuous, industrious, and worthy women. He condemned the "fashionable . . . slander" against working women; he condemned the prosecution's portrayal of Clem as a faithless wife. He would later be known as a champion of educational equality; "he believes in giving girls an equal chance with boys in the advantages of education," a subsequent "sketch" of "prominent citizens" noted, but the gender ideology he offered to Clem's jury was far more conventional.[25] In Hanna's rendition, female self-reliance—or a certain version of it—bolstered rather than threatened the institution of marriage. Making this argument meant turning a legal tale into a sentimental story, one that literally domesticated Nancy Clem. It was not Clem, Hanna claimed, but her future spouse, "act[ing] a better part than a mere fortune-hunter," who insisted on the by-now infamous ante-nuptial agreement. The Clem Hanna envisioned bore little resemblance to the self-reliant and God-defiant manipulator conjured up by prosecutors, let alone a Thug. "They seek to make a very extraordinary woman out of the prisoner, twisting all sorts of strong men about her ingenious fingers—twirling them around as boy would a stick." Hanna discerned "no such mysterious diabolism." Clem was "only a woman, with a capacity to feel and suffer as other women" with "a heart that can be broken by an unfounded prosecution."[26]

Being "only a woman," Clem possessed neither the initiative nor the legal knowledge to assert her rights; indeed, "rights" were absent from the argument. Hanna's story preserved Frank Clem's husbandly authority, entitling his wife to his symbolic protection. Nancy Clem had been faithful after all; she "managed her own estate" only because her husband suggested it. Countering the prosecution's portrait of an avaricious predator and faithless spouse, Hanna, as had Leathers, depicted his client as an able manager and dependable contributor to family coffers—just the sort of woman members of the jury might have married.[27]

Hanna's vision was neither new nor especially liberating. Rather, it tried to incorporate Clem's speculative ventures into older, predominantly rural traditions that viewed women's economic contributions as essential to family prosperity and survival. The fit was far from perfect; the Nancy Clem that defense attorneys fashioned exhibited little ambition, independence, or initiative. If prosecutors portrayed her as a grasping opportunist, Clem's attorneys took pains to emphasize her economic passivity. They denied that Clem was the "mastermind" behind the "ring." In neither the business of murder nor the business of business did she play a proprietary role; she was an innocent participant in a nefarious scheme organized and orchestrated by Young and other shadowy, unnamed, characters.[28] If prosecution portrayed her as an aggressive borrower, defense presented her as a naïve lender, attracted by the high rates of interest Young offered her.[29] The question of whether Clem had been a borrower or a lender involved the larger issue of motive: a lender would have wanted Young alive, not dead—a logic that both Leathers and Hanna argued. But the two terms had additional connotations. The prosecution's depiction of Clem as an aggressive borrower fit well with her alleged economic deviance and managerial powers. The defense's representation of a naïve lender, on the other hand, nicely complemented its definition of "faithful wife."[30]

■ ■ ■

Courtroom rhetoric offered two contrasting visions of gender, economy, and the expected duties of "faithful wives." One, articulated by the prosecution, was urban, and for its time and place, modern. In condemning Clem's "self-reliance," Dye, Fishback, and Duncan championed the ideology that historians have come to call the doctrine of separate spheres, a set of cultural principles that assigned men to the marketplace and women to the home. These beliefs had partisan overtones; Whigs, and later Republicans, were more likely than Democrats to embrace them.[31] But separate spheres was a concept that many Marion County residents—even as late as the 1860s—would have found unfamiliar. If female street brokers were rare, no one had to look very far to find evidence of women's active involvement in the city's economy. One needed to look no further than William J. Abrams's conspicuous consumption of firearms on the morning of the murder. Abrams—or someone who looked very much like him—encountered at least two businesswomen as he shopped for a shotgun. Rebecca Marot's second-hand furniture store had no guns for sale. The Exchange Store did, but Josephine Stevens, the twelve-year-old daughter of the proprietress, asked a higher price for a rusty double-barreled shotgun than the man was willing to pay. That he purchased the infamous weapon (newspapers would subsequently refer to it as "*that* gun") from a man—a clerk at Solomon Brothers pawnshop—was the result of a serendipitous combination of availability and price, not the absence of women from the urban marketplace.[32]

The gender ideology invoked by the defense reflected the necessities and sensibilities of a rural, and to a certain degree, Democratic society. Democrats believed that white men were the masters of their households, but they also believed that all who constituted those households, including faithful wives and dutiful daughters, had economic contributions to make. To the extent that their trial rhetoric reflected their beliefs, William Leathers and John Hanna had left the Democratic Party, but not its gender conventions, behind. Hanna's strident anti-capitalism placed him in opposition to the ascendant pro-business wing of his party, a faction that Fishback and Dye, Radical though they were, at least partially represented.[33]

Even as it stood, Hanna's carefully constructed moral universe was full of potential contradictions. His praises did not extend to *all* working people—or even to all women who stood before washtubs. To a certain extent, his choices were crassly instrumental. Witnesses who provided exculpatory evidence were honest, hardworking folk; those who gave damaging testimony failed to merit the "honor and respect" he accorded to "the laborer." He complained that the prosecution discounted Charlotte Bright's testimony because she worked as a seamstress, yet he included the illiterate dressmaker Ann Hottle in a list of the "doubly d——d" whose "machina-tions" had put his innocent client on trial. He urged jurors to discount the sworn statements of "the servant girl," Julia McCarty. He dismissed testimony in regard to Clem's allegedly newly purchased and hastily dis-carded shoes as evidence provided by "negro cooks and hard cases." An "earnest-working Republican," he nevertheless reserved special vitriol for Jane Sizemore, whom he described as "looking more like a fiend than a woman"—though he noted that "even that accursed nigger . . . testified to having heard Mrs. Clem laugh over at Hartman's before four o'clock that afternoon."[34]

Hanna's racial epithet would not have shocked his primary audience. Consider, for instance, the language of William Stuart, a man very much like those who sat on the jury. Stuart, a farmer from Johnson County just to the south, went to Indianapolis in the spring of 1869 in search of a neighbor's stolen horse: "Found him a niger [*sic*] on him . . . had him lock[ed] up."[35] In-diana Democrats were most notorious for their overt racism, but Republi-cans, apart from the Radicals represented in this case by Judge Chapman, John Dye, and the largely absent Benjamin Harrison, did not necessarily em-brace racial equality. Nor did they shy away from racist rhetoric. Apart from a minority of abolitionists even midcentury advocates for a free Kansas—a movement in which Hanna had been in the legislative if not the military forefront—were most interested in securing liberty for white men, a liberty they believed threatened by slavery. Indeed, in the context of the Kansas controversy, Hanna publicly declared his support for "the white laborer." If he had moderated his views by the late 1860s, he could still draw on a per-sonal reservoir of racial rhetoric when the occasion demanded it.[36]

Hanna's generous definition of "laborers"—farmers, housewives, the working and middle classes—reflected both the fluidity of social class and the myriad ways in which nineteenth-century Americans defined the con-cept. It also underscored the value he accorded to economic independence, an ideology that had deep roots in American soil but that had held particular importance for pre–Civil War Republicans. Hanna's denunciation of indi-gent porters and servant girls was strategic, but it also echoed his belief in self-reliance over servility, a belief in an ideal society constituted by indepen-dent (white) farmers and mechanics. By the late 1860s the days of this social vision were numbered.

■ ■ ■

The contrasting visions offered by prosecution and defense, first and foremost, were competing narratives constructed to serve a particular set of circumstances. They represented attorneys' best attempts to explain why a respectable woman was on trial for her life—and why she should be found guilty or innocent. But they also reflected tensions within the Republican Party—between former Whigs and former Democrats, between Radicals and moderates, between those who defended the labor theory of value and those who promoted industrial capitalism, between proponents of separate spheres and supporters of household patriarchy. These were tendencies, not ironclad categories; few individual party members lined up neatly along all axes. Still, the differences, especially between Hanna and Fishback, are striking. Hanna was not nearly as "destitute of legal learning and intellectual strength" as a condescending detractor—or Hanna's own language—implied, but he never joined the Indianapolis Literary Club; neither, one suspects, was he invited. Fishback's references to Thuggery, for all their racism, suggested a certain cosmopolitanism. Hanna, by contrast, championed a localism grounded in household economies, a localism that celebrated enduring ties to family, friendship, and place.[37]

These were the values on which Hanna drew as he opened and closed his six-hour defense of "the wife of an early and constant friend." He began by invoking Warren Township, where he and Frank Clem "grew together to man's estate" and "the church yard . . . [where] their parents were sleeping." He described Nancy Clem as "one who is nearer to me than anything in the world save the lady I call my wife." His final remarks condemned the "assault" on the alibi testimony of Chris Lout, discredited by the prosecution because he was the widower of Frank Clem's sister. "The wife of the witness is not living. She sleeps peacefully beneath the clods of the valley, unconscious that he who mourned her loss as a loving wife now stands unworthy in the eyes of the counsel."[38]

Whether Hanna had kept up with his "constant friend" is unknown. Whether he had even met the "one who is nearer to me than anything in the world save . . . my wife" prior to her arrest is unclear. Very likely these terms of endearment were rhetorical embellishments, meant to tug at the jurors' heartstrings, rather than genuine expressions of sentiment. Hanna's appeal, however sincere, did the work he intended. "His argument was very long, very powerful," the *Journal* reported, "and had a visible effect upon the jury." Or, as the *New Albany Daily Commercial* cynically observed, "Hanna pumped for 'salt water' and he got it."[39] In the end, his argument was every bit as brilliant, every bit as masterful, as that of his opponent. Of course, an argument that evoked communal bonds had its risks. Like John Hanna and Frank Clem, Silas Hartman, William J. Abrams, and Jacob Young had also "[grown] together to man's estate." If the prosecution's theory was correct, the very sorts of attachments Hanna valorized were those that led Young down the road to Cold Spring.

■ ■ ■

Judge Chapman issued a lengthy list of instructions, a task that occupied several hours. By and large, they favored the prosecution. Chapman noted, for example, that if the jury was convinced beyond a reasonable doubt of a conspiracy between Nancy Clem, William J. Abrams, and Silas Hartman, the guilt of any one party ensured the guilt of the defendant. Then the jury retired.[40] After deliberating for nearly two days, it failed to agree on a verdict. Prosecutors immediately submitted a motion for a new trial, which Chapman speedily granted. In the meantime Clem was to remain in jail.

■ ■ ■

As it turned out, John Hanna's moving statement *almost* worked. Eleven of the twelve jurors favored acquittal. No evidence regarding the substance of their deliberations survives, but newspaper accounts suggested that the members of the jury uniformly believed Clem guilty but only one beyond reasonable doubt. Put another way, only one was willing to convict. Certainly the case was a complicated one, requiring jurors to sift through a mountain of confusing evidence. Certainly the defense's version of marital economy better suited jurors' own common sense than did John Duncan's ill-advised critique of women who did their own work. Perhaps the responsibility of passing a judgment on a member of the gentler sex—regardless of whether she did her own work—was more than these eleven men could bear. "No jury in Indiana," the *Journal* proclaimed, "will ever hang a woman." Perhaps the outcome reflected the reputed clannishness of up-country southerners, men unwilling to condemn one of their own. Significantly, the sole dissenter, a man who "declared that he was so satisfied of [Clem's] guilt that he would not change his mind," was the only juror of foreign birth. Antone, also known as "Anthony," Wiese was a native Prussian. Too much could be made of his distinctiveness; Clem's own kin included "foreign" elements—Chris Lout, her brother-in-law by marriage, was also German. Indeed, the two men—both Democrats—lived in Warren

Township, the same locality in which Frank Clem and John had "[grown] together to man's estate." They were in fact neighbors, separated only by a few miles of farmland and a few pages of the census. Wiese's stand must have taken a fair amount of courage, courage that indeed would soon be put to the test.[41]

■ ■ ■

Whether prosecutors could persuade another jury to seriously consider hanging a woman remained to be seen.

CHAPTER SEVEN

Knowed It Was Them

Rumors spread near and far as Clem's second trial approached. Authorities had recovered a pistol and ladies gaiters from the Clems' backyard privy. Clem's words to Bill Abrams: "We put Mr. Young out of the way easy enough, but Mrs. Young fought like a good one." These tales proved groundless. One of the many facts reported in local and regional newspapers, however, seems to have been true: juror Anton Wiese, the "stubborn Dutchman" who held out against acquittal, received a death threat in the mail.[1]

The context had shifted in other, less dramatic, ways. During the six weeks or so that elapsed between the end of Clem's first trial and the beginning of her second, Indianapolis officials launched an investigation of the city's police department and brought charges against several officers. Among the police board's findings: members of the department had extorted payments—in cash and in kind—from the keepers of brothels and saloons; Indianapolis's finest regularly consorted with "confidence men, thieves and gamblers." (One especially poor loser went so far as to arrest fellow gamers to recover the money he had wagered.) Behavior of this sort was not unusual; to the contrary, it typified the petty corruption that plagued cities large and small. But coming as it did on the heels of a cold-blooded murder, the police investigation amplified fears of moral decay. It also threatened to influence the course of criminal justice. Although no one directly linked its findings to Clem's case, the inquiry implicitly cast doubt on the men responsible for her arrest and prosecution. Law and politics, nevertheless, made for strange bedfellows. Two of Clem's attorneys, John Hanna and William Leathers, defended policemen charged with various forms of wrongdoing. In the end they prevailed, amid accusations that the acquittals were politically motivated.[2]

Arguing unsuccessfully for the prosecution was Jonathan W. Gordon, one of the most prominent attorneys in the state. Well before the specially constituted police court finished its work, he had joined his erstwhile rivals as the newest member of Clem's defense team. Gordon was a man of many talents. The son of an Irish laborer, he began professional life as a doctor; a site in his native Ripley County nicknamed "Gordon's Leap" marks the spot where the young medical student, caught in the act of robbing a grave, supposedly jumped off a cliff to escape pursuing authorities. In the late 1840s, Gordon made another leap, abandoning medicine for law and politics. He won election to the Indiana House of Representatives in the late 1850s, serving two terms as Speaker. Like many of his contemporaries, Major Gordon was known for his military service, having volunteered in both the Mexican and Civil Wars. He also gained renown as a poet. His verses sound hackneyed to modern ears ("Bard of my soul, thy hallowed song sublime," begins his "Apostrophe to Milton"), but they merited inclusion in contemporary anthologies. A Republican but not a "rad," Gordon was prone to "isms," including both temperance and nativism. Remembered by a classmate at Hanover College as a "poor and awkward-looking country boy," he had risen considerably in the years since, having achieved particular recognition for his arguments opposing the jurisdiction of military commissions over civilian citizens of states that remained loyal to the Union. At the time of Clem's second trial, Gordon was by far the most "distinguished legal light" on either side. He had in fact given a young Benjamin Harrison his start. Now he would face off against his former protégé.[3]

Harrison had stayed in the background during Clem's previous trial, but this time he took an active part. An eloquent extemporaneous speaker, he eschewed the "florid and impassioned speech" that characterized mid-century courtroom performance, preferring instead to address juries in a conversational manner and tone. A stickler for preparation, Harrison devoted considerable time to "learning all the details of fact involved in a proposed prosecution or defense"—a quality well suited to this particular case. Clem's attorneys recognized the threat he represented, for on the opening day of the trial John Hanna presented a motion objecting to the employment of private attorneys, arguing that the county prosecutor should try the case on his own. Judge Chapman overruled the motion.[4]

Not the least of the many ironies that beset the Cold Spring case was that it placed Harrison in the position of prosecuting his neighbor. Before they ended up on opposing sides in court, Harrison and Clem must have had at least a passing acquaintance. It is unlikely they had anything more. In an era when churches structured much of the community's social life, the Harrisons were Presbyterians; the Clems, Methodists. The Harrisons were staunch abolitionists before the Civil War and Radical Republicans after it; the Clems, most likely neither. The Harrisons were not all that much wealthier than the Clems—by some estimates they were poorer—but

"Leading Legal Lights." Clem's trials engaged an impressive array of legal talent. George Henry Chapman (*top, left*), the former commander of Indiana's Third Cavalry and the first judge of the Marion County Criminal Court, was a stern jurist whose rulings and instructions tended to favor the prosecution. Three distinguished private attorneys, including Benjamin Harrison (*top, right*), assisted the young and inexperienced county prosecutor. Shown in his Civil War uniform, "General Harrison," like Judge Chapman, was a Radical Republican and uncompromising moralist. Clem's defense team included John Hanna (*bottom, left*), known for his "plain and unassuming manner" and described as resembling "an early Indiana circuit rider." Hanna's colleague, Jonathan W. Gordon (*bottom, right*), who joined Clem's defense in 1869, was a poet, doctor, and temperance advocate as well as a lawyer. Both were Republicans, but neither identified with the Radical wing of the party. General George H. Chapman, from the Records of the Office of the Chief Signal Officer (RG 111), National Archives; General Benjamin Harrison, 1865, courtesy of the Benjamin Harrison Presidential Site; John Hanna, public domain; Jonathan W. Gordon, from B. R. Sulgrove, *History of Indianapolis and Marion County, Indiana* (Philadelphia: L. H. Everts, 1884), following p. 180, courtesy of the Herman B Wells Library, Indiana University.

surpassed their neighbors in social capital. The grandson of a president, Benjamin Harrison was a graduate of Farmer's College and Miami University. Caroline Scott Harrison, a talented artist, held a degree from the Oxford (Ohio) Female Institute. "General Harrison" was a war hero, only recently returned from distinguished military service, and a lawyer of some renown. Finally, and perhaps not insignificantly, the up-and-coming attorney and the woman he would prosecute were temperamental opposites. Self-righteous, uncompromising, and reserved, Benjamin Harrison posed a striking contrast to Nancy Clem, a gregarious woman whose various conflicting alibis suggested at the very least a willingness to stretch the truth. These disparities aside, it would have been virtually impossible for the Harrisons, residents of North Alabama Street since 1861, *not* to have encountered the Clems and the Hartmans.[5]

■ ■ ■

The defendant herself appeared at the trial's opening session on February 9, 1869, fashionably but tastefully attired (wearing "apparently new gaiters," the *Sentinel* sarcastically noted). She retained her unnatural calm through her initial and subsequent appearances, the result, some said, of imbibing a daily pint of brandy.[6] Her genteel performances, as behind-the-scenes accounts make clear, came at considerable effort. When not in court, Clem was confined to a dark, dirty, vermin-ridden cell—only a few blocks away from her freshly painted and papered parlor. "The general appearance of her dress and person," noted one visitor, "like that of every one else immured in jail, was not suggestive of extraordinary cleanliness."[7]

Just as the jail's proximity to respectable residences—Harrison's as well as Clem's—reflected an as yet unspecialized urban geography, Indianapolitans' assessments of Clem's community standing revealed the lingering fluidity of their social order. One correspondent disputed reports that positioned Clem within "our best society." She described the accused as a woman who had "led the active, industrial life," one who did "not seem possessed of any natural refinement or education"—in other words, a woman who seemed entirely capable of uttering a colloquialism like "Mrs. Young fought like a good one." A longtime city resident remembered Clem quite differently: "a woman of social prominence . . . cultured beyond average." Another account agreed: Clem was "very prominent" because she was "the daughter of one of the best known and most highly respected of Central Indiana's pioneers." In a certain sense all three conclusions were true, for they reflected different measures by which a person's status might be judged. Newer standards that emphasized education, refinement, and— for women—retirement from "active, industrial life" overlay but did not entirely displace older definitions rooted in "pioneer" heritage. And within her circle, composed mainly of upland southerners, Clem *was* a woman of social prominence. How otherwise could she have attracted investors to her financial scheme? In more ways than one, Clem proved a difficult woman to pin down. In the years to come, she would move back and forth between competing indices of social worth.[8]

Most of the time, other people told Clem's story. At times, however, she seized the opportunity to declare her own sense of the status to which she was entitled. Jailers complied with her request to bunk with "a decent colored woman" (albeit one accused of murdering her husband) rather than a white prostitute, a move that confirmed her respectability and (as she would have seen it) her racial superiority. It also allowed her, however temporarily and incompletely, to replicate her previous domestic arrangements. In a remarkable display of noblesse oblige, she did so literally. When her cellmate was acquitted and released, Clem arranged for her to be employed at her house on Alabama Street.[9]

Frank, for his part, took his daily place at Clem's side, just as he had for the duration of her first trial. The *Sentinel* extolled his "manly conduct," which, it claimed, "has excited universal admiration." Representing Democratic opinion, it implicitly invoked southern notions of manliness that emphasized the importance of "honor," the maintenance of one's personal reputation. Certainly honor demanded that Frank stand—or rather, sit— beside his wife, whatever his suspicions regarding her innocence or guilt. Yet his posture in and of itself was an admission of defeat. Constrained by the rule of law, Frank could not exercise other prerogatives of southern manliness. He could not openly challenge Clem's accusers or detractors, although it is entirely possible that he was the author of the anonymous death threat sent to Anton Wiese. Moreover the general assumption of his ignorance and innocence rendered him an ineffectual patriarch, a man who could not control his wife. At worst it turned him into a laughingstock. The *Cincinnati Commercial Tribune* offered him a backhanded compliment: Frank was "a patient, plodding honest man [who] had no suspicion of . . . his wife's clever business transactions."[10]

■ ■ ■

Citing the extensive publicity their client's first trial had received, Clem's attorneys tried for a change of venue. It would be impossible, they argued, to find fair and impartial jurors among the citizens of Marion County. Among the several persons called before Judge Chapman were the editors of the *Journal* and *Sentinel*. Both testified that circulation had increased dramatically during the December proceedings. Nevertheless, Chapman ruled against the motion.[11]

The selection process came close to proving Chapman wrong. Over the course of nearly two days, attorneys questioned 132 potential jurors, dismissing the vast majority because they had already formed opinions on Clem's innocent or guilt, either by reading press accounts or conversing "with witnesses or jurors in the first trial." By the time the jury was seated the defense had used eighteen of its twenty peremptory challenges, the prosecution, four of six. A few potential jurors tried without success to avoid service. One, resorting to common euphemisms, raised the issue of his wife's pregnancy, explaining that "he had a sick wife, but she was not at present dangerously sick, but probably might become so." "Possibly another case of twins," the *Sentinel* remarked.

Apart from the presence of two Indianapolis mechanics, Clem's second jury, composed mostly of farmers from outlying townships, superficially resembled her first. Significantly and perhaps portentously, it included fewer who claimed southern origins. The *Sentinel* expressed optimism, arguing that the jurors' relatively advanced age ("Not one of them under thirty-five") would render them immune to Clem's charms. Others were not so sure that the gentlemen of the jury were up to the task. The *New York Tribune* pronounced the panel, which unavoidably excluded newspaper readers, "necessarily composed of unintelligent men." A correspondent for the *Cincinnati Commercial Tribune* minced no words: "Tis said but . . . one of the twelve could read."[12]

■ ■ ■

The trial itself finally got under way on the morning of Thursday, February 11, when William Pinckney Fishback delivered a brief opening argument. The prosecution's case would rely on circumstantial evidence; he promised "a chain of testimony coming from over one hundred witnesses" and "expected to show that the murder was the result of a deep laid conspiracy." Fishback suggested likely motives: the acquisition of the more than $20,000 Jacob Young carried on his person and "cover[ing] up some most extraordinary transactions of a financial nature, between the defendant and the deceased." Much of his rhetoric was familiar. "The defendant was a woman of most remarkable character," he proclaimed, "and seemed to exert a wonderful influence over all with whom she had business transactions." She "repeatedly called at Young's house at night time, on business of a most confidential character. . . . Young has been closeted with the defendant, at her home, on various occasions." Clem maintained her usual composure, though she did not look Fishback in the eye. She appeared relieved when he finished and brightened when John Hanna rose to speak.

Hanna's opening statement, similarly succinct, lasted scarcely an hour. He began by questioning whether a double murder had taken place, suggesting that Jacob Young had killed his wife and then himself. Given the prosecution's goal of proving a conspiracy between the three accused of murder, he briefly referenced evidence that exonerated William J. Abrams and Silas Hartman. Abrams was not the man who purchased the infamous shotgun; that man had been wearing different clothes from what Abrams had worn that day. "Persons whose testimony was far more reliable" than the witnesses previously called by the prosecution had seen Hartman on the road to Lanesville at the very hour he supposedly was heading to Cold Spring. "Good smiths" would prove that the shoes worn by the horse hitched in the bushes at the crime scene did not fit Pet's feet.

Hanna devoted the bulk of his statement to vindicating his client. Jacob Young had done business with many persons "interested in this trial" besides the defendant. Disputing the prosecution's claim that Clem had robbed the murdered man, he argued she "had more money in her possession before the murder than could be traced to her since." Next he launched into a now-familiar description of Clem's history and character: "She had married young, and during her widowhood was thrown upon her own resources. She took boarders, did her own work, sewed for those she boarded, and proved herself a self-reliant woman. Nothing whatever could be adduced against her virtue." This time Hanna focused less on championing the virtue of "working women" than on defending the integrity and business acumen of a penny capitalist, a strategy that better reflected Clem's own self-image and the facts of her case. "Her first husband left her some little property, and she had tended it with great business tact, and it would be shown that she could obtain money whenever desired, and in sums she desired years ago from the most influential bankers in the city." Clem did not need to stoop to robbery or fraud to carry on her business, Hanna insisted. True, "her lips were sealed regarding her business transactions." Then again, he noted, several of the state's witnesses were similarly reluctant to explain their dealings with Young.

Then, Hanna made a startling claim. Clem "was taken from her home, in the absence of her husband, and subjected to examinations before the Coroner's inquest, and before the Grand Jury, without being permitted the benefit of counsel. . . . [T]he persecution of the prosecution had gone so far, as to attempt to force a confession of guilt from her, with the muzzle of a pistol at her head."

Nineteenth-century police officers in search of confessions routinely resorted to psychological intimidation and physical violence. Most members of Hanna's courtroom audience would have found such methods entirely appropriate for run-of-the-mill criminals and common prostitutes. Indeed, the incident—if it actually took place—suggested something about local authorities' opinion of Clem, one that meshed nicely with the portrait presented by the prosecution. Faithless wives did not merit tender consideration; neither, perhaps, did "working women." Holding a gun to the well-coiffed head of a respectable matron, however, was beyond the pale. In accusing the state of "persecution" at gunpoint, Hanna called its entire case into question. A woman of unblemished character, a woman denied the protection of her husband, Clem hardly deserved the treatment to which she had been subjected. Instead she deserved the jury's sympathy. Little wonder she had uttered inconsistent statements. Despite her savvy dealing and "great business tact," Clem was hardly the "remarkable woman" the prosecution imagined. Rather, she remained a faithful wife. At the time the murders were committed, "she was in the city engaged in the prosecution of her household duties, doing her necessary shopping."[13]

■ ■ ■

Just before the proceedings commenced newspapers floated another rumor: Bill Abrams would testify for the prosecution. "It is believed he will be the first witness put on the stand by the State. It is said he will make a full confession of all he knows of the transaction," the *Cincinnati Commercial Tribune* reported.[14] Such claims failed to materialize; Abrams did not take the stand.

Indeed, much of the testimony would have been familiar to anyone who had followed the previous trial. Robert Bowman told his story of stumbling upon two bodies; the county coroner and attending physicians explained the results of the postmortem examination; the Locke children recalled seeing a man and two women on the sandbar; William and Julia Coleman remembered hearing two closely spaced "reports." (Julia Coleman elaborated on her previous testimony; now she claimed to have heard a woman's scream shortly after the first shot.) This time, however, under Harrison's direction, the state moved quickly to introduce evidence concerning the economic relations between Clem, Young, and Abrams. Rather than save the tedious testimony of bankers and bank clerks until last, they called these witnesses early, while jurors' minds were still fresh.[15]

New revelations emerged only on the sixth day. John Culp had previously testified to meeting Silas Hartman with a man he could not identify on Friday, September 11 on the Lafayette road—thereby corroborating Hartman's own account of his whereabouts on the day before the murder. Now Culp had a somewhat different story to tell. He was one of few people who could actually say that he knew Cravens Hartman, although he "was not personally acquainted with him." He had in fact last seen Cravens the previous summer. However, Cravens was not the man Culp had seen riding with Silas in September. "Think I told the Court, on former trial, that I had no impression as to who the man was with Hartman. . . . It has since come to my memory that Abrams was the man." Elijah Cooper, a farmer who had accompanied Culp that afternoon, confirmed his friend's account. Testifying before the court for the first time, Cooper stated that he had "known Hartman a good while, and Abrams about twenty years. The men in the buggy were Silas Hartman and W. J. Abrams. They were going North. I spoke to them as we passed." So did Culp, who said, "How are you, Syke?"[16]

Culp's and Cooper's testimony was significant for several reasons. First, it cast doubt on portions of Silas Hartman's previous testimony. Second, it suggested that Culp's faulty memory the first time around aimed to protect Bill Abrams, whom he had "known . . . longer than . . . Hartman." Third, while Culp and Cooper had not encountered either man on the fatal afternoon, they reported seeing Abrams and Hartman together in the general vicinity of Cold Spring on the day before the murders. Their statements bolstered prosecutors' claim that the crime "was the result of a deep laid conspiracy . . . committed after the most mature deliberation, in cold blood."[17]

The two John Wileys also recovered their memories. Sixteen-year-old John P. Wiley had previously testified that Clem "filled the bill." Now he was more certain. "Is this the same woman you saw in the buggy with Mr. Young and his wife?" Harrison asked Wiley as he pointed to Clem. "I think it the same woman I saw in the buggy." Asked to "indicate . . . the degree of certainty," young Wiley repeated his previous statement. "I think she is the same woman." Called to the stand the next day, his father also spoke with greater confidence. It was no longer simply the elder Wiley's "impression" that the woman he had seen riding in the Youngs' carriage was Nancy Clem. "The other lady in the buggy was Mrs. Clem, I think."[18]

Like many witnesses, Wiley was caught in a web of divided loyalties. He knew both Silas Hartman and Nancy Clem; both "were raised in our neighborhood." Clem's first husband had taught his children and plastered his house. Syke had worked on his farm; "Mr. Hartman and I had always been the best of friends." But Wiley had also known the Youngs; indeed, Nancy Jane Young had worked for his family before her marriage. Cross-examination revealed something of his dilemma. He denied having told various neighbors that he could not identify the second woman in the buggy. He claimed, rather, that he had said something more circumspect: "[I]f no one knew any more about the murder than I did that it would hang nobody, and told him he might tell Dan Hartman [Nancy Clem's brother in Pike Township] . . . and his friends so." Wiley's evasion reflected more than sympathy for the three accused murderers, people with whom he had "been quite intimate." It reflected his fear that these very people might find other means of silencing him. "I had been warned, and cautioned by different men in the County that it was not safe for me to go about especially after night for I would possibly be assassinated as it was supposed I was a material witness in the case."[19]

Wiley's predicament hints at a second drama, one that took place not in the Indianapolis courtroom but in the old Hollingsworth neighborhood. No overt violence related to Clem's case erupted in Pike Township, at least none for which evidence survives. Yet during the fall of 1868 and winter of 1869, tensions must have been palpable. Most obviously, the murders pitted the Hartmans and the Abramses against the family of Jonas Case. It also pitted friends and former neighbors of Nancy Clem and Syke Hartman against friends and former neighbors of Jacob and Nancy Young. As Wiley's difficulties revealed, it was quite possible to be both. Whether the animosities Clem's trials provoked had local consequences we cannot know; the historical record is silent. But we can easily imagine awkward and fearful encounters, veiled threats, and none-too-subtle pressure to take sides. Little wonder John H. Wiley was afraid to venture out after dark.

That same day, February 17, the state called three new witnesses. An insurance agent named Charles Chenoworth testified that he and his wife had driven to the Pike Township hamlet of Clermont on the afternoon of September 12. Sometime between 4:00 and 4:30 (Chenoworth admitted on cross-examination that "my watch was not very reliable") they almost collided with a buggy coming from the opposite direction, toward Indianapolis. "They were driving, I would consider, rather recklessly, and very fast," Chenoworth explained. The vehicle's occupants were "a man and a woman."[20]

Nancy Chenoworth told much the same story but added incriminating details. "I think" they drove "what is called a sorrel horse with white in its face, a blazed face," she observed of the people who nearly ran into them. She could not positively identify Pet (prosecutors had brought her to Sullivan & Drew's stable the previous day) but "thought it was the same horse." As for the offending buggy's female occupant, "My impression is that I saw the same woman in the court room last Tuesday week, and that the defendant is the person."[21]

Indianapolis newspapers largely refrained from comment, but "foreign" correspondents saw Chenoworth's testimony as a turning point. She "recognized Mrs. Clem to be the woman," the *Cincinnati Daily Enquirer* explained. "The woman is satisfied that she recognizes Mrs. Clem," noted the rival *Cincinnati Daily Gazette*.[22] Chenoworth's actual statements were more tentative. "My impressions were that she is the same woman, but I would not say positively," she testified during cross-examination.[23] But just as Culp and Cooper for the first time placed Abrams and Hartman together, Chenoworth was the first to swear under oath to seeing someone who closely resembled Nancy Clem coming *from* the scene of the crime driven by a horse that looked very much like Pet.

The third new witness, a brickmason named John C. Pierson, offered equally damaging testimony. The nephew of Clem's neighbor, Levi Pierson (a fellow bricklayer and part-time numbers runner), John had lived at his uncle's until his marriage five years ago.[24] Unlike the Chenoworths, who were newcomers to the city, he knew Nancy Clem and was "acquainted with Silas A. Hartman enough to know him when I see him." Indeed, he correctly identified Syke, who had been brought into the courtroom for that very purpose.[25] Sometime after four o'clock on the afternoon of September 12, Pierson testified, he saw a buggy at the corner of Illinois and Walnut Streets. The occupants were driving "a sorrel horse" with "a blazed face." They were, he stated, none other than Silas Hartman and Nancy Clem. "Knowed it was them," he insisted. Pierson's testimony, described by one commentator as "the clincher," shook Clem's usual composure. "Perceptibly agitated," she turned pale.[26]

The testimony of John Culp, Elijah Cooper, the two John Wileys, the Chenoworths, and John C. Pierson collectively strengthened the state's still-circumstantial case.[27] Culp's and Cooper's recollections suggested that Silas Hartman and Bill Abrams had driven to the scene of the crime the day before the murder to locate hiding places for Silas, his horse, and his buggy. Both Wileys previously claimed to have seen Syke following the Youngs as they drove to Cold Spring; now both were more certain that the woman riding with the victims was Nancy Clem. The Chenoworths had seen a man and a woman driving back to the city; Mrs. Chenoworth had the "impression" that Clem was the woman, although she "would not say positively." Pierson, however, *was* positive the two people driving a sorrel horse down Illinois Street were Silas Hartman and his sister Nancy: "Knowed it was them."

If these witnesses proved correct, Clem had ridden to Cold Spring with the Youngs and returned with her brother. Left behind were a shotgun, Jacob Young's fast horse still hitched to his top buggy, and the Youngs' horribly mutilated bodies. Satisfied with the evidence they had presented, prosecutors rested after calling eighty-eight witnesses instead of the "over one hundred" they had promised. The regional and national press declared that the state had made its case.[28]

■ ■ ■

Clem's attorneys had little choice but to repeat their previous strategies. Once again they summoned "good smiths" who claimed that the horse tracks at the scene could not have been made by shoes that fit Pet. Once again, shoe store proprietor David Cady testified that no. 3 was a common size of women's shoes.[29] Once again, Aaron Clem testified that Abrams had come to his grocery store on the morning of September 12 to buy peaches.[30] Silas Hartman took the stand and, again, steadfastly denied that he had driven the Lafayette road on Saturday and just as steadfastly defended Clem. "My sister was at no time with me in a buggy on that day," he insisted. During cross-examination Benjamin Harrison handed Hartman the shotgun that had killed Jacob Young, hoping to induce an impromptu confession or at the least, visible agitation. Holding the murder weapon had no discernible effect on the witness.[31]

Harrison's failure to rattle Syke Hartman was a rare setback for the prosecution. Defense attorneys did their best to challenge the new evidence but found themselves outmatched by his skillful cross-examinations and their own witnesses' dubious credibility. Silas White swore to having heard John H. Wiley utter the very words that he denied saying: "Tell Dan. Hartman and his folks to rest easy as to what I will swear about Mistress Clem, that I did not recognize her on the day of the murder, and could not swear that she was the woman that was with Mr. and Mrs. Young." White was an ideal witness, an upstanding citizen and prominent member of Pike Township society. But he was also Clem's former brother-in-law ("My first wife who died thirty years ago, was a sister of Mrs. Clem's"). Although White insisted that he was only "distantly" related to Clem and had "no family by my first wife," Harrison quickly undermined his claims to impartiality and distance. "I am very intimate with the Clems and Hartmans," White reluctantly acknowledged. "Have been to [Clem's] house, and stayed at Matthew Hartman's while attending the trial."[32] Albert Patton's status as the defendant's son rendered his testimony similarly suspect. He stated confidently—as he had during the previous trial—that Clem wore old gaiters on the trip to Richmond, but on cross-examination he admitted to Harrison that he could not recall what sort of dress his mother wore. Why would he remember shoes but not clothing? Harrison hoped that jurors would conclude that young Patton had been coached.[33]

Then on Saturday, February 20, the defense made the disastrous decision to call John Pierson. Hoping to cast doubt on his previous testimony, Hanna peppered Pierson with questions about the details of his movements on the afternoon of September 12 and the speed of his usual "gait." Armed with the results of a series of "experiments," the defense hoped to show that Pierson could not possibly have arrived at the corner of Illinois and Walnut at the stated time.[34]

It made sense to try to discredit one of the state's most important witnesses, but Hanna must have known that calling Pierson was a risky strategy. It was. Over Hanna's objection, which Judge Chapman overruled, Harrison began his cross-examination by asking Pierson why he had not testified during Clem's first trial. The answer was disturbing. Pierson, it turned out, had not exactly kept his sighting of Clem and Hartman to himself. To the contrary, he had told at least three people, including his uncle, *and* he had testified before the grand jury. But when the court summoned him, Pierson was nowhere to be found. In fact he had gone to visit his mother and stepfather in Shelby County some 15 miles to the south. Perhaps Pierson's absence reflected loyalty to family, a concern that influenced the testimony of many a witness. Both his uncle and cousin had taken the witness stand to support Clem's alibis, twelve-year-old Viola insisting once again that Clem was at home, broom in hand, around four o'clock on the day of the murder.[35] Perhaps Pierson's failure to appear reflected sympathy for—or fear of—his former neighbor.

Or perhaps Clem's attorneys had suggested that he leave town. If they had, they apparently believed that Shelby County was not far enough. Pierson testified that he was asleep at his mother's house when he was awakened by a visit from detective Peter Wilkins, one of the men involved in the search for a prostitute with no. 3 feet. Wilkins, Pierson explained, gave him a "little note" and $25. Pierson's recollections remained conveniently vague. He "thought at first [he] had left [the note] on the mantelpiece, but since remembered" having "burnt it the next morning." Although he could not remember what it said, it evidently suggested that he take a little trip. If so, Pierson complied. He left immediately for Pittsburgh and stayed there nearly for the duration of Clem's first trial.[36]

Monday's proceedings offered other surprises, none of them of the sort defense attorneys found heartening. Julia McCarty testified that Clem had returned home by four o'clock on the day of the murder. Cross-examination inevitably brought up the fact that she had lied to the grand jury at Clem's behest, a development the defense must have expected. Harrison extracted an additional piece of information from the obviously ill-at-ease witness. Asked what Clem was wearing late on the afternoon of September 12, McCarty describe a dark calico, not the buff gown Jane Sizemore laid out for her. Rebecca Hartman offered potentially exonerating testimony. Yes, she bought shoes for Julia and Pet a week before the murder, but not for Nancy Clem. Yes, she visited David Cady's store. She was not certain, however, if she made the purchases at Cady's or at another establishment. In addition to suggesting that her sister-in-law had *not* purchased new gaiters, and therefore could not have left behind the infamous footprints, Hartman, like McCarty, insisted that Clem had returned home at five minutes to four on the afternoon of September 12—only minutes before a crime was being committed some five or six miles away.[37]

Yet on the whole, Hartman's testimony did little to help the defense. For one thing she confirmed that upon her return, Clem was attired in an outfit very much like the woman various witnesses had seen riding in Jacob and Nancy Young's carriage. "She had on a dark hat and brown calico dress."[38] Cross-examination did further damage. Once again, Hartman was forced to admit her previous perjury. "The first time I was before the Grand Jury

I think I said that Mrs. Clem was at home all that afternoon. It was an untruth. Mrs. Clem had told me to say that she was at home all that afternoon." Further questioning revealed that Rebecca's "untruth" did not stem entirely from sisterly affection. Clem "did not make any threats to me," she explained in an admission that must have delighted prosecutors. "I heard she did . . . from the rest of the family."[39]

Other defense witnesses fared little better. Frederica Ginther testified to meeting Clem in the hosiery department at the New York Store, but Harrison forced the elderly woman to admit that her "memory is weak"—so weak that she could not remember the various places she had lived since moving to Indianapolis.[40] William J. O'Flaherty, a book salesman testifying for the first time, remembered calling at 266 North Alabama Street around 4:30 on the afternoon of the murder and addressing the woman who answered the door as Mrs. Clem. While he had "an impression," he refused to state with any certainty that the lady to whom he said, "Mrs. Clem, I suppose?" was indeed the defendant. He was testifying under oath, he said, "and it is a serious matter." Moreover, O'Flaherty explained, "I see at least from fifty to one hundred ladies every day, and it is a little hard to distinguish one from another." Asked by Harrison about his conversations with Clem's attorneys, O'Flaherty acknowledged that "one of the counsel for the defense met me in the hall just before I came in, and asked me if it was not earlier than half-past four o'clock when I left the house." By refusing this overture, O'Flaherty distinguished himself as a relative rarity: a credible witness for the defense. But his reluctant description of the encounter in the courthouse hallway lent further credence to those who believed Hanna, Gordon, and Leathers guilty of underhanded tactics. Timing aside, the testimony of a man who had only an "impression" and who encountered "so many ladies that it would be impossible for me to describe any of them" did little to establish an airtight alibi.[41]

After calling a few additional witnesses, the defense rested its case.

■ ■ ■

The prosecution immediately began calling rebuttal witnesses. Clem's former servant, a "German girl" named Christina Kellamyer, testified that the defendant had offered her $100 to swear she had seen her at home on the afternoon of the murder. A post office clerk stated that Clem had collected Albert's letter on the *morning*, not the afternoon, of September 12. Several Pike Township residents vouched for John H. Wiley's veracity and character.[42]

The most dramatic moment took place when prosecutors called Peter Wilkins to the stand. A detective famed for rounding up deserters during the Civil War, Wilkins was already something of a celebrity. He was also a master of evasion. Asked where he obtained the $25 he delivered to John Pierson, he replied, "I got it in Mr. Hanna's office . . . I do not know who gave me the money." Thus originated an oft-repeated local expression: "Who gave Peter Wilkins the money?"[43]

Shortly before three o'clock on the afternoon of Tuesday, February 23, the state called its final witness. After a motion from the defense asking that jurors be taken to the crime scene, a request Judge Chapman denied, John Dye began the first of six closing statements. He combined moral outrage with skillful presentation of the evidence. "Jacob Young and his wife were murdered in cold blood for the vilest of all motives for which man takes the life of a fellow creature—money." If Clem were a woman of "good moral character," a woman incapable of harboring vile motives, why had her attorneys not asked her neighbors to testify to that fact? In one of few victories for the defense, Chapman sustained Hanna's objection to an extended discussion of Clem's character. Dye managed nevertheless to cast doubt on her virtue. "She goes to Abrams' and Young's house night after night, and these men come to her house. No one but Mrs. Hartman knew of these transactions, not even her own husband. . . . Abrams, the man who bought the gun, seems to have held very intimate relations with her." Shifting from innuendo to brass tacks, Dye noted that Clem had repeatedly refused to explain the nature of her business; "secrecy," Dye insisted, "is always a badge [of] guilt." She had suborned some witnesses and had attempted to suborn others; she had falsely told the coroner's jury she had been at home the entire afternoon of the murder; she had asked Rebecca Hartman to hide a large sum of money, concealed in an old boot. These, he insisted, were not the actions of an innocent person.[44]

Dye's buttressed his argument that Clem had acted out of the "vilest of all motives" with a "carefully prepared" reconstruction of Clem, Young, and Abrams's financial transactions between April and September 1868; the *Journal* reprinted his "financial statement" in full. He noted that the three business partners typically squared their accounts on the eleventh or twelfth of each month. Florid rhetoric embellished his schematic—though no less confusing—summary of loans taken out and settled, interest paid. Shrewdly conflating the business of women with the business of murder, Dye proclaimed, "On September 12, the regular monthly settlement day, a final settlement was made at Cold Springs, and the debt canceled in blood." Clem, moreover, had "laughed on her way to the scene of slaughter and festival of blood." He closed with a vicarious return to the "scene of slaughter": "If you had seen the burnt and chared [*sic*] remains of Nancy Jane Young, and the bloody corpse of her husband on that sequestered sand bar, you would not then have fathomed the guilt of this woman. Make an example of this murdress [*sic*] to warn all others who come after her, of the dangers of the paths of wickedness and crime."[45]

William Wallace Leathers followed for the defense. He questioned the validity of circumstantial evidence. He noted various witnesses' inability to identify Clem, Hartman, or Abrams with absolute certainty. He doubted that someone as readily recognizable as Bill Abrams would have gone "stalking about the auction-rooms and pawn-broking shops, inquiring for a gun with which to commit a double murder. . . . Do persons intending crime act in this manner?" He suggested that John H. Wiley's testimony be taken with a grain of salt, for Wiley harbored "some unkind feeling for some members of the defendant's family." He underscored one of the most troubling aspects of the state's case: prosecutors insisted that killing Nancy Jane Young was part of the murderers' plan, yet Mary Belle Young had asserted unequivocally that her aunt decided to join her husband for an afternoon carriage ride only at the last minute.

Leathers took aim at the prosecution's characterization of his client, shifting the onus from Clem's relatively brief involvement in the venture to Young's somewhat longer "capitalist" career.[46] Clem, he insisted, was a lender, not a borrower. Using language that mimicked prosecutorial descriptions of the defendant, he marveled, "It is a matter of astonishment how this man gained the confidence of bankers and the way in which he carried on these gigantic financial transactions. . . . Why did they not tell us with whom Young, a year previous to his death, transacted his mammoth financial operations?" As everyone in the courtroom knew, the person Leathers intended to implicate was Robert Dorsey.[47]

■ ■ ■

The following morning a woman fainted in the close quarters of the courtroom stairwell as larger than usual numbers attempted to gain entrance. The crowd of spectators who nearly trampled each other did not come to hear county prosecutor John Duncan, who nevertheless gave a speech the *Journal* pronounced "highly creditable to one having no more experience

than he has had in criminal practice." Duncan focused on Clem's "subter-
fuges and prevarications"—her conflicting alibis, her insistence on concealing "blood money" in an old boot, her attempts to "blacken the souls" of
Julia McCarty and Pet and Rebecca Hartman with "perjury." This time he
wisely said nothing about her past history as a woman who had done her
own work.[48]

Jonathan W. Gordon, one of two voices not previously heard from, was
the day's main attraction. "Tall, well-formed" and "military looking" he,
like the other attorneys present, towered over "Little Ben" Harrison, who
stood at a mere five foot six. "A man of tender sympathies" who "could not
resist" aiding "the weak or the oppressed," Gordon would become Nancy
Clem's most fervent supporter.[49] His closing statement, which occupied the
remainder of the afternoon and a good part of the next morning, repeated
many of his colleagues' familiar arguments. Mrs. Chenoworth could not be
certain as to the identity of either woman or horse; Nancy Jane Young had
decided "by accident" to go to Cold Spring. "Dorsey knows more concerning Young's affairs than any other living person."[50] Confirming that he was
not by any means a "rad," he explained away Jane Sizemore's testimony
thus: "Of all persons I do think a colored servant girl is the most malleable
material for a witness."[51]

Yet in many ways, Gordon's was the most original speech of the trial. He
invited the gentlemen of the jury to "walk together through this case by the
light and reason of the nineteenth century." "Light" was provided "by our
Redeemer." It was important to have God on one's side, but Gordon was
much more interested in reason—or rather, reasons. He offered a hodge-
podge of contradictory theories: Jacob Young had committed suicide; someone killed Jacob Young but Nancy Clem and Silas Hartman were nowhere
near Cold Spring on the day of the murder; Silas Hartman killed Jacob and
Nancy Jane Young, but Nancy Clem was an innocent bystander who refused to implicate her brother.[52]

In what must have been one of the trial's most striking (and to some, entertaining) moments, Gordon demonstrated how Jacob Young might have
killed himself. "I could do it myself, as could any of you," Gordon told the
gentlemen of the jury. He then picked up the shotgun, "rested his right
cheek against the muzzle, and showed how it could have been discharged by
crossing the left foot over the right leg, so as to touch the triggers with his
toe." At least one observer found Gordon's explanation "absurd." Perhaps.
Yet Gordon skillfully combined forensic reconstruction with appeals that

would have resonated with his audience. For one thing, he staked his claim on the evidence of military experience. "[H]ow can you account for his legs being crossed? . . . No one ever saw a man lying on the battle field shot through the head and his legs crossed." For another, he conjured a scenario that would have been all too easy for jurors to imagine. Young had good reason to commit suicide, Gordon argued: "he was largely in debt, and was paying a ruinous interest . . . the victim of his own folly," Young "may have been driven to madness by the thought of his ruin; he may have loved his wife, and that would be a reason for taking her life. . . . You read of such instances every day." The gentlemen of the jury did not read of murder-suicides "every day"—if indeed given their apparently compromised literacy they could. But in an era punctuated by boom and bust, prosperity and bankruptcy, they read—or heard—of economic failure and its consequences often. By invoking the specter of failure, Gordon came close to rendering an "absurd" proposition plausible.[53]

More so than any other attorney involved in the case, Gordon relied on modern science, "the reason of the nineteenth century."[54] He employed a photographer to show that a camera held by the occupant of one carriage could not capture an image of the occupants of a passing vehicle; thus, he concluded, the two John Wileys could not have seen Silas Hartman as they passed him. Photographic evidence saw increasing use over the course of the nineteenth century, but investigators and prosecutors employed it mainly for purposes of identification and detection; Gordon's experiment remained a novel one.[55]

True to his reputation as a man of tender sympathies, Gordon relied as much on sentiment as on science. Both Frank Clem and Grandmother Hartman were present for his speech, an arrangement no doubt orchestrated by Gordon himself. "Almost at the outset of Major Gordon's remarks they were affected to tears," the *Sentinel* reported. So, too, was Gordon who "seemed to labor under a sympathetic affection": "When I look back and see that wife by her husband, that mother by her daughter, am I asking too much of you to look with the manhood of sympathy upon their distress?" he implored the jury. "Are you men? Have you families and children whose lives and character you guard as the apple of your eye? Have you mothers whose gray hairs you would not have go down to the grave in grief? Call around you all the circumstances and blessings of home; then look at William Frank Clem and ask yourself what you would do if your wife was on trial before you."[56]

■ ■ ■

Then—if subsequent commentary can be believed—came the moment that everyone had been waiting for, the reason the courtroom was packed to capacity, overflowing into the halls and stairways. At 11:15 on the morning of Friday, February 26, Benjamin Harrison rose to present the prosecution's third and final closing argument. It was, as numerous observers claimed, a brilliant performance.[57] Harrison's eight-hour discourse was clear and eloquent. Avoiding both rhetorical excess and obsequious folksiness, he fashioned a logical and easily comprehensible story from the jumble of available evidence—especially important given that Gordon, however unpersuasively, had managed to suggest a number of possible scenarios.

Harrison began by summarizing the findings of the postmortem examination of the Youngs' bodies, pronouncing Gordon's theory of murder-suicide patently false. "I will not so far discredit your intelligence," he told the jury, "as to think that you have any doubt that Nancy Jane Young came to her death by the hand of some person other than her husband." He moved next to Clem's business dealings, to evidence that placed Bill Abrams and Silas Hartman at the scene of the crime the day before the murder, and to testimony that identified Abrams as the purchaser of the shotgun on the morning of Saturday, September 12. He referenced testimony that suggested that Clem had left "her house in [a] clandestine manner" in order to accompany the Youngs on their fatal carriage ride, as well as evidence that suggested that Clem and Hartman returned together to the city. He dismissed Gordon's photographic experiment. "Just in so far as God's works always excel in delicacy and perfection the works of man, just so far does this eye, this window of the soul, this wondrous instrument by which we look out upon objects in the world around us, excel any thing that man has ever invented." He attacked the various alibis offered by Clem and her alleged accomplices. The "pitiable" story of Cravens Hartman was, he insisted, "a miserable fraud." Clem had first sworn that she had been home the entire afternoon, but she changed her story once her original version collapsed under the weight of evidence to the contrary. "A false *alibi* is always evidence of guilt."

Harrison's presentation was methodical but neither dry nor emotionless. He even managed a brief moment of humor. How was it, he mused, that Mr. and Mrs. Fee, the tollgate keepers, "who had probably never seen the mare [Pet] in their lives, . . . could tell you almost every spot there is on her"? How were they able to recall the number of stripes "on each side of each spoke of each of the wheels of the buggy"? More often, Harrison mar-shaled his well-known sense of righteous indignation. "The news of this fearful tragedy," he reminded jurors, broke on a "quiet Sabbath morning," disrupting "our contemplations of God's goodness, and turn[ing] our minds to thoughts of man's cruelty." He dismissed any suggestion of "suicide and wife murder": "It is cruel thus to stab the character of the dead."

Harrison made sure to touch on familiar cultural scripts even as he acknowledged the limits of their explanatory power. He condemned Clem's hypocrisy, her "giddy laugh" and "winsome talk" as she allegedly accompa-nied Jacob and Nancy Young to the scene of their demise. He could not re-sist hinting at sexual impropriety, even though he agreed that "it is very clear" that the motive "is money": "Business relations" were apparently "the cause of those frequent and mysterious visits paid to [Young] by Mrs. Clem." "It is hoped, for the sake of the accused herself, as well as for that of her hus-band, that that was the true explanation. Upon what other grounds could you explain these visits? She, a married woman—without the knowledge of her husband, and not only without his knowledge, but carefully concealing from him the fact—is found frequently visiting the house of Jacob Young, and going into a room with him privately and apart from others. What does this mean?"

At the heart of Harrison's argument was an assessment of Clem's char-acter. In an era before biological explanations of female deviance gained credence, he did not present Clem as physically or physiologically mascu-line. Instead he created a disturbing picture of an ordinary-looking woman who seized masculine prerogatives. Clem, he explained to the jury and to the assembled crowd, was hardly the "plain, innocent, simple-hearted woman" described by the defense. To the contrary, she was a woman who held power, a "terrible power," a "fatal power" over all who knew her—her family, her business associates, her alleged accomplices. She possessed "the wonderful power to get the mastery of strong men." She was "the central figure in [the] financial transactions." She was the mastermind who planned all facets of the plot: the purchase of the gun, the selection of "the route and place," and the execution of the murder and subsequent robbery. She was "the central figure in this whole transaction—the presiding genius of the whole conspir-acy, who both procured and directed all the other actors in this tragedy." Clem's refusal to abide by gendered expectations rendered complaints of "persecution" meaningless. A person such as this deserved to be the quarry of a legally sanctioned "woman hunt."[58]

For the most part, Harrison's closing argument simply repeated claims his colleagues had previously uttered. Yet he put his own stamp on the case by subtly shifting its emphasis. Clem in his telling was not only a murderess, a presiding evil genius, and a faithless (in the economic sense) wife. She was a corruptor of innocents. Drawing on John Dye's earlier pronouncements, Harrison enumerated the moral and spiritual damage Clem had inflicted on her niece. "We have seen little 'Pet,' a child just budding into womanhood, led through the fatal power of this woman over her, go before the grand jury and testify on oath to what she knows to be untrue! . . . I do not know which is the worse criminal, the one who takes the life of his fellow-man, or he who saps the foundations of childish innocence and truth." Here he may have missed his mark. Just as prosecutors had previously blundered by appearing to condemn "working women," Harrison conjured up an image of childhood that likely would have been foreign to the farmers and mechanics who sat in the jury box. By their standards, Pet was more woman than child. Harrison recognized this potential gaffe. His subsequent remarks rhetorically reversed the aging process, transforming Pet from "a child just budding into woman-hood" into a "little girl": "I say in all sincerity, that if that little girl who testi-fied here, were a child of mine, I would rather have walked behind her coffin and laid her in the grave, than to have seen her sit upon that stand and tell the story she had told. I would rather have laid her in the dust; for then I might have cherished the memory of a pure angel with her God."[59]

Harrison probably did speak "in all sincerity"; however disingenuous and hyperbolic by twenty-first-century standards, his proclamation re-flected his own keen sense of moral righteousness. It was also bound to res-onate with his audience. Nineteenth-century parents—even if they rejected idealized notions of childhood—walked behind their children's coffins all too frequently; Harrison himself had lost a daughter in infancy. And for Harrison, as for many who read or heard his speech, the wages of sin were all too real. Transforming a girl of a "tender age" from innocent to "felon" was more than a desperate act of a criminal who wished to escape suspicion. It was a crime that threatened Pet's eternal salvation. "My God! How shameful—how mournful a scene!" he exclaimed. Similarly, Harrison re-duced nineteen-year-old Julia McCarty to an "unfortunate girl": "How cruel and how shameful it was in Mrs. Clem to take advantage of [her] dependant [*sic*] position."[60]

"Children" who provided incriminating testimony deserved special praise in Harrison's book because they bravely stood on the side of justice.

Sixteen-year-old John P. Wiley "testified with" admirable "deliberation." Josephine Stevens was "that little girl who testified with so much sincerity and simplicity."[61] Harrison conveniently ignored Viola Pierson, the juvenile perjurer who refused to repent. Albert Patton, Wiley's elder by only one year, similarly escaped comment.

Harrison concluded his closing argument by urging jurors to forego sympathy for the defendant—a tacit admission that even the most damning evidence or logically formulated argument might not be enough to persuade them to condemn a respectable woman. "You are to speak the simple truth upon the question of her guilt or innocence of this crime, and it does not matter at all whether she has a husband, a son, an aged mother." Sympathy belonged to victims, not to perpetrators. "I only ask you," he implored the jury, "to remember the dead that are buried away out of sight; to remember the hearthstone whose fire has gone out forever. I ask you to remember that orphan child who is wandering fatherless and motherless to-day." This was the first and the last time anyone involved in the case made public reference to Ophir Homer Young.[62]

■ ■ ■

Reprising the part he played during the first trial, Hanna gave the final closing argument for the defense. "I have no fine spun theories to offer in this case," he explained. "I come before you simply to ask that you will try my client by the law and the evidence." Before turning to those twin pillars of wisdom, however, he insisted that sympathy, in contrast to Harrison's reasoning, *should* play a role in the jurors' deliberations. "If I thought I stood in the presence of men having no sympathy for humanity, I would take my seat. The large audience of ladies present every day since the trial commenced, show that they have sympathy for the accused." (This was at best a creative interpretation. By all accounts, the female spectators who crowded the courtroom were out for blood.)[63]

First, then, was the law. Hanna promised not to "read . . . long extracts" but quoted Blackstone on the high level of proof cases based on circumstantial evidence required. He then turned to section 12 of the Indiana criminal code: "And if the jury have a reasonable doubt about the existence of any necessary link in the chain of evidence, then they must acquit." Then there was the evidence. Reiterating arguments he had made the previous December, Hanna tried his best to weaken the links in the prosecution's chain. He did so with a logic and clarity that rivaled Harrison's. He began by disputing that the defendant had a motive. If Clem had received $21,000 *from* Jacob Young on the morning of his death, why would she subsequently murder him? Next he questioned nearly every facet of the state's argument. Charles Donnelan, Charlotte Bright, and Frederica Ginther testified to meeting Clem at the post office and at the New York Store on the afternoon of the murder. Chris Lout had seen her at home shortly thereafter. How could she have been at Cold Spring at the same time? Those who saw a woman riding in the Young's carriage could not be absolutely certain she was Clem; John H. Wiley told a neighbor he could not recognize the passenger because a veil partially obscured her face. The measurement of the woman's footprints at the crime scene had been taken with a most unreliable instrument: a green papaw stick. Even if one accepted its accuracy, Hanna reasoned, "there are, perhaps, three thousand women in Indianapolis that wear No. 3 shoes." Why would a man as "well acquainted in this city" as William J. Abrams shop so conspicuously for a gun? How could Syke Hartman be heading for Cold Spring at the very hour that Mr. and Mrs. Fee saw him pass through their tollgate on the Pendleton road? As for the mysterious Cravens Hartman, why had the state failed to produce the hotel register that showed that a "C. Hartman" had lodged at the Spencer House? And if John Pierson's recollection of seeing Clem and Hartman on Illinois Street shortly after 4:00 p.m. were correct, then the murderers must have made the trip from Cold Spring to downtown Indianapolis in five to ten minutes—a physical impossibility even with a very fast horse. (Hanna shrewdly ignored the issue of where Pierson had been during his client's first trial. He ignored altogether the question of who had given Peter Wilkins the money.)

For all his self-professed ignorance, Hanna knew a good deal about the importance, not just of tone, but of form. He knew, as did no one else—not even Harrison or Gordon—how to keep an argument ringing in his audience's ears, how to turn a legal speech into something like poetry. He concluded his presentation with a powerful and memorable refrain, one intended to convince jurors that the prosecution's case amounted to little more than a series of unsubstantiated conjectures. "You are asked to guess," he asserted, "that Abrams bought the gun." "You are asked to guess that Abrams, in some way, transferred the gun to Hartman." "You are asked to guess that a pistol was used by the defendant, although there is no proof that she ever had or ever saw a pistol." "You are asked to guess that the defendant was the woman who rode out of the city with Young and wife." "You are asked to guess that Hartman followed her." By the time he had finished, Hanna had enumerated more than a dozen such "guesses."

Hanna recognized that he needed to do more than raise doubts about the state's evidence; it was necessary to counter his opponent's assessment of Clem as an evil financial and criminal mastermind who possessed "fatal power." This time he was less effusive. He refrained from valorizing the "working classes" and "working women," though he once again praised his client's "habits of industry." Once again, he suggested that prosecutors had unfairly criminalized women's business. "What has these transactions to do with this charge of murder?" he asked the jury. "To handle money successfully, to be prompt, to have credit in bank, is that an evidence of crime?" Once again, he portrayed Clem as a lender, not a borrower—someone who would have had little to gain from Jacob Young's death.[64] Yet once again the strategic value of this description hinged as much on character as on motive. A passive investor was far less threatening than an aggressive borrower. Such a characterization relegated Clem—industrious and savvy though she might have been—to the economic margins. She could not have acted as "the central figure in [the] financial transactions." And once again, Hanna publicly suggested that other business partners of Jacob Young were better suited for the role of presiding genius, none more so than Robert Dorsey.

Hanna concluded by inviting his audience to examine Clem herself. "[I]f that awful crime, like a mountain of lead, had been weighing upon her conscience, do you believe that it is in human nature to have born[e] up, day after day and maintain her innocent expression of manner? No woman yet created, if guilty, could have so done." He concluded, "[D]o not imbrue your hands in the blood of that innocent women. . . . [B]e just to the State, be just to that woman." Jurors and spectators listened to Hanna's six-hour speech in "perfect silence," many of them moved to tears. Once again, "Hanna pumped for 'salt water' and he got it."[65]

■ ■ ■

Late on the afternoon of Saturday, February 27, it was Judge Chapman's turn to address the jury. For three long weeks, the twelve men had been confined to the jury box by day, sequestered in a boardinghouse at night. Now they sat for what must have been another couple of hours at the very least while Chapman read them his instructions, thirty-three in all. As in the previous trial, they favored the prosecution. Each party to a conspiracy was equally guilty, Chapman held, regardless of whether he had participated in the actual crime or was even present at the scene of the crime. He advised jurors that actual or attempted suborning of witnesses "should induce a most rigid scrutiny of all testimony . . . offered in behalf of the accused." Circumstantial evidence was "a most valuable and necessary instrument of justice," of "secondary character" only in instances where "direct evidence" could be obtained. Perhaps most important, Chapman burst Hanna's rhetorical bubble, chastising "counsel" for attempting to confuse the jury by "loose and unwarrantable use of the word 'guess.'" "An 'inference,'" he explained, "is not a 'guess,' but something more reliable, founded upon fact and builded [*sic*] with reason." The *Albany Journal* thought Chapman's instructions "masterly" but "possibly drawn out in too many subtleties of distinction for men unfamiliar with logical or legal analysis." They were better suited to "a jury of lawyers" than one of farmers, too complicated for "uncultured minds" to "easily grasp."[66]

Despite these concerns, observers predicted a speedy and decisive denouement. "There seems to be every indication that this trial will result in a conviction," the *Cincinnati Daily Gazette* proclaimed. The *St. Paul Daily Press* agreed: "Mrs. Clem is sure of conviction." The *New York Herald* considered conviction "highly probable."[67] Yet as the jury stayed out, first for hours, then for an entire day, confident pronouncements gave way to fear that "uncultured minds" might once again fail to agree. Indianapolitans in all walks of life—"rich and poor, business men, church goers, [and] loafers"— obsessively waited for news. As they congregated "in churches, drug stores, saloons, at the post-office, and on the streets" they asked, "Has the jury been heard from?" On Monday, March 1, at 11:00 a.m., after nearly two days of deliberation, the jury finally returned to the courtroom. The crowd that rushed in was disappointed; jurors had come not to pronounce a verdict but to ask the judge for clarification. Chapman obligingly reread the relevant instructions, a task that took him nearly an hour. The defense interpreted the jury's questions as a bad sign. Jonathan Gordon visited his client in her jail cell and advised her to prepare for the worst, a warning that left her "considerably affected." But when the jury announced two hours later that it had reached a verdict, Clem had regained her usual self-possession.[68]

Gordon's premonition proved correct. Jurors had spent their time debating not the verdict but the sentence, which Indiana law gave them the responsibility of pronouncing. They quickly agreed that Clem was guilty. Nine argued for first-degree murder and the death penalty, three (including a man who had once stood trial for murder himself) favored manslaughter and a short prison term. They eventually compromised on second-degree murder and a life sentence. Tears streamed down their faces as Judge Chapman read the verdict, but Clem displayed her "habitual composure." She turned to Frank and smiled, then tapped him on the shoulder, a signal that she wished to return to her cell. By some accounts she "shed a tear or two" as the bailiff escorted her from the courtroom. "I suppose the people are now satisfied," she said.[69]

CHAPTER EIGHT

I Wish I Was an Angel

The people for the most part *were* satisfied. "Public opinion has been against [Clem] from the first," the *Journal* reported. "Had it been left to a popular vote she would have been declared guilty by a large majority." Writing in her diary, Sarah Fletcher, the teenager who had observed Clem's first trial, offered a more succinct assessment: "She deserves it!"[1]

Not everyone was entirely satisfied. The *Journal* called the verdict of murder in the second degree "absurd," indicative of a dim-witted jury. "Taking this senseless verdict as an evidence of their average intelligence, society ought to congratulate itself that the dolts did not turn the fiend loose to murder somebody else," an editorial grumbled. In truth, second-degree murder, which Chapman's instructions had defined as murder "without premeditation," hardly suited the case the prosecution had proved. Evidently the jury had labored under the misimpression that a first-degree murder conviction mandated the death penalty; "no jury in Indiana will ever hang a woman," the *Journal* complained. Yet responsibility for the faulty verdict rested at least as fully with a learned judge as with a jury of supposedly ignorant farmers. At one point Chapman's instructions clearly stated that the penalty for first-degree murder was death, for second-degree murder confinement to "the State prison during life." Elsewhere, however, they declared that "if you shall adjudge her guilty, you will fix the punishment she shall be sentenced to undergo."[2] Little wonder jurors concluded that only second-degree murder would do if they wished to avoid hanging a woman.

■ ■ ■

Meanwhile, as Clem awaited sentencing and her alleged co-conspirators their respective trials, the three celebrity prisoners housed in the Marion County Jail resumed their routines. Clem bunked alone after the release of her "decent colored" roommate; an anonymous scribbler had drawn a snake over the door to her vermin-ridden cell and added the caption "Serpent's Den." Abrams and Hartman shared a small, dark, and dismal room, its only furnishing two beds, a shelf, and a "pocket" for holding small items on the back of the door. Still, by virtue of their previously respectable social status and probable prior acquaintance with the county sheriff, they occupied privileged positions within the jail hierarchy. Abrams was appointed "grub boss" and given the only iron bedstead in the jail; other prisoners slept on mattresses on the floor. All inmates were free to socialize during the day and early evening. But except for drunks, who slept in the hallway, Abrams and Hartman were the only male prisoners who were not locked in their cells at night. While men and women occupied separate corridors, Clem's cell was directly adjacent to Hartman and Abrams's. Brother and sister could communicate through one of the many holes the "boys" had gouged in the walls over the years. Nevertheless, Syke found jail a "hard place to stay in." He told a fellow inmate that he'd prefer "sudden death" to prolonged confinement. He asked what sort of poison "would produce the easiest death."[3]

■ ■ ■

Citizens who had followed Clem's trials obsessively found themselves at loose ends. They gathered outside the courthouse "looking as disconsolate and purposeless as bees burned out of a hive," the *Sentinel* observed. Those who turned to the local press for solace found plenty with which to vicariously occupy themselves. They read of mass meetings organized throughout the state to oppose the Fifteenth Amendment and honor the seventeen Democrats who resigned from the Indiana senate to prevent a vote on ratification. The *Journal* termed attendance at the Indianapolis demonstration "slender" and denounced the gathering as a "humbug" and a "failure." A subsequent editorial was quick to deny, however, that granting black men the right to vote would result in what Democrats feared: "social equality" between the races. (The Indiana General Assembly would ratify the amendment a month later by defining a quorum as two-thirds of the remaining state senators.) Other news touched more closely on the Cold Spring affair. The house of defense attorney Jonathan Gordon nearly burned down, destroying his personal papers and much of his library. A "brutal double murder" was committed in Lebanon, a town some 30 miles to the north. "The mystery and horror surrounding this affair is fully equal to that of the Young murder, while many of the circumstances connected therewith are equally suspicious," the *Journal* promised its readers.[4]

Circumstances directly connected to the Young murder would resurface soon enough. Only a day after his residential conflagration, Gordon filed a motion for a new trial, citing numerous grounds. Among the twenty reasons he enumerated were these. The court had erred by refusing to grant a

change of venue, by providing faulty instructions to the jury, and by "refusing to give the jury certain instructions at the suggestion of the defense."
Gordon also pronounced the "verdict of the jury . . . contrary to the law," and
accused four jurors of misconduct "by reason of their having both formed
and expressed decided opinions as to the guilt of the prisoner."[5]

Gordon's motion, however, was not the reason the courtroom was once
again "densely filled." Rumors that Bill Abrams would turn state's evidence had never materialized, but now there was talk that Silas Hartman
planned to confess. The many citizens who anxiously rushed to the courthouse were misinformed, for Hartman did not appear in open court. But he
did testify in secret before the grand jury. He also spoke to a jailer, who recorded his statement in writing—and quickly leaked it to the press. What
Hartman said to the grand jury remains unknown, but it seems to have
corroborated what the jailer wrote down. The statement, as published in the
Evening Mirror and reprinted in the *Journal*, *Sentinel*, and various other
venues, offered a story that implicated Abrams and exonerated Clem. Hartman claimed that Robert Dorsey was the mastermind behind the plot to rob
and murder Jacob Young. Clem had no previous knowledge and had not
been present at Cold Spring. Abrams, as prosecutors had already more or
less proved, purchased the shotgun, but at the Fruit House handed it over to
a brickmason named William Fiscus. Meanwhile a prostitute named "Frank
Clark" rode with Jacob and Nancy Jane Young to Cold Spring. There, Hartman maintained, Fiscus killed Mr. Young. Clark "shot Mrs. Young, but did
not kill her, and Fiscus hit her on the head and killed her." Hartman did not
deny involvement but limited his role to transporting Clark from the scene
of the crime. He hastened to add that he had not personally witnessed these
events but learned of them from Clark.[6]

The "confession" met with near universal skepticism. The *Journal* termed
it "a cooked up affair," the *Cincinnati Daily Gazette*, "a pretended confession"
and "improbable story."[7] "Is Generally Disbelieved," the *Chicago Tribune*
proclaimed.[8] Few believed Syke Hartman capable of coming up with this
story on his own. Some accounts held that the Hartman family collectively
decided he would take the blame for his sister; others attributed his tale to
Clem's influence over her brother. Despite its self-serving nature, Hartman's
confession betrayed a certain logic. For one thing, it mimicked the defense's
previous strategy. Although they had picked a different frail sister for the
honor of impersonating a murderess, Clem's attorneys had also attempted
to substitute a prostitute in the place of their respectable client. They had

seized on this tactic precisely because it reflected popular beliefs about the relationship between sexual vice and violent crime, beliefs that extended to the realm of the supernatural. Summoned by spiritualists the following summer, the ghost of Jacob Young chose to implicate Clark and exonerate Clem; on another occasion Nancy Young pointed a spectral finger at an unidentified "strange woman" (the minister Henry Ward Beecher's famous euphemism for prostitute).[9]

Nor was it any surprise that Hartman pointed *his* not yet spectral finger at Robert Dorsey, a man against whom Clem's defense had publicly and repeatedly cast suspicion. And although nothing could be proved against him, Fiscus had long been suspected of involvement; in fact, he had been one of the people arrested in the immediate aftermath of the murders. Hartman's attempt to implicate him may have been a preemptive move. The *Journal* reported that Fiscus was expected to testify that Syke had asked him to participate in the murder plot. Whether this statement bore any relation to the truth is unclear. If it did, the failure of the prosecution to call him as a witness during either of Clem's trials was a curious oversight. In the meantime, Fiscus was both embarrassed and an embarrassment. In late March, the *Sentinel* gleefully reported that he was a Republican candidate for city marshal. He did not win election.[10]

Abrams remained ignorant of his cellmate's confession until the day of its first publication, March 9, 1869, when Albert Harden, the turnkey, brought him a copy of the *Evening Mirror* (the city's only afternoon paper) at "just about locking up time" and advised him "not to have any words with Sike about the matter." Abrams handed the newspaper to a third inmate, Charley Hill, who was visiting their cell. Hill read the account, then passed it to Hartman, who read it silently while Hill played guitar. Hartman said nothing about the contents to either man but asked them both to step out into the corridor so that he could talk privately with Nancy Clem through the hole in the wall. "Dear sister," he reportedly told her, "I know all about this murder, and I know you are innocent. You shall not suffer much longer if I can prevent it." Soon after, he went to bed.[11]

Syke had been depressed and dejected, especially since his sister's conviction. He had spent much of the preceding afternoon alternately pacing the jail hallway and sitting with his head in his hands. Around lock-up time, he began singing hymns, among them "I Wish I Was an Angel," and "Hail the Power of Jesus' Name." "I wish I was out of here, and could be amidst good company and in good society," he told a fellow prisoner, Samuel

Thomas. Thomas, imprisoned for robbery and murder, replied that he him-self "loved to be in the society of people of the church."[12]

Hartman rose during the early morning hours and once again paced the corridor, this time in his underwear. Then he went back to bed. Around daybreak his groaning awakened his cellmate. Thinking his friend was suf-fering a nightmare Abrams shook him, only to discover Hartman covered in blood, his throat cut. Abrams called for help. Harden ran to get a doctor, leaving his keys with Abrams so that he could let the "boys" out of their cells on the off chance one of them could render medical assistance. It took Harden more than an hour to find a physician and bring him back to the jail. By that time it was almost seven o'clock, and Silas was beyond all help. Harden "fixed his hands"—presumably crossing them over his chest—a ges-ture that would irritate the coroner, who arrived shortly thereafter, because it disturbed potential evidence.[13]

Word of Syke's demise spread rapidly. A mix of policemen, jurymen, re-porters (including the *Journal*'s "phonographer"), and "several well-known citizens" crowded into the "cage" that connected the anteroom and the cell block. Indeed the cage was so packed that the door leading to the cells, which swung outward, could not be opened. Several members of the crowd grudgingly stepped back into the antechamber. Although it was by now after 8:00 a.m., cell no. 1 was so dark it had to be illuminated by candle. The *Journal* described the "truly fearful" scene in prose that would have made the editor of any penny dreadful proud. Hartman's bedclothes were "steep[ed] in . . . gore," his clothing "perfectly saturated by the effusion," and "his sandy beard bore . . . a carmine hue." Blood stained the floor and spattered the white-washed walls. "His throat displayed the marks of several gashes, from which blood still oozed."

Hartman's carotid artery had been severed, without a doubt, by an old bro-ken razor that belonged to Turnkey Harden but which "all the boys" used to shave with. Who had wielded the fatal instrument was as yet unclear. Coroner Garrison Allred, the same official who had presided over the Youngs' post-mortems, convened a jury on the spot to determine whether Hartman had died at his own hands or at the hands of the cellmate he had so recently im-plicated. Among the jurors was Erie Locke, the man who taken his children fishing at Cold Spring on the afternoon of September 12, 1868, and one of the "well known-citizens" who had crowded into the cage that morning.[14]

The members of the coroner's jury first questioned the attending physi-cian, who attributed Hartman's death to suicide. Next they interviewed

Abrams and several other prisoners. They sent for Nancy Clem, who for once behaved as her contemporaries thought she should. She was distraught—nearly hysterical—wringing her hands and pacing the floor of her cell. She had the presence of mind to refuse to speak to the jurors, on the grounds that she knew nothing of her brother's plans to kill himself. They did not press her. Two additional physicians examined the body and pronounced the wounds consistent with suicide. Their testimony, combined with inmate's statements concerning Hartman's state of mind, led the jury to formally conclude that he had taken his own life.[15]

Not everyone was convinced. "Was it suicide?" the *Cincinnati Gazette* asked.[16]

■ ■ ■

Syke's body was conveyed to the home of his brother Matthew, carried in through the same back door through which Clem had allegedly passed on her way to meet Jacob and Nancy Young, the same door at which Bill Abrams had instructed his brother Ben to knock. The corpse, attired "in a handsome black suit," was laid out in the Hartman parlor—"a handsomely furnished room," the *Journal* could not resist noting. Grandmother Hartman's palpable grief made for what the paper termed a "solemn scene": "Scarcely able to bear up," she exhibited "all the plainly manifested affection of a mother. . . . The affliction of the aged mother—so old, and herself so near the grave" was "deeply affect[ing]." Matthew spared no expense; Syke rested in a glass-topped rosewood coffin with silver handles, "*but no breast plate,*" the *Journal* reported. The *Sentinel* poked fun at its competitor's sensationalism, sarcastically recommending that the *Journal* republish its coverage of Hartman's suicide and funeral "every day for the benefit of a delighted public." "The idea of Syke Hartman's being buried 'without a breast plate' is as revolting as if he had been buried without an ichthyosaurus," the *Sentinel*'s editor sniffed. Melodrama aside, the Hartmans had good reason to prevent easy identification of Silas's remains. The corpses of criminals and suicides often ended up on anatomists' dissection tables; idle curiosity seekers and vengeful citizens were equally capable of desecrating criminals' graves.[17]

To discourage onlookers, the small funeral procession, two carriages in all, left for Pike Township an hour earlier than advertised. Grandmother Hartman—"too infirm to stand the fatigue of the journey"—remained at home. The funeral itself was well attended; nearly 150 people, most of them township men, filled the Methodist Church at Pleasant Hill. "Considerable crying . . . even by the men" accompanied the service; as the *Journal* explained, "the deceased was well known in that neighborhood." At one point "an old man, some sixty years of age . . . made some remarks"; the paper did not identify him by name. The speaker might well have been sixty-three-year-old Silas White, husband of Nancy Clem's and Silas Hartman's long-deceased sister—the man who had tried without success to discredit John H. Wiley's testimony. Whoever he was, the "gray haired man" presented Syke's sad end as a cautionary tale, encouraging "all young men and women present to take warning by what they saw and shun bad company and evil enterprises." This, too, "proved quite affecting." After the service, Hartman's coffin was carried to the graveyard across the road, on land once owned by his father but now the property of none other than Silas White. It was, the *Journal* noted, a "cheerless scene"—overcast and snowing with "a penetrating chill." "The deceased was left in a coffin, *without a breastplate*," the *Journal* concluded, "buried thus ignominiously on the farm where he had whiled away the hours of the spring time of childhood." Ignominious and anonymous. Even today, battered and broken headstones denote the final resting places of Nancy and Silas's parents, John and Nancy Hartman; of their older sister, Anna McCurdy; of Nancy Clem's first husband, William Patton. But no monument marks Silas Hartman's grave.[18]

■ ■ ■

The *Journal* did not take the *Sentinel* up on its suggestion that it continually reprint its account of Hartman's suicide "for the benefit of a delighted public." But a publisher who seems to have been closely associated with the *Journal* in a sense did. In June 1869, Alva C. Roach, a former Union soldier who had penned an account of his mistreatment in a Confederate prison camp, published a trial pamphlet with the sort of unwieldy and protracted title that typified the genre: *The Cold Spring Tragedy: Trial and Conviction of Mrs. Nancy E. Clem for the Murder of Jacob Young and Wife, With the Eloquent Speeches of Counsel, on Both Sides and Hon. Judge Chapman's Charge to the Jury in Full. To Which is Added the Confession and Suicide of Silas W. Hartman, Brother of Mrs. Clem and Her Accomplice in the Murder, and Many Interesting Facts Never Before Published.* Roach identified himself as the work's publisher; he did not specify an author. The pamphlet's introductory description closely resembled articles previously published in the *Journal*, not surprising given that Roach's office was situated in the "*Journal* Building" at Circle and Market Streets. While Roach hardly gave the *Sentinel* equal billing, he recognized the paper's journalistic contribution by republishing its account of Clem's conviction verbatim, albeit without attribution. He devoted the bulk of his booklet's 128 pages to reprinting the transcript of Clem's recently concluded second trial, which he rearranged in an effort to aid confused readers. Thus the testimony appeared not in chronological order but under subheadings such as "Shoes Worn by Mrs. Clem on the Day of the Murder," "Secret Financial Transactions of Mrs. Nancy E. Clem and Dr. W. N. Duzan," "Buying of the Gun," "Alibi Evidence," "Going to and Thence from Cold Spring," "Subsequent Conduct," and (here Roach admitted defeat) "Miscellaneous." *The Cold Spring Tragedy* reprinted "the eloquent speeches" of all the attorneys involved, except John Duncan's, and even included Fishback's "masterful" closing argument during the first trial. Despite the promise contained in its title, "facts never before published" were few and far between.

Nor did *The Cold Spring Tragedy* quite live up to the *Journal*'s promotional description, for it was not "profusely illustrated." It contained illustrations, to be sure, but only four. At least two were the work of Henry C. Chandler, an engraver who also kept his office in the *Journal* Building and who would become a founding faculty member of the city's first art school. In contrast to the sorts of images that had graced the pages of East Coast newspapers and trial pamphlets since the antebellum period, *The Cold Spring Tragedy* included only a tame re-creation of the crime scene. Its front cover depicted tiny figures, dwarfed by trees that surrounded them, recognizable only by their actions. In the lower left corner, Silas Hartman, hat pulled down over face, fires a shotgun at an unsuspecting Jacob Young, as he bends over to pick up fossil shells. At the scene's center, Nancy Clem points a pistol at Nancy Jane Young. While images of the burned and battered bodies of murdered prostitutes like Helen Jewett and Maria Bickford circulated widely in the penny press, Janey Young's reputation as a "pure [C]hristian woman" probably discouraged lurid visual depictions of her disfigured corpse.[19] She appeared instead beside her husband in an engraving that Chandler probably based on a photograph, perhaps a wedding portrait. As was typical of nineteenth-century portraits, both husband and wife wore sober expressions. Chandler nevertheless managed to capture something of Jacob Young's personality. He looked like a man who possessed "exemplary social qualities."[20]

In this respect, the engraving titled "Silas W. Hartman in the Act of Committing Suicide" (the only unsigned interior image) was less successful.

THIRD EDITION--20,000 COPIES SOLD.

COLD SPRING
TRAGEDY.

A. C. ROACH, Publisher, Indianapolis, Indiana.
BARCLAY & CO., Philadelpia, Pa.

The cover of *The Cold Spring Tragedy*, 3rd ed. (Indianapolis: A. C. Roach, 1869) imagined the murders in progress, adhering closely to the prosecution's version of the crime. In the lower left corner, Silas Hartman, hat pulled down over face, fires a shotgun at an unsuspecting Jacob Young, as he bends over to pick up shells. At the scene's center, Nancy Clem points a pistol at Nancy Jane Young, who cries out for help. The color-tinted original depicts Clem in a garish red and green outfit instead of the dark calico dress and black silk jacket witnesses described her as wearing. Courtesy of the Indiana Historical Society.

The man holding a razor to his throat sported a suitably maniacal appearance. But his features, like those of the sleeping William J. Abrams, were generic, devoid of individuality or personality. The illustration depicted the two friends and alleged partners in crime as nearly identical—a representation, to be sure, that lent support to prosecutors' claim that they tried to confuse potential witnesses by impersonating each other. It also suggested

The most sensational of the four illustrations in *The Cold Spring Tragedy* depicted Silas Hartman just about to cut his throat as his cellmate and co-defendant William J. Abrams slept. *The Cold Spring Tragedy*, 3rd ed. (Indianapolis: A. C. Roach, 1869), courtesy of the Indiana Historical Society.

that Abrams and Hartman were at best minor players in the "dreadful drama." The most arresting image, one conspicuously signed by Chandler, depicted the main attraction: Clem herself. It may have been a copy of the photograph enterprising street vendors hawked for the substantial sum of $10 apiece in December 1868, for it depicted Clem in the clothing she wore during her first trial. It also nicely illustrated one of the supposedly "many interesting facts never before published": both the author of the pamphlet's text and the artist who drew her portrait had decided that Clem did look a bit like a murderess after all. Words and image concurred: both depicted a woman with a "dangerous expression" on her face, a "sinister turn of her eye," and a "resolute set of her jaws."[21]

Despite its lack of originality and its tame and paltry illustrations, sales of *The Cold Spring Tragedy* were brisk. The *Journal* reported that the first edition sold out within days; by late June the second was "nearly exhausted" and plans for a third were in the works. Murder made for good business, a fact made clear by the notice that appeared on the pamphlet's back cover.

Here the Northwestern Mutual Life Insurance Company advertised that Jacob Young had been among its clients and advised "persons who are not insured" to "send for circulars containing information regarding this Company."[22]

The debate over the economic purview of faithful wives had been more muted during Clem's second trial, but it still formed a backdrop against which her actions might be judged. Hanna's characterization of the state's most recent case was not entirely off the mark. "Because she has handled large sums of money, and kept the fact to herself, you are asked to hang this woman," he told the jury.[23]

In the days that followed Hanna's unsuccessful plea, Clem herself brought matters of marital economy back to center stage. She had taken the stand in neither trial, probably because her attorneys believed her refusal to reveal the nature of her business or the names of her associates suggested guilt rather than innocence. Nevertheless she did testify, not in the courtroom, but in the pages of the city's two major newspapers. Here she presented two very different interpretations of women's proper business, images that mirrored, albeit imperfectly, the opposing interpretations of prosecution and defense. They also mirrored, again imperfectly, each paper's partisan ideology. Whether either interview faithfully recorded Clem's words is open to question. Of course, if she bore any resemblance to the woman prosecutors made her out to be, she was perfectly capable of telling successive reporters what they expected to hear.

Clem spoke to the Republican *Journal* on March 12, just two days after her brother's death, and to the Democratic *Sentinel*, some two weeks later, on March 29. Her conversation with the first reporter conjured up images of what one historian calls "Republican domesticity." Invoking sentiments that would have thrilled Pink Fishback, Clem emphasized her love of "home." She was a "home woman," she said. "She spoke very affectingly of her home and its attachments," the *Journal*'s correspondent reported. "[I]t was her delight to be there, and amidst its endearments." Clem said nothing whatsoever of her business.[24]

Clem told the *Sentinel* a different story, one that in at least some respects rang true. This time she spoke more freely, in part because she believed the *Sentinel* "fairer" than the *Journal*, in part because the *Sentinel*'s probable beliefs about faithful wives meshed more closely with her own.[25] Here Clem readily admitted her transactions with Jacob Young, although she denied any responsibility for his death. "Mr. Young was very prompt in his settlements," she explained, "and my confidence in him rapidly increased in consequence. I used every effort to obtain money to lend him whenever he required it." According to this version of events, *Nancy Jane* Young "first instigated . . . [Clem] to lend money to her husband": "I got quite intimate with Mrs. Young, as I thought her a very clever woman. . . . [S]he came to me and said she understood I managed my own affairs, and had some money; that her husband was engaged in a business in which he could make a good deal of money, and would pay me a high rate of interest for the use of mine."

Clem prudently presented herself as a lender, not a borrower. She avoided any hint of the avariciousness prosecutors attributed to her; she used her profits, she explained, for "repairing and refurnishing my home, and . . . to give my son a collegiate education." Yet the "clever woman"—a label that just as easily suited Clem—of the second interview deviated considerably from the "home woman" of the first. Clem matter-of-factly explained that she had concealed her business from her spouse. Nevertheless, Frank had "proved himself a good and true husband" one who held "a firm belief in my innocence." Intending to persuade the reading public of the same, Clem described herself as a faithful wife who was also a "clever" woman, a woman of "brain," if not "power." She offered a self-portrait that *Sentinel* readers might have recognized, for Democrats generally conceived of women as productive members of family economies. But her efforts to appeal to partisan beliefs—if indeed she intended to do so—only partly succeeded. Marital and monetary metaphors mingled in her telling, much as they had during her trials. Indeed, Clem executed a rhetorical maneuver very much like Fishback's: she reversed the sexes, speaking as much of husbandly obligations as of wifely duties. Her definition of a "true husband" was one who did not pry into his wife's business affairs. Careful readers, moreover, might have noted that the home on which Clem lavished so much attention was literally hers, not Frank's. If the stories crafted by her attorneys did not quite capture Clem's active pursuit of economic opportunities outside the bonds of matrimony, neither could Democratic narratives, which cast women's economic contributions in the context of men's household mastery, quite contain her self-reliance.[26]

Female breadwinning, as Clem seemed to recognize, had partisan implications. It also had larger political meanings, regardless of party. Men's right to vote no longer depended on property holding by the late 1860s, but the symbolic association between suffrage and economic independence remained strong. These connections were not lost on members of the woman movement, who hoped that women's wartime contributions and sacrifices would be rewarded with the vote and with access to previously "male" employments. Race implicitly entered these conversations along with gender, for women's rights advocates had only recently split into rival groups. One faction, headed by Susan B. Anthony and Elizabeth Cady Stanton, opposed the Fifteenth Amendment, which would be ratified the following year, because it stood to enfranchise only men; the other, led by Lucy Stone, supported it as a fulfillment of the movement's prewar abolitionist heritage and a step toward universal suffrage. Mary Livermore, a member of the latter camp and future vice president of the soon-to-be-formed American Woman Suffrage Association, was a featured speaker at the woman's suffrage convention held in Indianapolis during the summer of 1869. Livermore reiterated what she had said at earlier gatherings in New York, Boston, Syracuse, and Lowell: she considered the "closing of avenues of remunerative labor against them," like the denial of the franchise and limited access to education, a "wrong inflicted on women." Linking the political, the economic, and the marital, a "lady in the audience" expressed her hope that the vote would be granted not only to "Mrs. Livermore and other women of that class" but also "to the poor drunkard's wife, who, here in Indianapolis, spends his wife's earnings in the rum shop, and then beats her." Convention participants envisioned the possibility of refashioning both women's relation to the larger economy and their position in the more intimate political economy of marriage.

No one mentioned Nancy Clem in the course of this conversation; to do so would have attached added notoriety to an already controversial cause. ("We do not regard universal suffrage, or Woman's Rights—as they are called—as a means of grace, or even as one of the necessaries of life," the *Sentinel* snidely remarked.) Nor could Clem be easily incorporated into the sentimental tales fashioned by advocates of earnings laws—legislation that would grant gainfully employed married woman control over their wages. Unlike the "drunkard's wife," she was victim of neither a loutish husband nor a heartless marketplace.[27] Nevertheless, Clem's trials anticipated many of the questions the suffrage convention considered. Were women the independent economic actors that legal reforms increasingly suggested they should be? Or were husband and wife still "one" in practice, if not in the law? What exactly *should* women's business be?

■ ■ ■

Shortly after her interview with the *Sentinel*, Clem appeared once again in court to receive her sentence. Given that the jury had already spoken, this was merely, as Judge Chapman noted, a "formal duty." But it was a duty he took seriously. So did the spectators who once again crowded into the courtroom. "It . . . [is] not unfrequently the custom of judges," Chapman began, "when pressing judgment upon convicts, to address them such words of admonition as seemed proper under the circumstances." Yet given the nature of Clem's crime and what the evidence revealed of "her own individual character," he had "come to the conclusion that no words which he could utter, even in the trying position in which she was then placed, would produce upon her mind any good result." Despite this demurral, Chapman's statement was more a preamble than a closing. He did indeed utter further words—a good many of them—most with the stated purpose of deterring others from committing similar crimes.

Words may not have failed Chapman, but comprehension did. He confronted the same problem that had bedeviled prosecuting and defending attorneys, courtroom spectators, and ordinary citizens alike. He simply could not understand why a woman like Clem had involved herself in the "perpetration of a murder so revolting and diabolical." He could only fall back on the prosecution's definition of a faithful wife, appealing to the sort of stereotyped domesticity that had underpinned the state's case. Resorting to phrases that might have come straight from the pages of *Godey's Lady's Book*, Chapman noted that Clem had enjoyed "a beautiful home and pleasant natural surroundings." How could she, a woman who had "no useful want unsupplied," be "tempted by avarice"? How could such a woman stoop to murder? In closing, Chapman expressed his hope that Clem, "with a broken and contrite heart," would bow down "before the throne of that great and merciful Judge, whose power to save was sufficient to carry with Him, in his own blessed company, through the everlasting gates of glory, the soul of the repentant thief on the cross." He then pronounced her sentence: "It is the judgment of this Court that you be confined in the State Prison during your natural life."[28]

Clem, the *Cincinnati Daily Enquirer* reported, "remained perfectly calm." She smiled and bowed, not to God but to one of her attorneys. Then, accompanied by the bailiff, she left the courtroom.[29]

CHAPTER NINE

A Good Soldier

A crowd of Indianapolis residents gathered on the banks of the White River on September 12, 1869. They came to mark the first anniversary of the Young murders, and they timed their visit to coincide with the interval—between 3:30 and 4:30 p.m.—during which the crime was believed to have taken place. Some hoped that by virtue of their very presence, the mystery of the Cold Spring Tragedy would be revealed. They were disappointed. "Nothing new was developed," the *Sentinel* reported.[1]

There is no good time to be the defendant in a murder case. But this was a particularly inauspicious moment for William J. Abrams, whose trial for the murder of Jacob Young was just wrapping up. Abrams's day in court was initially scheduled to begin shortly after Clem's conviction and Hartman's suicide. The proceedings had been delayed by a series of mostly unfortunate events. On April 6, as the trial date approached, Abrams's attorneys (John Hanna, Frederick Knefler, William Wallace Leathers, and newcomer Joseph Ewing McDonald) asked, first, that Clem's departure for the Southern Prison be postponed until after she could testify in Abrams' defense, a request Judge Chapman denied. Clem left, as scheduled, for Jeffersonville at 2:00 a.m. on the morning of April 15. They asked, second, that their client be tried by a different judge on the ground that Chapman "was prejudiced against the prisoner and could not accord him a fair hearing."[2]

Chapman agreed to step aside and began the process of locating a new judge. He asked several, but found few takers. Finally, in mid-April, forty-eight-year-old Judge Nimrod Johnson of the Wayne County Criminal Court agreed to take on the case.[3] The *Journal* would remember Johnson as "one of the ablest and most brilliant lawyers in Eastern Indiana"—a backhanded compliment that limited the geographic scope of his achievements. He would also be remembered as a man of egalitarian principles who taught Sunday school to African American children.[4] Once Johnson had taken his seat on the bench, Abrams's attorneys filed a motion for a change of venue, arguing that finding a fair-minded jury in Marion County would be impossible given the massive publicity and considerable excitement Clem's trials had generated. Those who provided statements in favor of the request included the county sheriff, deputy sheriff, jailer Albert Harden, and Abrams

himself. The state responded with a series of counter-affidavits from supposedly representative citizens, among them three extraordinarily wealthy
men, G. H. Voss, an attorney; James H. McKernan, a real estate agent; and
William C. Smock, the county clerk. They also included a decidedly self-
interested individual, Silas A. Pollard, the man the newly jailed Abrams had
been so anxious to repay.[5]

Johnson overruled the motion, arguing that "no more prejudice against
Abrams existed in this county, than in other counties where the testimony
had been extensively read." He believed "that public sentiment here rather
favored Abrams, and he thought that a fair and impartial trial might be had
in this court." Certainly there were those who sympathized with the defendant. A reporter from the *Sentinel* interviewed Abrams as he visited with
his wife and daughter. His account, both sentimental and sympathetic, described three-year-old Cora's daily bedtime habit of saying a "little prayer
to God" for her "pa" and depicted the prisoner standing in the jail's "open
doorway . . . blowing kisses" to Maggie and Cora as they retreated from
sight. If Clem was a "home woman," Abrams was a home man. He "spoke
about his home with all the fervor of a man who loved the society of his
family and the heartfelt happiness that is only attainable under one's own
roof." Asked for their opinions, the Marion County sheriff and jailer described Abrams as a model prisoner. He conscientiously performed his
duties as grub boss; he could be counted on to "quell disturbances" among
the inmates, mediate their disputes, and protect those who were "imposed
upon." The *Journal*, more skeptical and less sympathetic, nevertheless acknowledged that Abrams did not look like a criminal. "He is not a bad looking man by any means, and . . . he is not the sort of man who would be picked
out of a crowd . . . as a murderer."[6]

Whether Abrams had succeeded in finding a sympathetic judge is an
open question; in any case, it quickly became a moot point. Shortly before
the trial was to begin, Johnson, the son of a physician, journeyed to Cambridge City, some 60 miles away, to visit his sick mother. The next day, feeling unwell himself, he stopped by his father's office and helped himself
to what he thought was "tincture of gentian, a mild tonic." Instead he swallowed a dose of aconite, a harmless analgesic taken in small quantities, a
deadly neurotoxin ingested in larger amounts. The mistake quickly discovered, an emetic was administered but to no avail. On Thursday, April 29,
newspapers published accounts of Johnson's "melancholy death."[7]

Judge Jeremiah Wilson, of Indiana's Fourth Circuit Court—a jurisdiction that encompassed several southern counties—agreed to replace Johnson, but he was unavailable until July. The trial did not actually begin until the tail end of August. As might have been predicted, procuring a fair and impartial jury was easier said than done. Selection took nearly two days. Some potential jurors took "the usual question of whether they had formed or expressed an opinion" a bit too literally; they replied they believed the defendant guilty. Although Abrams joined in the "general laughter" that "invariably" ensued, his attorneys were not amused.[8] They once again requested a change of venue, a request that once again was denied.

A jury was finally seated, but only after prosecuting and defense attorneys examined more than two hundred potential candidates. As in Clem's trials, its members consisted primarily of farmers from outlying townships, none, of course, from Pike. One, the *Sentinel* reported, had previously been tried for but acquitted of stealing a $75 cow. The *Journal* described the jury as "almost universally regarded as being quite as intelligent as the average." It "has vindicated Judge Wilson as well as Judge Chapman, in the belief expressed by them that a fair and impartial jury could still be obtained in this county," its editor confidently concluded.[9]

As an attorney, Wilson was renowned for his skill at cross-examination. As a judge he was a no-nonsense courtroom manager. The *Journal* commended him for ensuring that Abrams' trial progressed as speedily as possible, a cost-cutting strategy that partly mitigated the considerable expense the county incurred from trying Clem twice, and, now, of transporting and lodging Abrams's new judge. The defense agreed to cross-examine witnesses only "where the testimony tends to connect Abrams directly with the case." After brief opening statements from county prosecutor John Duncan—now all of twenty-two years old—for the state, and William Wallace Leathers, for the defense, testimony began.[10]

■ ■ ■

Maggie and Cora appeared each day, but this time the courtroom was far less crowded.[11] A respectable woman on trial for murder was a sight worth seeing; a man, even one of hitherto respectable character, less so. Two stars of the previous proceedings, Jonathan Gordon and Benjamin Harrison, sat this one out. Sheer monotony provided the most likely explanation for "very slim" attendance. Despite the *Sentinel*'s promise of "a great deal of new matter . . . not [previously] brought to light," anyone who had paid attention during Clem's trials had heard it all before. Notable differences were few. Elisha Kise (who had wanted to be certain that he had correctly identified the Youngs' bodies) and William Coleman testified to the defendant's strangely unconcerned response to the news of Jacob and Nancy Jane Young's probable deaths. Otherwise, most of those called to the stand by the prosecution, including Coroner Allred, Robert Bowman, Erie Locke and his children, Rebecca Marot, Joseph Solomon, Isaac Sweede, and Josephine Stevens, Jane Sizemore, Rebecca Hartman, Robert Dorsey, the two John Wileys, and Dr. Duzan had testified previously. Their statements differed little from what they had said only six months before.[12]

Few of them were eager to take the stand. When only a portion of those called appeared in court on the first day of testimony, Judge Wilson threatened to attach the property of those who failed to present themselves the next day. One of the no-shows was Dr. Duzan. Despite his eventual testimony and his explanation that "he had been absent professionally in another county," he was fined for his initial failure to appear. John Pierson also failed to come when called, but he turned up the following day to testify to seeing Nancy Clem and Silas Hartman "driving in a buggy, a sorrel mare" on the afternoon of the murder. This time he neglected to add that he "knowed it was them."[13]

■ ■ ■

Leathers's opening argument acknowledged the difficulty of defending a client whose alleged co-conspirator—and an extremely high profile one at that—had already been convicted. "No case ever tried in this State has been so notorious," he told the jury—or so the *Journal* reported. The *Sentinel* raised the rhetorical stakes; its coverage claimed Leathers said "no case ever before tried *in the United States* had excited so widespread a notoriety" [emphasis added]. The defense, Leathers made clear, intended to refute the state's claim that Abrams was part of a scheme orchestrated by Clem and Hartman to murder Jacob and Nancy Young. "The State must prove that a conspiracy existed . . . and they must show beyond a reasonable doubt, that it was a conspiracy to commit the crime of which this defendant stands indicted, and that he was a party to it." Clem's and Hartman's guilt or innocence mattered not, Leathers declared, because Abrams had no *criminal* connection to either, and no one, not even the prosecutors who tried Clem, had placed him anywhere near Cold Spring on the afternoon of the murder.

Nor, Leathers added, should the jury rely on "the evidence of pawnbrokers and second-hand auctioneers." William J. Abrams, in implicit contrast to these morally suspect sorts of people, offered a different sort of evidence, the evidence of "good character in his past life."[14]

The defense scored a few minor victories. A witness who claimed to have seen Abrams near Illinois Street on the fatal morning admitted he had previously mistaken one man for another. Twelve-year-old Josie Stevens, who identified Abrams as the man who tried to buy a shotgun at her mother's store, acknowledged that poor eyesight had forced her to withdraw from school. Taking the stand for the first time, Frank Clem corroborated Abrams's account of his activities on the morning of September 12: the defendant had been at his grocery buying peaches. Any advantages Frank's testimony gained for the defense evaporated under Fishback's cross-examination. "I testified before the grand jury that we had quit visiting Abrams because we were afraid he was making money too fast," Frank admitted.[15]

Although a subpoena had reportedly been served, Nancy Clem did not testify. Why is not certain. Abrams believed she could exonerate him, but his attorneys may have thought otherwise. There was also a practical matter to consider: transporting Clem from Jeffersonville would cost money. It was already becoming abundantly clear that Abrams—despite the early infusion of cash extracted from a boot in the Hartmans' basement—did not have the funds to pay the costs of his defense.[16]

It was also becoming apparent that the defense could offer only a feeble challenge to the prosecution's evidentiary claims. Too many people testified to Clem, Young, and Abrams's business relations; too many people, even if they were "pawnbrokers and second-hand auctioneers," testified to Abrams's determination to buy a gun on the morning of the murders. Given these circumstances, Abrams's attorneys relied primarily on the evidence of character, a tactic foreshadowed by Leathers's initial remarks. They called a long string of witnesses, forty in all, who testified that Abrams was "honest," "humane," "honorable," "kind hearted," "law-abiding," and above all that he had been "a good soldier." One who swore to this latter fact was none other than Abrams's own attorney, Frederick Knefler.[17]

Judge Wilson made good on his promise of a speedy trial. On Friday, September 10, after only seven days of testimony, the closing arguments began. These, too, were brief in comparison to the six- and seven-hour speeches given at Clem's trials. William Pinckney Fishback, Frederick

Knefler, and John S. Duncan finished their statements in the course of a single day, and John Hanna had time to begin his own before court adjourned until the following morning.

The state's case hinged on proving that Clem, Abrams, and Hartman had engaged in a conspiracy to murder Jacob Young; such a finding, Fishback explained to jurors, rendered Abrams guilty even if he was not "physically present when the crime . . . [was] committed." It also hinged on circumstantial evidence, "a safe and reliable means of getting at the truth." Ever eloquent, Fishback once again quoted *Hamlet*. "The dangerous people of the world are those 'who can smile, and smile again, and still be a villain,'" he explained. They included Clem, "the woman who can smile with her neighbor one minute, and kill her the next," and Abrams, "the sweet voiced man who can buy a gun to kill his friend with that day." Citing recent vigilante action against the notorious train-robbing Reno Gang in the southern part of the state, Fishback issued a grim warning to any juror bent on "leniency." If crimes such as Abrams's were "not punished, we can welcome as relief, the Seymour hangings, or New Albany mobs."[18]

Just as prosecutors' case against Clem depended on deviant femininity, their case against Abrams found him lacking in manly virtues. Fishback suggested that in this respect, as with the crime itself, Abrams was guilty by association. Reprising arguments presented the previous December, he reminded jurors that the key piece of material evidence against the defendant—the shotgun that had killed Jacob Young—had come to light only through a draft dodger's cowardice. "Had he who fired the gun been as brave as his accomplice, the gun would have been thrown into the river, and this means of tracing the murderer lost. But he was a coward, and when he had done his work of blood, dropped his gun and fled, leaving the work of rifling the clothing of the dead man to his female accomplice."[19]

In contrast to the now-deceased Silas Hartman, Abrams could be accused of neither cowardice nor evasion of military service. But as an erstwhile carpenter with no apparent means of making a living, he *could* be accused of being a loafer. In explaining to the jury why Abrams had visited Clem's house on the afternoon of September 12 (to "hear the news of the murder") Fishback conjured up a curiously distorted domestic scene, one that linked diminished masculinity and symbolic infidelity. "His wife was canning peaches that afternoon," Fishback sneered, "but [Abrams] . . . could not help her; he must go down and help Mrs. Clem's colored woman."[20]

Despite its Radical cast, the prosecution was just as capable as the defense of pandering to jurors' racial prejudices.

Frederick Knefler had not taken a speaking part during Clem's trials. This time he had a starring role. Knefler had the most unusual background of any of the "leading legal lights" who participated in the various iterations of the Cold Spring case. Born Knoepfler Frigyes to a Jewish family in Hungary, he served as a teenage soldier in the unsuccessful Hungarian revolution of 1848. As did many "forty-eighters" in the wake of the repression that followed, he immigrated to America, settling briefly in New York—where "Knoepfler" became "Knefler"—before moving to Indianapolis. There his father, a physician, was among the founders of the city's first synagogue. Like his client, Knefler learned carpentry. But he also studied law on the side. In the years before the Civil War he became the assistant to the Marion County clerk. In 1861 he enlisted as a first lieutenant in the "famous Seventy-ninth Indiana Regiment"; four years later he mustered out as a brevet brigadier general. Shortly thereafter he became John Hanna's law partner. Despite his ethnicity and religion, Knefler was unquestionably a member of the city's elite. Next to Benjamin Harrison, he was the city's most famous Civil War veteran.[21]

Immediately after the noon recess, Knefler, who had already testified in Abrams's defense, rose to give his closing arguments. Abrams was not merely his client but one of his former soldiers. He was "an old friend, a man who has stood within the sound of my voice, while in the army, for a year." "The only reason I stand here in his defense," Knefler avowed, "is on account of the great friendship I owe him." Knefler disputed the state's claim of conspiracy. Abrams was at Clem & Brother's grocery store buying peaches at the very moment prosecutors placed him at the pawnbrokers. Testimony regarding the appearance and identity, even the clothing and facial hair of the man who shopped for a shotgun was, Knefler insisted, contradictory and inconsistent. (Fishback had accounted for these discrepancies by suggesting that Abrams brought two hats along with him on the morning of the murder, changing them frequently to confuse potential witnesses.) Knefler offered what was by now a shopworn refrain: shouldn't suspicion fall on others who did business with Jacob Young, namely Robert Dorsey? "You must bear in mind that [Abrams] is not on trial here for his money transactions," he reminded the jury.[22]

Abrams's "money transactions" surely *were* on trial. So, too, was his manhood. As testimony presented by the defense made clear, the outcome would depend a good deal on jurors' perceptions of his character, a notion inseparable from gender. One measure of manhood, on which John Hanna would shortly rely, emphasized breadwinning. Another, which Knefler shrewdly invoked, rested on soldiering. As Knefler must have known, at least some of the jurors were veterans themselves.[23] He must have known that appeals to wartime courage were bound to sway all but the most recalcitrant Copperheads. The memory of the Civil War touched nearly every aspect of postwar life. Civilians retained their military titles long after war's end; "General Knefler," who in the 1890s would oversee the construction of Indianapolis's Soldiers and Sailors Monument, was a case in point. Martial metaphors and paramilitary organizations structured political campaigns. In this atmosphere "waving the bloody shirt"—an accusation Democrats would hurl at Republicans in the decades to come—proved as useful a courtroom strategy as political tactic. In 1869, only four years after Appomattox, honorable military service provided persuasive proof of a man's moral character and social worth.[24]

Now Abrams's former commanding officer would personally acknowledge what numerous witnesses had already established: that Abrams was a man of "excellent" character. "In the army I knew him intimately, and a better soldier never served his country. He was a brave soldier, an honest man, and through the terrible battles of Stones River, Chickamauga, Chattanooga, the Atlanta campaign and the battle of Nashville, his conduct was as brave and as gallant as that of any man in the United States army." Knowing that jurors likely disagreed over the war's meaning, Knefler settled for vague appeals to patriotism. Abrams had not fought to end slavery, put down a rebellion, or even save the Union; he had merely "served his country," albeit with courage and distinction. A "brave and gallant" soldier, Knefler would have the jury believe, could never be a shifty criminal. No one, not even members of the prosecution, mentioned a curious paradox. If Abrams had been a good soldier that meant in part that he had been a good killer, perhaps more likely to commit murder than one who had never seen combat. Soldiers who fought in the American Civil War experienced violence on a hitherto unimaginable scale. Countless veterans suffered the continuing effects of wartime trauma, descending at times into drunkenness and violence. These were things that Knefler must have known but did not say. Aside from referencing "terrible battles," he presented an idealized war and an honorable soldier-hero who had returned unscathed to civilian life. Such a man, Knefler implied, was incapable of complicity in the murder of a friend and would-be comrade.[25]

John Duncan followed. The young prosecuting attorney remembered the lessons he had learned the previous December; his argument (which the *Journal* termed "perfect, logical and cover[ing] all of the ground") stuck closely to nuts and bolts, though he could not resist criticizing Abrams for "blast[ing] the reputation of his dead friend" Jacob Young by accusing of him of killing his wife.[26]

John Hanna was in fine form, praising both judge (a man whose conduct "inspire[d] continued confidence in the American judiciary") and jury ("twelve intelligent, impartial, unbiased and fair men"). He focused on discrediting witnesses' accounts without disparaging the witnesses themselves. "Little Josie [Stevens]" was "honest in her impression," he acknowledged, "but the man she describes is not the defendant. . . . He had no such beard as she describes, and was not dressed in the speckled suit she describes; neither did he wear the low round-crown black hat which she describes." Similarly a Mrs. McMullen, who testified that she could not be certain Abrams was the man she had encountered on Illinois Street, won Hanna's praise. She was "an intelligent woman" with a "pure heart." Even the "colored man Sweede" gained Hanna's qualified endorsement. "He will not and does not swear the defendant is the man."[27]

Hanna made character the centerpiece of Abrams's defense. He repeated what his colleague Fred Knefler had already said: Abrams was a brave soldier; "no braver or better man went to die that his country might live." Abrams was also a good family man, the earner of a family wage that supported his wife and child. His "small cottage"—which, Hanna failed to mention, had recently been mortgaged to pay attorneys' fees—hardly amounted to "extravagant and luxurious living." Rather it represented the fruits of honest labor. "Why was it he came down town that morning?" Because "at the breakfast table his wife said she wanted the article which he afterward purchased." It was on this humble domestic "mission" that Abrams had visited the Clem grocery. Hanna made explicit what Knefler had only implied. Abrams's "good character," he claimed, "is utterly incompatible with the accusation against him; murderers, cold-blooded money murder[er]s are not made of such material. . . . Who can prove a better character, from his boyhood through all his life than has William J. Abrams?" he asked.[28]

Hanna could not resist a dig at the prosecuting attorney's youth and inexperience. "I am sorry that my young friend Duncan spoke rather lightly of character yesterday. His father and mine taught us differently and I can but feel that he did it without thought and intent to belittle the value of character."[29] Hanna's rejoinder suggest the beginnings of a generational change in legal thought, that belief in the value of appearance, demeanor, and character was slowly giving way to methods that focused on supposedly dispassionate analysis of factual evidence. "Character" would remain—and still remains—important. But it would become increasingly clear over the course of the nineteenth century that otherwise respectable people were capable of committing violent crime. One of them might have been William J. Abrams.

John Dye's closing argument, only incompletely reproduced in the *Journal* and *Sentinel*, covered familiar territory. He largely avoided the self-righteous indignation that characterized his rhetoric during Clem's first trial, cleaving more closely to the strategy he employed in the second. His rhetoric was almost stodgy; catchy phrases like "self-reliant and God defiant" were absent from his presentation. Instead, he settled for a point-by-point refutation of the defense's evidentiary arguments. He did not, however, avoid the issue of character entirely. Taking a page from Hanna's book, he praised prosecution witnesses as "intelligent and honest." Josie Stevens was "bright, intelligent, and candid . . . at an age when the powers of observation are quick—when the memory is retentive."[30]

Joseph Ewing McDonald, a newcomer to the Cold Spring case, gave the concluding statement for the defense. McDonald was a figure of considerable prominence. Like Hanna and Knefler, he was a self-made man, one who began his career as a harness maker before turning to the law. He was also a former congressman and state attorney general. In 1864 he ran unsuccessfully for governor against incumbent Oliver Morton. He would be elected to the Senate only a year after his courtroom appearance in Abrams's defense. Variously known as "a man of the people," "Old Saddle Bags," and the "war horse of the Hoosier Democracy," he was the only Democrat enlisted thus far to serve on either side's legal team. The *Journal* reported McDonald's closing argument was "logical and eloquent, covering every point in the case." In a clearly partisan swipe, it did not bother to reproduce even an abbreviated version.[31]

It did reprint Judge Wilson's instructions, which might be read as a rebuke to the defense in general and to Hanna in particular. Wilson admonished jurors not "to swerve . . . a hair's breadth from the evidence." Evidence counted, not character.[32]

■ ■ ■

The hasty proceedings, the limited cross-examinations, the "slim" attendance, the increased responsibilities granted young John Duncan, the absence of Major Gordon and General Harrison, the abbreviated speeches and curtailed coverage—all suggested that Abrams's trial was something of an afterthought, its outcome a foregone conclusion. But the jurors took their responsibilities seriously, holding "prayer meetings every night for light and guidance."[33] Their deliberations lasted first one day, then two, sparking fears of another hung jury. They failed to materialize. On the morning of Wednesday, September 15, just three days after the impromptu anniversary gathering at Cold Spring, jurors returned to the courtroom to announce that they had reached a verdict. They found Abrams guilty of first-degree murder, but they rendered a sentence of life imprisonment rather than death. A signed recommendation accompanied the verdict. "In the discharge of our duty, and under the solemnity of our oaths, [we] found the defendant guilty of murder in the first degree; yet believing that the crime committed by him was the result of wicked influences surrounding him, and not the result of a bad heart, we would respectfully ask the Governor to commute his sentence to ten (10) years' imprisonment."[34] It was a curious piece of jurisprudence, one that would lend weight to calls for overhauling a judicial system that gave juries the duty of pronouncing sentences as well as verdicts. The sentence and verdict followed Judge Wilson's instructions; both were grounded in evidence. The appended document, however, was based on the evidence of character. Abrams, the jury believed, was not a bad man at heart.

For Abrams, the jury's decision was a mixed blessing. Most obviously, it dashed his hopes for acquittal. Still, it spared him the noose and offered the prospect of future release. But it also publicly proclaimed him a weak man, a man unable to resist "wicked influences," a man who could be twirled around a scheming woman's fingers.

■ ■ ■

At the time of his jailhouse interview, the home of which Abrams had so fondly spoken was just a few blocks away. Now he would have to remember domestic bliss from a greater distance. He asked to be assigned to the

Southern Prison at Jeffersonville. More than 100 miles from Indianapolis, this would put him far from his wife and daughter but closer than would the Northern Prison in Michigan City. Like many of his previous requests, this entreaty was denied. "Probably he thought he would share in the *Clemency*," the *Cincinnati Daily Enquirer* quipped.[35]

"Clem-ency," much to the *Enquirer*'s chagrin, seemed to be in full force at the Southern Prison, where Abrams's alleged accomplice supposedly "live[d] off the fat of the land." Convinced of Clem's innocence and eager to give a respectable female inmate her due, the warden, Colonel Lawrence S. Shuler, had arranged to have her cell wallpapered and carpeted in advance of her arrival. Celebrated as a humanitarian reformer in some circles, ridiculed as gullible dupe in others, Shuler, the *Cincinnati Daily Enquirer* complained, treated his celebrity prisoner "more like a distinguished guest than a murderess expiating one of the most dreadful crimes on record."[36]

"Clem-ency" eluded William J. Abrams for the time being. Nancy Clem had been whisked away to Jeffersonville in the wee hours of the morning, shielded from curious onlookers. Abrams received no such consideration. On the morning of October 25, "a large crowd"—few of them well-wishers— "assembled at the depot . . . to see [him] off." The scene seemed designed for maximum humiliation, although probably not intentionally, for both the sheriff and the jailer had grown fond of their model prisoner. Despite the reputation they had acquired for "criminal negligence" (or perhaps because of it), they followed what passed for procedure. They shackled Abrams to the other convicts bound for Michigan City. He left Indianapolis in chains.[37]

One of his attorneys grumbled that he would be lucky to "get fifty cents on the dollar, for his share of the fees."[38]

CHAPTER TEN

Lebanon

The year 1871 began inauspiciously for the remaining Cold Spring conspirators. On the fifth of January, Bill Abrams's house was sold at auction to pay his legal expenses. This transaction only increased his bitterness toward his attorneys, who he believed had failed to adequately represent him. As he told a reporter who interviewed him in his Michigan City prison cell, "one of his counsel would rather spend a thousand dollars to keep him in prison than to get him out." Abrams's conviction and incarceration put an end to his family's short-lived prosperity. His wife and daughter moved to rented quarters on Mississippi Street, in a decrepit and disreputable neighborhood. Maggie took in sewing to make ends meet.[1]

On the very day that the proceeds from the sale of Abrams's house and lot were conveyed to John Hanna, Frederick Knefler, and William Leathers, Grandmother Hartman ate a hearty breakfast at Matthew's house and went next door to the Clems'. Shortly after, the eighty-year-old matriarch collapsed onto a sofa and died. The *Journal* identified her only as the mother of Matthew Hartman, the plasterer and the mother-in-law of "Mr. Frank Clem"; the *Sentinel*, however, described the deceased as none other than the mother of the infamous Nancy Clem, now housed only a few blocks away in the Marion County Jail, awaiting her third trial. The *People*, Indianapolis's newest paper and the city's answer to the *National Police Gazette*, dispensed with propriety altogether: "The mother of Mrs. Nancy E. Clem, the alleged murderess of Mr. and Mrs. Jacob Young, and the mother of Sike Hartman, who committed suicide in the county jail, while awaiting trial for complicity in the murder, died Thursday morning quite suddenly at the residence of Mr. Frank Clem." Even so, journalists conceded Clem her privacy. No one reported her reaction to her mother's death.[2]

If Abrams was resigned to his fate by the spring of 1871, Clem had reason for optimism. Public opinion had previously, as the *Journal* put it, "largely been against her," indeed, some accounts suggested that the threat of a potential lynching had pushed jurors toward a guilty verdict in 1869.[3]

Attitudes toward Clem were more varied by the early 1870s. In part this was because the state supreme court had granted her a new trial on the grounds that Judge Chapman had not clearly explained the meaning of "consent" when he instructed the jury "if the murder was perpetrated with her knowledge and consent or connivance, she is a principal." Most citizens paid little attention to the higher court's reasoning, focusing instead on the decision itself, which suggested judicial corruption to some, innocence to others. In part it was because feelings toward the case increasingly reflected partisan and regional identities. City Republicans, by and large, remained convinced of Clem's guilt; Democrats and many country dwellers belonging to either party were no longer so sure. Clem herself told the *Louisville Courier-Journal* that the Democratic *Sentinel* "was fairer" to her than was the *Journal*, although, like its rival it had "said some hard things."[4]

Despite her mother's death and a recent bout of serious illness, Clem reportedly was "in excellent health and spirits" as her third trial approached. Numerous delays—due for the most part to the busy schedules of the attorneys involved—ensured that proceedings did not get underway until midsummer. On the morning of July 9, 1871, Clem made her third opening appearance in the Marion County Criminal Court. Once again citing the intense local publicity her case had received, Clem's attorneys requested a change of venue. This time, the presiding judge, David Banta, complied. After consulting both prosecution and defense, he transferred jurisdiction to the Boone County Circuit Court.[5]

Boone County was a reasonable choice. Just 30 or so miles to the north, it was close enough to facilitate the transportation of the more than one hundred people who would once again be called to testify. Even so, stingy Marion County authorities refused them the relatively expensive luxury of passenger service from Indianapolis to Lebanon, the Boone County seat. The court had to adjourn on at least one occasion because an overloaded freight had failed to stop to pick up witnesses waiting at the Indianapolis depot.[6]

Bolstered by Judge Banta's decision, Clem was confident of acquittal. At least one reporter questioned her wisdom, for few Boone County residents, he believed, objected to capital punishment. Others wondered whether changing to this particular venue would accomplish its intended purpose. Indeed, prosecution and defense questioned over one hundred potential jurors before they settled on the twelve men, "mostly farmers, men in middle life," who would decide Clem's fate. "If the object of a change of venue be to secure a jury who know nothing of the matter they are to try, it is in this instance a signal failure, for the call of the *venire* showed that the people of Boone are eminently a reading people and as familiar with the subject in hand as the people of Marion," the *Journal* complained.[7]

But as the *Journal*'s grumblings intimated, Boone offered Clem particular advantages. Indeed, she could not have asked for a better locale. The Boone County was largely populated by rural folk, many of them upland southerners like Clem herself—in fact, Boone's population was significantly more southern than Marion's.[8] These were literally Clem's people. Boone's southeast corner bordered Pike Township; early settlers had paid little attention to county lines as they laid out homesteads that put them in close proximity to kin. Clem still had relatives in the "state of Boone." Her first cousin Anna was married to Silas Lee, a wealthy Lebanon banker and attorney, prominent local Republican, and a former county clerk. The editors of both local papers, the Republican *Weekly Patriot* and the Democratic *Pioneer*, believed her innocent.[9] Clem had reason to expect a favorable verdict.

■ ■ ■

Boone County was home to fewer than twenty-three thousand inhabitants. Only about fifteen hundred of them lived in the county seat, so named because a stand of hickory trees reminded a founding town commissioner of the biblical cedars of Lebanon.[10] Like many small Midwestern towns, "Leba-nen," as Hoosiers pronounced it, aspired to greater things. "The first object of interest" a newcomer would notice, was the Boone County Courthouse, a rare application of Gothic Revival architecture, complete with a tower "somewhat after a pattern of castles of the olden time." Completed in 1857 at a cost of some $40,000, it embodied town boosters' hitherto unrealized hopes.[11]

As in many other instances, Clem provided enterprising citizens with opportunities. For once, the county courtroom—unusually commodious for a town of Lebanon's size—filled. In fact, it was often bursting at the seams. "The city is full of strangers who are here to hear the case, which is creating a profound sensation in our ordinarily quiet town," the *Weekly Patriot* observed. While some locals departed for the state fair in Indianapolis, a "Great Flood of Strangers" descended on Lebanon like locusts, filling the town's hotels and boardinghouses to capacity. They included "foreign" correspondents from other parts of the state and nation, curiosity seekers of all stripes, and, more reluctant sojourners—witnesses subpoenaed to testify yet again. They also included attorneys from various parts of Indiana and nearby states, who came to watch legal luminaries in action and witness the still novel prosecution of a case based on circumstantial evidence.[12]

Boosters quickly recognized the potential advantages this "profound sensation" offered. Taking their cues from enterprising Indianapolitans,

Lebanon businessmen linked their merchandise to the case. "IF the Clem trial is going off at present that does not keep Holloway from selling sewing machines," read an advertisement published in the *Pioneer* in mid-October.[13] The *Weekly Patriot* went a good deal further, publishing a several-part "Pencil Sketch of the City and Its Attractions." It began with cliché—a now-familiar story of hardy white pioneers wresting a wilderness from savage Indians. "Boone County was named for the celebrated 'Indian fighter,' Daniel Boone, whose name will ever be held in high esteem by frontiersmen." The *Patriot* emphasized the exceptional obstacles would-be settlers encountered in order to tell a story of progress that "almost reads like a tale of the Arabian Knights." Boone County had been no mere wilderness but "an absolute wilderness . . . one of the very last in the State to be freed from the blighting existence of an Indian Reservation." While "thirty-nine years ago there was not the vestige of a town here," now even the log cabins inhabited by the first generation of settlers had given way to "evidence of a higher civilization, of progress in the arts, and of development of material wealth." An "elegant court house," "substantial brick business blocks," and "many attractive residences" stood where once there had been only forest; "graveled turnpikes" replaced "impassable morass[es]." The "pencil sketch" sang the praises of various churches, of which Lebanon "is amply supplied," and affirmed the superiority of Lebanon's public school, "which presents to the advanced students all of the advantages of an Academy." Lest a visiting witness or courtroom spectator miss the point, the author, most likely editor D. E. Caldwell, concluded his first installment thus: "We ask those who are looking for new home to visit Lebanon. . . . Our people have acquired wealth; and the future offers as many attractions, yes, more than at any other time. The climate is healthful, the soil productive, and the resources almost unbounded."[14]

Despite Caldwell's disclaimer that schools and churches—indicators of the "intellectual and moral status of the community"—were as important as "mercantile prosperity," he devoted his three subsequent sketches to a "review" of the town's "principal business houses." The Lebanon Bank, the "conservator of the monied [*sic*] interests of the community," took pride of place, as did the members of the firm that operated it, who included Clem's cousin by marriage, Silas A. Lee. The pencil sketch and subsequent mentions, one featuring his acquisition of a new racehorse, another his selection to represent the town lodge at a regional meeting of the Masonic order, and still another detailing a minor injury to his young son—all in the space of two months—confirmed the *Indianapolis Sentinel*'s impression that Lee was indeed a prominent citizen of "this burg."[15]

Lee made his influence felt. When the Marion County jailer escorted Clem from Indianapolis to Lebanon, he allowed his celebrity prisoner to stop for dinner with the Lees in exchange for a promise from the Boone County sheriff, Richard S. Camplin, to afterward convey her to the town jail. Camplin conveniently forgot to collect her. "The result," the *Sentinel* reported, "was that Mrs. Clem enjoyed, for the first time in nearly three years, the blessing of home comforts under a Christian roof." Even after she returned to the sheriff's custody, she received special treatment, a charge local officials emphatically but unconvincingly denied. Town officials prepared the jail "for her reception" by evicting "several vagrants and persons committed for drunkenness." If drifters and drunks were not allowed to share Clem's quarters, Frank Clem was. A Lebanon resident, writing as "Justice," insisted that the jailor, not the Lees, supplied Clem's meals, but he acknowledged that she was allowed occasional outside strolls, a decision "regarded by the citizens here as a simple act of humanity."[16]

Buoyed by various acts of humanity and local sympathy, Clem "did not exhibit the anxiety of previous years." She exhibited instead a renewed attentiveness to performance. On Tuesday, September 26, 1871, the opening day of her third trial, she entered the courtroom "dressed with becoming taste," wearing "a black luster dress, paisley shawl, and black velvet hat." Upon taking her seat, she boldly threw back her veil, symbolically communicating that she had nothing to hide. As the *Weekly Patriot* observed, she appeared "entirely self-possessed."[17]

■ ■ ■

The most recent proceedings reconvened a familiar cast of characters. It also introduced some new ones. William Pinckney Fishback had relinquished the law in favor of editing the *Journal*, but Benjamin Harrison and John Dye once again represented the state. This time they joined a newly elected prosecuting attorney, John Duncan having left public service for private practice. Thirty-year old Henry C. Guffin began his appointment with a good deal more experience than had his predecessor; still, Clem's case was far too important to be left entirely at Guffin's disposal. John Hanna, Jonathan Gordon, William Wallace Leathers, and Frederick Knefler once again served as Clem's defense. Each side retained the assistance of local attorneys as well, men who mostly remained on the sidelines. Thomas F. Davidson, judge of the Boone County Circuit Court, presided. The *Journal*—or more accurately, Pink Fishback—approved. Davidson, an editorial noted, "unites in an unusual degree those peculiar qualities, the combination of which make a good judge—firmness, clearness and felicity of expression."[18]

John Dye opened for the prosecution, as he had twice before. His language differed slightly, but his message was the same: Clem was no longer "self-reliant and God defiant" but a woman "actuated by mercenary motives" who made "frequent and stealthy visits to Young's house." The initial testimony covered familiar territory. Robert Bowman recounted his story of discovering the bodies of Jacob and Nancy Jane Young. Drs. L. D. Waterman and William Wands described the postmortem examination, Waterman also testifying to his subsequent discovery of the footprints left behind at the crime scene. Millie and Seymour Locke, now seventeen and fourteen, once again told the court about seeing two women and a man walking along the sandbar and later noticing the reclining "lewd couple." Their father's decision to leave "for the West . . . in opposition to the wishes of the prosecution" caused the first potential delay and the first significant deviation from previous scripts. After some grumbling, Clem's attorneys agreed to read Erie Locke's testimony from the last trial into the transcript.[19]

There were other changes. Mary Belle Young, now a "pale, frail child" of thirteen, had been shunted off to another set of relatives; she had to be brought from Attica, a tiny town some 50 miles northwest of Lebanon, where she lived with an aunt. Clem's mother and brother Silas were dead. So, too, was Madeline Everson, the neighbor who had recorded what turned out to be fictional accounts. Judge Davidson sustained the state's objection to introducing Grandmother Hartman's previous testimony, but allowed Erastus Everson to testify for the prosecution on his deceased wife's behalf. The younger John Wiley—the boy who once said, "Here comes Syke Hartman"— initially failed to appear because he had his own legal troubles. He had absconded to Illinois after being accused of robbery.[20]

■ ■ ■

The two Boone county papers, both weeklies, gave Clem's trial ample coverage, although the Democratic *Pioneer* was forced to admit that it simply did not have the space to publish "all the evidence" unless it omitted all other news. Indianapolis publications devoted less attention to the case—editors, reporters, and readers had heard it all before.[21] Bill Abrams provided a sensational exception. The news that he would be brought from the Northern Prison to testify for the state broke the monotony that had settled over the proceedings. Rumors circulated that the prosecution had promised him a pardon in exchange for evidence that incriminated his one-time partner Nancy Clem. The *Evening Journal* predicted that Abrams's testimony would resolve "the mystery that has encircled the Cold Spring tragedy . . . as effectually as if the victims themselves could appear on the witness stand." The *Cincinnati Daily Gazette* proclaimed, "There is little doubt that his testimony will be fatal to Mrs. Clem." The *People* went so far as to report that Abrams had confessed to the sheriff who escorted him from Michigan City "that he knew the murder was contemplated, that he purchased the gun, but had no active hand in the murder, and declared that Mrs. Clem was the ruling spirit in the tragedy from first to last."[22]

A standing-room-only crowd waited eagerly for Abrams's appearance on Saturday, September 30, the fifth day of the trial. The spectator who had the most to lose maintained her usual composure, betraying no sign of nervousness as he entered, save "brightened color to her face." Abrams bore the marks of his nearly two and a half years of confinement. Lips and face blistered from a recent bout with fever, the man once described as tall and broad-shouldered, appeared diminished in both stature and spirit. A reporter for the *Lebanon Weekly Patriot* depicted him as "a small or medium sized man, with a small narrow head, [and] a face indicating but little intelligence."[23]

Both the *Journal* and *Sentinel* settled for brisk summaries of evidence provided by the usual suspects—Ann Hottle, Dr. Duzan, Robert Dorsey, Rebecca Marot, Josie Stevens, John Drew—but chose to print Abrams's testimony verbatim. In retrospect, it proved a waste of precious space. Those who hoped for "the complete unraveling of the entire mystery" were doomed to disappointment. Abrams's demeanor provided the first clue: he did not act like a man eager "to make a clean breast of it." He spoke haltingly, not decisively, his voice barely audible to the jurors and most likely entirely inaudible to the throng who had come to hear him. Equally significant, Benjamin Harrison's questions focused solely on Abrams's financial transactions with Jacob Young and Nancy Clem, an odd choice for a prosecutor who had supposedly secured a confession to complicity in murder. It was an attorney for the defense, Jonathan W. Gordon, who first broached the central issue. When Gordon asked during cross-examination, "Did you buy that weapon?"

Abrams barely had time to answer "I never did" before Harrison objected. Judge Davidson sustained the objection, ordering that the question and answer be stricken from the record: "You may not cross-examine in regard to matters not enquired about in chief," he told Gordon, although he agreed to give the defense until Monday to submit an appeal.[24]

To be sure, Abrams said little that helped Clem's case. His elaborate, albeit hesitant, recollections of his business dealings suggested he had been a victim of her financial scheming rather than her full-fledged business partner. He had lent her considerable sums; she paid him "profits" on his investments but rarely repaid his principal. As the *Evening Journal* put it, "If his history of the financial relations with the defendant is to be credited, he was another of the dupes who . . . were bamboozled by the defendant into the belief that she had intimate business relations with the leading banks of Indianapolis, and was making a great deal of money." Abrams confirmed that Clem had behaved suspiciously in the immediate aftermath of the Cold Spring tragedy; she had come to his house a few days after the murders, "asked if I had any of her letters or notes sent me on occasions that she wanted to see me, with her name attached, and requested that if I had any such that I should destroy them." And to the defense's chagrin, Abrams denied that prosecutors had promised him a pardon in exchange for "making a clean breast of the whole thing." He acknowledged that a reporter, Laura Ream, had visited his jail cell and encouraged him to confess. "She wanted me to tell something that I could not tell."[25]

On Monday, Davidson allowed the defense to recall Abrams to the stand. Once again, Gordon asked his question, this time sure that the answer would become part of the official record. "Mr. Abrams, did you buy that gun with which those parties were killed?" "No, sir, I did not."[26]

The *Journal* had promised its readers that "new and important testimony for the State has been discovered."[27] Abrams failed to deliver. Mattie Pugh, the wife of an Indianapolis painter, did. On Wednesday, October 4, the eighth day of the trial, Mrs. Pugh, who had testified in neither of the previous two trials, took the stand. On the afternoon of Saturday, September 12, 1868, she explained, she had been walking down Market Street on her way to the post office. Sometime between one and two o'clock, she saw "a lady clothed in a dark calico dress and short black silk sack," a woman "she recognized unequivocally" as Clem, flag down a buggy occupied by a man and a woman. Clem got in and the buggy drove away, headed northwest on Indiana Avenue—in other words, in the direction of Cold Spring. The *Evening Jour-*

nal's headline that afternoon recognized the import of Pugh's testimony: "EXAMINATION OF A NEW WITNESS FOR THE STATE. THE WOMAN WHO GOT INTO THE YOUNG BUGGY IDENTIFIED AS MRS. CLEM." So, too, did Clem's defense, which "subjected" Pugh "to a lengthy and searching cross-examination."[28]

Most of the remaining prosecution witnesses provided little new information. Those who did only added to the general confusion. Jane Sizemore offered yet another explanation for the disappearance of the infamous ladies gaiters, albeit one that did not cast the defense in a particularly good light: defense attorney William Leathers "took away" a pair of shoes shortly after Clem's first interview before the coroner's jury.[29] The elder John Wiley repeated his previous account of passing Silas Hartman on the Lafayette Road, but he added a new and curious twist: shortly after his encounter with Hartman, he had seen William Fiscus, the man Hartman's confession had implicated, walking in the direction of Cold Spring "with a double barreled shot gun across his shoulder."[30]

■ ■ ■

The next day Jonathan W. Gordon opened for the defense. He suggested three possible scenarios, each of which demonstrated the innocence of his client. The first deemed Clem entirely "guiltless." The second rendered her "an innocent witness" to a crime committed by her brother. "The law allows her the right, she being innocent, to screen her brother's guilt, if he was the criminal, even though she stood by and saw him commit the crime, and the Court will so instruct you," he told the jury. Here, perhaps, he stood on the firmest ground. Some Indianans, unwilling to stomach the idea of a respectable woman pulling the trigger, had come to doubt a key episode in the prosecution's story. In their imaginary reconstruction of the crime scene Silas Hartman had brandished both the shotgun *and* the pistol as Clem watched him kill Jacob and Nancy Jane Young. However, they generally believed—contrary to Gordon's retelling—that Syke was doing his sister's bidding. Gordon's third possibility rehashed his argument during the previous trial: "Young first shot his wife and then took his own life." Finally, in support of his assertion that his client was "guiltless," Gordon promised to produce evidence that implicated another woman in the crime.[31]

This time the defense called fewer witnesses, only eighteen in all. Clem's attorneys dispensed with parts of their previous strategy. They did not try to prove that she had been at the post office or the New York Store; they did not try to show that Syke Hartman had *not* been at Cold Spring. Still, much of the resulting testimony would have been familiar to those who had followed the previous proceedings. Albert Patton, with whom Clem had an "affecting interview" during a noon recess, swore that his mother had worn "a pair of old gaiters" on the train to Richmond and that he "did not notice any new shoes she had about the house the day I left home." Chris Lout testified to seeing Clem at her house shortly after four o'clock on the day of the murder. Aaron Clem maintained that Abrams had purchased peaches from his grocery on the morning of September 12, a statement corroborated by his clerk.[32]

Then the defense called a man who had not previously testified. Major Oliver M. Wilson had all the trappings of a credible witness. An assistant United States attorney, he was the former secretary of the Indiana senate, a legal scholar, and, as his title indicated, a Civil War veteran. He would shortly serve as the reporter for the Indianapolis superior court, and some years later he would chronicle the history of the Grand Army of the Republic.[33] He was a man who knew his way around a courtroom, a man compelled by neither family feeling nor (as far as can be discerned) financial gain.

Wilson was a boon to the defense in more ways than one. First, he suggested that Clem was the victim of mistaken identity. Gordon's opening statement had promised that subsequent testimony would reveal that "a woman greatly resembling Mrs. Clem—so much so as to be often mistaken for her—was seen running away from the scene of the alleged murder." Wilson was the source for this claim. The story he told on the witness stand had the woman proceeding at a somewhat more leisurely pace, but it otherwise corroborated Gordon's account. Wilson, who had been en route to a Republican rally in Pike Township, testified to having seen her "in the vicinity of Cold Spring" on the afternoon of September 12, "walking along the road from the direction of the scene of the murder." Important as these details were to Clem's defense, the full impact of Wilson's statement lay in the unnamed woman's social identity. Clem's lookalike, Wilson revealed, was "a well known woman of the town."[34] Casting suspicion on Clem's disreputable doppelganger brought the case back into familiar cultural territory. "A woman of the town" was a likely murderess; a respectable woman who lived in a respectable neighborhood *in* the town was not. And this time the information derived not from underhanded detective tactics or a suicidal codefendant but from a man with impeccable social, professional, and legal credentials.

The state called Congressman John Coburn as a rebuttal witness. General Coburn was an attorney, a former judge, and a Civil War hero who had fought alongside Benjamin Harrison. Like Harrison, he was a Radical. Coburn testified that the meeting Wilson recalled attending had taken place on a different Saturday afternoon. Wilson responded by retracting his testimony, explaining that he must have encountered the "frail sister" on August 22, not September 12. Most likely he simply wished to correct an honest mistake; in a busy electoral season it was easy enough to mistake one meeting for another. In fact, Wilson originally said he saw the woman "on a Saturday in September, 1868, can not fix the date," only to decide during cross-examination that "it must have been the day of the murder."[35] Perhaps he had purposely lied under oath, only to be foiled by General Coburn. Or perhaps Coburn deliberately misstated the date as a favor to his political ally and army comrade. "I can not but wonder yet that I should be so widely mistaken as to the date of this meeting," Wilson wrote in his letter of correction. The reasons for Wilson's initial testimony and his about-face, like the answer to "Who gave Peter Wilkins the money?" remain unknowable.

Testimony ended on Saturday, October 7, and attorneys began their closing arguments. John Hanna followed a relatively brief two-hour oration from the Boone County prosecuting attorney. Given the setback Wilson's changing testimony posed, Hanna "touched but lightly upon the evidence in the case, his remarks being general and of the character of a special pleading." He continued speaking the following Monday, but by that time coverage of Clem's trial had been eclipsed by news of the Great Chicago Fire. The fire, which raged from October 8 to 10, was undeniably a newsworthy event— although historians have long noted that the contemporary press devoted markedly less attention to the far deadlier conflagration in Peshtigo, Wisconsin. In Chicago, the Great Fire destroyed much of the commercial downtown, decimated working-class neighborhoods on the city's south side, and left hundreds dead and nearly 100,000 homeless. Like their counterparts elsewhere, Indianapolis and Boone County papers offered blow-by-blow accounts of horrid deaths, heroic rescues, properties destroyed, and blocks burned. Indianapolitans took pride in the performance of city firemen who, along with colleagues from Cincinnati, Milwaukee, Dayton, and St. Louis, rushed to Chicago to help douse the flames. But they also experienced their own "fire panic" as strong winds blew through the Hoosier capital at the very moment the better part of the Indianapolis Fire Department was fighting fire in Chicago.[36]

These fears proved unfounded: no "careless spark" imperiled Indianapolis. The Chicago fire, however, ensured that the text of the closing statements in the Clem case has been lost. Similar editorial decisions might have prevailed even in the absence of other big news; by 1871 the Young murders and their aftermath had lost their novelty. No one printed or even summarized the remainder of Hanna's speech or the substance of John Dye's remarks. No one, not even the *Journal*, published Benjamin Harrison's seven-and-a-half-hour-long address. No one published Jonathan W. Gordon's rejoinder.[37] Thus we do not know precisely what arguments were made on behalf of the state or in Clem's defense, although it is likely their content deviated little from previous performances. Presumably, Gordon failed to mention the "well known woman of the town."

The twelve men entrusted with deciding the case spent less time in the jury box than their predecessors, a little over two weeks rather than three. They faced much the same dilemma: they contemplated a case based largely on circumstantial evidence, strengthened to be sure by Mattie Pugh's testimony. Added to the mix was the suggestion that a fourth perpetrator, as yet unprosecuted, had taken part in the crime. Many predicted another hung jury. They proved correct. After twenty-two hours of deliberation, the jurors failed to reach a verdict. Six believed Clem guilty; six, innocent.[38]

■ ■ ■

The *Evening Journal* acknowledged that "this Clem business is getting troublesome" but insisted that "the majesty of the law must be sustained if it takes the last dollar, and Mrs. Clem must submit to trial after trial until a verdict is reached, if it takes all her life." Joseph J. Bingham, the editor of the *Sentinel*, by contrast, was exasperated. "This prosecution has already cost the county a very large sum of money," an editorial fumed, "and it is estimated that the expenses of the trial just closed at Lebanon, including counsel fees, will foot up some twenty thousand dollars or more." For Bingham, the voice of Indianapolis Democrats, the unsuccessful attempt to prosecute Clem a third time had implications well beyond the fate of one woman. "It seems to be mainly to give General BEN HARRISON princely fees for prosecuting the suit, and a professional reputation that will make him the next Radical candidate for Governor. . . . BENJAMIN has succeeded in getting princely fees," Bingham sneered, "but he has failed most utterly in the reputation business. His management of the prosecution at Lebanon came very near acquitting Mrs. CLEM, and if she can succeed in retaining him as her prosecutor it is altogether probable he will secure an acquittal on the next trial."[39]

In invoking BENJAMIN's "Radicalism," Bingham invoked not only his Democratic opposition to a potential Republican gubernatorial candidate but the national debate over Reconstruction. Indeed, at the very moment witnesses were taking the stand in Lebanon, Indiana, federal authorities, empowered by the recently enacted Ku Klux Klan Act, were arresting and prosecuting hundreds of Klansmen in North and South Carolina. The law represented one of the high points of Radicalism, for it made crimes committed by the Klan—terrorizing African Americans and their white supporters, preventing newly enfranchised citizens from exercising rights guaranteed them by the Fourteenth and Fifteenth Amendments—federal offenses, subject to prosecution by federal authorities and, in certain circumstances, to federal military invention. Northern Democrats in Indiana and elsewhere viewed accounts of Klan violence as exaggerated, fantasies invented to reinvigorate and unify an increasingly divided Republican Party and encourage newly enfranchised African Americans to vote Republican. "The Radicals seem anxious to keep alive all stories about outrages at the South," the *Fort Wayne Weekly Sentinel* complained. Most of all, Democrats and a growing number of Republicans condemned legislation such as the Klan Act as evidence of the growing power of an increasingly tyrannical national government.[40]

If Bingham lodged his complaints against a national backdrop, the concerns he expressed were local. Reconstruction entailed more than the process by which former Confederate states were readmitted to the Union, even more than the federal government's guarantee of the rights of newly freed slaves. At the state and local level, especially in northern cities, Reconstruction meant an expanded role for government, a phenomenon that manifested itself in newly professional police and fire departments, the establishment of local health departments, the expansion of existing institutions, and the creation of new ones. Indianapolis was no exception, and many of these developments ran counter to Democratic faith in limited government. "A few CLEM cases under BEN. HARRISON's manipulation, and the building of another Poor Asylum and Court House under Radical Commissioners, would bankrupt the county," Bingham complained.[41]

■ ■ ■

"Another Court House" was indeed in the works. Even as attorneys, witnesses, and spectators assembled in Lebanon's outsized Gothic courthouse, Indianapolis was building its own monument to justice. Intended to complement what local boosters saw as the Circle City's growing prominence and bolster faith in the power of an activist state, county authorities approved the construction of a new courthouse. More practical considerations accompanied these lofty goals. The city's population was growing rapidly, and with it the need for courtroom space. No one had demonstrated this better than Clem herself.

Indianapolis's response reflected both local exigencies and national trends. The second half of the nineteenth century witnessed a frenzy of courthouse construction—often accompanied by substantial corruption. Such endeavors were by no means limited to Republicans; most famously—or rather infamously—the never-completed $13 million New York County Court House was the brainchild of the Democratic machine boss William M. Tweed. At a cost of $1.4 million, the new Marion County Courthouse, completed in 1876, was a comparative bargain. Still, as Bingham's grumbling suggested, not everyone saw matters in this light. A correspondent for the *People* dubbed the new building, a four-story structure that would occupy an entire city block, "Our new Two Million Dolly Varden Court House" after a popular and elaborate style of women's dress.[42] The analogy between form and frippery was apt, for the building, a structure that one historian has called "the most elaborate example of French architecture of the Second Empire in Indiana" struck many as unnecessarily fussy—festooned with no fewer than three towers, numerous decorative sculptures, and abundant ornate details. The "Dolly Varden Court House"—a phrase the *Sentinel* picked up as well—provided its detractors with a convenient shorthand, equating those who endorsed its construction—"Radical" county commissioners and their supporters—with extravagant women, the kind of women who presumably did *not* "do their own work."[43]

The ceremony that celebrated the laying of the cornerstone was ostensibly nonpartisan and remarkably inclusive, featuring brass bands, "distinguished" and ordinary citizens, representatives of "military companies, secret societies, trade unions, benevolent societies," as well as fraternal organizations, including a "large representation of colored Masons and Odd Fellows." But as the conspicuous presence of African Americans suggested, the new courthouse, unlike "the house that Tweed built," was, as Bingham noted, a "Radical" project. Their "large representation" was testament both to the rapid growth of the city's black population (from just under five hundred in 1860 to nearly three thousand in 1870) and their increasing importance as a reliable bloc of Republican voters.[44]

In the context of Reconstruction in Indianapolis and in the nation at large, the new courthouse assumed larger political meanings. So, too, did successive attempts to prosecute Nancy Clem. If Radicalism assumed a commitment to "trial after trial," Clem's story in a certain sense mirrored the story of Reconstruction.

CHAPTER ELEVEN

The Indiana Murderess

For the meantime, Radicalism prevailed. Construction on the Dolly Varden courthouse proceeded and prosecutors declared their intention to try Clem a fourth time. They met with resistance. Continuing in an earlier vein, the *Sentinel* pointedly cited the $1,000 apiece Benjamin Harrison and John Dye earned for Clem's most recent prosecution. They "have a nice thing of it," an editorial complained, "and doubtless would not care if the 'regular spring trial' came on four times a year." In a "card" sent to the same newspaper, "Marion" suggested that Clem's prosecution might better be described as "persecution": "Several of our prominent citizens are interesting themselves in behalf of the accused, who declare they will leave no stone unturned to secure her acquittal—thus saving the county the expense of further useless and vexatious trials."[1]

Some of these anonymous citizens convinced one of the famous names in Indiana politics to join Clem's defense team. Daniel W. Voorhees, a prominent attorney, former congressman and soon-to-be senator, had long been a key figure in the Democratic Party at both state and national levels. Like his political nemesis, Abraham Lincoln, a man to whom he was often compared, Voorhees was a renowned orator. Like Lincoln, he stood over six feet in height—hence his nickname, the "Tall Sycamore of the Wabash." Voorhees, in the words of one biographer, was an "ultra-Democrat." He was an unabashed racist and an ardent opponent of abolitionism—he famously defended one of John Brown's accomplices in the raid on Harper's Ferry by giving an eloquent speech that endorsed states' rights and slavery. During the Civil War, Voorhees was a vocal critic of the Lincoln administration and a reputed member of the Knights of the Golden Circle, a secret society of Confederate sympathizers. A fierce opponent of congressional Reconstruction, he was the antithesis of Radicalism. Benjamin Harrison was his political, ideological—and now—legal rival. At the time of Clem's fourth trial, Voorhees had temporarily put aside public life for private practice, enhancing his already widespread reputation as a formidable defense attorney. Soon, however, he would reenter the political fray. He would defeat Harrison in the senatorial election of 1878, part of the Democratic resurgence as northern support for Reconstruction waned.[2]

Most likely it was not Voorhees's politics but his success some seven years earlier in securing the acquittal of Mary Harris, a young woman accused of murdering her former fiancé, that attracted the attention of Clem's supporters. His participation nevertheless gave the latest proceedings a sharper partisan edge. Indeed, at a time of intense political turmoil, both Voorhees and Harrison remained true to their parties. Harrison had only recently lost the Republican nomination for governor, in part because he lacked the common touch—his opponents labeled him a "stinking little aristocrat [who] never recognized men on the street"—in part because the state party's leader, the former governor and current senator Oliver Morton, saw him as a threat to his own political ambitions. Still, Harrison refused to endorse Morton's rivals, the Liberal Republicans, a breakaway movement that opposed the corruption of Ulysses S. Grant's administration but also advocated sectional reconciliation, the end of Reconstruction, and the return of white supremacy. The Liberal Republicans attracted many Democrats— their standard-bearer, Horace Greeley, stood as the presidential candidate for both parties—and provided a mechanism by which many prewar Democrats-turned-Republicans would reclaim their partisan heritage. But although he agreed with the Liberals on Grant, Reconstruction, race, and Radicalism, Voorhees, after a brief flirtation, declined to join them.[3]

To be sure, prosecution and defense in Clem's fourth trial, which began in June 1872, did not line up neatly according to party lines any more than previously. Jonathan Gordon did not forsake the regular Republicans; neither, apparently, did John Hanna or William Leathers.[4] All were willing to work with Voorhees, not because they endorsed his political views but because his very presence increased their chances of winning their case. Still, a trial that pitted Daniel Voorhees against Benjamin Harrison promised a good deal of political drama; indeed, contemporaries would remember "the great struggle" between them as a grand showdown. Hanna, Gordon, and Leathers planned what the *People* termed a "grand coup detat," intending to keep Voorhees's participation a secret until the opening day of the new trial. They believed that "his very appearance would secure an acquittal or at least a disagreement among the jury." The coup failed. The *Sentinel* leaked the news that the Sycamore of the Wabash would defend the "the Indiana murderess."[5]

And by the 1870s that was exactly how newspapers from Massachusetts to California described Nancy Clem: "the Indiana murderess." As successive trials cast her into a national spotlight, she would become not just an

In 1872 the defense added a fifth attorney to its roster. Clem's fourth trial generated considerable excitement because it pitted Benjamin Harrison (*left*) against his political rival, the "ultra-Democrat" Daniel W. Voorhees, nicknamed the "Tall Sycamore of the Wabash." Voorhees would defeat Harrison in the 1878 senatorial election. Benjamin Harrison, probably 1870s, courtesy of the Benjamin Harrison Presidential Site; Daniel Wolsey Voorhees, ca. 1865–1880, Brady-Handy Collection, Library of Congress.

infamous—or persecuted—woman but a symbol of the Hoosier state itself.[6] As her notoriety grew, so, too, did sympathy for her plight. J. Harrie Banka's *State Prison Life, by One Who Has Been There* appeared in late September 1871, during the course of Clem's third trial.[7] Penned by a former convict, *State Prison Life* was part exposé, part memoir. Clem figured prominently in a chapter titled "Life-Time Women." Banka commented approvingly on her deportment, reporting that she "associated very little with the inmates of her department," most of them incarcerated for prostitution, and "was usually alone in her cell, or sitting apart from the rest, busily engaged with her work. Sometimes we would see her sitting for hours under a little shade-tree in the yard of the department, plying her needle, the tears all the while dropping from her great soft eyes." While Banka's account read as if Clem were "busily engaged" in fancy parlor needlework, "plying her needle" was her required prison job; she fashioned a humbler product, pants worn by male prisoners. Banka's status as a former co-resident of the Southern Prison lent his narrative a certain credibility, but his saccharine prose suggested he found a respectable murderess a difficult proposition to fathom. "Sometimes she would come up to the library, and passing into the chapel, stand at the barred windows and gaze out upon the world with a blank despair, or such a longing look as was painful to witness. We have seen her stand at the library window that overlooks the yard, when the prisoners were marching in long lines to their meals, and weep like a child. 'Poor fellows,' she would say, 'how many wives and mothers, and children are waiting for you!'" Lest his readers miss the point, Banka took care to make it: "This did not look to us like the actions, nor did her plaintive words sound like the language of a murderer."[8]

No one commanded greater sympathy than Bill Abrams. In March 1872 a reporter for the *People* interviewed him along with a handful of other renowned inmates under the appealing title of "The Northern Prison: Sketches of the Condemned." Abrams "insisted that had he been allowed by his counsel to go before the grand jury he would have beyond a doubt settled the matter as to his own innocence, or had he been allowed to testify in Mrs. Clem's first trial," the correspondent explained. Deliberately or not, the *People*'s reporter appropriated Banka's mawkish sentimentalism. "He showed me his little girl's picture, and talked for some time about her, and exacted a promise from me that I should call on my return and tell her about him. He evidently worships his child."[9]

The story had an unanticipated unhappy ending, one that befitted a sentimental novel and gave the anonymous reporter a starring role in another sort of "tragedy." As her father chatted with the reporter, seven-year-old Cora Abrams lay gravely ill with the measles. "Neither of us thought at the time of the heart-breaking anguish he would soon be called upon to endure in the news of her death. Calling at the house on my return to Indianapolis, I found the convict's little idol dead, and the sorrow-stricken wife in paroxysms of grief and so prostrated mentally and physically as to be confined to her bed." Abrams's reaction, while doubtless genuine, was similarly scripted: "The strong man wept." Conrad Baker, Indiana's "kind-hearted"—and outgoing—governor, had no objections to Abrams attending his daughter's funeral, but he left the decision to the prison's warden, who refused the request. Such treatment further embittered Abrams against his former associate: "We have heard it said he now declares that after the next trial of Mrs. Clem, he will reveal certain matters connected with the Cold Spring tragedy that have hitherto failed to see the light."[10]

■ ■ ■

Thus in the early summer of 1872, as sentimental representations of Clem and Abrams competed for popular sympathy and after several continuations and postponements, the usual suspects once again assembled in the outsized Gothic courthouse with the peculiar tower. Once again, Clem made the journey from the Marion County jail to the little "burg" of Lebanon. Once again, her arrival generated considerable excitement; "the town was filled," the *Sentinel* noted on June 4, "as though a political barbeque, district fair, or a circus was holding within its limits." This time, however, she occupied new quarters. Describing the Boone County jail as "the most unhealthy and poorly ventilated dungeon in the State," the Honorable Thomas Davidson, still the circuit court's presiding judge, ordered her housed in a room on the upper floor of the courthouse; Frank Clem was allowed to stay there as well. Though observers noted that the effects of nearly four years of confinement were beginning to show, Clem exhibited her previous assurance and expressed her confidence that she would be found innocent. This was the verdict that the Lebanon papers predicted—at worst, they believed, another hung jury might result.[11]

Those who hoped for a different outcome repeated arguments ventured during Clem's second trial, three years earlier. They reasoned that the jurors selected were more likely to convict because they were, on average, older and wiser than their predecessors, presumably less vulnerable to the defendant's legendary charms. Indeed, their average age was fifty-two. Thirty-seven-year-old William Roberts, a farmer "of robust form," was the youngest; sixty-seven-year-old Fielding Denny, the eldest. Collectively these twelve "men of mature judgment and unquestioned integrity"—seven of them Democrats, five of them Republicans—had considerable legal experience. Four were former justices of the peace; one, the "robust" William Roberts, currently held the office. The most prominent member of the jury, fifty-seven-year-old Colonel W. C. Kise ("too well known in this county to need description," the *Patriot* reported), a Civil War veteran and substantial farmer, was a former constable and clerk of the court.[12]

Everyone—including the jurors, who surely were already familiar with the case—knew what to expect. As the *Journal* put it, "the grooves in which the testimony runs have become so smooth from long use that no piece of machinery could move more satisfactorily."[13] Despite the case's familiar contours—or perhaps because of them—spectators and journalists often packed the courtroom. Among the latter was a tall, dark-haired woman, "stately, dignified . . . interesting, if not attractive." She was Laura Ream, the reporter who had visited Abrams in jail. Like many of the people present, Ream, "the first woman in the state to engage in regular newspaper work," owed her career to Nancy Clem. "At the time of the murder of Mr. and

Mrs. Young," noted one account, "Miss Ream commenced corresponding with the *Cincinnati Commercial.*" It was Ream, writing in her capacity as the *Commercial*'s Indianapolis correspondent, who had described Frank Clem as "plodding" and characterized his wife as a practitioner of "the active, industrial life" rather than a "member of our best society."[14]

In many respects, Ream represented what Nancy Clem might have become. Both women were quick-witted, persuasive, and observant. Both were willing and able to take advantage of any maneuvering room their respective cultures allotted them. "She takes her place, as reporter . . . wherever her journalistic life may call her, without ostentation, and without diffidence, as a matter of right," the *Indianapolis Sentinel* wrote of Ream in 1872. The graduate of a private academy in Indianapolis and a Catholic boarding school in Kentucky, Ream had the advantage of education. Initially that was not enough. A year before the Young murders, the forty-something "maiden lady" with literary pretensions was a figure of fun. In the spring of 1867 Ream made headlines—nationally as well as regionally—not for her compositions but for her unsuccessful breach of promise suit against her erstwhile fiancé, an Indianapolis attorney. "So far as outward appearances are concerned, she is not beautiful," the *San Francisco Daily Evening Bulletin* noted, "and the defendant certainly never admired her on account of her personal charms."[15]

Only a few short years later, "the lady news writer" had gained both respect and influence. The *People* termed her "a careful, truthful and entertaining correspondent," the *Patriot*, "the most accomplished newspaper lady writer in Indiana." Despite her association with a Republican-leaning paper (she now served as one of the two editors of the *Evening Journal*), Ream had risen in the ranks of the state's Democratic Party, narrowly missing a patronage appointment as the state librarian. Active in various literary and charitable endeavors, she confined her writing to politics, disdaining "woman's special interests" in favor of "general public affairs": "We take pleasure in saying that she does not belong to that class of strong-minded females who are eternally lifting up their voices against the tyrant man, and bewailing their own miserable and oppressed condition," the *People* proclaimed. The *Sentinel*—opposed, as were most Democratic voices, to woman suffrage—concurred. Ream, it noted approvingly, "has no ultra ideas of woman's rights" and "mak[es] no racket about female suffrage."[16]

For the time being, Ream's influence extended to neither of the surviving defendants. Despite repeated requests for interviews, Clem refused to speak to her. Abrams evidently followed suit. Whatever inducements he had been offered failed to sway him; so, too, did his newfound bitterness against Clem. His much-anticipated second appearance on the witness stand elicited no new evidence. "He gave his account of his whereabouts on the day of the murder much according to the programme of all the former trials," the *Journal* explained.[17]

■ ■ ■

Some aspects of the "programme" had changed, however. Though still a firm believer in his client's innocence, Jonathan W. Gordon took a less active part, ceding the job of main cross-examiner to John Hanna. It was a role Hanna relished. He seldom missed a chance to ridicule prosecutor John Dye's "very red whiskers," asking witnesses tasked with recalling the features of particular faces, "How does the person's hair or mustache compare with Mr. Dye's whiskers?" Dye remained silent but "look[ed] daggers." And as in the previous proceedings, the passage of time altered the programme as well. Pet Hartman, now nineteen and newly married, was called to the stand as "Mrs. Kurtz." Even the physical terrain of the crime scene had perceptibly changed. One recent visitor to Cold Spring "could scarcely recognize the scene of the horrid murder of over three years ago," the *People* reported. The spring had run dry and the underbrush had been cleared. Only the willow tree on which Jacob Young had draped his coat remained. "There is nothing about the place to denote the dreadful tragedy that was there enacted," the *People* explained. "Could the stones on the bar speak, the mystery of several years might be revealed—but they are dumb, like those who know the secret but will not tell it."[18]

Stones did not speak, but witnesses did. A neighbor, called by the state for the first time, testified that she had never seen the defendant wearing "ragged shoes" except when she worked in her garden. Hence, the prosecution hoped to suggest, it would have been inconceivable that the fashion-conscious Mrs. Clem would have accompanied her son to college with old gaiters on her feet.[19] Another new witness was John Harbert, a Pike Township farmer described by the *Journal* as "an elderly gentleman of excellent appearance"—he was, in fact, only fifty. Harbert had passed the Youngs as they drove toward Cold Spring and noticed "a strange lady" sitting beside them. He had appeared before the coroner's jury in the fall of 1868, where he testified that he thought the woman looked about thirty-five years old—that is, about the same age as Nancy Clem.[20]

The substance of Harbert's initial appearance in the Boone County courtroom in the summer of 1872 has been lost. What is known is this: a "legal accident" occurred during cross-examination, when John Hanna asked Harbert why he had not testified during Clem's previous trials. There was a reason: Harbert had been present when detectives hired by the defense "tried to put [the prostitute] Cal. Prather into Mrs. Clem's shoes." He had been subpoenaed by the prosecution in 1868, 1869, and 1871 but had never taken the stand, his testimony ruled inadmissible because the state could not demonstrate that Clem had known about or participated in the plan to implicate Prather. Now, John Dye seized his opportunity and recalled Harbert. Hanna strenuously objected as Dye's questioning broached the topic. But Judge Davidson decided that "as the defense had called out a part of the conversation the State was entitled to the rest."[21]

Thus, on Saturday, June 8, 1872, a trial jury heard for the first time the story of Harbert's encounter with ex-sheriff Robinson and the deputy marshal Scudder on a Sunday evening just days after Clem's arrest. Harbert's colorful recollections of Robinson and Scudder's visit to his farm made him a compelling witness. Robinson did the talking. "John, I have a woman in the carriage I want you to look at," he told Harbert as the latter "sauntered" into his yard. "It is not Mrs. Clem," Robinson insisted. "This is the woman." "What does John T. Dye say about it?" Harbert asked. "John T. Dye says this is the woman," Robinson reportedly replied, "and 20 of the officers about the Court house say she is the woman and I can prove it by half of the citizens in Indianapolis that this is the woman and that Mrs. Clem is not the woman." Harbert initially was inclined to agree, but demurred: "Colonel, it is too dark. I cannot see well enough to give an opinion, and I will not."

When the trio returned in the light of day, Harbert decided that Prather was not the woman he had seen the afternoon of the murder. "There is a difference in the shape of her face," he explained. Prather was "not so good looking a woman" as the one he saw riding in Jacob Young's buggy—a compliment Clem surely could have done without. Robinson continued to pressure Harbert, insisting (falsely) that the Wileys had identified Prather as the Youngs' traveling companion. When Harbert voiced his suspicion of "a dog in the well," Robinson replied, "No, no, John, there is not. You do not think I would take advantage of you?" Harbert answered, "I do not know who to trust these days." Robinson started scribbling in a notebook, but refused to let an increasingly nervous Harbert see what he was writing.

In the end, the colonel prevailed. After "studying the matter over . . . and not wanting to do any person any injury" (least of all, one suspects, himself), Harbert asked the foreman of the coroner's jury to correct his statement, substituting "thirty" for "thirty-five," thereby rendering the "strange lady" closer to Prather's actual age. Now he reverted to his previous opinion; the woman he saw riding with the Youngs was around thirty-five years old.[22]

That, perhaps, was the least of the damage. Harbert relayed a story of witness tampering and illegal confinement—Robinson had admitted during the course of their conversation that he and others were holding Prather under guard in a room above an Indianapolis piano factory.[23] Like the tale of Peter Wilkins (who had also participated in the detention of Prather and two other women) and the mysterious money, Harbert's account suggested that Clem's attorneys were utterly without scruples, willing to employ local authorities (Robinson, it is true, was at the time the former sheriff, not the incumbent) to intimidate potential witnesses. To borrow Harbert's phrasing there was indeed a dog in the well.

■ ■ ■

George Hollingsworth, a member of the prominent Pike Township family, had appeared for the defense in the winter of 1868, placing his friend and former neighbor William J. Abrams in downtown Indianapolis at 5:00 p.m. on Saturday, September 12. Now, in the summer of 1872 he took the stand on behalf of the prosecution. Around three o'clock on the afternoon of the murder, Hollingsworth stated, he saw a man he thought was Silas Hartman and another man he had never seen before drive by in a buggy pulled by a sorrel mare, with a double-barreled shotgun sitting between them. They were headed in the direction of Cold Spring.

Hollingsworth's testimony supported the state's case but introduced new mystery. Who was the man sitting next to Syke Hartman? Hollingsworth may have confused Friday with Saturday; Bill Abrams had been seen with Hartman in the vicinity of the crime scene on the afternoon before the murders. But Hollingsworth was adamant: the man was *not* Abrams.[24] If there was a second man in the buggy, he might have been William Fiscus, implicated from the beginning (even arrested) but never charged. During Clem's third trial the previous summer, John H. Wiley had testified to seeing Fiscus— shotgun in tow—in the vicinity of Cold Spring. Or possibly the mysterious stranger was Cravens Hartman, the man whose very existence Benjamin Harrison publicly questioned.

Cravens Hartman, it turned out, did exist, although his presence in Indianapolis in mid-September 1868 could not be confirmed. Indeed, testimony would show that defense attorneys had enlisted none other than Peter Wilkins to bring him from Missouri to take the stand on his cousin's behalf. Wilkins made three attempts. The first time, he found his man. Cravens agreed to make the journey to Indianapolis "but did not come." An article published two decades later embellished this first encounter, claiming that Cravens suggested Wilkins return to Indianapolis immediately "for his own safety." Quite possibly this version of the story bore some relation to the truth; Peter Wilkins was a man of few words, not a man to admit defeat. When Wilkins returned to Missouri a few weeks later, Cravens was nowhere to be found. A third trip also met with failure. The daring detective who reportedly had arrested and detained some seven hundred Union army deserters, the man who single-handedly subdued eight armed men, could not apprehend Cravens Hartman.[25]

Any number of reasons might explain Cravens's failure to appear. Perhaps, as Syke had suggested, the "coolness" between the two branches of the Hartman family was enough to make him stay away. Perhaps Cravens was a man of integrity who refused to swear he was on the Pendleton Pike on a day he had been at home in Missouri. Perhaps he feared a charge of perjury. Or perhaps he did not wish to incriminate himself.

Accounts of the murder written many years after the fact took it for granted that Cravens had been at Cold Spring. Some identified him as Clem's cousin, others as "another brother." A retrospective published by the *Journal* in the late 1890s imagined Nancy Jane Young improbably conversing with Nancy Clem at the scene of the crime. "That's your brother Crave. You brought us here to murder us."[26]

A later article confidently asserted another "fact" that had never been proven: Nancy Clem, Silas Hartman, and "Crave" had poured coal oil on Nancy Young's body and set it alight. A more immediate reminder of Young's fate surfaced during the course of the trial. On June 13, 1872, the *Weekly Patriot* reported the tragic story of a woman whose clothing caught fire when her coal oil lamp exploded. The efforts of "several men who wrapped their coats about her and smothered the fire" came too late to save the victim, who lived in Attica, the same town where Mary Belle Young now resided. No one mentioned the gruesome similarities between the woman's demise ("Her whole body was horribly roasted," the *Patriot* explained) and that of Mary Belle's aunt.[27]

The resemblance, one suspects, would have been lost on no one. Like the footprints suggesting a perpetrator had fled the crime scene, the chain of evidence led away from the carnage at Cold Spring toward a mundane if somewhat disreputable world of secondhand stores, pawnshops, and mysterious business transactions. Apart from the graphic postmortem descriptions that opened each trial, the victims largely disappeared from view. The Attica incident, had anyone cared to dwell on it, was a tangible reminder of the lives—and deaths—of Jacob and Nancy Jane Young.

■ ■ ■

On June 14, 1872, the prosecution called a final witness. Silas Gist had served alongside Abrams during the Civil War. He had not testified during Clem's previous trials. Now he recalled a jailhouse conversation that had taken place in the fall of 1869. "Bill, there is one thing I would like for you to tell me—that is, if you feel safe," Gist asked his army buddy. "Is Mrs. Clem guilty or not guilty?" "She is guilty, Sike," he answered. "She is guilty."[28]

■ ■ ■

In the preceding trial, the defense had counted on Major Wilson to make its case. Now that his testimony proved useless, Clem's counselors reverted to earlier strategies, calling fifty witnesses instead of the eighteen previously summoned. The first was Bill Abrams. Perhaps not feeling quite so "safe," or perhaps simply being truthful, he took the stand to refute Gist's testimony. Gist had been "considerably intoxicated" at the time of their meeting, Abrams claimed. "I do not think there was anything said about Mrs. Clem."[29]

None of the remaining forty-nine witnesses provided appreciably new information, but perhaps that was not the point. Defense attorneys hoped the sheer weight of their evidence would furnish convincing proof of reasonable doubt. Wilson, needless to say, did not testify. Neither did Charles Donnelan. The one-eyed veteran who had previously sworn to seeing Clem at home on the afternoon of the murder did not appear when summoned. The combined efforts of three detectives hired by Frank Clem and a "vigorous pursuit" by a posse organized by the Boone County sheriff failed to locate him.[30]

On June 18 the defense rested its case. Just before closing arguments were to begin, star juror Colonel Kise became gravely ill, delaying the proceedings and spawning talk of a mistrial. Ever the optimist, Clem, annoyed by the postponement and confident of acquittal, expected to be home shortly. The *Pioneer* supported her prediction. "Reason suggests," its editor declared, "that it is possible that the murderers of Jacob Young and his wife have never yet been under arrest.[31]

Three days later Kise had recovered enough to resume his duties, listening to closing arguments while he lay on a lounge. Texts of the speeches have not survived. By all accounts, Benjamin Harrison made a forceful, logical case for conviction. Daniel Voorhees's eagerly anticipated closing statement proved a disappointment. It was not the grand oration listeners expected. Democrats did their best to justify his performance. In the words of the *Cincinnati Enquirer* it was a "brilliant effort." "It is said by those who listened to it to have been very effective, although he disappointed all by the calm, conversational tone in which it was delivered," the *Pioneer* explained. The Republican *Patriot*, on the other hand, pronounced Voorhees's address "a complete failure." Even the Tall Sycamore's children, who compiled and published a sampling of their father's speeches, must have decided that his closing argument in the Clem case was not his best effort, for they failed to include it in *Forty Years of Oratory*.[32] Everyone seems to have agreed on one point: the strength of Harrison's performance forced Voorhees to devote the full five hours allotted him to a point-by-point refutation of his opponent's argument, largely preventing him from advancing an argument of his own.[33]

Two clues regarding the content of Voorhees's statement can be gleaned from contemporary newspapers. He frequently invoked biblical references. He also employed "facetious" avian analogies that ridiculed his opponents. Voorhees likened John Dye to a woodpecker who "has been pecking away at his tree for a worm for the past four years, but has not got his worm yet." He decided that "Brother Harrison . . . was not like the eagle, for when the eagle swooped down upon his prey, if he failed to get it he flew off . . . and was seen no more." Instead, he concluded, Harrison was "more like a pheasant" who "scared little boys who mistook its drumming upon a log for thunder, but after all it is only a little pheasant that is drumming away with a harmless sound."[34]

Any phrases Voorhees may have uttered that referenced the Hoosier Democracy's vision of virtuous womanhood have been lost to history. If his successful defense of Mary Harris provides any hints, he may have focused less on the dignity of working women and the nobility of feminine self-reliance than on the evidence provided by appearance and demeanor. "Am I to be told that this heart-broken young girl, with her innocent, appealing face, and look of supplicating dependence on you, is the fierce and malignant monster of guilt which is described in the indictment and in the inflammatory language of the prosecution?" Voorhees had asked the jury charged with deciding Harris's fate. "Am I to be told that her heart conceived and her hand executed that crime for which the Almighty marked the brow of Cain?"[35] Whatever else he might have said, the task of answering Harrison so exhausted Voorhees that after concluding his statement he lay down on the courthouse lawn. Or as the *Journal* sarcastically noted, "the Wabash Sycamore waved so violently during his speech in defense of Mrs. Clem that he was obliged to stretch his manly form upon the bosom of Mother Earth upon emerging from the court room."[36]

The *People* reported "the general impression . . . that the jury will either acquit or disagree." Disagreement seemed a likely outcome. The jury deliberated five hours before asking Judge Davidson for clarification. Then it once again retired. The next morning, twenty-four hours after first receiving their instructions, jurors announced that they had reached a verdict. Clem walked in smiling. Her attorneys, on the other hand, "looked gloomy."[37]

Those who believed that the jury would disagree were partly correct, for deliberations hewed closely to previous "programmes." In the end its members agreed that Clem was guilty, although, once again, they disagreed on her sentence. Fielding Denny, the eldest of the twelve jurors, held out for manslaughter, the others for first-degree murder. They compromised on murder in the second degree, a life sentence, and a recommendation for executive clemency (advice two successive governors would ignore). As the verdict was announced, Frank Clem and Albert Patton began to weep. The defendant kept her composure.[38]

On July 4, 1872, the same day that Judge Davidson sentenced Nancy Clem to life imprisonment, D. E. Caldwell of the Republican *Patriot* announced that his rival, Benjamin A. Smith of the Democratic *Pioneer*, had accepted $200 ($4,000 in 2014 currency) from Clem's attorneys in exchange for favorable coverage of their client. "We can find no words to express our contempt for the newspaper man who will thus barter the influence of his editorial columns," Caldwell complained. Meanwhile, Voorhees decided to throw his support to the Liberal Republicans. "The tall Sycamore of the Wabash has come down with a crash," the *Journal* reported.[39]

■ ■ ■

The "sold out editor" and the sell-out politician aroused less controversy than did the verdict itself. The *Journal*, no longer in Pink Fishback's hands, was nevertheless indignant: "It is probable that other considerations have influenced the jury besides a strict construction of the law and a fearless ap-plication of the evidence. Whether those considerations have grown out of the increasing opposition to capital punishment, or whether they have root in a sentimental unwillingness to inflict so terrible a penalty on a female criminal, we can not say. Either consideration is one that ought not to weigh with a jury sworn to find a true verdict according to the law and evidence."[40]

The *Patriot* expressed greater sympathy. "Although this verdict accorded with the views of many in the court room, yet the faces of all assumed a serious air, which indicated sympathy for the brave little woman who had with-stood the terrible four years ordeal that she had." The *Sentinel* concurred, noting Frank Clem's and Albert Patton's anguished reactions. No one in the crowded courtroom rejoiced at the verdict, it claimed. Even Ben Harrison lamented his duty—or so journalists remembered years later. According to a widely reprinted 1896 article that circulated under titles including "He Has a Soft Heart," "Won't Prosecute a Woman," and "Quite a Lady's Man," Harrison never referred to Clem as anything except the "unfortunate defen-dant." Asked by Voorhees why "he had been so easy in his remarks against the defendant," he replied, "Dan, no matter what she may have done, she is still a woman and I won't abuse her." "When the jury had retired," "He Has a Soft Heart" continued, "he went over to Mrs. Clem, who was crying, and asked her forgiveness for anything he had said that might have injured her feelings. As he turned away he said to Judge Palmer, who was hearing the case, 'Judge, I'll never prosecute another woman,' and he kept his word."[41]

This touching rendition of Harrison's courtroom behavior, composed several years after the fact, was probably apocryphal. For one thing it got the judge's name wrong (an understandable mistake—a Judge Palmer *would* figure in Clem's story, but not this time). For another, it was part of a public relations ploy meant to counter the controversy surrounding Harrison's impending marriage to a much younger cousin—a union his now-grown children opposed.[42] And while it is indeed possible that the man who had once publicly condemned Clem for her "terrible power," "fatal power," and "mastery over strong men" softened his approach, such posturing probably spoke less to inherent gallantry than to professional prudence—he would not have wanted to antagonize a potentially sympathetic jury.

The *Journal* for its part eschewed "maudlin sentimentalism." In an edito-rial titled "THE LESSON," it offered "some reflections on" the "moral and ethical bearings" of the case. The lesson, the *Journal* opined, "is this: that it pays under all circumstances to enforce the laws and to pursue crime to the bitter end. . . . There have been times during the progress of this trial, when even good citizens have wearied of the prosecution and have said, 'what is the use of wasting more time and money in this prosecution? Discharge the woman, and let us have an end of this worry and expense.'" These naysayers "forgot . . . that a great principle was involved, and that the State can better afford to sacrifice thousands of dollars than on principle. . . . Flagrant crime[s], committed at our doors, for money, in broad daylight, should be ferreted out with all the energy and resources of the State."[43]

Justice had been done, albeit imperfectly, for Clem had been sentenced to life imprisonment rather than the gallows. Still, the *Journal* believed, the prolonged prosecution and expense had been worth it. "When it comes to enforcing the law there should be no maudlin sentimentalism, no false economy, no wavering purposes." Radicalism, as the Liberal insurgency demonstrated, was under attack; a little more than a month after Clem's sentencing African American "wideawake" Grant supporters were battling Irish American Greeleyites on the Indianapolis streets. If regular Republicans, who ultimately prevailed in the 1872 elections, were beginning to retreat from their commitment to racial equality, local manifestations of "Radicalism" survived. The Clem verdict not only avenged the Youngs' tragic deaths, it upheld Republican law and order, and, as the *Journal* might have put it, the Republican ideal of an energetic state. The successful conclusion of the case temporarily silenced those who condemned the expenditures Marion County had allocated to it, which by now amounted to nearly $40,000.[44]

The national press was inclined to agree. "The conviction of a criminal nearly four years after the commission of the crime is an illustration of the occasional sureness of slow justice," the *Brooklyn Eagle* opined.[45] Many assumed the case was over. A lengthy summary of the Young murders and the subsequent trials first published in the *St. Louis Democrat* circulated widely. Beginning with the discovery of the bodies at Cold Spring, recounting various incidents under subheadings such as "The Purchase of the Gun," "The Horse and Buggy Tracks," "Who Was the Woman?" "Motive for the Murder," "Bribery of Witnesses," "The Shoes She Wore," and "Mysterious Financial Transactions," and concluding with Clem's conviction for second degree murder, "Circumstantial Evidence" consigned the case to "history."[46]

Not everyone was sure that Cold Spring was indeed history. The *Chicago Tribune* feared that "some legal quibble" would induce the Indiana Supreme Court to order a new trial.[47] The prediction proved correct. Once again, in a manner of speaking, Benjamin Harrison would prosecute a woman.

CHAPTER TWELVE

Indiana Justice

A nyone who believed that Cold Spring was history underestimated the determination of Clem's attorneys—and of Clem herself. Convinced of his client's innocence, Jonathan Gordon (newly shorn of his mustache and therefore resembling a "heathen" in the eyes of the *Lebanon Weekly Patriot*) immediately filed a motion for a new trial. Among the several irregularities his appeal specified was this: alcohol might have clouded jurors' judgments. William Roberts, the "robust" farmer, had been seen entering a saloon during the course of the trial; the ailing Colonel Kise had been treated with "stimulants" including whiskey and, by some accounts, morphine.[1]

Gordon's argument was entirely in keeping with his principles. A longtime advocate of total abstinence, he had served as editor of the *Temperance Chart*, an Indianapolis newspaper sponsored by the Sons of Temperance, in the 1850s.[2] Gordon must have suspected, however, that a claim based on the effects of alcohol consumption would resonate with the larger reading public. An argument about inebriated jurors was easier to understand than one grounded in arcane legal technicalities.

Gordon was hardly alone in his beliefs. Temperance had been a divisive political issue in Indianapolis and the state at large since the earliest days of Euro-American settlement. The evils of alcohol were among the topics a young Henry Ward Beecher had covered in his public lectures to young men in the late 1840s. In 1855 a coalition of Know-Nothings and Republicans passed Indiana's short-lived answer to the famous "Maine Law"—an act outlawing the sale and consumption of alcoholic beverages except for medicinal and manufacturing purposes.[3] Advocates of a statewide prohibition law tried and failed to pass a similar measure twenty years later. Partisan divisions—Republicans in favor, Democrats opposed—were still very much in evidence, but so, too, were divisions between town and country. "Some folks, perhaps, won't believe it," the *People*'s "People and Things" columnist, "Hathaway," wryly noted, "but both editors at Lebanon, Indiana, use lemonade as a beverage." Indeed, supporters of the doomed legislation carried the rural areas, once known for their liberal use of whiskey. Temperance did not fare so well in Indianapolis, which included a significant number of Irish and German voters, as Frederick Knefler learned when he stood as the unsuccessful "woman's candidate" (so-named for his teetotal views) for the city council. Clem might have counted herself among the ranks of teetotalers. Her daily tippling, newspaper accounts implied, was medicinal, necessary for her health.[4]

Whatever *his* personal feelings on the temperance issue, Judge Davidson found none of Gordon's arguments persuasive. Clem's counsel had failed to challenge jurors who admitted to having formed opinions, he noted. They had not insisted that the jury be sequestered. The "stimulants" ingested by both Roberts and Kise had been prescribed by physicians. Clem's attorneys, moreover, had been consulted and had not objected to the treatment. Nor had medicinal alcohol impaired their performance. Davidson "regret[ted] to differ with learned counsel" but encouraged them to take the case "to another court . . . where it may have the consideration of judges more learned in the law, and who have time to consider it, and who in addition will have the benefit of each other's learning and judgment." That said, he overruled the motion for a new trial and sentenced Clem to life imprisonment. Clem's attorneys asked that she be allowed to remain in the Marion County Jail for sixty days while they prepared their appeal; Davidson gave them forty. Clem returned to her "old quarters" in Indianapolis, where family and lawyers could easily visit her. Someone gave her a Newfoundland "pup" to keep her company. The *People* considered this an injustice, an example of class privilege. "Crazy Kate," a local woman committed to the county insane asylum, was not allowed to bring along her beloved poodle and sole companion, but a "murderess" could keep a pet in her jail cell.[5]

The tears shed in the Boone County courtroom notwithstanding, the *People*'s attitude reflected near universal condemnation. The newly "nonpartisan" *Sentinel* continued to complain about the cost of Clem's trials. But it no longer advocated Clem's release. Instead it condemned her attorneys' decision to appeal once again to the state supreme court, a strategy that threatened further depletion of the public coffers.

■ ■ ■

In September 1872 the Indiana high court denied Clem's petition for "further suspension of sentence," forcing her to return to the Southern State Prison, evidently without the pup. The court, did, however agree to hear her appeal. "Nancy Clem, the Indiana murderess, proposes to relieve the monotony of the Courts again by appealing for another trial," the *Chicago Tri-*

bune reported, a quip various newspapers around the nation repeated more or less verbatim.[6]

The mere fact that the court had agreed to consider the case inflamed tempers. Concern continued to center on cost, but more ominous rumblings began to surface. "The recent trials of Mrs. Clem have cost the taxpayers thousands of dollars," complained "LEX," in a letter to the *Sentinel*. "Although all were willing to allow her as fair a chance as could be desired and no one begrudged the money spent," he continued somewhat disingenuously, "yet, the injustice of making the community at large suffer, pecuniarily speaking, for the crimes of an individual, is apparent." LEX suggested that convicted criminals be required to pay the costs of their trials. He also noted that, "the more summary the trial the less chance there is of . . . Lynch Law."[7]

As the case progressed, law itself seemed to be on trial. In arguments that sound strikingly modern, various commentators seconded LEX's opinion that arcane legal technicalities were incompatible with justice. "The widely known and never-ending Clem case bids fair to become chronic with our legal lummaries [*sic*] [and] State Judiciary," the *Sentinel* grumbled. "It would seem, indeed, that whenever time begins to hang heavy on the minds of our leading disciples of Blackstone, they all turn in and give the inevitable case another twist." In mid-December, shortly after the "legal lummaries" on both sides had completed their arguments before the supreme court, the *Sentinel* published an article aptly titled "Try, Try, Try Again." It provided "a brief review of the progress of the cause [*sic*]" and led uninitiated readers through "THE MAZES OF THE LAW." Some months later it sustained the metaphor, comparing Clem's case to Charles Dickens's famous depiction of the British chancery courts in *Bleak House*.[8]

Those who hoped for a "summary" decision (including Clem herself) were disappointed. The court took the case under advisement but decided to wait until an additional justice could be appointed to issue a decision. In the meantime, Clem waited in her cell at Jeffersonville, the effects of confinement beginning to wear on her, despite the relatively comfortable accommodations she and other female lifers enjoyed at the state's expense. "The word cells can scarcely be properly applied to these apartments either, for they look more like well though plainly furnished rooms in a hotel," one reporter complained. A group of journalists who visited the prison in the early winter of 1873 could not resist the opportunity to interview "the observed of all observers." Clem, as usual, was reluctant to speak with them.

She took the opportunity, however, to assert her innocence and "the conviction that the 'real murderer' will yet be found."[9]

■ ■ ■

In mid-June 1873 the Indiana Supreme Court finally issued its decision—to grant Clem another trial. The court acknowledged the "other questions presented and argued" but based its ruling on two considerations. First, it found that Judge Davidson's instructions to jurors, intended to encourage them to reach a verdict, were in error. "No number of minds can agree upon a multitude of facts, such as this case presents, without some . . . deference to the opinions of others, without what some might call compromise of different views," Davidson advised the gentlemen of Clem's fourth jury. The justices of the state's highest court disagreed: "Each juror must act upon his own judgment of the facts as they are presented to him, in the evidence adduced, and cannot rightfully yield his honest convictions to those of some one else, or even to those of the other members of the jury." Second, the court called the legitimacy of the previous two hearings into question. In 1868 and 1869, Clem stood trial for the murder of Nancy Jane Young, prosecutors reasoning perhaps that the brutal killing of a "pure [C]hristian woman" would more likely result in conviction than the demise of a somewhat shady businessman. They had also hedged their bets, reserving the option of trying Clem for Jacob Young's murder in the event of an acquittal. Now, in 1872, Clem's attorneys argued (successfully it turned out) that her prior conviction for second-degree murder automatically acquitted her of first-degree murder. Prosecutors had anticipated this maneuver, for in 1871 and 1872, determined to secure a conviction of murder in the first degree, they tried Clem for the murder of *Jacob* Young—a change to the "programme" most press accounts overlooked. In their argument before the high court, Gordon, Voorhees, Leathers, Hanna, and Knefler made the ingenious claim that the murders of Jacob and Nancy Young constituted a single crime. The Indiana Supreme Court agreed and reversed Clem's most recent conviction.[10]

Journalists descended on Jeffersonville as the news spread, hoping to catch Clem's reaction. She did not disappoint. A reporter for the *Sentinel* described her response to the news—"a sudden paleness, deep agitation and a fervent 'Thank God!' "[11]

Few shared her elation. Fewer still defended the court's decision. One such brave soul was "W.," an attorney from the town of Franklin. "I am a lawyer," he wrote, "loving my profession with that kind of passion that may warp my judgment a little on the subject about which I write, but I think not." Criticizing the press for "moulding public opinion" against the law, he cautioned that the "very technicalities" that newspaper editorials roundly condemned "were invented, not to shield the guilty, but to protect the innocent."[12] Almost no one thought Clem deserved such protection. The *Journal* accused the Indiana Supreme Court of corruption, implying that its justices, much like the "sold-out editor," accepted bribes in exchange for ordering a new trial. Newspaper articles with titles such as "Murderers' Loopholes" and "How the Murderess Heard the News" suggested little doubt concerning Clem's guilt. "It is the earnest hope of those who love justice that the Judges will do all that befits their high place in expediting the final conviction of the wicked woman whose fate hangs in the balance," the *Sentinel* opined. "If there are points of law which seem uncertain in the recently rendered decision, let us have them reviewed, so that the woman shall have no possible loophole nor any hope in prolonging this unseemly contest. No man who has watched the case can doubt for a moment the utter irremediable guilt of the woman."[13]

Popular feeling, as far as the press "moulded" it, agreed. "Contrary to expectations on the part of Mrs. Clem and her friends, the public opinion against her in Indianapolis is as strong and bitter to-day as it was at the time of her first trial. Prominent public men in Indianapolis were heard to say . . . that 'the next jury should hang her,'" the *Sentinel* reported. "Two-thirds of the people of Marion county, if not nine-tenths, believe Mrs. Clem to be guilty of the Young murder, and the prospects are that they will always think so, whatever opinion may be given hereafter by courts and juries to the contrary." Clem's jailers were so concerned for her safety that they arranged for her transfer to the Boone County jail for her fifth trial to be made in secrecy. Even the conductors and baggage handlers of the Jeffersonville and Lafayette Railroads were unaware that a famous passenger rode in their cars on Saturday, June 23, 1873.[14]

The news that Clem's next hearing would be delayed until September further inflamed tempers. Newspaper editors complained of "the law's dishearteningly tedious delays": "How long, oh Lord, how long, shall murder be impossible of punishment?" implored the *Sentinel*. It then repeated what had become a popular refrain: law was not on the side of justice. "There seems no earthly reason that the rehearing should have been postponed," its editor complained. Delays were simply "intervals . . . seized by the ferocious criminal and her advisors as passages of final escape from punishment. . . . If the popular voice could have had the dictation of the time, the rehearing would have been to-day."[15]

Some commentators feared *both* law *and* lawlessness. Or, as LEX had warned the previous winter, "the law's delays" might encourage citizens to take the law into their own hands. Clem's secret journey from Jeffersonville to Lebanon was one indication that lynching was a distinct possibility. So, too, was the fact that extralegal executions, if not exactly commonplace, were a reality of Hoosier life. The editor of a northern Indiana newspaper, the *Rochester Democrat*, claimed that the lynching of an alleged murderer in the southern Indiana town of Salem could have been avoided had those responsible "been assured that the murderer would have been tried with all decent haste, convicted and executed. . . . If society had not grown into the habit of disregarding the law and shrinking from assuming the responsibility of shedding blood, they would not have labored under the misconception that it was their duty to become riotous murderers." The *Democrat*'s editor moved quickly to what he saw as the larger implications of legal and judicial sloth. "The recent decision of the Supreme Court of Indiana, in the case of the murderess Mrs. Clem has evidently shaken the confidence of the people in the administration of justice. . . . No wonder that all reverence for law is lost when its ministers are seen conspiring to defeat its aims."[16]

The *Democrat* feared that "the law's delays" in the Clem case would plunge all of Indiana into the violence and lawlessness that supposedly plagued the southern part of the state. Other observers feared that Clem's appeal, combined with various newsworthy acquittals, foreshadowed a nationwide tolerance for violent crime. "Stokes may shoot Jim Fisk, McFarland may murder Richardson, Mrs. Clem may butcher husband and wife, Mary Harris may shoot a recreant lover, . . . Daniel Sickles may murder the paramour of his wife, Cole may shoot Hiscock down," the *Sentinel* complained. In this telling, Clem joined a pantheon of celebrity murderers, including Edward Stokes, who gunned down his financial and romantic rival, financier Jim Fisk; Daniel Sickles, George Cole, and Daniel McFarland, each of whom murdered his wife's lover; and Mary Harris—(successfully defended by Daniel Voorhees)—who shot and killed her erstwhile fiancé. Each escaped punishment despite overwhelming evidence of guilt. Stokes received a four-year sentence for manslaughter. Sickles, Cole, and McFarland were acquitted by juries who believed that husbands had a customary if not legal right to protect their honor. Harris became the first defendant to be acquitted on the grounds of temporary insanity—a verdict many attributed to Voorhees's brilliant closing argument.[17]

The *Sentinel*'s list of perpetrators who got away with murder signaled the beginnings of an important cultural shift. In the late 1860s, Indianapolitans were astonished that a respectable woman like Mrs. Clem could commit murder. By the early 1870s, as the various cases enumerated by the *Sentinel* suggested, it had become abundantly clear that gentlemen could be murderers—and ladies murderesses. The Nancy Clem who emerged in the public prints was unquestionably a lady, even if she was unquestionably guilty.[18] Prosecution and defense presumably continued to argue over the respectability of "working women" and competing definitions of marital fidelity. But the Clem casual readers encountered was *not* a working woman, even though prison regulations required her to labor. In a twist that must have filled prosecuting attorneys with dismay, they read about a prisoner who hewed much more closely to their own definition of virtuous womanhood than to the disreputable villainess they had tried to create. Influenced by a series of high-profile cases featuring refined criminals, commentators presented a Clem who was not only eminently respectable but positively genteel. They created what many nineteenth-century Americans would hitherto have termed an oxymoron: a genteel murderess.

By the late nineteenth century, associations between class and criminal behavior had loosened; the era's most famous murderers were not clerks, manual laborers, or people with previous criminal histories but men of relative wealth and standing. Stokes was a wealthy speculator and scion of a distinguished family, Sickles a congressman, Cole a doctor and Civil War hero. Although he was much better educated, McFarland, a failed land speculator and teacher of elocution who falsely represented himself as a distinguished attorney, bore the closest resemblance to the protagonists in the Cold Spring saga. And, then, two years later, the renowned clergyman Henry Ward Beecher became the nation's most notable defendant—accused, to be sure, of adultery, not murder. Taken together, these cases suggested that it had become possible to conceive of respectable people committing serious crimes, even murder—even if it might not be possible to imagine convicting them. In short, genteel murderers (as opposed to defendants who derived their gentility from perceptions of innocence) had become recognizable cultural types.[19] Their very existence provided contemporaries with a means of classifying Clem—ladylike, *but* guilty.

Nevertheless she fit awkwardly into this cast of characters. Accounts that likened her to the perpetrators of sensational crimes committed by genteel criminals inadvertently underscored her uniqueness, for her alleged "butchering of husband and wife" was no crime of passion in either the unintentional or (despite prosecutors' arguments) sexual sense of the term. A correspondent for the *Chicago Times* recognized as much. Terming Clem "the most remarkable murderess of the West," he noted that she was not a killer "of the Miss Harris kind, who shot for love," but rather one who acted according to "cool calculation." But his was the minority view; if the conventional wisdom linking class and crime had been shaken, the more common insistence that Clem somehow *was* "the Miss Harris kind" suggests that associations between sexuality and murder had not.

Still, while supporters of Sickles, Cole, and McFarland argued that husbands' rights (or—in Harris's case—a lover's callous betrayal) justified their actions, no one offered any justification for Clem's alleged crime. Her inclusion among criminal members of the relative elite was notable in another respect, for it exemplified a strange form of upward social mobility. That Harris, the child of Irish Catholic immigrants, could also be depicted as ladylike suggests that women were especially likely candidates for these sorts of makeovers. Yet Harris was a woman wronged. Her gentility stemmed from her status as the victim of a heartless lover and an "irritable" reproductive system. *No one* who believed Clem guilty depicted her as a victim. More to the point, Clem, unlike Sickles, Cole, McFarland, and Harris had *not* been acquitted. She had only been granted an appeal.[20]

The longer Clem remained in the public eye, the more genteel she became in the eyes of her beholders—even among those utterly convinced of her guilt. Few commentators seconded J. H. Banka's faith in Clem's innocence. Yet most accounts took their stylistic cues from his sentimental portrait in *State Prison Life*, even as they disputed his judgment. Newspapers across the nation collectively created a portrait of a genteel murderess who exemplified "quiet and resigned submission" and "lady-like deportment." Successive accounts depicted a model prisoner who kept her cell "neat and clean by her own hands," "cheerfully" performed her assigned duties, and knelt in prayer before "her little iron bedstead every night and morning." The *Chicago Inter Ocean* described "the notorious Mrs. Clem" as "very much a lady in her appearance, dressing neatly and with great taste."[21]

Clem had always been "respectable." Yet the social standing she carried, as the daughter of a middling farmer and the wife, first, of a prosperous craftsman and, later, a successful grocer, differed from the status on which journalists would increasingly rely. Or to put it another way, there was a difference between antebellum and (immediate postbellum) respectability and Gilded Age gentility. The distinction, slippery though it may be, tells us much about the remaking of the middle class in the late nineteenth century. It was part and parcel of what one historian has described as the "transition from the sentimental culture of early Victorianism to the theatrical culture of high Victorianism." It also marks a historical moment in which local and regional notions of respectability gave way to—and sometimes clashed with—broader national definitions of propriety and refinement. Gentility, as journalistic depictions of Clem suggested, emphasized appearance and outward behavior over inner character. Gentility required stylish but tasteful dress; it necessitated a bearing and an accent that identified one not as a provincial bumpkin but as a member of a nation of refined people. For women, genteel status was largely incompatible with visible labor.[22]

Of course accounts that transformed a poorly educated confidence woman into a genteel murderess are testimony to the limited interpretative frameworks nineteenth-century commentators had at their disposal. What to think of a *woman* who allegedly murdered not a husband or lover but a business associate? A woman who allegedly killed with a pistol rather than poison (the usual female weapon)? In their efforts to pin her down, to prove her innocence or guilt, attorneys, reporters, and ordinary citizens lurched from one available cultural script to another. Thus it is tempting to conclude that the potentially guilty if socially rehabilitated Nancy Clem who appeared in print was merely a figment of journalistic imagination. But she also reflected Clem's own sense of the status to which she believed she was entitled—and something of her own social aspirations, aspirations symbolized by her previous request to bunk with "a decent colored woman" instead of a white prostitute.[23] Like many a prisoner, before and since, Clem dedicated much of her time to self-education, "read[ing] a great deal." A reporter who bucked the general trend by noting that she was "not a person of culture" explained that "she is naturally observing, and knows how to make good use of what she sees and hears."[24]

Attentive to her appearance and to the particulars of interior decoration, Clem was already something of a fashion plate at the time of her arrest in October 1868. Six years of incarceration and almost as many trials only increased her fondness for stylish apparel, an inclination aided and abetted by a prison system that allowed female inmates to wear their own clothes.[25] As her fifth trial approached, a half-literate woman of upland southern origins had become an icon of fashionable refinement. Surely Clem understood, as her attorneys must have as well, the potential (if not always persuasive) connections between appearance and deportment and perceptions of innocence. Her performances of innocent gentility, if indeed they were such, left her open to charges that she was an "actress." The *Sentinel* described a woman attired "in a neatly fitting calico dress, with jewels in her ears" and "a gold pin [that] held a white collar at the throat." Confronted with this "noble specimen of physical womanhood—a study worthy the pencil of a master artist," the reporter could only confess his confusion. "She is one of the most accomplished actresses in the land, or else she is innocent of the brutal crime of which she has been several times pronounced guilty by a jury of her countrymen."[26]

Still, Clem maintained a distinctly unsentimental interest in economic affairs, even while incarcerated. If newspaper reporters mostly ignored the economic initiatives that underwrote her alleged crime, glimpses of a more believable Nancy Clem occasionally surfaced. Depictions like one that noted that the famous prisoner relieved the monotony of her confinement by "mark[ing] all the real estate transactions and comment[ing] on them in a vivacious and knowing manner" rang truer than Banka's account of her weeping over "poor fellows."[27]

■ ■ ■

In the end, money, not law, threatened justice. As Clem's fifth trial, scheduled to begin on April 27, 1874, drew near, rumors began to circulate that the Marion County commissioners were unwilling to allocate funds for her prosecution. "No more money is to be spent in the Clem case," the *Sentinel* announced as early as February. William B. Walls, the Boone County prosecutor, declared his intention of trying Clem should Marion County refuse. This was an empty pledge, for it depended on "the state of Boone's" unlikely willingness to foot the bill. But it proved a shrewd preemptive maneuver guaranteed to protect his reputation, if not his job.[28]

Preparations for the Clem's fifth trial took place in a different context than had previous proceedings. In the words of one local historian, the Panic of 1873, which ushered in the nation's worst depression to date, "struck Indianapolis with peculiar force." During the next three years, an estimated one thousand of the state's businesses failed. Banks closed; many that remained open refused to allow depositors to withdraw much needed cash.

Factories, retail establishments, and workshops laid off employees and re-
duced wages. While the worst of the labor unrest was yet to come, workers
in several industries (including typesetters for the *Journal* and *Sentinel*) went
on strike—with few successes—to protest wage cuts. While the city hired out-
of-work men to labor on its roadways, it refused to distribute funds directly to
needy residents.[29]

In this atmosphere even the most "Radical" county authorities found the
prospect of a funding a fifth Clem trial a difficult proposition. This one,
moreover, was expected to be especially expensive, analysts estimating that
it would add $18,000 to the considerable sums already spent. Key witnesses
for the prosecution would have to be transported from considerable distances. Erie Locke had stayed in California; by now his family had joined
him in Pasadena's "Indiana Colony." Dr. Duzan had moved to Dallas, laying
him open to charges that he had deliberately vacated the state to avoid testifying—an accusation that sparked angry exchanges in Indianapolis newspapers. Other important witnesses, including the mother of "little Josie Stevens," the girl who had offered a too-expensive shotgun to Bill Abrams, and
Jacob Young's sister, Mary Server, had died, weakening the potential case
against Clem.[30]

■ ■ ■

On March 18, 1874, the Marion County commissioners made the expected
announcement; they "decline[d] to make any further appropriation from
the country treasury to aid in such prosecution, believing that enough has
already been done in that behalf by the county of Marion." Boone County
officials quickly followed suit, despite Walls's previous pledge. "He tried early
and late to induce the authorities to do their duty, but he was disregarded,"
the *Sentinel* grumbled.[31]

Both the local and national press protested the commissioners' decision.
"Let the woman Clem escape without another trial and go forth into the
world," the *Sentinel* complained, "[and] it will be an encouragement to
criminals in every state of the Union to flock here for the perpetration of
crime. No man's life would be safe." The failure to prosecute Clem was, in
its editor's eyes, "a stain upon the procedure of a state . . . an open invitation
to all criminals to make Indiana the field of their operations." Last but not
least, "it is a reminder to imprisoned law-breakers, that by perseverance they
may escape the penalties already visited upon them, and escape prison by
the formal processes of the law."[32] "Justice appears to be not only blind in

Boone County, Indiana, but to be reduced to an extraordinary condition of impecuniosity," San Francisco's *Daily Evening Bulletin* observed.[33]

Various constituencies appealed to newly elected Thomas Hendricks, the first Democratic governor of a northern state since the Civil War. Hendricks claimed to have only a few hundred dollars at his disposal; he could not request the legislature to allocate funds, he explained, because it was not currently in session. Instead he encouraged prosecutors to proceed and ask the state's lawmakers, once they reconvened, for reimbursement. Benjamin Harrison and John Dye declined the suggestion. Hendricks responded with a partisan put-down, blaming the poor quality of prosecuting attorneys for the state's failure to make Clem's conviction stick.[34]

■ ■ ■

On April 27, Boone County prosecutor Walls stood before the recently appointed judge of the newly constituted twentieth circuit, Truman Palmer, and entered a plea of *nolle prosequi*. Walls based his motion on three arguments: "the indisposition of Marion county and the state to assist the prosecution," the expense of transporting witnesses from considerable distances, and Boone County's inability to prosecute another county's case with no guarantee of reimbursement for expenses.[35]

Judge Palmer took two days to make a ruling. A crowd gathered in the Boone County courtroom on the morning of April 30 to hear it. Those who hoped "to catch . . . a glimpse of the old lady" were disappointed, for Clem chose to remain in her room on the second floor. Frank Clem, Jonathan Gordon, John Hanna, Williams Leathers, and Frederick Knefler listened as Palmer read his decision, Frank "white with anxiety," Gordon "graciously nodding his approval" as it became clear that Palmer had, as expected, decided to approve Walls's motion. From the vantage point of many local spectators the judge had shown himself "a faithful democrat," who acted "in the interests of tax payers as well as justice and right."[36]

Frank rushed to his wife's room, attorneys in tow. Displaying the same mixture of maudlin sentimentality and righteous indignation that had characterized previous reporting, newspaper accounts depicted an "affecting scene": "The scene that followed may not be described," the *Indianapolis News* reported. "The sobs of the husband and wife could be heard by those in the hall outside. . . . [T]he jailor came from the room, his eyes filled with tears." Yet, the *News* concluded, "the feeling is very general that one of the

grandest mistakes has been made in closing this trial without either an acquittal or conviction."[37]

Clem quickly regained her composure. "A faithful husband and able,
persevering lawyers have saved me; may God bless you all," she exclaimed,
as she clasped John Hanna by the hand. "I want you to live long. . . . I want
all my counsel to live long." Described by the *Journal* as "almost besides
himself with joy," Hanna telegraphed a friend: "Mrs. CLEM is discharged,
free as the air. God bless you."[38]

Numerous visitors, invited and uninvited, crowded into Clem's neatly
furnished "cell" on the second floor of the courthouse, among them reporters from the *Sentinel* and *Inter Ocean*. She once again thanked her family
and her attorneys. She offered particular praise to her husband, who had
"sacrificed business, property, and even his social position for my sake." To
repay Frank and Albert for their unstinting devotion, she pledged to "pass
the remainder of her days in making them as happy and comfortable as it
was in her power." Asked if she planned to stay close to home because she
might find it "annoying to have every one staring at you as if you were in a
circus procession," Clem answered, "[B]y no means. Why should I? Have I
not the rights of other ladies?"[39]

Then Clem, her husband, her son, and her attorneys boarded the 2:46
train to Indianapolis. Learning that they sat in the same car as the Indiana
murderess, two "ladies" exercised *their* rights and insisted on changing their
seats. When Frank, Nancy, and Albert arrived at the Indianapolis depot,
they took a carriage to the corner of Massachusetts Avenue and Delaware
Street, where Frank Clem now lived on the upper floor of the building that
housed Clem & Brother's grocery store. Nancy Clem announced plans to re-
model her house on Alabama Street as well as her intention to go into the real
estate business.[40]

■ ■ ■

Another bit of drama attended the news that Clem had been released. The
Journal had agreed to furnish the *Sentinel* a copy of Judge Palmer's order, an
offer that turned out to be too good to be true. When the promised report
failed to materialize, the *Sentinel* took desperate measures to avoid being
scooped. The paper's editor, accompanied by a reporter, roused W. H. Vandegrift, the assistant superintendent of the Cincinnati, Lafayette, & Indianapolis Railroad, from his bed. Vandegrift commandeered a locomotive

and fireman and volunteered, as the *Sentinel* put it, to "run mit der ma-cheen." The quartet made an exciting "midnight whiz" toward "the state of Boone," traveling "a mile a minute. . . . WITH WHAT RECKLESSNESS the engine, with its precious freight, plunged into bridges, rumbled through them and thundered on its way!" Once the engine thundered into Lebanon, the two journalists raced to awaken Judge Palmer, who "appeared at the door" of his hotel room "en dishabille to receive his unseasonable visitors. . . . And thus the readers of the *Sentinel* were permitted to peruse the decision that gave the celebrated Mrs. Clem her liberty," the May 4 morning issue smugly concluded.

The *Sentinel's* report exaggerated the perils of the journey, though a speeding locomotive without freight or passenger cars was indeed danger-ously unstable. But it provided comic relief, made for good copy, and gave the *Sentinel* an opportunity to publicly question the "supposed honor" of its journalistic rival.[41]

The "midnight whiz" aside, the general mood was grim. Few people in Marion County or the nation at large seem to have agreed with the "demo-cratic" principles espoused by Judge Palmer and his fellow townsfolk. "She is free because the law officers refuse to prosecute her further, because it will cost money; free because Marion county, which can build a magnificent court house as a mockery of justice, can not afford to pay the expenses of her prosecution," the *News* thundered. "It is a shame, a disgrace, an out-rage." The *Sentinel* complained, "Mrs. Clem has triumphed over what may be called the law and order of Indiana."[42]

The *New York Times* rendered the harshest criticism. In an article enti-tled "Indiana Justice" published just after the Marion County commission-ers had made their intentions known, the paper termed their decision—"the most extraordinary circumstance in connection with this most extraordi-nary case"—"a disgrace to the State." It went further once Clem was free, neatly underscoring the gendered dimensions of the case by connecting the state's history of liberal divorce (here the *Times* failed to point out that a recently passed statute requiring two year's residence had put an end to quick divorces) to its supposed tolerance for other sorts of crimes. "Indiana has for many years enjoyed the doubtful distinction of being the 'champion' divorce State of the Union. It has now earned the right to be called the murder-ers' paradise. . . . Was there ever such a farce enacted in a civilized country?" the editorial continued, "a woman about whose guilt there was scarcely a second opinion, allowed to walk out of jail for the lack of means to continue her prosecution?" The *Times* spared no one—not the commissioners, not the governor, not the prosecutors (who "failing to procure retainers... washed their hands of the business and retired"), not the citizens of the Hoosier state. "The people of Indiana, it is said, are greatly 'excited' and 'deeply indignant' at this most disgraceful failure of justice, and well they may be, for though they had more than six weeks' notice of the intention of the Marion Commissioners, no movement was made to avert the reproach by public subscription."[43]

Newspapers across the nation took up the *Times*'s refrain. "Indiana Justice Hard Up" read a *San Francisco Daily Evening Bulletin* headline, while the *Chicago Inter Ocean* pronounced Clem's liberation "A Specimen of Indiana Justice." The *Cincinnati Gazette* was content to merely repeat the title of the *New York Times* story. The *Times* itself continued to use "Indiana justice" as shorthand to denote what it considered the state's aversion to properly punishing criminals. While an article thus titled concerned two murderers who received life sentences instead of hanging failed to mention Clem, no one needed to be reminded of the original reference.[44]

As a variety of commentators, national and local, lamented the sad state of Indiana justice, the newly liberated "Indiana murderess" enjoyed the "same rights of other ladies." "Every day that the sun shines she is seen upon the streets," the Indianapolis correspondent for the *Inter Ocean* reported, "either riding in her carriage, or walking at the side of her husband, dressed in the height of fashion, and compelling everyone to stop and gaze at her."[45]

Gradually the outrage dissipated, as sensational coverage of new crimes slowly pushed Clem out of the spotlight. Yet the Young murders remained in the news. Efforts to secure Bill Abrams's release accelerated. "It doesn't look hardly fair that Abrams should spend his life in the penitentiary, while Mrs Clem goes free," the *News* complained. And the case, to be sure, remained a touchstone, a point of reference by which other outrages might be evaluated. A year or so after her release, the *Sentinel* enumerated "the most important murder trials since that of Mrs. Nancy Clem." The *National Police Gazette* wrote of an 1880 murder, "Not since the Clem trial has any case attracted as much interest."[46]

■ ■ ■

William Wallace Leathers would not live long. He died on December 16, 1875, aged thirty-nine years. His obituary, which described his legal talents and identified his most famous assignment as defending Nancy Clem, served as a fitting epitaph for the Cold Spring tragedy.

Another "sequel" to the case preceded Leathers's death by eight months. On April 17, Maggie Abrams filed for divorce.[47]

CHAPTER THIRTEEN

I Kept It Rolling

Nancy Clem expected to live over the Clem grocery only temporarily. She announced plans to "brighten and furnish up" her Alabama Street residence, only a stone's throw away, which Frank had rented out in her absence. Neither the move nor, as far as can be discerned, the renovations came to pass. A tenant also occupied her house on North Pennsylvania Street, a dilapidated "old-fashioned one-story cottage," its run-down condition, in the eyes of some observers, a fitting symbol of the character of its owner. These portents aside, the Clems returned to a semblance of ordinary life, "roosting" in the "pleasant" and "commodious" upstairs rooms on Massachusetts Avenue. Frank continued in the grocery business, apparently prospering. Albert, now a plasterer like his father and uncle, resided with his mother and stepfather until 1877, when he married Beulah Wilcox, the daughter of a railroad engineer, and moved to a house next door to his in-laws, some four miles away. For a while it seemed that the Indiana murderess, despite her ill-advised penchant for promenades, would live quietly—and perhaps even live down her reputation.

Clem did, in a manner of speaking, go into real estate. She also pursued business of another sort. In fact, she resumed the same sort of informal banking enterprise that previously brought her notoriety—taking out loans, promising high rates of interest, and loaning borrowed funds. Or as the *New York World* would explain, "she has been operating extensively of late as a capitalist on the plan formerly adopted." This time Clem dealt with less illustrious partners than the leading men who supposedly backed her previous operations—"guileless old grangers ... capable widows, and shrewd spinsters."[1] And this time her unhappy business associates lived to tell the tale.

■ ■ ■

In November 1876, only two and half years after Clem's release from prison, newspapers reported that Lena Miller, a boardinghouse and hotel keeper, was suing the alleged Indiana murderess in civil court for failing to repay the money she loaned her.[2] Shortly thereafter the "guileless granger," a farmer named Hezekiah Hinkson, also filed suit—and retained Benjamin

Harrison as his attorney. In the spring of 1877, Clem was summoned to the law offices of Harrison and Dye to give a deposition, where she fielded questions from her old adversary. This time she took preemptive action, requesting an interview with the *Sentinel*, the paper she had always believed "fairer," to tell her side of the story. According to the *Sentinel*'s account of the "chat," Clem claimed that Harrison did her "her great injustice in compelling her to undergo an examination to which the other parties to the suit are not subjected." She then launched into a detailed explanation of her transactions, one in which she figured as lender rather than a borrower. "She said much more," the *Sentinel* explained, "but lack of space prevents its appearance."[3]

Various observers marveled at Clem's willingness to risk her newfound freedom. The *New York World* attributed her behavior to habitual criminality. "The man who has once been arrested for drunkenness is soon likely to see the inside of a station-house again. A thief who is just out of State Prison may safely be accused of the first burglary that takes place in his neighborhood, and a person who is guilty of homicide and escapes hanging for it rarely rests, satisfied with one murder." Others believed that her escape from punishment had only deepened her conviction that she was above the law.[4]

More commonplace concerns may have inspired "the noted murderess'[s]" resumption of "her old business." The "height of fashion" did not come cheaply. Frank had spent a small fortune on five trials' worth of attorneys' fees, which he may not yet have fully paid. On the surface, Clem's promise to spend the rest of her days providing for her family's comfort suggests a renewed commitment to industrious domesticity. Quite possibly, she meant something different: supplying "comforts" by making as much money as possible. And she may well have decided to do so by returning to the principles enumerated in her ante-nuptial agreement and "manag[ing] her own business affairs." Or perhaps a woman known for eagerly scanning the real estate pages was bored with domestic life. The *New York World*'s correspondent may have come closest to the truth when he suggested that Clem "was too full of excitement to forego her old business." Clem's own words, recorded in the spring 1877 deposition, suggest as much: "Whenever . . . [I] . . . would make anything I kept it rolling."[5]

Clem kept it rolling, but as the economic depression worsened, much else came to a halt. In June 1877, only a few months after she gave her deposition, angry mobs of unemployed Indianapolitans threatened to riot. Mayor John Caven, a Republican sympathetic to working people's plight, responded by purchasing hundreds of loaves of bread out of his own pocket and distributing them to the hungry crowd, a measure that prevented violence and assured Caven a prominent place in the city's folklore. A month later the wheels of freight and passenger trains literally stopped rolling, as the Great Railroad Strike, a nationwide response to far-reaching wage cuts, reached Indianapolis. Violence was again averted in the "Railroad City," although elsewhere, especially in Pittsburgh, lives and property were lost. Benjamin Harrison's membership on Committees of Public Safety, which organized volunteer militia companies, and Arbitration, which promised to investigate the cause of low wages but "counseled obedience to the law," earned him a reputation as a friend of capital and foe of labor.[6]

The state of the economy may have enhanced the appeal of dubious financial schemes that dangled "the deceptive bait of getting something for nothing." If Clem's new business proved less dangerous than her previous endeavors ("She has not, to be sure, been accused of a second murder," the *World* noted), her post-release financial operations assembled an even more colorful cast of characters than those who populated the original "ring." Hinkson, "the guileless granger," was the least colorful but in some ways the most important, for he gave Clem her "start"—that is, seed money for further investments. Intrigued by the alleged murderess's legendary financial abilities, Hinkson, a man "after big percentage," asked an "old army comrade" to arrange a meeting with Clem even before she had been released from prison. The old comrade was Peter Wilkins, the detective who could not say who had given him the money.[7]

At first Hinkson was pleased with the arrangement, for Clem repaid his initial investments with "big interest." But she did not return his principal. Nor, initially, did she put their agreement in writing. "Hinkson never asked me for a note," she claimed, "until he got scared." By the time he became sufficiently alarmed, $8,000 of his money was in Clem's hands. Hinkson's insistence on IOUs proved Clem's undoing. The complaint he lodged with authorities accused her of cheating his son-in-law William Wishard. Wishard, who also happened to be the younger brother of a man who served as a juror during Clem's first murder trial, had come to collect his father-in-law's money. Clem, he claimed, tendered a packet made up of newspaper cut in the size and shape of bank bills and tore up the promissory notes (worth $3,000) before he discovered the deception.[8]

Clem kept it rolling. Hinkson's "start" financed a range of investments. Money passed through many hands, funds borrowed from one lender used to pay another. "Mrs. Clem's remarkable financial operations," the Indianapolis *News* concluded, are not so much proof of transcendent powers on her part as of transcendent foolishness of her victims." Clem claimed that she invested $5,000 in Lena Miller and Eliza J. King's Enterprise Hotel, an establishment directly across the street from her rooms at 99 Massachusetts Avenue. Miller would deny this assertion, insisting that *she* was an aggrieved lender, not the profligate borrower, originator of "loose business practices," and initiator of "foolish trades" Clem made her out to be.[9]

Whether they lent Clem money hoping for "big interest" or borrowed it from her, those who had business dealings with the alleged Indiana murderess joined strange and disreputable company. The floor above the Clem grocery housed a veritable hive of illicit business activity, a "roost" where Nancy Clem consorted with counterfeiters and gamblers. Her associates included Joseph W. Bugbee, a notorious forger, and Henry W. Cook, a "doubtful commercial traveler" and gambler, who operated out of rooms rented by Clem's neighbor Eunice Barnes, a fifty-one-year-old widow. Cook, Clem claimed, "borrowed my money"—an assertion he would dispute—"and paid me interest, too, good interest." Cook also paid Barnes and Clem to guard the doors during the gaming hours. Clem admitted to preparing meals for the gamblers who joined Cook's card games and even boarding them, services for which she was also paid. And she and Barnes worked together to ensure that Hinkson never crossed paths with those who made use of his money. On one occasion, Clem reported, "Mr. Hinkson was sitting in the sitting room, and Cook was hid in the bed room. . . . They were all here and there dodging around through holes in the wall. [I]t was just like rats in a barn down there."[10]

"Was hid in the bed room." "Like rats in a barn down there." "Pretty damned comfortable" (Clem's almost certainly less than truthful description of Hinkson's situation). Clem's words, faithfully recorded perhaps for the first time, reveal something of the woman herself, a woman who more closely resembled an "uneducated . . . wife of a small grocer" (as the *New York World* described her) than the refined heroine of J. H. Banka's *State Prison Life* or newspaper descriptions of a genteel murderess.[11] Banka had recorded Clem's statements in flowery prose. The verbatim testimony of the deposition reveals a different idiom—a fondness for folksy expressions, spoken no doubt in the upcountry accent that rendered "Indianapolis" into "Nopolis."

Whatever the truth of the story Nancy Clem told Benjamin Harrison, the deposition and subsequent proceedings exposed a business world that accommodated both sexes. Both women and men participated in the wheeling and dealing, albeit in gendered ways. In her successful lawsuit, Lena Miller testified that she started the Enterprise Hotel with only $50 to her name; the *News* concluded that Clem's financial dealings "rate into insignificance when compared to the achievements of Lena Miller." Eunice Barnes revealed a similar entrepreneurial bent, turning the apartments she rented from Frank and Aaron Clem into a gambling den, "cut up into little rooms, with dark halls."[12]

Such scenarios would have been familiar to nineteenth-century Americans, who routinely condemned hotels and boardinghouses as places of vice that put respectable and unsuspecting people in the company of gamblers, confidence men, and women of ill repute. Revelations of the goings on in the rooms above 99 Massachusetts Avenue confirmed their worst fears. But they also showed that women eagerly embraced both the legitimate and illegitimate economies. If the local press routinely ridiculed Miller's spinsterhood and her credulity in trusting her hard-earned dollars to the notorious Nancy Clem, the *News* article suggested that there were those who admired her "shrewdness" in both business dealings and the law. "The fact that Miss Miller has been able to secure judgment . . . does go far towards establishing the claim" that she was the better businesswoman, the *News* explained. Only a few years later a booster publication would heap praise on Miller's "active business career" and "executive ability rarely excelled by men." And of course there were those who admired the reputed shrewdness of Nancy Clem—enough to trust her with their hard-earned cash.[13]

All of these shenanigans supposedly went on under (or more accurately, above) Frank Clem's nose. Since "Mr. Clem didn't want me to do business," Nancy once again took pains to conceal her dealings from Frank, enlisting Eunice Barnes to "stand guard" against her husband as well. Deception took its toll. "We had such dragging around and dodging about," Clem admitted. "It was behind my husband's back, and I had the responsibility of meals on my hands, and my family coming to dinner and there was no dinner. And they would want to know where I had been. . . . Oh, Mr. Harrison!" Clem exclaimed to her interrogator, evidently hoping for sympathy from the softhearted ladies' man. "I had a terrible time."[14]

■ ■ ■

Frank, too, was having a terrible time. He learned that something was amiss when rumors spread that his wife had forged the signatures "of some Boone county people to paper that was floating about the city." Visibly "affected" by this news, "he walked the floor all night."[15] Frank would soon find additional reasons to lose sleep.

This time around, not everyone was convinced of Nancy's self-reliance. The *Saturday Herald*, a newly minted paper that occupied much the same journalistic niche as the *People*, published a scathing letter to the editor by Lena Miller, who dubbed Frank Clem "incognito." Another contributor commented, "The theory of such supernatural relations between husband and wife, always difficult to understand, is now giving place to the more plausible theory that a mutual understanding existed between them." These observers may have had a point. "My husband has sacrificed property, business, and even his social position for my sake, and it has grieved me more than tongue can tell that an innocent wife should be the cause of it," Clem informed the *Sentinel* upon her release.[16] In this instance she evidently spoke the truth; Frank spent the early 1870s working as a clerk for his brother's firm, a demotion, both social and economic, that suggested he had sold his share of the business to finance legal expenses. By 1876, however, he was once again a partner in A. Clem & Co. No existing evidence decisively links Nancy Clem's return to "capitalism" to Frank Clem's return to partnership, but perhaps the timing was less than coincidental. Perhaps Frank "wanted her to do business" after all, if not precisely the kind of business in which she evidently engaged. As one writer put it, "When Nancy E. Clem signalized her discharge by the re-opening of her business, the questions naturally arise: Who are her helpers and her confidential advisers? With whom does she live, and where does the money all go?"[17] Meanwhile a reporter poked fun at Frank, who supposedly told the *Journal* that he supported capital punishment. "Justice, like charity," the *Herald* quipped, "should begin at home." Other commentators, like the "Citizen" who penned a letter to the *Herald*'s editor, were more sympathetic, casting him as the victim of his wife's corrosive influence on her "kith and kin. . . . It is unaccountable that she should have been permitted to enter into the secret intimacy of home relations after it was discovered that she possessed such wonderful influence over others."[18]

Once admired—at least by some—for "manfully" sitting at his wife's side through her innumerable trials, Frank now appeared as an ineffectual patriarch, a gullible victim—or a potential suspect. And, for the first time, he became directly entangled in his wife's legal difficulties. Lena Miller sued both Clems. In part this was merely necessary; Nancy Clem had relinquished her feme sole status in deference to legal constraints (in the eyes of the law, a convicted felon, a condition Clem temporarily assumed, was civilly dead) and evidently had neglected to regain it. But as Miller's letters to the *Herald* made clear, she held "Incognito" equally responsible for her plight. And she retained Jonathan W. Gordon as her attorney. The irony was lost on no one. "The man who was mainly instrumental in saving . . . [Clem] from the gallows, is now one of the counsel against her," the *New York World* reported. Gordon worked his customary magic, but this time to the disadvantage of his former client. After a two-week trial, a lengthy proceeding by nineteenth-century standards, the jury found in favor of the plaintiff, awarding Miller $8,000 in damages ($160,000 in current dollars).

Hinkson, for his part, retained Benjamin Harrison to sue Nancy, Frank, *and* Albert. Frank and Albert hired one set of attorneys, including John Hanna, and Nancy, another. Quite possibly the family believed this arrangement would protect individual assets—perhaps Nancy had managed to retain some property in her name. Whatever their intentions, it was easy to imbue them with more ominous meanings. "Nancy E. Clem employs none of her old counsel to defend her in the civil suits brought against the family," the *Herald* noted, "while her husband and son show their appreciation of services rendered by retaining for themselves a part of the counsel who restored to them a wife and mother."[19]

Frank and Albert suffered significant financial losses by losing civil suits. Only Nancy, accused of larceny for destroying the promissory notes she had given to Hezekiah Hinkson, faced criminal charges. If the authorities initially proved reluctant to prosecute a case based on the credulity of an "old fool," events that transpired during the spring and summer of 1878 solidified official resolve.

First came the "confession" of former Boone County prosecutor William B. Walls. Walls claimed that two recently publicized confessions—Florida attorney general Samuel B. McLin's admission that he had committed voter fraud in the disputed presidential election of 1876 and Mrs. Elizabeth Tilton's acknowledgment of her adulterous affair with her minister, the Reverend Henry Ward Beecher—prompted him to make his own. By linking these disparate revelations, Walls drew a curious connection between political malfeasance and marital infidelity, suggesting the continuing appeal, if actual irrelevance, of illicit sexuality to Clem's case. Walls's own confession was banal by comparison. And it was not exactly a confession after all but a statement designed to implicate someone else—Truman Palmer, the judge who presided over Clem's abortive fifth trial. Walls told the *Journal* that the Clems had "delegated" him "to ask Judge Palmer whether he would sustain my motion to nolle the case if $1,000 were tendered to him." Palmer reportedly agreed, insisting on receiving the money in advance. Equally galling, Walls claimed that Clem's attorney, Jonathan W. Gordon, was the real author of the "elaborate decision" that Palmer delivered from the bench. Walls had an axe to grind; Palmer had been instrumental in disbarring him for "unprofessional conduct." In revealing the judge's own alleged misconduct, the former attorney saw an opportunity to settle the score.[20]

Palmer emphatically denied the accusation. The lawyers of Frankfort, Indiana, Palmer's hometown, quickly organized an "indignation meeting," which passed "resolutions expressing their confidence in his judicial and personal integrity." The *Chicago Tribune* was inclined to agree with Palmer's supporters. "Walls is a disreputable character. He has been indicted twelve times for forgery, perjury, and other crimes,—twice at the insistence of Judge Palmer, and, although he has been acquitted, is regarded as a scaly lawyer." Palmer, on the other hand, the *Tribune* continued, "is an old-fashioned, quiet, reputable man."[21] The *Tribune*'s local rival, the *Inter Ocean*, agreed, terming Walls "one of the most unscrupulous of men." It lost no time in heaping blame on an Indiana newspaper for believing Walls, "who is vouched for by the *Journal* as the best Prosecuting Attorney Boone County ever had. . . . It is generally thought that the *Journal* put its foot in it clear up to its ears."[22]

Walls's allegation, nevertheless, sparked calls for reopening the Young murder case. Doing so was a technical possibility if not an especially practical one. The *nolle prosequi* motion merely declared the state's intention not to prosecute; it was not a ruling on the merits of the prosecution's case. The legal logic of the supreme court's 1873 decision suggested that Clem could not be retried for first-degree murder, but theoretically she could still face charges of murder in the second degree. "There is no single excuse for this woman's freedom," thundered the *Saturday Herald*. "Her partners in the crime have their punishment. One takes refuge in suicide—'and suicide is a confession'—the other is in prison under a life sentence. Why should she be free, except for the intolerable cowardice, the crime-stained parsimony of this society? . . . It matters not whether she was discharged through bribery of officers, or whether she was discharged without this. In either event the community and the law officers of this county are blameable [*sic*]." Echoing previous reactions to the *nolle prosequi* ruling, the *Herald* concluded, "No wonder the law is held in contempt by the criminal class." Once again, Clem's freedom reflected poorly on local governance. "Marion county is the only county known to have a murderess not even tried because she has money."[23]

Prosecuting Clem once more for the Young murders, nevertheless, posed what most legal experts, Benjamin Harrison included, believed were insurmountable problems. Authorities were determined to take advantage of other opportunities. On June 14, 1878, more than a year after Clem had given her deposition to Harrison, the Marion County grand jury returned an indictment for grand larceny, based on Clem's destruction of the two promissory notes that registered her debt to Hezekiah Hinkson. Less than two hours later, Nancy Clem was under arrest. "In well feigned tones," as the *Herald* put it, she "expressed her astonishment and her entire innocence of any offense against the law. . . . She wore the expression of a much persecuted and injured woman." Albert paid her bail, set at the relatively high sum of $2,500. Frank, for the moment, was nowhere to be found.[24]

Newspapers spread the word, none of it complimentary. "The Notorious Mrs. Clem Arrested for Larceny," read a headline in the *Cincinnati Gazette*. "That Dreadful Woman," a letter to the editor of the *Saturday Herald* complained. The *Louisville Courier-Journal* described "Mrs. Clem, of Indianapolis," as "the wickedest and most irresponsible woman in the world." The *Chicago Tribune* reported that "Indiana's noted murderess and money-broker" had been arrested. The *Cincinnati Enquirer* intimated that Indianapolitans, faced with Clem's "Satanic power," might resort to lynch law. Some expressed disappointment that the indictment was for larceny, not for murder, but hoped, as did the *Saturday Herald*, that "the next grand jury will do its duty. . . . What is the use of arresting this woman for so trivial an offense while the monstrous charge of triple murder hangs over her, and is not prosecuted because prosecution is too expensive?" (Here the *Herald* implied what the *People* would soon state plainly: that the Cold Spring murders included a third victim, the Youngs' unborn child.)[25]

Only a few weeks after her arrest and release on bail, newspapers reported that Clem "had no fear of the indictment." Her attorneys devised a novel defense, though hardly one designed to salvage their client's reputation. Journalists predicted that Clem would "unblushingly plead" that the promissory notes given to Hinkson had been forged, so therefore no larceny had been committed. The statute of limitations for forgery prosecutions had expired. Rumors circulated that she had powerful protectors. "This woman had better be let alone," warned the *Kokomo Tribune*. "If persecuted much longer she will 'squeal,' when a host of persons will fall. When Mrs. Clem decides to tell all she knows there will be a rattling of dry bones."[26]

■ ■ ■

A second sensation emboldened those who wanted Clem prosecuted for *something*, even if she could not be retried for murder. It also lent credence to the argument that "Indiana's noted murderess and money-broker" exerted an influence far beyond her immediate environs. On July 3, only two weeks after Clem's arrest and after years of petitions, William J. Abrams finally received his pardon. Abrams had come close to freedom two years before. "Not satisfied that his guilt was sufficiently established," Governor Thomas Hendricks, who left office in early 1877, favored a pardon on the grounds that Abrams was "failing in bodily and mental strength." Already facing heavy criticism for granting what his political opponents considered an excessive number of pardons (more than 280) he left the decision up to his successor, James Douglas Williams.[27]

Like Hendricks, "Blue Jeans" Williams, a longtime fixture of the state assembly and single-term congressman, was a Democrat. He was a self-proclaimed man of the people, the first farmer to ascend to the state's highest office. The man he defeated in the 1876 gubernatorial election was none other than Benjamin Harrison. Observers interpreted the contest in light of national events. The *New York Herald* described the "the contrast between Ben Harrison and Blue Jeans" in the familiar terms of Reconstruction versus reconciliation, civil rights versus white supremacy. Harrison "waves the bloody shirt and asks his hearer to keep up the bitter feeling of the North against the South"; Williams "preaches the Christly doctrine of 'peace on earth, to men good will.'" The "Christly doctrine" would prevail; as part of the infamous Compromise of 1877, newly elected president Rutherford B. Hayes would withdraw the last remaining federal troops from the South, formally ending Reconstruction and the nation's commitment to enforcing the rights of southern freedpeople. White voters in Indiana voters cared about the course of Reconstruction, but like many northerners they cared more about economic matters by the late 1870s. Hence Williams's supporters focused on class more conspicuously than they did on race, contrasting their candidate's blue jeans to Harrison's "Broadway fashion." In this respect, ironically enough, Harrison had something in common with his old nemesis, Nancy Clem. Neither seemed to understand that dressing to the nines was in poor taste in the middle of a depression.[28]

Would a nattily attired Governor Harrison have pardoned William J. Abrams? Probably not, unless Abrams had agreed to talk. In any case, given the election results, it was up to Blue Jeans to bestow or withdraw "good will." The new governor visited Abrams at the Northern Prison, evidently more than once, hoping to convince him to "break his stubborn silence" in exchange for release. He failed but issued a pardon anyway, persuaded by Abrams's "unexceptionally good" behavior as a prisoner, petitions from constituents, including eight former members of Abrams's jury, and the jury's original request (now nearly due) that Abrams receive only a ten-year sentence.[29]

Public commentary vacillated between hope that the newly liberated felon would reveal what had happened at Cold Spring and certainty that Clem had secured Abrams's pardon in exchange for his silence. A letter to the *News* from "One of Your Readers" deplored "the idiotic action of an old man"—that is, the state's seventy-year-old governor. "Abrams claims that the newspapers have treated him badly, but, doubtless, appreciates the Clem-ency of our blue and noble governor," the *Herald* snidely remarked. Writing under her own name, albeit from the relative safety of rural Cartersburg (a town some 20 mile west of Indianapolis), Lena Williams sarcastically offered her "compliments to Governor Williams. . . . I should like to introduce him to Nancy E. Clem. I should like to hear her thank him for liberating Abrams."[30]

A woman did in fact bear a great deal of responsibility for Abrams's liberation, but she was not Nancy Clem. Even as they speculated about Clem's influence, Indianapolis papers credited reporter Laura Ream, who commanded significant influence in Democratic circles and who counted Daniel Voorhees, Thomas Hendricks, and Blue Jeans Williams among her personal friends. "The lady news writer" had never succeeded in interviewing the notorious Mrs. Clem, but she did talk—at least once—with Abrams. Ream became convinced of his innocence or at least concluded that his punishment did not fit his crime. While the details of her campaign are unknown—largely the result of a tornado that demolished her house and destroyed her papers—Ream dedicated several years to Abrams's cause. Whatever might have been said privately, no one—Democrat or Republican—publicly chastised "Miss Ream" for her role in gaining Abrams's release. Just as surprisingly no one publicly suggested that the now fifty-year-old Ream had a crush on Bill Abrams. "Miss Ream," the *News* reported, learned of the pardon on July 4, "and this news was the capsheaf to her enjoyment of the day."[31]

If Governor Williams hoped that Ream's involvement would quiet public reaction to his decision, he was sadly mistaken. Pundits returned to familiar arguments, suggesting that Abrams's pardon would only embolden criminals. As the *Herald*'s reference to "our blue and noble governor" made clear, such commentary often assumed a partisan cast. Republicans styled themselves as upholders of law and order, condemning the Democratic administration that pardoned Abrams. "Since our governor has by his actions declared that murderers shall not be punished according to law, murders are on the increase," ONE OF YOUR READERS wrote to the *News*. "The lives of the people of Indianapolis, nay, the whole state, are endangered, and no longer protected by the law as executed. The demoralizing influence of our present executive is too apparent not to press upon our minds the question, 'What can we, the citizens, do to protect ourselves against the lawless which our state executive so persistently protects?'" ONE OF YOUR READERS hinted that extralegal action might be necessary; after all, the citizens of Seymour, a town in southern Indiana, had recently lynched several members of the Reno Gang.[32]

As Abrams made his way south from Michigan City, the hope remained that he might yet reveal what he knew of the Young murders and in the process implicate Nancy Clem. He did neither. As his train approached Indianapolis, Abrams became "exceedingly nervous" and "gazed eagerly from the windows on both sides as though looking for familiar landmarks." He "said that he felt as if he had risen from the grave." Still, nearly a decade after the infamous event, he stubbornly maintained both his innocence and his ignorance. "I know nothing whatever of the murder," he explained to a "friend" who met him at the Indianapolis depot and who lost no time in reporting the substance of his conversation to city newspapers. Asked if he might testify against Nancy Clem, he replied, "I never did her any harm, and am not going to now." Then he boarded the train for New Augusta en route to his brother's farm in Pike Township. He "comes home an afflicted man," the *Journal* reported, "his child is dead, and his wife has divorced him and remarried." A correspondent for the *News* sighed, "His release will not aid in bringing the Young murderers to justice unless something turns up which will show all his assertions of last night to have been false."[33]

As prospects for re-prosecuting Clem for the Young murders faded and the likelihood she would escape the larceny charge became increasingly evident, Benjamin Harrison, the man who had vowed to never again prosecute a woman, had an idea. He suggested that Clem could be indicted for perjury. After all, in her deposition in his law office she had denied ever seeing the notes that Hinkson claimed she snatched out of his son-in-law's hands. In the meantime, Henry Cook, the gambler, joined the list of plaintiffs suing Clem for failing to repay borrowed money. "Do not talk 'greed' and 'large per cents.' to the present victims; please wait and hear the evidence. They do not yearn for sympathy so much as for justice and their own preservation," he wrote the editor of the *Herald*.[34]

As both plaintiffs and the general public—eager to see her tried in both civil and criminal court—complained of "the law's delay," Clem continued to serve as a reference point for discussions of law and order. The *Herald* likened Kate Cobb, a Connecticut woman accused of poisoning her husband, to Nancy Clem. "Everybody speaks well of her before the murder. Even her enemies admit that she was a kind wife, a devoted mother, a generous friend and neighbor." Here the comparison faltered, once again suggesting that Clem simply did not fit the cultural frameworks nineteenth-century commentators invoked when tried to understand women who had committed crimes. Clem, if indeed she was guilty as charged, had not used poison. Her alleged victim was not her husband.[35]

Law soldiered on. In February 1879, Eliza J. King's suit "against the Clem banditti" resulted in an award of $6,000 in favor of the plaintiff. In April, Cook, too, won his case—after a trial in which Clem took the stand. "This remarkable woman was as calm and self-possessed, as shrewd and strong, as when being prosecuted for the murder of Mr. and Mrs. Young," the *Sentinel* marveled. "The lawyers could not rattle her in the least, though the ordeal lasted two hours."[36]

Criminal proceedings against Clem, amended to include perjury in addition to larceny, were postponed due to the trial of a man accused of murdering his former lover. In the meantime, the *Herald* took heart in the conviction of Anna Hayden Smallman, a San Francisco confidence woman it termed "a rival of Mrs. Clem." The "elegantly dressed" Smallman had "a suave manner, fine figure, and handsome face," the *Herald* explained. "Her face, always sweet to look upon, had assumed a thoughtful expression and her manner was that of an injured woman. Had she studied to enlist from the outset the jury's sympathies she could hardly have appeared better." To make its point, the *Herald* described Smallman's trial as "quite a matinee. . . . Could such beauty fail to win?" it asked. Much to the correspondent's relief, it did. "California justice occasionally is awake," he noted approvingly. Indiana justice, he implied, might awaken as well.[37]

Clem's portrayal in the pages of the press provided one indication of the direction in which Indiana justice might turn. Newspaper reports stripped away any hint of sentimentality or refinement. Gone was any reference to beauty. "Mrs. Clem . . . is a portly woman of more than middle size," explained the *San Francisco Bulletin*. "She has grown much fatter than she was when tried for murder a few years ago," noted the *Herald*. The *News* concurred. "Mrs. Clem is somewhat stouter than when she first appeared in the role of defendant to a criminal proceeding twelve years ago, but aside from a settled hardness in the face, which robs her of whatever claims she may have had to good looks, she has not greatly aged since then." Whatever resemblance these depictions bore to reality, they functioned less as factual descriptions than as moral indicators. The once-genteel murderess now appeared "as to dress and figure, like the buxom wife of a thriving countryman."[38]

■ ■ ■

A reporter for the *Saturday Herald* likened the newly released Abrams to Rip Van Winkle. The *Journal* agreed: "Every improvement that came within his range of vision was noticed, and as he had not been in Indianapolis since 1869, it may readily be imagined that he saw little that was familiar."[39] The pardoned felon did indeed confront an alien landscape when he returned from the Northern Prison in 1878. Nine years earlier he had left behind a city of forty-eight thousand; now its inhabitants numbered nearly seventy-five thousand. The liberated prisoner could not have missed the "Dolly Varden" courthouse, completed in 1876, or the vacant lot on Washington Street where the recently condemned capitol building had stood. The erection of the new state house for $200,000 less than the $2 million appropriated for it would stand as Blue Jeans Williams's crowning achievement.[40]

Numerous commercial and industrial "improvements" would have greeted Bill Abrams upon his arrival, and as various accounts of the Indianapolis's "rise and progress" made clear, they would only continue to multiply as the city emerged from the nearly decade-long "Great Depression." New commercial blocks, such as the magnificent flatiron Vance Block at the intersection of Washington, Pennsylvania, and Virginia Streets graced the city's downtown. The Spencer House, site of the Abramses' and the Young's double wedding, remained a local landmark but now competed with newer ventures like the Enterprise Hotel (operated until recently by Lena Miller and Eliza King), the Grand Hotel, the Brunswick Hotel, and the Wagner Hotel;

in 1880 the dazzling New Denison Hotel would dwarf them all. (The Denison, at various junctures, would host the meetings of the Indianapolis Literary Club, founded in 1877. George Chapman, Jonathan Gordon, and William Pinckney Fishback were among its charter members; Benjamin Harrison joined soon after.) Joining these various commercial monuments were the equally resplendent buildings that housed various fraternal lodges: the Masons, the Odd Fellows, the Knights of Pythias. Some portions of this fraternal landscape (for example, Odd Fellows Hall, "a sort of cross between a Gothic chapel and the Taj Mehal," completed in 1856) predated Abrams's conviction, but much of it was new.[41]

A new belt railway, the brainchild of Mayor Caven, encircled the city. Indianapolis's more than eight hundred factories included fixtures such as the Western Machine Works and Kingan's meat-packing plant, both of which expanded substantially during the late 1860s and early 1870s, and James M. Buchanan's agricultural implements manufactory. They included newcomers such as Ott & Madden, makers of sofa beds (the invention of "ingenious mechanican" L. W. Ott); the Adams Packing Company, producers of "mince meat, fruit-butters, jellies [and] preserves"; and the pharmaceutical manufacturing firm of Eli Lilly & Co., which *Manufacturing and Mercantile Resources of Indianapolis* would describe (correctly) in 1883 as "An Enterprise Ranking among the leading and Most Successful in the Country."[42]

By the late 1870s the city spilled far beyond its original boundary, encompassing nearly 20 square miles by end of the following decade. This recently acquired acreage accommodated the factories, warehouses, and stockyards that clustered on the edges of the growing metropolis as well as the equally numerous subdivisions (or "additions," as booster publications preferred to call them) that sheltered the city's growing population. The end result was a more segregated municipality, one in which divisions of class, race, and ethnicity, though never fixed or stable, were more firmly entrenched in the Circle City's topography. On the west side stood an expanding African American community; to the south and southeast, existing Irish and German enclaves put down deeper roots.[43]

If neighborhoods differentiated by race and ethnicity were nothing new, class mattered in a way it had not before. Members of Indianapolis's elite, including Benjamin Harrison and William Pinckney Fishback, built Victorian mansions on the city's "fashionable streets"; Harrison's handsome new Italianate home on North Delaware, completed in 1875, cost nearly $30,000.

It did nothing to diminish his reputation as an aristocrat and lent credence to the claim—not circulated until the 1888 presidential campaign—that at the height of the 1877 railroad strike he had said "that one dollar a day was enough for any working man."[44] Other wealthy Indianapolitans settled in exclusive neighborhoods such as Woodruff Place. Irvington, a streetcar suburb laid out in 1870, catered to middle-class professionals, while Brightwood, the addition to which Aaron Clem moved in mid-decade, developed from land he owned, was decisively working class, dominated by the families of men employed by the "Bee Line" railroad. With progress, of course, came poverty, as the recent bread riot and railroad strike made clear. The distinction between a locality populated by "workingmen's cottages" and a slum was often in the eyes of the beholder, since most homes, even those inhabited by the city's poorest residents, were single-family dwellings. By 1880 the old North Alabama Street neighborhood was by no means a slum, but it had lost much of its heterogeneity. Although still home to prosperous tradesmen (including Matthew Hartman and "Mrs. Clem's broker," former county treasurer Arthur Wright, now a carpet dealer) it included no white-collar professionals save a Baptist minister.[45]

Clem's release from prison predated Abrams's by four years, but she, too, had returned to a changed city, one in which her position was far from secure. In part this outcome was predictable; meeting a flesh-and-blood murderess was a far different matter than reading about her in the papers. Like the ladies who moved to a different train car, many people preferred to avoid the encounter. And, indeed, Clem fell from social grace in part because her brand of "capitalism"—exposed by both civil suits and her forthcoming perjury trial—dispelled any lingering doubts regarding her guilt in the Cold Spring affair. In part, her descent from "noble specimen" to "buxom wife" can be explained by the fact that her business dealings so blatantly defied the tenets of genteel femininity; Clem failed to understand that street brokers could not be ladies. But by the late 1870s there was less space for self-fashioning. During the five and a half years in which she occupied various jail and prison cells, Clem had remained outside of real time and space, unmoored from the usual markers of social distinctions. Her ill-advised return to "capitalism" aside, the same changes that rendered Bill Abrams a veritable Rip Van Winkle made it difficult for her to play the lady outside prison walls. Upcountry heritage, criminal history, and metropolitan "rise and progress" made for a potent mix, consigning her to liminal social and residential spaces. Neither elite nor working-class nor part of an increasingly numerous educated bourgeoisie, Clem remained downtown, no longer the dwelling place of genteel or even, perhaps, respectable people, "roosting" over a grocery store. Left to her own devices, she failed to grasp the nuances of genteel performance, overplaying her hand by dressing too fashionably and promenading too conspicuously. Her new clients were "guileless old grangers . . . capable widows, and shrewd spinsters" not only because they were "guileless" but because the social geography of later nineteenth-century Indianapolis rendered encounters between leading men and the wife of a sometimes grocery clerk, sometimes grocer increasingly improbable.

In the spring of 1880, the *People* published an illustration of Nancy Clem to accompany its coverage of her perjury trial. It pictured what recent press accounts had described in words: a fashionably dressed, middle-aged woman, perhaps a bit portly. It captured Clem's "glare of defiance." Its caption—"A Relic of the Cold Spring Horror"—aptly summarized Clem's circumstances, perhaps even more so than the portraitist realized. True, she was a relic of a twelve-year-old crime that had never been decisively solved. She was also a relic of an older Indianapolis, one in which the Harrisons were the rough social equals of the Clems, a half-literate southerner could still be respectable, and the status of "old settler" a mark of social worth.[46]

Clem's sixth criminal trial assembled a mix of familiar and unfamiliar characters. Preoccupied with his political career (in that very year he would be elected to the Senate), Benjamin Harrison remained more or less true to his pledge not to prosecute another woman—if one discounts the civil suit in which he represented Hezekiah Hinkson. Thirty-four-year-old John Babb Elam, the recently elected Marion County prosecuting attorney (he would later join Harrison's law firm), argued the case for the state, assisted by W. A. Brown, an attorney who left few traces in the historical record. The defense included two old hands. Frederick Knefler's appearance might have been predicted. In a curious twist, albeit one the city's legal fraternity would have found unsurprising, John S. Duncan, now an established private attorney, joined Clem's defense.[47]

Opening skirmishes began in late February 1880, when Clem's attorneys asked for a change of venue, citing widespread local coverage and community prejudice. "The principal business of Indianapolis," the *Saturday Herald* quipped, "seems to be to try Mrs. Clem." Edward C. Buskirk, judge

Indianapolis's *People* published this image on the front page of its March 20, 1880, issue, during Clem's trial for perjury. The portrait visually confirmed newspaper commentary that described Clem as "portly" and aptly captured her "glare of defiance." Courtesy of the Indiana State Library.

of the Marion County Criminal Court, denied the motion. The defense succeeded however in gaining a "change of court"; Buskirk agreed to step aside in favor of Judge Joshua G. Adams, of the Nineteenth Circuit. The absence of two witnesses, the daughters of Mary Gohl, Clem's laundress, further delayed the proceedings. After a week, the presiding jurist had had enough. "Judge Adams says that the trial shall go on if all the witnesses are absent," the *News* reported. "One that knows" claimed the Gohl sisters were in Chicago, sent there by Mrs. Clem.[48]

The trial finally began—without the sisters—on March 15, 1880. On the witness stand Mary Gohl denied that Clem met with Hinkson's son-in-law on the evening she had supposedly torn up the now-famous promissory notes—a statement called into question by another witness's testimony that Clem had given Gohl $10 "to keep her mouth shut." Frank testified in his wife's defense, denying that she ever said, "I've got those notes." Then Clem herself took the stand and "emphatically and broadly denied every material allegation made by the witnesses for the state."[49]

Clem's trial for perjury was exceedingly well attended. "Such a jam of people as is present in the criminal court today has never been there before," the *News* observed. "Not even the murder trials attracted such a throng." This was partly a matter of capacity; the new courthouse, which accommodated many more spectators than its predecessor, made better attendance possible. Lena Miller's testimony commanded particular attention. "These old partners, having enjoyed very intimate relations as friends in former times, were well posted as to the weak points in each other's armor, and neither was adverse to striking below the belt," the *Herald*'s coverage of Clem's "exciting trial" explained. "So they made it interesting for the crowd of spectators in attendance. Of course, each denied all the other said, and gave the denial all the emphasis possible."[50]

Clem's notoriety brought East Coast journalists to Indianapolis to cover what was on the surface a run-of-the-mill perjury trial. They included an artist employed by the *New York Graphic*. Once again, natural disaster upstaged Mrs. Clem. The Great Chicago Fire had pushed coverage of her third trial off the pages; now, the same cyclone that destroyed Laura Ream's house changed the illustrator's plans. The *Graphic* published images depicting the storm's aftermath but not the planned sketches of Clem's trial. One may have survived; very likely it was the *Graphic*'s portrait that graced the *People*'s front page.[51]

After six hours of closing arguments (the contents of which have not survived) Clem spent the night of March 19 in jail to await the verdict, as procedure required. Neither Frank nor Albert was in the courtroom when the members of the jury announced their decision. They found her guilty of perjury and fixed her punishment at a $100 fine and four years imprisonment. As usual, Clem "did not betray any emotion." "We will apply for a new trial, will we not?" she asked one of her attorneys. "Yes, madam," he replied. She then asked that he send for Frank.[52]

Judge Adams denied the motion for a new trial. There would be no appeal. On April 11, 1880, Clem began serving her four-year sentence. According to a thoroughly disillusioned Jonathan W. Gordon, "it isn't half what she deserves."[53]

CHAPTER FOURTEEN

Aunty Smith

W hen Nancy Clem crossed the threshold of the Indiana Reformatory Institution for Women and Girls she joined a grand social experiment. The latest addition to the city's institutional landscape, the nation's first prison designated solely for women, placed Indiana in the forefront of modern methods of detention. It stood "at the head of establishments of that kind in the United States," one observer explained, a "model to be followed by such houses of correction everywhere." Intended to rehabilitate rather than merely incarcerate, the Reformatory was notable in second respect: its administration was entirely in the hands of women. Thus, in the spring of 1880, Superintendent Sarah Jane Smith, a "mild-looking old Quakeress" known to the inmates as "Aunty Smith," assumed the challenge of reforming the notorious Mrs. Clem.[1]

■ ■ ■

Like most such experiments, the Female Reformatory was a response to the inadequacies of existing practice. Judging by the scandal emanating from the Southern Prison, which housed the state's female offenders, reform was long overdue. Lurid tales of the goings-on at "Old Jeff" circulated widely in the late 1860s, chronicling the "high carnivals" that regularly transpired, evidently with the knowledge, consent, and occasional participation of the warden, a Civil War veteran named James B. Meriwether. Drunken prison guards indulged their sadistic desires by whipping half-naked women. They "amused themselves on Sundays" by forcing female inmates to run nude "Olympic" races. Amusements of this sort naturally culminated in "outrages" and other "dark deeds." "My reader, this is not fiction," J. Harrie Banka's *State Prison Life* insisted. Some of these deeds generated profits as well as gratification; corrupt prison officials ran a prostitution ring based on the unwilling participation of female prisoners. The appointment of a new warden, Colonel Lawrence S. Shuler, put an end to these abuses; Banka devoted Part II of his treatise ("Advantages of the New") to chronicling the "sunshine" Shuler brought to prison life. Clem herself basked in the sunshine of Shuler's compassionate supervision, having had the good fortune to arrive shortly after he assumed charge of the Jeffersonville facility.[2]

Nevertheless, proposals for a separate women's prison, long advocated by Quaker reformers, continued to gain public support as the "horrors of the old system" came to light. In May 1869, only a few months after Shuler assumed leadership of the Southern Prison, the Indiana legislature passed a bill authorizing the construction of a separate facility for female inmates.[3] Four years later, the Indiana Reformatory Institution for Women and Girls opened its doors, and the women residents of the Southern Prison boarded a train to Indianapolis.

They entered an institution designed to effect their reformation. Inspired by widely held faith in the transformative power of nature and in keeping with a half century of asylum-building tradition, the Reformatory's board of managers situated the new facility on a 15-acre site adjacent to the county orphan asylum, 2 miles east of downtown Indianapolis. (This relatively isolated setting offered the added benefit of discouraging attempts at escape.) The building itself reflected prison reformers' belief in the value of persuasion over coercion. The managers commissioned the architect Isaac Hodgson to design a structure that was "graceful and imposing" but "not very prison-like." Dispensing for the most part with the flourishes that characterized his Dolly Varden courthouse, Hodgson adopted what his contemporaries called a "modern or American utilitarian" style. The result was a 530-by-116-foot building that resembled an oversized Victorian mansion.[4]

This, too, was deliberate. Like the benefactors who founded "homes" for a variety of institutional populations—elderly men and women, orphaned children, "rescued" prostitutes, patients afflicted with mental illness—the founders of the Female Reformatory took an idealized middle-class home as their model. As Superintendent Smith saw it, staff and inmates ideally constituted "a quiet orderly family." Believing that "refinement" itself would speed reformation, Aunty Smith did her best to replicate bourgeois domesticity inside the Reformatory's walls. Inmates sat at tables covered with linen tablecloths and decorated with vases of flowers; they ate from plates of "simple but attractive china." This homelike setting served both vocational and inspirational purposes; Smith and her colleagues endeavored to prepare their charges "to occupy positions assigned to them by God, viz., wives, mothers and educators of children." Tempering idealism with realism, they recognized that most inmates would first be released to the "homes" of employers, where they would "occupy positions" as servants, before they could hope to inhabit homes of their own. Thus the Reformatory trained its residents in various domestic pursuits, rejecting labor-saving machinery

The Indiana Reformatory Institution for Women and Girls. Designed by architect Isaac Hodgson, the building that housed the nation's first women's prison (opened in 1873) was intended to be "graceful and imposing" but "not very prisonlike." Clem served her sentence for perjury here where, in contrast to her previous incarcerations, she received no special treatment. Conditions had deteriorated considerably by the time she arrived in 1880. *The Development of Public Charities and Correction in the State of Indiana, 1792–1910* (Jeffersonville, Ind.: Indiana Reformatory Printing Trade School, 1910), 94. Courtesy of the Indiana State Library.

because "it is best for them to learn these much-needed branches of labor thoroughly by hand, hoping it may help them to get homes when their term expires."[5]

From the beginning, Smith and her lieutenants had to make compromises. They initially rejected prison uniforms as being unduly degrading and therefore detrimental to reformation. They were, however, equally horrified by prisoners who arrived from Jeffersonville attired in "white tucked skirts and morning wrappers" bearing "trunks full of fine clothing." Their solution was to require inmates to don "simple, well-fitting dresses, protected by tidy aprons"—clothing that, despite the disavowal of uniforms, marked its wearers as prisoners. More important, the Reformatory's founders had hoped to house juvenile offenders and adult inmates in separate facilities. But a stingy state legislature forced them to make do with one structure instead of two. Smith divided the "not very prison-like" building into "Reformatory" and "Penal" departments, each of which had "its own kitchen, laundry, and yard"—one for delinquent girls and one for adult felons. In practice it proved impossible to keep the two populations separate; annual reports routinely lamented the inability to shield still-impressionable girls from hardened criminals.[6]

As their rhetoric suggested, Reformatory administrators envisioned their ideal inmate as a wayward girl, young enough to contemplate a future position assigned to her by God. While they gave lip service to the notion that *all* prisoners could be "reclaimed," Smith and her assistants focused their emotional energies on juvenile offenders, certain of older inmates' corrosive influence, ambivalent about grown women's rehabilitative potential. Whether Aunty Smith believed the notorious Mrs. Clem capable of reformation or even worth the effort is an open question. Nevertheless the law she had championed required the Reformatory to accommodate all of the state's female offenders. In April 1880, whatever her thoughts on the matter, she had no choice but to add Clem to her roster.

Assigned as a matter of policy to the Penal Department, Clem joined approximately forty adult prisoners, most in their late teens and early twenties. At age fifty, she was the eldest of the institution's approximately two hundred inmates, the vast majority girls incarcerated for various forms of delinquent behavior. If a regimen designed for adolescents poorly served the needs of mature women, the Reformatory's accoutrements and routines proved particularly ill suited to its most famous inmate. Clem had never claimed membership in the "best society," but previous exposure to china plates and linen tablecloths rendered her immune to their transformative powers. She was already a wife and mother; she was, in fact, as one newspaper reporter sarcastically observed, a "crowing grandmother." She was a former employer of servants rather than a prospective servant herself. She expected, and had received, special treatment.

This time she would not receive such treatment. During previous confinements Clem enjoyed delicacies procured by relatives, friends, and, by some accounts, jailers; now she ate bread that "was at times very bad and some times good" and "victuals [that were] generally not good, very cheap and very poor."[7] If conditions at "Old Jeff" had allowed her to play the lady, the Reformatory—despite linen tablecloths, china, and other trappings of "refinement"—offered no such option. Clem wore the same simple dress and apron as everyone else.

■ ■ ■

In a way, her arrival was overdue. Had she not been remanded to the Marion County Jail while awaiting her fifth trial, Clem, too, would have been transferred from the Southern Prison to the Female Reformatory when it opened in 1873. Conditions had deteriorated by the time she reached what many considered her rightful destination. While the Reformatory's 1881 *Annual Report* described the Penal Department's "large, well lighted rooms, letting in the cheering rays of the sun," an investigative committee appointed by the Indiana House of Representatives that same year painted a different picture. Committee members discovered dirty and dark "cells" and food supplies ravaged by insects and other vermin. "The printed reports of the institution have been extremely rose-colored from the beginning," the *Cincinnati Commercial* observed.[8]

More serious allegations surfaced as the investigation continued, revealing a disciplinary regime very much at odds with stated principles, which rejected physical punishment in favor of gentle persuasion, "constant employment," and "the loving power of the Christian religion."[9] Staff members, including Smith herself, allegedly struck and kicked uncooperative inmates, at times dragging them by the hair. Worst of all was "the bath" in which handcuffed women and girls were hosed down with cold water. The brutality of these punishments and their sexualized nature ("stripped naked," newspapers continually reported) suggested that the Female Reformatory was no better than Old Jeff had been under the Meriwether administration. Dubbing the Reformatory "Another Andersonville," the Republican *Commercial* summarized conditions thus: "The angelic Aunty Smith jerks sick babies out of bed by the arms and ducks big girls with cold water and spanks them. She strips children naked and beats them with a strap and pounds their heads against the wall until their hearing is sometimes permanently injured." The *Commercial* lost no time in noting that the Reformatory, while signed into law by a Republican governor, operated under the auspices of a Democratic administration, with only one "representative of Republicanism" on its board. More sympathetic observers claimed that the investigation was politically motivated given that "the institution," as the *Kansas City Star* put it, "[has] always been under democratic control." Still others claimed that Democrats within the legislature initiated the inquiry and that "Republicans are enjoying the fight as spectators, and are perfectly willing that Democrats shall convict Democrats of mismanagement and incapacity to govern the benevolent and penal institutions of the State."[10]

Among the current and former inmates interviewed by the committee was the notorious Mrs. Clem. Betraying no sense of irony, the *Chicago Inter Ocean* reported that the testimony furnished by Clem, "now undergoing a four-year sentence for falsely swearing" was "a fair sample for all." No one pulled Clem's hair or subjected her to the "bath." But she claimed to have seen others brutally whipped, even to witnessing Aunty Smith yank an inmate out of bed by the hair. Clem herself "was forced to wash and work very hard as punishment."[11]

If Clem had been the committee's sole informant, the furor would have died down quickly. But as witness after witness recounted stories of hair-pulling, beating, and waterboarding ("They threw [water] in my face until it strangled me," one former inmate testified), the future of the Female Reformatory, especially of its current administrators, looked increasingly grim. "If the half is true that is being written down as testimony in the case, officers of the institution need reforming quite as much as the inmates," the *Cincinnati Gazette* observed. Some suggested that the sixty-something Aunty Smith was too old to manage the institution. Others claimed she had "become hardened by constant intercourse and association with fallen women, and now under her placid Quaker exterior lurks a cruel disposition."[12]

In the end Aunty Smith prevailed. A veteran administrator with long experience in lobbying for benevolent causes, she speedily orchestrated an effective response. Smith assembled her own roster of inmate witnesses, who testified to kind treatment and wholesome meals. By most accounts it was her own appearance before the committee that turned the tide in her favor. "Mrs. Smith's testimony seems to have made a very good impression upon the public," the *Commercial* observed. Smith explained that an epidemic of "self-abuse" (masturbation) among the girls necessitated drastic action; "I could not stop it by any other mode of punishment than by using cold water." She admitted to slapping self-abusing inmates in the face and beating them with shoes, but only with soft-soled slippers, which she exhibited before the committee. "There is now a general insurrection going on in the Institution since the commencement of this investigation," Smith complained.[13]

Smith's job had been at stake, but the superintendent had charmed a hostile group of legislators. Institutional life returned to normal, and Smith's subsequent *Annual Report* proclaimed that the Reformatory management had been "fully exonerated." Nevertheless the investigation left behind scars. Smith hoped that her successors could avoid future "ordeals" based on "the suggestion of some . . . ungrateful inmate confined for murder, perjury or theft." She complained that the investigation "so demoralized our quiet, orderly family that little Reformatory influence could be exerted. We fear it will take years to repair the injury."[14]

■ ■ ■

Nancy Clem was now the very person her former attorney John Hanna once had valorized: a woman who stood before the washtub. As she told the investigative committee, she considered her assignment to the Reformatory's laundry "punishment." She was correct. Laundering was hot, dirty, back-breaking labor; washing other people's tidy aprons meant soiling one's own. Of all the employments the institution offered—sewing, knitting, chair caning, cooking, and gardening—laundry was the worst. "This is not a favorite branch of industry," an annual report acknowledged.[15]

The laundry was indeed an industry. Reformatory laundresses washed their sister prisoners' clothes. But they also took in washing from local residents willing to risk injury to their garments and linens in exchange for a discounted price and the satisfaction of supporting a good cause. Still, as management saw it, the value of the institution's laundry was moral, not monetary; "it does not bring us any net profit in financial terms." Moral profits came in two forms. Aunty Smith believed in the redemptive power of labor, or as she put it, "constant employment." A stint in the prison laundry work also promised inmates "good homes" upon their release. "Many come to the institution almost incapable of even washing their own clothing," Smith explained, "but leave it qualified to take charge of any family washing—at all times a recommendation to a good home."[16]

Clem must have resented the servile associations of laundry work as much or more than the physical toil it extracted. Washing was the chore middle-class housewives were most likely to delegate to servants—hence Smith's comment that a qualified laundress could "at all times" find "a good home." As a young widow, Clem had done her boarders' laundry. Later in life she hired various "girls," including Jane Sizemore, to do her washing. Even as she "roosted" above her brother-in-law's grocery, she had employed a laundress (and allegedly paid her an extra $10 to keep her mouth shut).

In late-nineteenth-century Indianapolis, as elsewhere in the nation, laundry work was largely the province of Irish and African American women; a prison laundress occupied the same symbolic footing. Smith and her assistants were as likely to disregard racial and ethnic hierarchies as they were to follow them, a choice that reflected Quaker belief in racial equality. White as well as black inmates could be found toiling alongside

Clem in the laundry; white as well as black inmates worked at chair caning, sewing, and cooking.[17] Still, as Clem's complaint suggested, Smith probably envisioned particular work assignments as means of inducing humility. What better way to take a high-class prostitute down a peg than assign her to the prison laundry? What better way to put the notorious Mrs. Clem, a woman who believed herself entitled to special treatment, in her place?

■ ■ ■

News of Nancy Clem surfaced periodically after the legislative investigation concluded. When a religious revival swept through the city's churches and Female Reformatory in the summer of 1881, the celebrity inmate was among the converts. "If the signs fail not, a divine hand has been laid notably on the city of Indianapolis," the *Journal* observed. Clem made another "public confession of [her] faith in Christ" when a second revivalist visited the prison a year later.[18] Early in 1883, a prisoner known as "Black Jennie" fingered Clem as the mastermind behind an unsuccessful "insurrection" supposedly involving "the most vicious characters in the laundry room."[19] Nothing came of the accusation and word of the alleged rebellion died down quickly.

In 1881, after years of lobbying by woman's rights activists, the Indiana legislature passed an act giving married women ownership over the wages they earned—a law that certainly would have been of interest to Nancy Clem had she been a free woman. But Frank Clem rendered these new rights irrelevant. Only a few months after circulating rumors of the abortive Reformatory uprising, newspapers reported another "sensation," this one with definite merit: Nancy Clem's husband had filed for divorce. Some wondered why he had waited so long. "It seemed strange to many people that he should have remained constant to his wife during all the years that she was fighting for her life on the charge of the Young murder, and since then in her succeeding troubles, to ask for a separation now," the *St. Louis Globe-Democrat* observed.[20]

Convinced that Frank was "the victim of all sorts of rascalities," Nancy contested the proceedings. But there was little she could do from behind bars, and her felony conviction for perjury gave him legal grounds. "One who knows" suggested that he was taking a risk: "There will be 'tremolo music and red fire,' if she unlocks her lips, which she now threatens to do," the *News* reported. An article published some fifty years later offered greater specificity, claiming that Clem had warned her husband, "If you divorce me,

I will tell." The allusion to a possibly apocryphal conversation suggested, as had the *Saturday Herald*, that Frank had somehow been involved in his wife's business dealings, perhaps even in the Young murder. If such a threat passed Nancy's lips, it proved ineffectual. "He divorced her and she didn't tell." The divorce, initiated on March 23, 1883, was granted a mere two weeks later, on April 9.[21]

Clem made the papers yet again the following month, when Beulah Patton, Albert's estranged wife, appeared before a grand jury. Patton testified that she had been forced at gunpoint to sign a mortgage transferring the family property—and any claim she had to it—to Frank's attorney. Newspaper reports of the affair were tantalizingly vague, failing to specify *who* had wielded "a drawn revolver" as a "persuasive argument." Had not Clem taken her daughter-in-law's part, Albert would have been a likely suspect. But her willingness to testify on Beulah's behalf suggested that the culprit was Frank. So, too, did the *Cincinnati Enquirer*'s observation that the "considerable bitterness" engendered by divorce "accounts for Mrs. Clem's present effort to get her late husband into trouble." Frank seems to have stayed out of trouble. Evidently the grand jury seconded his lawyer's opinion that Patton's claim was "preposterous." No charges were ever filed; the anticipated "very interesting developments" that promised to shed "light upon the Young murder" did not materialize. Beulah returned to her new home in Chicago, where she died six years later.[22]

Frank left town.

CHAPTER FIFTEEN

Mrs. Dr. Patterson

Aunty Smith must have had a keen sense of poetic justice. She discharged her most famous inmate on September 12, 1883, the fifteenth anniversary of the Cold Spring murders.[1]

The beneficiary of recently passed legislation that shaved time off convicts' sentences in exchange for good behavior, the newly liberated Nancy Clem moved with Albert to rented quarters, a multifamily brick building west of downtown on the edge of an expanding African American neighborhood. She attempted to preserve a modicum of dignity by listing herself in city directories as the widow of Franklin Clem.[2] Frank was very much alive, though he put a fair number of miles between himself and his former spouse. For a time he lived in Louisville; in 1887, when Nancy once again petitioned unsuccessfully to invalidate the divorce, rumor had it he was in Winfield, Kansas. By the early 1890s Frank had returned to his home state, but he chose to settle in Anderson, a town about 40 miles northeast of Indianapolis, where two of his brothers resided. Although some accounts claimed he hadn't smiled since the Young murders, he recovered sufficiently by mid-decade to court and marry a fifty-five-year-old widow. Divorce and distance restored his reputation. The man who may have held a pistol to his daughter-in-law's head was once again a "respected citizen."[3]

Nancy Clem was not. Friends and family once convinced of her innocence now abandoned her. Only Albert remained loyal. "She was always a good mother to me," he insisted.[4]

■ ■ ■

In the late 1880s or early 1890s, Clem once again went into business. Perhaps Albert, still a plasterer, had difficulty supporting her. Perhaps his mother sought an outlet for her famous "avariciousness," what some would term a "monomania." Perhaps she remained determined to leave her son a sizable inheritance. Or perhaps Albert's remarriage in 1892 prompted the self-identified "home woman" to leave home for life on the road.[5] Whatever the reason, she became a traveling saleswoman for Slavin's Infallible Female Tonic.

Slavin's was the brainchild of another striver. Michael Slavin, the son of an Irish day laborer, had worked as a driver for the city fire department since the age of sixteen. Some twenty years later he left his job for what he must have hoped would be a more lucrative pursuit: in 1888 he and two partners applied for and received a patent for the "female tonic."[6]

Like similar medicines, Slavin's Infallible Female Tonic was advertised as a remedy "for all female complaints," including "weakness, change of life," and "painful or suppressed menstruation." Both its name and the symptoms it purportedly cured implied none-too-subtly that Slavin intended his concoction to be used as an abortifacient. Not only was it "infallible," it was a "Female Regulator" that could be taken to treat "suppressed menstruation." As its rather ecumenical description suggested, however, Slavin's formula was also a "tonic" intended to boost the energies of tired housewives, mothers, servants, and seamstresses. Clem herself claimed that "it was for the blood."[7]

The purveyors of various types of what one historian has called "black market birth control" included large firms like Goodyear and Sears & Roebuck but also numerous smaller concerns, many of them headed by immigrant and female entrepreneurs. Ostensibly outlawed by the Comstock Act of 1873, which banned the sale and distribution of "obscene" materials, businesses like Slavin's, always vulnerable to prosecution, survived through euphemistic advertising—and because consumers very much wanted their products. Nevertheless, "S.I.F.T." was one of many entries into a crowded market."[8] The tonic failed to bring riches to its creator; after nearly a decade in the patent medicine business Slavin was still living in "a modest little cottage" in a mixed-race working-class neighborhood on the city's west side, not far from where Clem had lived with Albert. Indeed, he would return to the fire department in 1901, leaving the tonic business in the hands of a daughter.[9]

Female remedies would seem to require female drummers, but how Nancy Clem came to join Slavin's sales force remains a mystery. A longtime resident of the city, Slavin could not have been ignorant of her notoriety. Perhaps he was among those who considered Clem an unjustly persecuted victim. Or perhaps he figured that if he wanted an effective saleswoman, he could do no better. Clem had repeatedly demonstrated her powers of persuasion, enticing potential investors, convincing hard-boiled attorneys and ordinarily skeptical newspaper editors of her innocence. If this was Slavin's line of thinking, his hunch proved correct. "She was," he said, "the best salesman he ever knew . . . a pleasant and convincing talker" who "worked on commission and made as high as $50 a week frequently and rarely made less than $20 a week." If these figures bear any resemblance to the truth, Clem earned two to five times an unskilled workingman's take-home pay.[10]

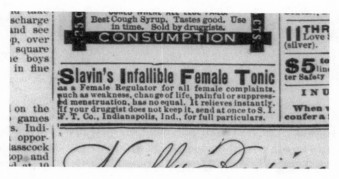

Slavin's Infallible Female Tonic advertised in the *Indianapolis Freeman*, the city's African American newspaper. The description suggested that S.I.F.T. was intended to be used as an abortifacient. Clem's final employment was selling the tonic door to door; proprietor Michael Slavin described her as "the best salesman he ever knew." In 1892 an African American Civil War veteran, John Martin, died shortly after she prescribed him three bottles of Slavin's tonic. *Indianapolis Freeman*, August 17, 1889, courtesy of the Indiana State Library.

Some Indianapolitans recognized the woman who sold "patent medicines and nostrums from door to door," but many did not. "She always spoke to me as she went by," a neighbor of the Slavins remembered, "but I never knew her name."[11] Young people and newcomers to a city whose population had doubled since 1868 might have read about the Cold Spring murders, which popped up in the newspapers from time to time, but would not have recognized a woman whose likeness had appeared only twice—in Alva C. Roach's now out-of-print pamphlet and the now-defunct *People*. Clem's sales territory, moreover, was a large one, encompassing not just Indianapolis but smaller towns and cities in Indiana and neighboring states, places where "she seemed to prefer to work," undoubtedly because they guaranteed her anonymity. In Indianapolis, she catered to the city's poorest residents, including the inhabitants of the black community on the city's northwest side. Her assignment may have been less the result of personal initiative than her employer's marketing strategy; advertisements for Slavin's appeared in the pages of the *Freeman*, Indianapolis's recently established African American newspaper.[12]

Still, Clem's position gave her ample latitude in which to exercise her considerable skills. As an itinerant peddler of S.I.F.T., "epsy salts," and miscellaneous remedies, she once again demonstrated her understanding of the power of performance. She made her rounds dressed in "the cheapest clothing," a fact that embarrassed Albert, who repeatedly offered to buy her new clothes. Clem demurred, explaining that poor people were unlikely to trust a well-dressed person. "It helps business," she explained. "People won't buy unless they think I am in need of the money."[13]

■ ■ ■

In mid-December 1892 just as Indianapolis newspapers were advertising CHRISTMAS PRESENTS!, John Martin, a fifty-eight-year-old African American Civil War veteran, died after drinking three bottles of Slavin's Infallible Female Tonic. Lame as a result of a wartime injury, Martin, a retired janitor, had been confined to his bed for several weeks. Upon his death, his wife Amanda summoned Cassius M. Clay Willis, the city's sole black undertaker and a pillar of the city's African American community.[14] Willis, however, could make no arrangements until Martin's attending physician, a Mrs. Dr. Patterson, signed his death certificate.

Formalities of this sort were relatively recent developments; only ten years earlier family members had buried loved ones who died of natural causes without interference from the state. Like the "$2 million courthouse" and the Female Reformatory, county health departments empowered to impose quarantines, regulate the disposal of garbage and offal, and keep vital records represented both a growth in governmental power and faith in its efficacy, the enduring legacy, one might say, of Radicalism. Now, health department regulations delayed Martin's burial. Willis searched in vain for Dr. Patterson but could not find her. In keeping with state protocol he turned the case over to William S. Beck, the county coroner. Through means unknown, Beck made a startling discovery: Mrs. Dr. Patterson was none other than the notorious Mrs. Clem.[15]

Beck's initial search for Clem proved similarly fruitless, so the city police, aided and abetted by the press, assumed the responsibility for finding her. Papers as far away as Chicago and New Orleans published articles titled "A Search for a Female Doctor" and "Police Searching for Mrs. Nancy Clem."[16] Clem learned from D. L. Rogers, the physician she regularly recommended to her customers, that she was wanted by the coroner. She took the initiative, making it know that she wished to meet him. An interview was arranged for noon on December 14. Beck described the encounter to local reporters, who published detailed accounts in the next day's papers. Attired in a black alpaca dress, a brown shawl, and "an undecorated," albeit veiled, hat, "the historical little old woman," as the *News* dubbed her, walked into the coroner's office just before the clock struck the hour. The smiling, dowdily dressed visitor, now about sixty years of age, retained much of the Nancy Clem of old. "She is a cunning little woman," Beck told the *Journal*, "and knows how to get around the evidence as quick as a flash, and is nothing if not wonderfully self-contained."[17]

Beck had a point. Clem's responses—at least as the papers reported them—suggest that her longstanding acquaintance with the law had schooled her well in the art of evasion. "Oh, dear me, no. I am no physician," she told Beck, "and all that I do for sick people is what I have learned from the sicknesses in my own family." She represented herself not as Dr. Patterson but as *Mrs. Patton*. "I love my first husband," she explained, "and will go by his name as much as I can, though I have nothing that I am ashamed of in my past life"—a statement that the coroner and many *News* readers must have found disingenuous.[18] Clem explained that she had been calling on the Martins in her lay capacity since the previous summer. Asked why she prescribed a female tonic to a man, she replied that Slavin's infallible remedy "was used by families promiscuously without regard to sex, age or character of illness." Furthermore, she claimed, "If he had taken any of that, it would have injured him no worse than water." The Martin children even drank the infallible tonic "because they liked the medicine, which tasted sweet." Nevertheless, while she acknowledged bathing John Martin's sore foot, Clem was careful to explain that *Mrs.* Martin had purchased the tonic and that she had merely "heard" that Mr. Martin used it as well. She admitted that she had also provided Martin with a liniment, "the contents of which she did not know" given her by "a lady" who told her it was a formula from *Gunn's Prescription Book*.[19]

Clem attributed Martin's death to "neglect . . . as to cleanliness and diet," as well his refusal to heed her recommendation that he go to the city hospital. Determined nevertheless to help, she claimed that "out of the fullness of my heart, and because I wanted to do a charitable thing, and try to earn my crown in heaven," she went to Dr. Rogers, who wrote a prescription. She decided not to fill it when she learned from the druggist that it would cost her 90 cents. He offered to "fix me up something for 30 cents that would give Mr. Martin an appetite"; this sum she willingly paid and took the "something" to the Martins. Clem insisted that she had already extended them considerable charity. They had failed to pay her for "seven or eight bottles of medicine I had furnished." During her final visit to the Martin household, she tried to collect what they owed her. "Instead of my being able to collect anything, Mrs. Martin wanted to borrow $2 from me, and bless her heart, for she is a good woman, and I believe her to be honest. I would have done it if I had had the money." As the lengthy subtitle of the *News* article suggested ("Medicine Furnished Good For All Sorts Of Ills and Perfectly Harmless— Her Action 'Charitable' To Assure a Heavenly Crown"), journalists—and their readers—greeted Clem's account with considerable skepticism.[20]

Amanda Martin told a different story. She insisted that the woman who treated her husband answered to Mrs. Dr. Patterson and represented herself as a "regular physician." According to Mrs. Martin, the impoverished family had paid the erstwhile doctress $10. Faced with competing accounts of a suspicious death, Beck ordered an autopsy, which attributed Martin's demise to peritonitis but revealed that he suffered from numerous ailments, including a "tubercular affection of his kidneys." No amount of liniment or foot bathing could have healed his lameness; that would have required surgery that Martin certainly could not have afforded. In the end, the role Slavin's tonic and the druggist's "something" played in his demise could not be ascertained.[21]

City newspapers hinted at another mysterious death, this one involving a "colored woman" prescribed patent medicine by a female physician who bore a striking resemblance to Mrs. Dr. Patterson, but Indianapolis authorities took no further action. Indeed, predictions that Clem would be prosecuted for manslaughter or practicing medicine without a license failed to materialize. While Dr. Rogers came in for his share of the suspicion—the unfilled prescription he wrote for Martin was notable for its failure to include dosage or frequency—no one pursued him either. Slavin, too, was questioned but escaped further scrutiny by insisting he had given Clem "strict instructions to prescribe . . . [his] preparation for none but women."[22] Had she treated someone of greater importance—someone wealthier or white—Clem's latest brush with the law might have ended differently. In the end, city and county authorities cared little about the fate of "colored" men and women. Radicalism in its original sense had vanished from the scene.

Much like the confidence schemes she supposedly masterminded, peddling "patent medicines and nostrums from door to door" gave Clem a means of making a living but placed her on the margins of the legitimate economy. These particular margins, it should be made clear, were crowded commercial territory. Clem's own history gave the story of Mrs. Dr. Patterson an especially sensational slant, but the good doctress had plenty of company in the largely unregulated world of late-nineteenth-century medicine. Numerous self-taught practitioners, some offering remedies that were unorthodox but effective, others outright frauds, assumed the title of Dr. or Professor, presenting their potions as the latest scientific formulas. Many such people, Clem included, targeted—one might say preyed upon—the poor and the gullible.[23] Both authorities' failure to press charges and the jocular attitude of press accounts suggest that the Indiana murderess no longer posed a threat—at least to the people who in their estimation mattered. As the *Journal*'s description implied, by the early 1890s Clem was a "historical" figure.

■ ■ ■

Matthew Hartman was spared the embarrassment of the Martin episode, for the sixty-nine-year-old master plasterer had died four months earlier, a victim of "coronary ossification" (what we would today call hardening of the arteries). No one reading the city newspapers that summer would have guessed he was the brother of the notorious Mrs. Clem. The *Journal* described him as "one of the best known citizens in the eastern part of the city," a longtime member of the Roberts Park Methodist Church, and a man "loved and respected by all who knew him." The *News* reported that Local 46 of the Plasterer's Union attended his funeral "in a body." After the services its members met and passed a resolution "remembering him as courteous to his employes [*sic*], a good citizen, a kind father and a loving husband."[24]

These tributes aptly illustrate one historian's observation that late-nineteenth-century Indianapolis was both a "large country town where 'everyone knew everybody else'" and a thriving metropolis. They also expressed nostalgia for a rapidly vanishing social order, one that could bestow the title of well-known citizen on a working man. They expressed longing as well for a mythic past in which employers and employees shared common interests. In a city all too often riven by labor unrest (a streetcar strike, the most dramatic recent example, brought Indianapolis to a standstill for nearly two weeks the previous February), the eulogies that accompanied the death of a man like Matthew Hartman carried considerable cultural weight. Hartman, though in ways considerably different than his sister, represented "history."[25]

■ ■ ■

"The historical little old woman" kept on selling Slavin's infallible remedy after the Mrs. Dr. Patterson incident, though she seems to have increasingly frequented the smaller cities and towns where no one knew her. Despite the economic depression that followed the Panic of 1893—or perhaps because of it—she continued to earn "big wages" by peddling S.I.F.T. to unsuspecting customers. Now in her mid-sixties, the shabbily dressed saleswoman looked younger than her years. Her face was unlined, she had few gray hairs, and her small hands resembled those of a much younger woman. But early in 1897 she began experiencing symptoms of what was then termed Bright's disease, an inflammation of the kidneys that might have manifested itself in back pain, vomiting, or swelling. She fell ill after returning from a sales trip and asked to stay at the Slavins' while she recuperated.[26]

She never recovered. Clem remained clear-headed for a time—by some accounts for one week, by others, three. Thereafter she "seemed to lose her reason and never talked coherently afterward." Some versions had her lapsing into unconsciousness, others described her behavior during her final days as "deranged." At any rate, Clem knew she was dying. During periods of lucidity she spent much of her time praying and talking with Slavin's daughter "about religious matters," an ecumenical meeting of Roman Catholic and born-again Protestant minds. Lillie May Slavin read to Nancy Clem from the Bible; no one reported which passages.[27]

The ailing Clem had Cold Spring on her mind. "I know that the Lord will forgive all my sins," she told Lillie May. "I have not done anything very wicked in my life, though I have been accused." At another moment she was more direct: "I am not guilty of the Young murder, and all these years I have borne the blame for what another did. I think I could put my hand on the man who killed the Youngs." The Slavins' notorious house guest uttered additional cryptic remarks during the course of her illness: "A statement may be made for me after my death, if the man will come forward and make it. I have borne the blame for a great crime that I had nothing to do with. It would have done great harm to others besides the guilty ones, if I had told all I know." "A banker will probably have something to say about my financial affairs after I am gone." She summoned Albert to tell him about a secret bank account. She insisted that if she "died even one minute before midnight, that she should be buried the next day."[28]

On Wednesday, June 8, a little after eleven in the evening, the historical little old woman passed into history. Those who hoped that she would reveal what she knew of the Young murders were disappointed. "[S]he died with her lips sealed," the *News* reported. Clem's wish for a speedy burial was granted. Late Thursday afternoon, as children gathered on the street arguing over whether the hearse that stood outside the Slavin house was "as 'pretty' as one that had recently taken away a child from the neighborhood" and curious neighbors "crane[d] their necks," a dozen mourners, Albert among them, assembled in the Slavins' parlor. The Reverend C. L. Berry, a Baptist, presided. The service was brief: "A hymn was sung, a few words were spoken, a prayer was said, another hymn was sung, then the coffin was closed."[29] No one recorded which hymns were sung; if "In Expectation Sweet"—the song that had ushered the Youngs from this world to the next—was one of them, journalists and subsequent historians lost the chance to ponder the irony.

Commentators saw Clem's hastily arranged and poorly attended funeral as a fate befitting a notorious criminal. "There were hardly enough men to serve as pall-bearers," the *News* reported smugly. Its correspondent only dimly understood the cultural and practical matters at play. Clem invoked her North Carolinian heritage when she insisted on next-day burial if she died before midnight. If a speedy internment was a concession to "superstition"—an artifact of the white southern "barbarism" that Hoosiers of New England extraction increasingly deplored—it was also a means of avoiding publicity. "The curious crowd that might have been attracted had it been known that the funeral of Nancy E. Clem was to be held, was absent," the *News* admitted. The public did not learn of Clem's death until after the pretty hearse, accompanied by only two carriages, had made its trip to Crown Hill Cemetery and laid its occupant laid to rest. Fearing grave robbers as well as the possibility of desecration, Albert had his mother buried in an unmarked location. Some months later he had her remains moved to his wife's family plot. Still, he remained cautious. Clem's headstone reads simply "Mother."[30]

■ ■ ■

Knowing that she "made big wages" while working as his "salesman," Michael Slavin was sure that Clem had squirreled away a large sum. Albert had his doubts. When he visited the bank she named in her deathbed delirium, he "learned that his suspicions were correct. There was no money there belonging to his mother."[31]

Epilogue

Benjamin Harrison became president of the United States, and Bill Abrams died in a soldiers' home. It would be claiming too much to draw a direct connection between these events, but at the same time it would be wrong to say they were completely unrelated. Harrison's performances during the trials of Abrams's alleged accomplice did much to secure the future president's reputation as a brilliant attorney, a reputation that launched his political career. Yet in a strange sense Abrams was also Harrison's beneficiary, for Harrison was a steadfast supporter of government assistance to Union veterans.[1]

Poles apart by almost any measure, Harrison and Abrams had wartime service in common. Commissioned as a second lieutenant, Harrison raised a regiment and moved up quickly, mustering out as a brigadier general—his promotion a reward for his bravery during the Atlanta campaign. Though he never rose above the rank of private, Abrams, too, acquired a reputation for courage, recognized by an official commendation. To many, including Frederick Knefler, his attorney and former commanding officer, Abrams's military performance revealed good character, a quality that helped persuade jurors to spare his life.

■ ■ ■

After his pardon and release, Abrams returned to carpentry, a trade he had also practiced in prison. He lived and worked for a time in Pike Township, where he built a barn for a member of the Hollingsworth family. Shortly thereafter he returned to the city, finding a job in the Indianapolis lumberyard run by Abel Streight, a former Civil War colonel famously outfoxed by Nathan Bedford Forrest at the Battle of Day's Gap. At some point during his post–Cold Spring career (available sources do not say when) Abrams worked as a janitor in the Marion County Courthouse—one of many truths that turned out to be stranger than fiction.[2]

Abrams did not stay at Streight's lumberyard long. He may have found his notoriety too vexing or his memories too painful, for only a few years later he moved to Peru, Nebraska, to live with his sister, Jane, her husband, Lewis Reade, and their six children. In contrast to his ne'er-do-well brother-in-law, "Esquire" Reade, a prosperous farmer, was a pillar of his community, having served as Peru's first justice of the peace. Whoever answered when the census taker knocked on the Reades' door on June 5, 1880, described Abrams as a carpenter—and a widower. Perhaps this lie contained a germ of truth, for Maggie, alas, vanishes from the historical record after obtaining her divorce.[3]

A widowed man was a better catch than a divorced one in the late nineteenth century. If this was Abrams's thinking, he succeeded. In March 1883, now nearly fifty, he married forty-three-year-old Phebe Hester Neal, the widow of a local farmer, at Peru's Methodist Episcopal Church. Whether Hester knowingly married a convicted murderer or whether Abrams kept his past a secret we do not know. Perhaps like many a spouse before and since, she believed her new husband's professions of innocence, professions he may have believed himself.[4]

Whether Abrams's neighbors were aware of his history is similarly unknowable. Evidence suggests that he lay low. John H. Dundas, the garrulous author of *Nemaha County*, painstakingly chronicled murders, drownings, fires, and epidemics but failed to mention that a participant in one of the nation's most notorious crimes had taken up residence among the good people of Peru. Nor did Abrams appear on a roster of Civil War veterans residing in the county in 1887, though the list included several who had served in Indiana regiments.[5]

Abrams once again benefited from his military service, even if he shunned the publicity associated with it. In 1888 he filed an application for a government pension, claiming to be an invalid suffering from rheumatism he had contracted during the war. Whether Abrams truly merited support is anyone's guess; he was just as likely to have acquired rheumatism during his nearly nine-year stay at the notoriously damp and dank Northern Prison as in a Civil War encampment. This distinction would have mattered little had he applied two years later, for the Dependent Pension Act, passed by Congress in 1890 at President Harrison's request, granted pensions to incapacitated Union veterans, regardless of whether their disabilities derived from the battlefield or the postwar home front. At any rate, Abrams's application was approved and he was awarded the standard sum of $12 a month.[6]

Abrams's subsequent history suggested that his disability was real. In the late 1890s he began a remarkable odyssey, embarking on a national tour of federal and state institutions that housed disabled veterans. Choice, not desperation, governed his particular decisions, for he would later declare that he "never was refused" admission to "any National or State Home." He entered the Marion (Indiana) Branch of the National Home for Disabled Volunteer Soldiers in 1897, listing his brother Benjamin, who now lived in Indianapolis, as his nearest relative. Two years later he transferred to the Western Branch in Leavenworth, Kansas, probably to be closer to Hester, who had stayed behind in Peru (national homes did not admit wives and children). Abrams was discharged at his request in October 1900 and returned to Nebraska. In 1903 he listed his home as Hall County, some 150 miles west of Peru. He did not tarry long. He spent May through December of the following year at the Pacific Branch in Yountville, California (not far from where Millie Locke, now Mrs. Charles Watts, lived), perhaps hoping to find relief for his aching joints.[7]

Abrams gained admission to the Indiana State Soldiers' Home in Lafayette in January 1904. Hester, who had spent the last two years in that city, living with a daughter, joined him a month later. Bill completed the application form in a shaky hand. He unwittingly produced a document that revealed far more of his character and personality than any of the statements journalists attributed to him. To someone who knew nothing of his previous history, Abrams's application appears commonplace; to one familiar with his past, it poignantly reveals the high personal cost of his alleged transgressions. The sixty-nine-year-old admitted to possessing only "a few Dollars in Cash" and claimed to suffer from "lumbago, rhumatisem, piles, [and] catarh of bladder," a series of ailments the "home surgeon" translated into "Chronic Cystitis, Chronic rheumatism, [and] Slight Internal Hemorr[hage]." In answer to "What is your occupation?" Abrams answered, "a Carpenter." To "How many children have you now living?"—a query intended to ferret out other possible sources of financial support—he replied "none at all." He assented to the provision requiring inmates to undertake "a reasonable amount of work in and about the Home": "yes Sir all in reson." He asserted, "I have read [the Rules for Admission]. I agree [to abide by them] to the best of my ability."[8]

Even at this late date, Abrams did not stay put. He and Hester were discharged from the home in May 1905, returning for readmission just a little less than a year later. Where they went in the intervening months is anybody's guess. It is possible that it was during this time that, in a supreme instance of poetic justice, Abrams served as a janitor in the Marion County Courthouse. In the spring of 1906, Hester and Bill came home to stay. There,

Bill died of pneumonia in 1910 on the first day of June. He was seventy-six years old. Taciturn to the end, he made no deathbed confessions. Indiana newspapers took the opportunity to reprise his role "in the most sensational murder Indianapolis had ever known" but had little to say about his later life.[9]

■ ■ ■

If Abrams could be likened to Rip Van Winkle upon his release from prison in 1878, the analogy would have been even more apt if he did indeed return to the city in the oughts to push a broom across the courthouse floors. Indianapolitans numbered more than 169,000 at the turn of the twentieth century, making their city the twenty-first largest in the nation. Nopolis still lagged far behind New York, Boston, and—closer to home—Chicago, St. Louis, and Cincinnati, but its rapid growth represented partial fulfillment of boosters' dreams. The city's spatial boundaries continued to expand, as factories, stockyards, and residential additions swallowed up much of the surrounding farmland. The landscape inside the original mile square was transformed as well. The Clem and Hartman houses survived the turn of the twentieth century, but by then most of the neighboring residences had been replaced by apartment buildings with names like the Colonial, the Oxford, the Alexander, and Belmont Flats. Territories once situated on the rural fringes had been absorbed into the commercial downtown.[10]

Changes in the public cityscape were equally impressive. The new economically constructed Indiana Statehouse, built on the site of its predecessor, opened for business in 1888. Designed to accommodate all branches and agencies of an ever-expanding state government, it was an impressive structure built in the shape of a cross, its four wings connected by a dome-topped central rotunda. Indianapolis finally found a use for its central circle, the site of the never-occupied and long ago demolished governor's mansion: a 284-foot obelisk called the Soldiers and Sailors Monument. Abrams would live to see the completion of this shrine, which commemorated his military service and that of thousands of his comrades; Frederick Knefler, his former commanding officer and defender and chair of the committee tasked with overseeing its construction, would not. (Neither would Benjamin Harrison.) Abrams would also live to see the transformation of a site that commemorated a sorrier episode in his life. In the late 1890s the city purchased Cold Spring and the surrounding area for its hitherto largest public park. The 950-acre Riverside Park boasted a "splendid boulevard . . . along the river

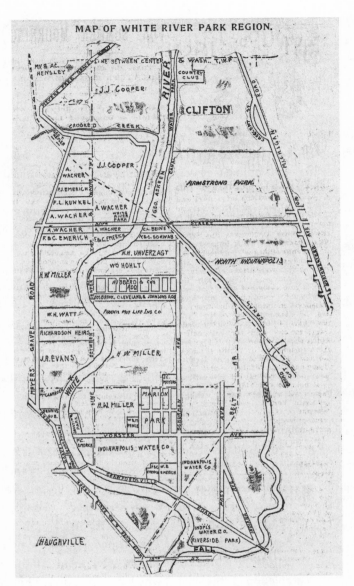

MAP OF WHITE RIVER PARK REGION.

Proposed site of Riverside Park. Even as they contemplated a major transformation of their landscape in 1898, Indianapolitans remembered their past. The text of the accompanying article noted that the future park included "an historic spot in the criminal history of Marion county, being the scene of a murder mystery that attracted public attention throughout the country." The illustrator who created the map marked the location where Jacob and Nancy Jane Young's bodies were found with an "X," visible just above the "White" in "White River." *Indianapolis News*, June 18, 1898, courtesy of the Herman B Wells Library, Indiana University.

bluffs," a golf course, and a menagerie. Only a few years later, in 1903, enterprising entrepreneurs erected an amusement park right next door. Patrons
brave enough to keep their eyes open could look down from the top of the
double-eight roller coaster onto the scene of a long-ago crime.[11]

Many of the "improvements" an elderly custodian named Bill Abrams
might have witnessed, like the Soldiers and Sailors Monument or Riverside
Park, were tangible. Changes in the nature of daily encounters, patterns of
sociability, and measures of social standing, less readily apparent, were
no less important. Abrams could "regain [his] lost place in society" only by
leaving Indianapolis behind. But the social ground on which his former
peers stood was subtly shifting. Take a respectable man like Aaron Clem, for
example. In the 1850s he had been the rough equal of Benjamin Harrison
and William Pinckney Fishback. No one would describe him as such by
the late 1880s, a fact confirmed by residence and patterns of association.
True, Harrison and Fishback often stopped to drink at the pump outside
of the Clem grocery as they walked home to their North Delaware Street
mansions—chance meetings with its proprietor must have been supremely
awkward encounters. True, Aaron Clem moved to the suburbs, but to a far
from fashionable location.[12]

Aaron Clem was not working-class, certainly not in the sense that the
city's eleven thousand or so factory hands were. In fact, he was by many
standards a wealthy man. But as an old settler, a relic of a "pioneer" past,
neither could he claim membership in the ranks of an educated white-collar
middle class. The *News*'s condescending assessment of John Hanna could
just as easily apply to Clem: "He was a fine type of western man, on whom
the influences and privations of pioneer life had left an ineffaceable stamp,
and who had not been polished by the contacts of later life." Aaron Clem and
John Hanna were not only "western men"; they were also southern men at a
time when being southern had become a social liability. Local historians
ridiculed early settlers from the upland South—ignorant, shiftless, and
superstitious folk who spoke a strange unintelligible "dialect." In 1888
crusading minister Oscar McCulloch published his "study in social degradation," a treatise that detailed the moral and physical depravity of people he
dubbed the "Tribe of Ishmael," several generations of impoverished Indianapolitans who originated "mostly from Kentucky, Tennessee, and North
Carolina." He even blamed the "Clem murder" on this "tribe."[13]

Still, Aaron Clem had little in common with the troglodytic degenerates
who populated McCulloch's fertile imagination. When he died in 1901 he

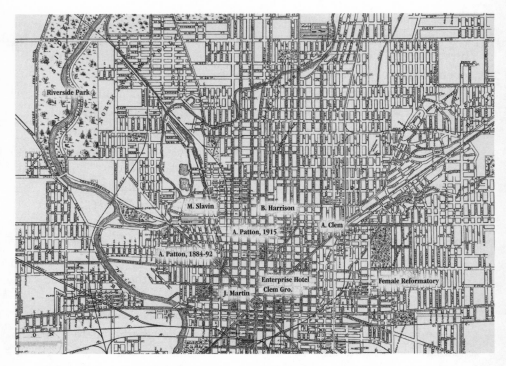

By the turn of the twentieth century, Indianapolis had spread far beyond its original boundaries, and Indianapolitans had sorted themselves into more precisely calibrated residential categories. Michael Slavin's "modest little cottage," Albert Patton's apartment and subsequent rooming house, and John Martin's residence were located in mixed-race working-class neighborhoods on the city's west side. Benjamin Harrison had moved to "fashionable" North Delaware Street and Aaron Clem to Brightwood, a somewhat less fashionable suburb. The site of the Cold Spring murders had been incorporated into Riverside Park. Map by Ian Byers-Gamber, adapted from Fred Dessecker and Theo. Sandstrom, *Bicycle & Driving Map of Indianapolis* (Indianapolis: Topographical Map & Survey Co., 1899), courtesy of the Herman B Wells Library, Indiana University.

merited a prominent obituary in the *News*. The coverage was respectful, purposely omitting any mention of Clem's connection to his former sister-in-law (a retrospective published four years earlier had noted that he was not "connected to this celebrated case in any invidious way"). The article celebrated his fifty years as a grocer, a man with a reputation for hard work and honest dealing. Yet the *News* also made a point of noting "the peculiar drawl in his speech." In a city in which southerners were becoming an "undesirable element," drawls—once commonplace—were now "peculiar."[14]

■ ■ ■

Boosters and self-styled historians quantified many facets of Indianapolis's economic history—miles of track laid, products manufactured and articles sold, acres of farmland converted to rich men's mansions and workingmen's cottages. The parameters of the city's informal economies are more difficult to measure. As various accounts made clear, confidence men and women continued to profit at the expense of their hapless victims. Shaving notes continued to be a time-honored, if increasingly disreputable, strategy parlayed by bankers and brokers. Corporations such as the Security Mortgage Loan Company offered to lend "$5, $10, $15, $20, $50, $100, $150 . . . ON FURNITURE, PIANOS, HORSES AND WAGONS," promising "low rates" and "plenty of time to pay it back." While newspapers railed against the underhanded practices of "professional money lenders" (complaints that often shaded into anti-Semitism), they said little about the activities of people who loaned money on a casual basis, episodes in the social history of capitalism illuminated only when scandal unfolded or murder ensued.[15]

There is little reason to doubt the survival of personal banking, even if its existence cannot be documented with any degree of precision. Lending money to friends and neighbors—and collecting interest when the loans came due—was a type of business open to anyone willing to risk the resources at his or her disposal. And it was a business uniquely accessible to women. Ventures of this sort could be easily combined with housework and childcare, small-scale profits hidden from tax collectors, nosy relations, and meddlesome husbands.

Woman's rights advocates who lobbied for legislation that would allow married women ownership over the wages they earned were not thinking of female street brokers, like Nancy Clem at her most innocuous, or even proprietors like her nemesis, Lena Miller. Mary Livermore's list of working women—"saleswomen, cashiers, bookkeepers, telegraphers, compositors, stenographers, type-writers, watchmakers, chemists, pharmacists, journalists, authors, lecturers, physicians, lawyers, clergywomen"—was notable for its exclusion of entrepreneurs. Livermore justified both earnings laws and vocational training as a hedge against "incompetent" husbands, rather than a right to which women were entitled. "Many men make neither good nor competent husbands. Many are incompetent, others are invalids, some are dissolute and idle, and not a few desert entirely both wives and children," she declared in her most famous speech, "What Shall We Do with Our

Daughters?" Such a position was, of course, strategic, far more likely to sway the members of all-male legislatures than a bold declaration of rights.[16] It left a crucial question unanswered: did women married to competent and prosperous husbands have the right to engage in business on their own accounts?

Neither a stenographer nor a clergywoman, but undeniably a woman of business, Nancy Clem raised precisely this question. Her trials took place before the passage of Indiana's earnings act in 1881; hence her legal ability to "manage her own business affairs" depended on a prenuptial agreement rather than a general statute. The men who served on successive juries were charged with determining whether she was guilty or innocent of murder, not whether she had a right to the profits she had earned. Yet competing interpretations of the political economy of marriage were central to the narratives constructed by her prosecution and defense. They echoed a cultural conversation that took place in many arenas—in feminist demands; in statehouses, as legislators contemplated revised married women's property acts and earnings laws; in courts, as judges considered women's claims; and in myriad negotiations between husbands and wives. The proper exercise of female self-reliance–especially as it applied to married women—would remain contested. Both prosecution and defense agreed that faithless wives deserved to be punished. But each had proposed its own definition of fidelity. The subtle but significant differences between them created a slender continuum between wifely dependence and limited autonomy, granting ambitious women a narrow cultural space in which to maneuver. The question, as journalist and advice writer Martha Rayne would put it twenty years later, of "What Can a Woman Do?" did not have a definitive answer.[17]

This was in part because Rayne, as she undoubtedly knew, posed a partisan question, one of many issues that determined whether one leaned Republican or Democratic. Republicans championed the doctrine of separate spheres, which gave women authority within the home and provided a justification—in the name of protecting it—for their activism outside it. At the same time, it celebrated the distance of true women from a corrupt marketplace. Democrats, by contrast, emphasized white men's household mastery but recognized women's contributions to family economies and, increasingly, their role as price-conscious consumers.[18] In Clem's case, partisan identities only imperfectly reflected these distinctions, for with the exception of Daniel W. Voorhees, the Sycamore of the Wabash, both those who prosecuted her and those who defended her belonged to the Republican Party. Yet as their own definitions of faithful wives revealed, men like John Hanna and William Wallace Leathers had once been Democrats.

If gender furnished the text of the Cold Spring case, race was its subtext, for Clem's initial trials took place at the height of Reconstruction. They pitted Radical prosecutors against a Moderate defense team, who in 1872 added a Democrat to their ranks. While Voorhees remained an unreconstructed racist, it would be easy to make too much of Republican differences. John Hanna, who termed the Republicans "a white man's party" in 1860, spoke twelve years later to a largely black audience at a rally celebrating the anniversary of the ratification of the Fifteenth Amendment; so did Jonathan W. Gordon, despite the fact that he was "not a rad." By the late 1870s, if not before, Gordon was giving speeches "heaping abuse" on Voorhees, now his bitter political enemy. The Rads, for their part, did not always distinguish themselves from the Moderates. Harrison was initially a reluctant endorser of black voting rights. Even Pink Fishback, an avowed Radical, could make derisive comments about "colored women." And by 1872, now editor of the *Journal*, he would retreat from Radicalism and throw in his lot with the party of reconciliation, the Liberal Republicans. So would Voorhees.[19]

In the context of Clem's trials, race mattered most when it helped to make the case. John Hanna's description of Jane Sizemore as "that accursed nigger" and Jonathan W. Gordon's characterization of "colored servants" as inherently unreliable informants were, first and foremost, calculated maneuvers, intended to discredit the testimony of a key witness for the prosecution. At a time when African Americans' right to testify was subject to lingering doubts, this was a shrewd, if repugnant, strategy. Whatever their personal convictions, Hanna and Gordon knew they were speaking to jurors who, more likely than not, accepted their claims as common sense— nothing more, nothing less. This was, indeed, the conventional wisdom that newspapers implicitly invoked by adding the modifier "(colored)" when they reprinted the testimony of black witnesses. If race was woven into the very fabric of the case, it was because race was an intrinsic feature of Gilded Age society. In Indianapolis its continuing salience was evident in segregated schools, churches, and neighborhoods, selective enforcement of civil rights laws, and unequal justice. It was evident, not least, in Mrs. Dr. Patterson's careless exploitation of impoverished African American consumers and authorities' less-than-thorough investigation of John Martin's death. Race inhabited the very scene of the original crime—or rather, very close by it; Riverside Amusement Park admitted whites only except for the annual "Colored Frolic Day."[20]

■ ■ ■

On the evening of Tuesday, September 21, 1915, a lodger in the rooming house at 31 West St. Joseph Street in Indianapolis, site of a former firehouse occupied by the city's African American firemen, found the bathroom door locked. Whoever was inside failed to respond to repeated knocking, knob-rattling, and shouts. As other roomers, aroused by the commotion, gathered in the hallway, they realized that the bathroom was probably occupied by a sixty-five-year-old lodger nicknamed "Dad." Dad, who had only recently taken up residence, had a heart condition. His housemates feared the worst.[21]

When two of the city's "bicyclemen" police officers arrived to break down the door, they found that Dad had indeed expired. The *Indianapolis News* reported that his real name was Albert Patton (the *News* spelled his last name "Patten") but that his identity remained a mystery. No one knew of his origins or next of kin. It took two days for reporters to make the connection. On September 24, the *News* acknowledged that Patton was the son of Nancy Clem. Patton, the *News* explained, "was an honest, quiet, law-abiding citizen" whose "life was a quiet and mournful struggle against the notoriety that came to him, not from any wrongdoing of his own, but because of his mother."[22]

It was by every indication a lonely life, especially at the end. His second wife, Carrie, died almost three years before him. The Pattons had no children. No conclusive evidence survives to tell us what became of Daisy, his daughter by his first wife, Beulah. It is entirely possible that when Albert Patton died, so too did the last direct descendant of the notorious Mrs. Clem. He was laid to rest in Crown Hill Cemetery, with Carrie on his right and "Mother" on his left, closest to his heart.[23]

■ ■ ■

"Mother" faded from historical memory, albeit not entirely. Even before her death—and long after—some Hoosiers were convinced that Ferdinand Ward, the "Young Napoleon of Finance" who swindled Ulysses S. Grant out of his entire fortune, had learned his trade from Nancy Clem during his brief tenure as an Indianapolis bank clerk. When the exploits of Cassie Chadwick, a confidence woman who obtained enormous loans by representing herself as the heiress of Andrew Carnegie, surfaced at the turn of the century, Indianapolis newspapers remembered their own "counterpart" with a certain amount of pride. Clem, in the words of the *News*, was the "first of the Chadwicks."[24] Well into the twentieth century, successive generations of law students at the University of Indianapolis practiced the Cold Spring case in the school's moot court. A centennial edition of the *Indianapolis Star* included Clem, in company with the founding of the Female Reformatory (it failed to connect the two), in its summary of key events in the city's history. Even today, plays about the Cold Spring murders are periodically performed at the Benjamin Harrison home.[25]

Still, the woman who at one time was arguably the nation's most famous murderess has been eclipsed by others with more lasting claims to fame. Lizzie Borden inspired a more memory ditty: "Who gave Peter Wilkins the money?" has nothing on "Lizzie Borden took an axe." Borden's case, one might argue, was the more sensational; in addition to the sheer horror and brutal intimacy her alleged crime evoked, Borden, a bona fide member of her city's elite, had farther to fall. By the time she stood trial in the early 1890s, newspapers had multiplied, both in number and bulk, reaching even wider audiences and providing even greater detail than in Clem's heyday. Surely the different narrative arcs of each case have something to do with their relative staying power. Even though many people believed her guilty, Borden was acquitted and therefore could not be tried again. The widespread sense of justice denied, coupled with Borden's subsequent behavior (having inherited her father's estate, she lived the rest of her life in ostentatious style) fixed the case in public memory. Clem's tale might well have followed the same trajectory had she stayed out of further trouble with the law. The fact that she *was* punished, albeit not for murder, gave her story a resolution that Borden's lacked.[26]

Yet Clem stubbornly resisted standard narratives. She may have been the first of a new breed of "middle-class" murderesses who killed for money, not for love. But unlike Mary Sheedy, who may have murdered her husband, or Belle Gunness, the "Lady Bluebeard," who murdered successive husbands, or even Lizzie Borden, who almost certainly hacked her parents to death with an axe, Clem's was neither a sexual nor a familial crime.[27]

Nancy Clem, a woman purportedly unable to write, left behind no diaries or letters. She offered few clues to her motivations; in the words of the *New York Times*, she was "a perfect psychological enigma." This much is clear: she relished the art of the sale. And like virtually all salespeople, she did not always tell the truth. Perhaps she might have directed her energies into safer channels had not educational deficiency and gender conventions limited her prospects. Perhaps not. A "German friend" remembered Clem as a financial genius who "knew more of the business world than many of the business men" in the city. His description erred on the side of generosity, for the evidence in favor of her business acumen is decidedly mixed. Clem was charming and persuasive, and she convinced people who should have known better to part with their money. But she did not always play her hand well. She was a confidence woman, but not an entirely accomplished one. She was a woman, however, who may have gotten away with murder.[28]

Prologue

1. Federal Manuscript Population Census (hereafter, FMPC), 1870, Indianapolis, roll M593-340, p. 217A, and (2nd enum.), roll M593-338, p. 233; testimony, Seymour Locke, *Indianapolis Sentinel*, Dec. 3, 1868, 4; testimony, Millie Locke, *Nancy E. Clem v. State of Indiana* (1869), Office of Supreme Court Records, Indianapolis, Indiana.

2. *The Cold Spring Tragedy: Trial and Conviction of Mrs. Nancy E. Clem for the Murder of Jacob Young and Wife*. . . (Indianapolis: A. C. Roach, 1869), 6–8; FMPC, 1870, Center Township, Marion County, Indiana, roll M593-337, p. 339.

3. "Horrible and Mysterious Affair," *Sentinel*, Sept. 14, 1868, 4.

4. Ibid.; "The Cold Spring Tragedy," *Sentinel*, Dec. 1, 1868, 4.

5. "Horrible and Mysterious Affair," *Sentinel*, Sept. 14, 1868, 4; "Appalling Double Murder," *Indianapolis Journal*, Sept. 14, 1868, 8.

6. *Cold Spring Tragedy*, 9–10; "The Cold Springs Murder," *Journal*, Sept. 15, 1868, 8. See Leigh Darbee's entry in *The Encyclopedia of Indianapolis*, ed. David J. Bodenhamer and Robert G. Barrows (Bloomington: Indiana University Press, 1994), 456, for an excellent summary of the Cold Spring case.

Chapter 1 · New Year's Day

1. "Emancipation," *Indianapolis Journal*, Jan. 3, 1868, 2; "Carrier's Greeting," *Journal*, Jan. 1, 1868, 2; "Before Esquire Curtis," *Journal*, Jan. 6, 1868, 5; "An Employes' [*sic*] Dinner," *Journal*, Jan. 3, 1868, 2; "Holiday Festival of Trinity Church," *Journal*, Dec. 27, 1867, 2; "Social Reunion," *Journal*, Jan. 1, 1868, 2.

2. Frederick D. Kershner Jr., "From Country Town to Industrial City: The Urban Pattern in Indianapolis," *Indiana Magazine of History* 45, no. 4 (Dec. 1949): 329.

3. "Descriptive List of Convicts in the Indiana State Prison, South," 142, Indiana State Archives, Indianapolis; "Mrs. Clem: An Hour's Talk with Her," *Indianapolis Sentinel*, Mar. 29, 1869, 4.

4. "Five Trials for Murder," *Northern Light* (Indianapolis), May 14, 1959, n.p., clipping file, Benjamin Harrison Presidential Site, Indianapolis, Ind.; Robert Underwood Johnson, *Remembered Yesterdays* (Boston: Little, Brown, 1923), 25; Walter S. Smith, "The Uncalled Witness," *Indianapolis Star*, Aug. 18, 1907, SM1; "The Cold Spring Tragedy," *Sentinel*, Dec. 1, 1868, 4, and Dec. 2, 1868, 4; "The Young Murder. First Day of the Trial," *Journal*, Dec. 2, 1868, 5; *The Cold Spring Tragedy: Trial and Conviction of Mrs. Nancy E. Clem for the Murder of Jacob Young and Wife*. . . (Indianapolis: A. C. Roach, 1869), 16. *The Cold Spring Tragedy*, dedicated to depicting a likely murderess, found additional physical defects. Most accounts, however, portrayed Clem as an attractive woman.

5. John Hartman family tree, Ancestry.com, http://trees.ancestry.com/owt/person.aspx ?pid=119943854; Federal Manuscript Population Census (hereafter FMPC), 1830, Stokes County, North Carolina, roll 125, p. 275; Early Land Records of Pike Township, Pike Township Historical Society, http://www.in1.org/pike/tract.htm; Smith, "The Uncalled Witness"; "Behind the Bars: Prison Life of Mrs. Clem: A Half-Hour with the Lady from Indianapolis," *Louisville Courier-Journal*, May 7, 1869, 4; "Rural Historical and Architectural Resources of Eagle Township (Boone County) and Pike Township (Marion County), Indiana, 1820–1956," www.in .gov/dnr/historic/files/eagletownship_mpd.pdf, 2–3, 7–10; John Lauritz Larson and David G. Vanderstel, "Agent of Empire: William Conner on the Indiana Frontier, 1800–1855," *Indiana Magazine of History* 80, no. 4 (Dec. 1984): 301–382; John Hartman's will, in *First Wills of Marion County, Indiana, Compiled by Miss Lucy Campbell, Chairman, Mrs. Norman E.*

(Ethel Corbin) Patrick of the Genealogical Records Committee, Caroline Scott Harrison Chapter, D.A.R. (Indianapolis, 1935), 1:110. On the limited extent of literacy and schooling in Indiana in general, see James H. Madison, *The Indiana Way: A State History* (Bloomington: Indiana University Press; Indianapolis: Indiana Historical Society, 1986), 111–115, and James H. Madison, *Hoosiers: A New History of Indiana* (Bloomington: Indiana University Press; Indianapolis: Indiana Historical Society, 2014), 113; for Marion County in particular, see Oliver Johnson, *A Home in the Woods: Pioneer Life in Indiana* (1951; repr., Bloomington: Indiana University Press, 1991), 61.

6. *Cold Spring Tragedy*, 16; testimony, Mrs. Erastus Everson, *Journal*, Dec. 8, 1868, 2. Other sources suggested Nancy could both read and write, though likely not well; see "Descriptive List of Convicts in the Indiana State Prison, South," 142, 339; "Free: Nancy Clem at Large," *Sentinel*, Apr. 30, 1874, 5; and "The Nancy Clem Case," *Chicago Inter Ocean*, Apr. 27, 1874, 2. Gregory S. Rose, "Hoosier Origins: The Nativity of Indiana's United States-Born Population in 1850," *Indiana Magazine of History* 81, no. 3 (Sept. 1985): 201–232; Rose, "The Distribution of Indiana's Ethnic and Racial Minorities in 1850," *Indiana Magazine of History* 87, no. 3 (Sept. 1991): 224–260; Dorothea Kline McCullough, " 'By Cash and Eggs': Gender in Washington County during Indiana's Pioneer Period" (PhD diss., Indiana University, 2001), 142–165; Richard F. Nation, *At Home in the Hoosier Hills: Agriculture, Politics, and Religion in Southern Indiana, 1810–1870* (Bloomington: Indiana University Press, 2005), 109–112; Laurel Thatcher Ulrich, *Good Wives: Image and Reality in the Lives of Women in Northern New England, 1650–1750* (New York: Vintage, 1991), 18–34; Joan M. Jensen, *Loosening the Bonds: Mid-Atlantic Farm Women, 1750–1850* (New Haven: Yale University Press, 1986); Nancy Grey Osterud, *Bonds of Community: The Lives of Farm Women in Nineteenth-Century New York* (Ithaca, N.Y.: Cornell University Press, 1991); Jeanne Boydston, *Home and Work: Housework, Wages, and the Ideology of Labor in the Early Republic* (New York: Oxford University Press, 1990); Susan Sessions Rugh, *Our Common Country: Family Farming, Culture, and Community in the Nineteenth-Century Midwest* (Bloomington: Indiana University Press, 2001), esp. 20–21, 23–24, 65–70; Tamara Gaskell Miller, " 'Seeking to Strengthen the Ties of Friendship': Women and Community in Southeastern Ohio, 1788–1850" (PhD diss., Brandeis University, 1994), 67–107; Madison, *Hoosiers*, 61–72, 86–87; O. Johnson, *Home in the Woods*, 25–26, 31, 34–38; John Hartman family tree; marriages, Anna Hartman and James McCurdy, Polly Hartman and Silas White, in Indiana, Marriage Index, 1800–1941 (online database, Ancestry.com, 2005), http://search.ancestry.com/search/db.aspx?dbid=5059; "Rural Historical and Architectural Resources," 6–7.

7. Marriage Nancy E. Hartman and William N. Patton, in Marriages through 1850 (online database, Indiana State Library, n.d.), www.statelib.lib.in.us/INMarriages1850/marriages_search.asp. According to some accounts, Hartman married at the age of fifteen; genealogies suggest that she would have been nineteen. Census takers recorded various ages. See Jonathan Gordon, closing argument, *Sentinel*, Feb. 16, 1869, 4; John Hartman family tree; FMPC, 1850, Center, Marion County, roll M432-159, p. 195A, and 1860, Indianapolis, roll M653-279, p. 163. Testimony, William N. Duzan, *Nancy E. Clem v. State of Indiana* (1872), 2426; testimony, John H. Wiley, *Nancy E. Clem v. State of Indiana* (1869), 972–973, 985–986. Both transcripts are held by the Office of Supreme Court Records, Indianapolis.

8. *Journal*, Aug. 1, 1853, 3; Carl Abbott, "Indianapolis in the 1850s: Popular Economic Thought and Urban Growth," *Indiana Magazine of History* 74, no. 4 (Dec. 1978): 296; "Old Alabama Street House Still Holds Mystery of Famous Clem Murder Case," *Star*, Aug. 30, 1930, 2.22.

9. B. R. Sulgrove, *History of Indianapolis and Marion County, Indiana* (Philadelphia: L. H. Everts, 1884), 20, 25–27, 90; Abbott, "Indianapolis in the 1850s," 294; John H. Holliday, *Indianapolis and the Civil War*, Indiana Historical Society Publications 4:9 (Indianapolis: Edward J. Hecker, 1911), 525; Hugh McCullough, quoted in Shirley S. McCord, comp., *Travel*

Accounts of Indiana, 1679–1961 ([Indianapolis]: Indiana Historical Bureau, 1970), 142–143; Jeffrey Tenuth, *Indianapolis: A Circle City History* (Charleston, S.C.: Arcadia Publishing, 2004), 28–29; Edward A. Leary, *Indianapolis: The Story of a City* (Indianapolis: Bobbs-Merrill, 1971), 12–13; Ann Lieberman, *Governors' Mansions of the Midwest* (Columbia: University of Missouri Press, 2003), 18–19.

10. Sulgrove, *History of Indianapolis and Marion County*, 111, 123–124, 129–130, 147; Robert G. Barrows and Leigh Darbee, "The Urban Frontier in Pioneer Indiana," *Indiana Magazine of History* 105, no. 3 (Sept. 2009): 268–282; *A. C. Howard's Directory for the City of Indianapolis* (Indianapolis: A. C. Howard. 1857), 14, 18, 259; Rexford Newcomb, *Architecture of the Old Northwest Territory: A Study of Early Architecture in Ohio, Indiana, Illinois, Michigan, Wisconsin, and Part of Minnesota* (Chicago: University of Chicago Press, 1950), 56, 60; Ferencz Pulszky, quoted in McCord, *Travel Accounts of Indiana*, 202.

11. David W. Peat, *Indiana Houses of the Nineteenth Century* (Indianapolis: Indiana Historical Society, 1962), esp. 43–50; John Hartman family tree. The absence of birth and death records (Indiana did not create a state Department of Health that required the keeping of such statistics until 1882) makes it impossible to learn whether Nancy Patton and Rebecca Hartman gave birth to other children who did not survive. "Funeral of Mrs. Clem," *Indianapolis News*, June 10, 1897, 8; Jacob Piatt Dunn, *Greater Indianapolis: The History, the Industries, the Institutions, and the People of a City of Homes* (Chicago: Lewis Publishing, 1910), 1:599; Sulgrove, *History of Indianapolis and Marion County*, 608–610; Riley B. Case, "'An Aggressive Warfare': Eli Farmer and Methodist Revivalism in Early Indiana," *Indiana Magazine of History* 104, no. 1 (Mar. 2008): 91; Nathan O. Hatch, *The Democratization of American Christianity* (New Haven: Yale University Press, 1989), 193–195, 201–205. J. T. Palmatary's *View of Indianapolis* (1854) includes an unnamed "Methodist Church" in addition to Roberts Chapel and Wesleyan Chapel, but since the North Street Church was not completed until the very end of 1854, the illustration probably depicts the Asbury Chapel at South and New Jersey Streets.

12. "Relics of Barbarism," *News*, Mar. 19, 1883, 3; George S. Cottman, "Old-Time Slums of Indianapolis," *Indiana Magazine of History* 7, no. 4 (Dec. 1911): 170–171; Nicole Etcheson, *The Emerging Midwest: Upland Southerners and the Political Culture of the Old Northwest, 1787–1861* (Bloomington: Indiana University Press, 1996); Harry J. Sievers, *Benjamin Harrison*, vol. 1: *Hoosier Warrior: Through the Civil War Years, 1833–1865* (New York: University Publishers, 1952), 173–174. For occupations and birthplaces of neighborhood residents, see, for example, FMPC, 1860, Indianapolis, roll M653-279, pp. 158–160.

13. See Mary P. Ryan, *Cradle of the Middle Class: The Family in Oneida County, New York, 1790–1865* (Cambridge: Cambridge University Press, 1981). Much recent work on the middle class takes Stuart Blumin's magisterial *The Emergence of the Middle Class: Social Experience in the American City, 1760–1900* (Cambridge: Cambridge University Press, 1989) as its starting point. Increasingly, however, scholars argue that class, like gender and race, is at least partly socially constructed. See especially the essays in *The Middling Sorts: Explorations in the History of the American Middle Class*, ed. Burton J. Bledstein and Robert D. Johnston (New York: Routledge, 2001); Daniel J. Walkowitz, *Working with Class: Social Workers and the Politics of Middle-class Identity* (Chapel Hill: University of North Carolina Press, 1999); Jocelyn Wills, "Respectable Mediocrity: The Everyday Life of an Ordinary American Striver, 1876–1890," *Journal of Social History* 27 (Winter, 2003): 323–349; Robert D. Johnston, *The Radical Middle Class: Populist Democracy and the Question of Capitalism in Progressive Era Portland, Oregon* (Princeton: Princeton University Press, 2003); the recent special issue on the "Middle Class in the City," *Journal of Urban History* 31 (Mar. 2005); and "Symposium on Class in the Early Republic," *Journal of the Early Republic* 25 (Winter 2005): 523–564. For an opposing view, see Seth Rockman's contribution to the *JER* symposium and Rockman, *Scraping By: Wage Labor, Slavery, and Survival in Early Baltimore* (Baltimore: Johns Hopkins University Press, 2008).

William Wallace Leathers, closing argument, *Journal*, Dec. 19, 1868, 2; John Dye, closing argument, *Sentinel*, Feb. 25, 1869, 4; "Musty Pages of History Opened," *Jeffersonville National Democrat*, Dec. 6, 1899, 4; see also *Fort Wayne Daily Gazette*, Apr. 27, 1869, 1.

14. William Patton, gravestone, Pleasant Hill Cemetery, Pike Township, Marion County, Indiana; testimony, James W. Hill, *Sentinel*, Feb. 18, 1860, 4; testimony, James W. Hill, *Sentinel*, Oct. 4, 1871, 3. William Patton apparently died intestate (no will has survived). James W. Hill, a local farmer who had known both William and Nancy, was appointed administrator of William's estate and Albert's guardian. Guardians ensured that minor children were provided for and protected the estates they would inherit when they reached adulthood. The terms of settlement, absent extant legal documents, are difficult to decipher. Hill's statements, all the evidence that survives, contradict themselves. On one occasion, he described Nancy's "realty" as "amount[ing] to the house and lot where she lived and a house and lot on Pennsylvania street"; on another, he claimed that the Alabama Street house was hers, the Pennsylvania Street house Albert's. The latter version hews more closely to legal practice. *The Revised Statutes of the State of Indiana* (Indianapolis: J. Chapman, State Printer, 1852), 1:25; Lawrence M. Friedman, *A History of American Law*, 3rd ed. (New York: Simon & Schuster, 2005), 323; Joseph R. Long, *A Treatise on the Law of Domestic Relations* (St. Paul: Keefe-Davidson, 1905), 170.

15. Testimony, Matthew Hartman, *Sentinel*, Dec. 12, 1868, 2; John Hanna, closing argument, *Journal*, Dec. 21, 1868, 6; Wendy Gamber, *The Boardinghouse in Nineteenth-Century America* (Baltimore: Johns Hopkins University Press, 2007). Patton did not advertise her services in city directories. Some years later, however, her family physician would testify that she "kept a boarding house." Testimony, William N. Duzan, *Clem v. Indiana* (1872), 2429.

16. Testimony, Ann Hottle, *Sentinel*, Oct. 4, 1871, 3; William P. Fishback, closing argument, in *The Cold Spring Tragedy: Trial and Conviction of Mrs. Nancy E. Clem for the Murder of Jacob Young and Wife . . .* (Indianapolis: A. C. Roach, 1869), 100; "Funeral of Mrs. Clem," *News*, June 10, 1897, 8; Kershner, "From Country Town to Industrial City," 329. The now-thirty-year-old Clem told the enumerator of the 1860 census that she was twenty-six; FMPC, 1860, Indianapolis, roll M653-279, p. 159.

17. "A Christmas Visit to Mrs. Clem," *Cincinnati Enquirer*, Dec. 27, 1876, 8; FMPC, 1850, Warren Township, Marion County, roll M432-159, p. 372A; "Aaron Clem Dead. For Fifty Years a Grocer in Indianapolis—Widely Known," *News*, Oct. 14, 1901, 10; Indiana, vol. 67, p. 26, R. G. Dun & Co. Collection, Baker Library, Harvard Business School, Boston, Massachusetts (microfilmed records for Marion County are located at the Indiana Historical Society); Internal Revenue Service, Indiana, District 6, Annual Lists, 1862, M765, roll 23, p. 2; 1863, roll 23, p. 17; 1864, roll 25, p. 177; 1865, roll 26, p. 225, in U.S. IRS Tax Assessment Lists, 1862–1918 (online database, Ancestry.com, 2008), http://search.ancestry.com/search/db.aspx?dbid=1264. In 1865, the Clem brothers reported annual income of only $250; "Measuring Worth: Seven Ways to Compute the Relative Value of a U.S. Dollar Amount, 1774 to Present," www .measuringworth.com/uscompare.

18. Virginia Dill McCarty, "From Petticoat Slavery to Equality: Women's Rights in Indiana Law," in *The History of Indiana Law*, ed. David J. Bodenhamer and Randall T. Shepard (Athens: Ohio University Press, 2006), 179–180; Fishback, closing argument, *Cold Spring Tragedy*, 100; "Funeral of Mrs. Clem," *News*, June 10, 1897, 8.

19. "An Error," *New Albany Daily Ledger*, Apr. 26, 1869, 2; "Behind the Bars: Prison Life of Mrs. Clem," *Louisville Courier-Journal*, July 5, 1869, 4. The error was understandable; the Hartmans named their firstborn son John Wesley (see John Hartman family tree), and Pike Township's Pleasant Hill Methodist Church stood on the land John Hartman donated. Clem herself described her father as "a prominent member of the Methodist Church." "City News: Hartman Suicide," *Journal*, Mar. 12, 1869, 4; John Hartman's will, in *First Wills of*

Marion County, 1:110; "Rural Historical and Architectural Resources," 4–6, 14–15; *Map of Marion County, Indiana* (Indianapolis: Condit, Wright, & Hayden, 1855), in Historic Indiana Maps (online database, Indiana University–Purdue University at Indianapolis, n.d.), http://ulib.iupui.edu/digitalscholarship/collections/HIM; Federal Manuscript Agricultural Census, 1850, roll 3893, p. 361; Nation, *At Home in the Hoosier Hills*, 29, 80–127; Madison, *Indiana Way*, 66–67; O. Johnson, *Home in the Woods*, 29–32; testimony, Benjamin Abrams, *Journal*, Dec. 7, 1868, 2. According to the terms of John Hartman's will, the family farm—too small to be divided—would be sold upon the death of "his beloved wife," the proceeds distributed equally among his ten surviving children. His widow, the elder Nancy Hartman, would live another thirty years. Hartman also owned two lots in the tiny Boone County town of Eagle Village; the sale of these lots in 1847 provided his children with small inheritances. Jane Eaglesfield Darlington, *Marion County, Indiana: Complete Probate Records, January 1830–August 1852* (n.p.: n.p., 1994), 149–150.

20. *The Seventh Census of the United States: 1850* (Washington, D.C.: Robert Armstrong, 1853), 769; *Population of the United States in 1860* (Washington, D.C.: Government Printing Office, 1864), 121; Warren E. Roberts, *Log Buildings of Southern Indiana* (Bloomington, Ind.: Trickster Press, 1996), 194–198; Robert Cottrell, "From Cellar to Shingles: Nineteenth-Century Building Trades," in *Building a Home, Preserving a Heritage: The Story of the Conner House*, ed. Stephen L. Cox and Timothy Crumrin (Fishers, Ind.: Conner Prairie, 1993), [n.p.]; *Century Old Houses in Pike Township* (n.p.: Pike Township Historical Society, [1976]); testimony, Silas Hartman, *Journal*, Dec. 14, 1868, 2.

21. Testimony, Matthew Hartman, *Journal*, Dec. 12, 1868; testimony, Silas A. Hartman, *Journal*, Dec. 14, 1868. See also testimony, "Grandmother Hartman," *Journal*, Dec. 16, 1868, 3. John Hartman's will, *First Wills of Marion County*, 1:110; FMPC, 1880, Peru, Nemaha County, Nebraska, roll T9-752, p. 100B; "The Cold Springs Murder," *Journal*, Sept. 17, 1868, 5; "Letter from Indianapolis. The Clem Murder Case—The Mystery Increases," *Cincinnati Daily Gazette*, Dec. 14, 1868, 1.

22. According to Jonathan Gordon, Jacob Young was five feet eleven inches tall—Gordon, closing argument, *Journal*, Feb. 26, 1869, 5. "Appalling Double Murder," *Journal*, Sept. 14, 1868, 8; "Horrible and Sinister Affair," *Sentinel*, Sept. 14, 1868, 4. See entries for Samuel Young, FMPC, 1850, Lost Creek, Miami County, Ohio, roll M432-711, p. 43A, and 1860, roll M653-101, p. 244. The 1840 census lists a William Young in Pike Township but no Youngs except Jacob in subsequent years; FMPC, 1840, Pike Township, Marion County, roll 88, p. 254. Numerous people with the last name of Young lived in neighboring Boone County in 1850, but their relation to Jacob Young—if any—cannot be determined. Jacob Young's sister Mary moved to Indianapolis with her husband, Granville Server, but they followed him rather than preceded him. An Indianapolis physician recalled treating Jacob Young's brother; see testimony, Dr. William M. Duzan, *Sentinel*, Sept. 30, 1871, 2.

23. "The Cold Springs Murder," *Journal*, Sept. 17, 1868, 5; *Journal*, Sept. 16, 1868, 8; FMPC, 1860, Pike Township, Marion County, roll M653-280, pp. 930, 945. In 1860, Young lived with the Gill family, evidently tenant farmers since they owned no real estate and held personal property valued at only $100.

24. Genealogies date Nathaniel Case's death at 1850, although the evidence is contradictory. See, for example, Teresa's Family, Ancestry.com, http://trees.ancestry.com/tree/11820 356/person/-300223491, and Smith Family Tree, Ancestry.com, http://trees.ancestry.com /tree/5818538/person/-1375170981. Nancy Jane's mother may have died around this time as well, for she vanishes from extant records. Janey and her younger brother David were farmed out to different branches of the Case extended family. Extant records provide no clues as to Nancy Jane Case's exact relationship to Jonas Case. In 1868 he would be appointed legal guardian of her child; *Journal*, Oct. 13, 1868, 2. In his trial testimony Robert Dorsey referred to Case

as Jacob Young's brother-in-law; see *Clem v. Indiana* (1869), 510. FMPC, 1850, Liberty Township, Hendricks County, Indiana, roll M432-150, p. 84A; FMPC, Pike Township, Marion County, roll M432-159, p. 429A; FMPC, 1860, Waltz Township, Wabash County, Indiana, roll M653-304, p. 9; FMPC, 1860, Pike Township, Marion County, roll M653-280, p. 966. Pre-1880 census records did not designate family relationships, so it is possible that Jonas Case *was* her biological father and that the family members with whom she lived in 1850 were cousins or other relatives. On helps, see Faye Dudden, *Serving Women: Household Service in Nineteenth-Century America* (Middletown, Conn.: Wesleyan University Press, 1983), 12–43, and (for an earlier period) Laurel Thatcher Ulrich, *A Midwife's Tale: The Life of Martha Ballard, Based on Her Diary, 1785–1812* (New York: Vintage, 1991), 81–82. In 1860, Case was "serving" in the family of Elisa Cotton, but she had met Jacob Young while working for James Raveal. See FMPC, 1860, Pike, Marion, Indiana; roll M653-280, p. 266, and Raveal's testimony before the coroner's jury in "The Cold Springs Murder," *Journal*, Sept. 15, 1868, 8. John Duncan, closing argument, *Journal*, Sept. 11, 1869, 2.

25. Testimony, Silas Hartman, *Journal*, Dec. 14, 1868, 2; FMPC, 1850, Pike Township, Marion County, roll M432-159, p. 445B; Myers Family Tree, Ancestry.com, http://trees.ancestry .com/tree/30884819/person/12495361040. William and Jemima Jones moved to Wayne Township sometime after 1850, apparently leaving Margaret behind, and returned to Pike Township by 1870. Margaret was listed twice in the 1860 census, as living with her parents in Wayne Township *and* as a servant in Pike Township. FMPC, 1860, Wayne Township, Marion County, roll M653-280, p. 280, and Pike Township, Marion County, roll M653-280, p. 945; FMPC, 1870, Pike Township, Marion County, roll M593-337, p. 464B; marriages, Jacob Young to Nancy Jane Case and William J. Abrams to Margaret Jones, *Sentinel*, Sept. 18, 1860, 2; *Sentinel*, Sept. 16, 1868, 4.

26. Testimony, Silas Hartman, *Journal*, Dec. 1, 1868, 3; FMPC, 1860, Pike Township, Marion County, roll M653-280, p. 945; *Journal*, Sept. 16, 1868, 8; *Sentinel*, Sept. 18, 1860, 2; "Arrest of William Abrams," *Sentinel*, Sept. 16, 1868, 4.

27. Testimony, William J. Abrams, *Journal*, Oct. 2, 1871, 5; *History of the Seventy-Ninth Regiment Indiana Volunteer Infantry in the Civil War of Eighteen Sixty-One in the United States* (Indianapolis: Hollenbeck Press, 1899), 29; Frederick H. Dyer, *A Compendium of the War of the Rebellion* (1908; repr., Dayton, Ohio: Press of Morningside Bookshop, 1978), 1147; U.S., Civil War Soldier Records and Profiles, 1861–1865 (online database, Ancestry.com, 2009), http://search.ancestry.com/search/db.aspx?dbid=1555; National Park Service, U.S. Civil War Soldiers, 1861–1865 (online database, Ancestry.com, 2007), http:// search.ancestry.com/search/db.aspx?dbid=1138; Draft Enrollment Lists [1862], Marion County, Indiana State Archives, roll 7, p. 263; *Journal*, Sept. 16, 1868, 8; testimony, Robert S. Dorsey, *Journal*, Dec. 11, 1868, 2, and *Sentinel*, Dec. 11, 1868, 2; *Journal*, Sept. 14, 1868, 8; Eric Foner, *Reconstruction: America's Unfinished Revolution, 1863–1877* (New York: Harper & Row, 1988), 19.

28. *Cold Spring Tragedy*, 100; "The Young Murder: Another Bloody Chapter," *Sentinel*, Mar. 11, 1869, 4; Holliday, *Indianapolis and the Civil War*, 572; Robin W. Winks, *The Civil War Years: Canada and the United States* (Montreal: McGill-Queen's University Press, 1998), 203–204; U.S., Civil War Draft Registrations Records, 1863–1865 (online database, Ancestry .com, 2010), http://search.ancestry.com/search/db.aspx?dbid=1666.

29. Matthew Hartman succeeded in gaining an exemption (for reasons unknown) from the 1862 draft overseen by the state of Indiana and administered by county commissioners. Federal authorities nevertheless considered him eligible a year later. Hartman's "Class II" status as a married man between the ages of thirty-six and forty-four (he was thirty-nine at the time he was registered) offered him some protection since younger, single men were the first to be called up. Frank Clem, however, was only thirty-two and thus in Class I. Draft

Enrollment Lists [1862], Marion County, roll 7, pp. 29, 31; Civil War Draft Registrations Records; Richard F. Nation and Stephen E. Towne, *Indiana's War: The Civil War in Documents* (Athens: Ohio University Press, 2009), 44–45; Thomas E. Rodgers, "Liberty, Will, and Violence: The Political Ideology of the Democrats of West-Central Indiana during the Civil War," *Indiana Magazine of History* 92, no. 2 (June 1996): 133–159; Rodgers, "Copperheads or a Respectable Minority: Current Approaches to the Study of Civil War–Era Democrats," *Indiana Magazine of History* 109, no. 2 (June 2013): 114–146.

30. Holliday, *Indianapolis and the Civil War*, 570; Nation, *At Home in the Hoosier Hills*, 205–206. Matthew Hartman was a delegate to the Sixth District Democratic convention in 1864; see "Sixth District Democratic Convention," *Indiana State Sentinel*, Jan. 11, 1864, 3; see also "Democratic Township Convention," *Journal*, Dec. 9, 1867, 1. For Aaron Clem's Republican identity, see "City Council," *Journal*, Mar. 15, 1867, 5.

31. Holliday, *Indianapolis and the Civil War*, 582–583, 595.

32. Richard S. Skidmore, "Civil War," in *Encyclopedia of Indianapolis*, ed. David J. Bodenhamer and Robert G. Barrows (Bloomington: Indiana University Press, 1994), 441–443; Holliday, *Indianapolis and the Civil War*, 574.

33. Holliday, *Indianapolis and the Civil War*, 594, 576–577, 584, 589–590, 593; Richard S. Skidmore, "Civil War," in Bodenhamer and Barrows, *Encyclopedia of Indianapolis*, 441, 443; Madison, *Indiana Way*, 197–198; Nancy F. Gabin, "Women," in Bodenhamer and Barrows, *Encyclopedia of Indianapolis*, 218.

34. Holliday, *Indianapolis and the Civil War*, 555; testimony, Matthew Hartman, *Journal*, Dec. 12, 1868, 2; testimony, William J. Abrams, *Journal*, Oct. 7, 1871, 5; *History of the Seventy-Ninth Regiment*, 217–218.

35. See, for example, James Alan Marten, *Sing Not War: The Lives of Union and Confederate Veterans in Gilded Age America* (Chapel Hill: University of North Carolina Press, 2011), 75–94.

36. Hester Anne Hale, *Indianapolis: The First Century* (Indianapolis: Marion County / Indianapolis Historical Society, 1987), 3; *Journal*, Sept. 9, 1869, 2; *Manufacturing and Mercantile Resources of Indianapolis, Indiana* (n.p.: n.p., 1883), 576; John Duncan, closing argument, *Journal*, Sept. 11, 1869, 2; FMPC, 1870, Indianapolis, roll M593-340, p. 91A, and 2nd enum., roll M593-338, p. 169B. See also Sean Wilentz, *Chants Democratic: New York City and the Rise of the American Working Class, 1788–1850* (New York: Oxford University Press, 1984), 132–134. Indianapolis newspapers in the late 1860s included references to carpenters who built entire houses, presumably with the assistance of journeymen, as well as advertisements for firms such as Campbell & Bratton, Carpenters and Jobbers. See, for example, *Journal*, Apr. 21, 1866, 4 (Mrs. Hanlyn), and "Carpenter," *Journal*, May 2, 1866, 5.

37. *Journal*, Sept. 14, 1868; *Journal*, Sept. 17, 1868, 5; testimony, S. K. Fletcher, *Journal*, Dec. 15, 1868; testimony, Robert Dorsey, *Journal*, Dec. 11, 1868, 2.

38. "The Cold Springs Murder," *Journal*, Sept. 17, 1868, 5; testimony, Dr. William Duzan, *Journal*, Dec. 10, 1868, 2; testimony, "Grandmother Hartman," *Journal*, Dec. 16, 1868, 3; testimony, Jane Sizemore, *Sentinel*, Feb. 17, 1869, 4.

39. "The Young Murder," *Sentinel*, Sept. 22, 1868, 4; Fishback, closing argument, *Journal*, Sept. 9, 1868, 2; "Nancy Clem," *Fort Wayne Weekly Sentinel*, May 20, 1874, 1.

40. Holliday, *Indianapolis and the Civil War*, 595; David W. Blight, *Race and Reunion: The Civil War in American Memory* (Cambridge, Mass.: Harvard University Press, 2001).

Chapter 2 · Business

1. "Horrible and Mysterious Affair," *Indianapolis Sentinel*, Sept. 14, 1868, 4; "Appalling Double Murder," *Indianapolis Journal*, Sept. 14, 1868, 8; "Mrs. Clem: An Hour's Talk With Her," *Sentinel*, Mar. 29, 1869, 4.

2. "The Cold Spring Horror," *Sentinel*, Sept. 15, 1868, 4; testimony, Lizzie Henry, *Journal*, Dec. 5, 1868, 5; Walter S. Smith, "The Story of the Uncalled Witness," *Indianapolis Star*, Aug. 18, 1907, SM1.

3. "Appalling Double Murder," *Journal*, Sept. 14, 1868, 8; testimony, Lizzie Henry, *Journal*, Dec. 5, 1868, 5; W. W. Leathers, opening statement, *Journal*, Sept. 3, 1869, 4.

4. "Horrible and Mysterious Affair," *Sentinel*, Sept. 14, 1868, 4; testimony, Mary Belle Young, *Journal*, Dec. 5, 1868, 5; "The Cold Spring Tragedy," *Sentinel*, Dec. 1, 1868, 4; William B. Atkinson, M.D., *The Philadelphia Medical Register and Directory* (Philadelphia: Collins, 1875), 199–200. The Philadelphia Training School for Feeble-Minded Children was founded in 1854. For census takers' imprecise definitions of "idiocy" and insanity, see E. Fuller Torrey and Judy Miller, *The Invisible Plague: The Rise of Mental Illness from 1750 to the Present* (New Brunswick, N.J.: Rutgers University Press, 2002), 235.

5. Testimony, James Raveal, *Journal*, Sept. 15, 1868, 8; *The Cold Spring Tragedy: Trial and Conviction of Mrs. Nancy E. Clem for the Murder of Jacob Young and Wife . . .* (Indianapolis: A. C. Roach, 1869), 10.

6. Testimony, E. F. Ritter, *Journal*, Sept. 9, 1869, 2; John Duncan, closing argument, *Journal*, Sept. 11, 1869, 2; testimony, Flora Ellerhardt, *Journal*, Dec. 14, 1868, 3.

7. Testimony, H. A. Pollard, *Journal*, Sept. 9, 1869, 2; testimony, John Bowers and Lea W. Munhall, *Journal*, Sept. 10, 1869, 2; John Dye, closing argument, *Journal*, Sept. 14, 1869, 2; W. P. Fishback, closing argument, *Journal*, Sept. 11, 1869, 2; John Duncan, closing argument, *Journal*, Sept. 11, 1869, 2; "Arrest of William Abrams," *Sentinel*, Sept. 16, 1868, 4; "Indianapolis Letter," *Cincinnati Commercial Tribune*; Mar. 16, 1869, 4; testimony, W. F. Clem, *Journal*, Sept. 10, 1869, 8.

8. "Funeral of Mrs. Clem," *Indianapolis News*, June 10, 1897, 8; "Appalling Double Murder," *Journal*, Sept. 14, 1868, 8; "The Cold Spring Tragedy," *Sentinel*, Dec. 1, 1868, 4; "The Cold Spring Tragedy," *Journal*, Sept. 16, 1868, 8; testimony, Louisa B. McKibben, *Journal*, Dec. 9, 1868, 2; testimony, Rebecca Hartman, *Journal*, Sept. 6, 1869, 5.

9. Existing evidence does not tell us whether or not Young and Abrams purchased the $100 broker's license the state of Indiana required; odds are they did not. Apart from this probable lapse, they were theoretically law-abiding citizens. *The Revised Statutes of the State of Indiana* (Indianapolis: J. P. Chapman, 1852), 1:356.

10. Testimony, Robert L. Dorsey, *Journal*, Sept. 8, 1869, 2; "Arrest of William Abrams," *Sentinel*, Sept. 16, 1868, 4; "The Cold Spring Tragedy," *Sentinel*, Dec. 1, 1868, 4; "Mrs. Clem: An Hour's Talk with Her," *Sentinel*, Mar. 29, 1869, 4. See Jonathan Levy, *Freaks of Fortune: The Emerging World of Capitalism and Risk in America* (Cambridge, Mass.: Harvard University Press, 2012), 16–18.

11. John Dye, opening statement, "The Young Murder: First Day of the Trial," *Journal*, Dec. 2, 1868, 4; testimony, Julia McCarty and Rebecca Hartman, *Nancy E. Clem v. State of Indiana* (1869), Office of Supreme Court Records, Indianapolis, Indiana, 1132–1133, 1182–1183.

12. Testimony, Mary M. Server and Mary Belle Young, *Journal*, Dec. 5, 1868, 5; testimony, Alfred Rooker and George Rooker, *Journal*, Dec. 7, 1868, 2.

13. Testimony, Mrs. Erastus Everson, *Journal*, Dec. 8, 1868, 2; Federal Manuscript Population Census (hereafter FMPC), 1870, Indianapolis (2nd enum), roll M593-338, p. 136B.

14. Testimony, William N. Duzan, S. K. Fletcher, and Arthur Wright, *Journal*, Dec. 10, 1868, 2; testimony, Robert S. Dorsey, *Sentinel*, Dec. 11, 1868, 2; testimony, Ann Hottle, *Sentinel*, Dec. 7, 1868, 2; *Cold Spring Tragedy*, 29–39; FMPC, 1870, Indianapolis, roll M593-340, p. 8B, and (2nd enum.), roll M593-338, p.17A; FMPC, 1870, Center Township, Marion County, roll M593-337, p. 344B; Nicole Etcheson, *A Generation at War: The Civil War Era in a Northern Community* (Lawrence: University Press of Kansas, 2011), 65; Gayle Thornbrough, Dorothy

Riker, and Paula Corpuz, eds., *The Diary of Calvin Fletcher*, vol. 6: *1857–1860* (Indianapolis: Indiana Historical Society, 1978), xvi.

15. *News*, June 9, 1897; *Star*, Nov. 11, 1971, B3; Jacob Piatt Dunn, *Greater Indianapolis: The History, the Industries, the Institutions, and the People of a City of Homes* (Chicago: Lewis Publishing, 1910), 1:60; Stephen Mihm, *A Nation of Counterfeiters: Capitalists, Con Men, and the Making of the United States* (Cambridge, Mass.: Harvard University Press, 2007), 343, 347–350. On the history of banking in Indiana, see Emma Lou Thornbrough, *Indiana in the Civil War Era, 1850–1880* (Indianapolis: Indiana Historical Society, 1965), 424–439.

16. "The Young Ring," *Sentinel*, Oct. 7, 1868, 4; "Special Correspondence of the Enquirer," *Cincinnati Enquirer*, Nov. 28, 1876, 2. On corruption, see, for example, "Police Board Investigating Court," *Sentinel*, Jan. 14, 1869, 4, and "Police Investigation," *Sentinel*, Jan. 15, 1869, 2. Timothy J. Gilfoyle, *A Pickpocket's Tale: The Underworld of Nineteenth-Century New York* (New York: W. W. Norton, 2006), 243–254.

17. "From Indianapolis: The Trial of Mrs. Clem for Murder—Proceedings of the Court Yesterday," *Cincinnati Daily Gazette*, Dec. 8, 1868, 3. See, for example, "From Indianapolis," *Cincinnati Daily Gazette*, Mar. 27, 1868, 3, and "Imposter," *Sentinel*, Feb. 15, 1869, 4. See also Bessie K. Roberts, "Crime and Crinoline," *Indiana Magazine of History* 41, no. 4 (Dec. 1945): 388–394, and Gilfoyle, *Pickpocket's Tale*, 82, 204–222.

18. Testimony, William N. Duzan, in *Clem v. Indiana* (1869), 397; testimony, William N. Duzan, *Nancy E. Clem v. State of Indiana* (1872), 2426, Office of Supreme Court Records, Indianapolis, Indiana; *Cold Spring Tragedy*, 29, 31–33.

19. Testimony, William N. Duzan, *Sentinel*, Feb. 13, 1869, 4; Gilfoyle, *Pickpocket's Tale*, xiiii, 209–210; Mihm, *Nation of Counterfeiters*, 347–51. On the continuing salience of localism, Morton Keller, *Affairs of State: Public Life in Late Nineteenth Century America* (Cambridge, MA: Harvard University Press, 1977), 35, 50–51, 106–121, 162–196. For a recent example of a Ponzi scheme that resembles the one that Clem, Young, and Abrams undertook, see William Yardley, "A Fraud Played Out on Family and Friends," *New York Times*, May 26, 2011, A13.

20. *Cold Spring Tragedy*, 33; "Measuring Worth: Seven Ways to Compute the Relative Value of a U.S. Dollar Amount, 1774 to Present," www.measuringworth.com/uscompare; "Death of Nancy E. Clem," *News*, June 9, 1897, 8; Lawrence M. Friedman, *Crime and Punishment in American History* (New York: Basic Books, 1993), 438–439.

21. "Indianapolis Letter: The Hand of God," *Cincinnati Commercial Tribune*, Feb. 1, 1869, 2.

22. "Appalling Double Murder," *Journal*, Sept. 14, 1868, 8; "The Cold Springs Murder," *Journal*, Sept. 17, 1868, 5; "The Cold Springs Tragedy," *Sentinel*, Dec. 1, 1868, 4; John T. Dye, closing argument; *Journal*, Dec. 18, 1868, 2.

23. Thornbrough, *Indiana in the Civil War Era*, 435–436. On informal money-lending, see Suzanne Lebsock, *A Murder in Virginia: Southern Justice on Trial* (New York: W. W. Norton, 2003), 13, 130–131. See testimony, Silas A. Pollard, *Journal*, Sept. 9, 1869, 2; testimony, Silas Hartman, *Journal*, Dec. 14, 1868, 2; testimony, Ann Hottle, *Journal*, Dec. 7, 1868, 2–3.

24. Testimony, Ann Hottle, *Journal*, Dec. 7, 1868, 2–3.

25. "A Few More Notes," *Journal*, Dec. 25, 1868, 3; testimony, Rev. T. A. Goodwin, *Journal*, Dec. 15, 1868, 3; "Wanted—To Loan—Money," *Sentinel*, Oct. 25, 1872, 2.

26. M. S. Emery, *Every-Day Business: Notes on Its Practical Details Arranged for Young People* (Boston: Lee & Shepard, 1890), 88–91; "Shaving Notes—By Henry Ward Beecher," *Cambridge (Ind.) City Tribune*, June 22, 1871, 5; "Enjoyment—Happiness," *Williamsport Review Republican*, Aug. 17, 1871, 4; "Who Bids?" *Journal*, Jan. 3, 1868, 5; "A Broker's Love Affair," reprinted from *Harper's Monthly* in *Journal*, Mar. 19, 1868, 7; "A Card," *Greencastle Weekly Indiana Press*, Dec. 30, 1868, 3.

27. *Cold Spring Tragedy*, 12.

28. Testimony, James Raveal, *Journal*, Sept. 15, 1868, 8; William J. Abrams to Robert L. Dorsey, May 8, 1868, reprinted in *Journal*, Sept. 8, 1869, 2; *Clem v. Indiana* (1872), 2414–2419.

29. "Mrs. Clem: An Hour's Talk with Her," *Sentinel*, Mar. 29, 1869, 4; testimony, William H. Brown, Alfred Rooker, and George Rooker, *Journal*, Dec. 7, 1868, 2; testimony, Jane Sizemore, *Journal*, Dec. 10, 1868, 2; testimony, James D. Brown, *Journal*, Dec. 8, 1868, 2; "Behind the Bars: Prison Life of Mrs. Clem," *Louisville Courier-Journal*, July 5, 1869, 4.

30. "Mrs. Clem: An Hour's Talk with Her," *Sentinel*, Mar. 29, 1869, 4; "Behind the Bars: Prison Life of Mrs. Clem," *Louisville Courier-Journal*, July 5, 1869, 4; John Hanna, opening statement, *Sentinel*, Feb. 12, 1869, 8; Hanna, closing argument, *Journal*, Dec. 21, 1868, 6.

31. Testimony, John Patterson, *Journal*, Dec. 9, 1868, 2; testimony, George Knodle and Jane Sizemore, *Journal*, Dec. 10, 1868, 2; testimony, Dr. W. N. Duzan, *Journal*, Dec. 10, 1868, 2; Thomas D. Hamm, *Earlham College: A History, 1847–1997* (Bloomington: Indiana University Press, 1997), 33, 42–45, 60, 62; Thomas Hamm, Curator of the Quaker Collection & Director of Special Collections, Earlham College, email message to author, July 22, 2015. Albert evidently was not quite ready for college, for he enrolled in Earlham's Preparatory, not its College, Department.

Chapter 3 · Cold Spring

1. "The Cold Spring Horror," *Indianapolis Sentinel*, Sept. 16, 1868, 4; "The Cold Spring Tragedy: Arrest of William J. Abrams for the Crime," *Indianapolis Journal*, Sept. 16, 1868, 8.

2. "Appalling Double Murder," *Journal*, Sept. 14, 1868, 8, and Sept. 15, 1868, 8; *The Cold Spring Tragedy: Trial and Conviction of Mrs. Nancy E. Clem for the Murder of Jacob Young and Wife . . .* (Indianapolis: A. C. Roach, 1869), 26–28; testimony, Lizzie Henry, *Journal*, Dec. 5, 1868, 5.

3. "The Cold Springs Murder," *Journal*, Sept. 17, 1868, 5; "The Cold Springs Murder: To the Editor of the *Indianapolis Journal*," *Journal*, Sept. 18, 1868, 5. Newspapers alternated between "Julia McCarty" and "Julia McCarthy." I have chosen "McCarty" as both the 1870 census and official trial transcripts identify her thus. By 1872 she had married and answered to Julia Shaughnessy. Federal Manuscript Population Census (hereafter FMPC), 1870, Indianapolis, roll M593-340, p. 9B; *Nancy E. Clem v. State of Indiana* (1869) and *Nancy E. Clem v. State of Indiana* (1872), 3322, Office of Supreme Court Records, Indianapolis, Indiana, 1130.

4. "The Cold Springs Murder," *Journal*, Sept. 17, 1868, 5.

5. "The Cold Spring Murder," *Sentinel*, Sept. 18, 1868, 4.

6. "City News: The Cold Springs Murder: Arrest of Silas A. Hartman Yesterday," *Journal*, Sept. 22, 1868, 4; testimony, Silas Hartman, *Clem v. Indiana* (1869), 1384–1385; Benjamin Gresh, in FMPC, 1870, Indianapolis, roll M593-340, p. 23B; "The Cold Spring Murder: Trial of Mrs. Clem: Tenth Day's Proceedings," *Sentinel*, Dec. 12, 1868, 2; "The Young Murder," *Sentinel*, Sept. 22, 1868, 4.

7. *Cold Spring Tragedy*, 47–48, 58–59.

8. "The Young Murder Trial," *Sentinel*, Oct. 24, 1868, 4.

9. Testimony, William H. Brown, *Journal*, Dec. 7, 1868, 2; testimony, James D. Brown, *Journal*, Dec. 8, 1868, 2; testimony, Jane Sizemore and Nancy Hartman, *Clem v. Indiana* (1869), 851–852, 1784–1785, 1794–1795.

10. John T. Dye, opening statement, *Journal*, Dec. 2, 1868, 4; testimony, Lucy Brouse, *Journal*, Dec. 17, 1868, 2, and *Clem v. Indiana* (1869), 1073–1074; testimony, Charles Donnellan, Charlotte Bright, Christina Ginther, and Nancy Hartman, *Clem v. Indiana* (1869), 1579–1594, 1722–1728, 1742, 1745–1746, 1787.

11. Testimony, William H. Brown, *Journal*, Dec. 7, 1868, 2; testimony, James D. Brown, *Journal*, Dec. 8, 1868, 2.

12. Testimony, Lucy Brouse, *Journal*, Dec. 17, 1868, 2, and *Clem v. Indiana* (1869), 1073–1074.

13. Testimony, Jane Sizemore, *Clem v. Indiana* (1869), 851–852.

14. "Horrible and Mysterious Affair," *Sentinel*, Sept. 14, 1868, 8; "The Cold Spring Horror," *Sentinel*, Sept. 15, 1868, 4.

15. "Appalling Double Murder," *Journal*, Sept. 14, 1868, 8; "The Cold Spring Tragedy: Arrest of William J. Abrams for the Crime," *Journal*, Sept. 16, 1868, 8; testimony, Millie Locke, Seymour Locke, and Julia Coleman, *Journal*, Dec. 3, 1868, 4; testimony, Julia Coleman, *Clem v. Indiana* (1869), 393–395.

16. "Horrible and Mysterious Affair," *Sentinel*, Sept. 14, 1868, 8.

17. "Abrams Pardoned," *People* (Indianapolis), July 6, 1878; "Nancy E. Clem!" *People*, Mar. 20, 1880, 1.

18. "Site of Young Murder," *Journal*, June 10, 1897, 8; testimony, Luther D. Waterman, *Clem v. Indiana* (1869), 378; "Extinguishing Burning Clothes," *Godey's Lady's Book* 77 (Sept. 1868): 263; "A Funereal Fashion," *Albion*, May 1, 1858, 213; "Dangerous Dresses," *Albion*, Feb. 4, 1865, 51–52; and "A Coroner on Crinoline," *Ohio Medical and Surgical Journal*, Mar. 1, 1863, 155–156. See also "Burnt to Death," *Littell's Living Age*, Sept. 14, 1861, 674; "A New Kind of Willful Murder," *Saturday Evening Post*, Jan. 31, 1863, 3; "The Disadvantages of Crinoline," *Liberator*, Sept. 1, 1865, 139; and "Dangers and Fears," *Harper's Bazaar*, Jan. 11, 1868, 162. "Horrible and Mysterious Affair," *Sentinel*, Sept. 14, 1868, 4.

19. Jacob Piatt Dunn, *Greater Indianapolis: The History, the Industries, the Institutions, and the People of a City of Homes* (Chicago: Lewis Publishing, 1910), 1:596.

20. "Obituary," *Journal*, Sept. 17, 1868, 8; *Hymns for the Use of the Methodist Episcopal Church, with Tunes for Congregational Worship* (New York: Carleton & Porter, 1857), 84.

21. Peggy McDowell and Richard E. Meyer, *The Revival Styles in American Memorial Art* (Bowling Green, OH: Bowling Green State University Popular Press, 1994), 133–144.

22. Mary Thomas Crismore, comp., "Volume One Cemetery Records of Marion County and Some Adjoining Counties" (Indianapolis: Caroline Scott Harrison Chapter of the National Society Daughters of the American Revolution, 1970–1971), 52; *Cemetery Readings of Pike Township Marion County, Indiana* (Indianapolis: Genealogical Society of Marion County, 1998), 104.

23. "A Singular Phenomenon," *Journal*, Sept. 17, 1868, 8; Dunn, *Greater Indianapolis*, 1:60; "Police Board Investigating Court," *Sentinel*, Jan. 13, 1869, 4; "Appalling Double Murder," *Journal*, Sept. 14, 1868, 8.

24. Testimony, Charles E. Harris, *Journal*, Dec. 9, 1868, 2.

Chapter 4 · Detection

1. Testimony, Lou Monroe, *Indianapolis Journal*, Dec. 3, 1868, 5.

2. *The Cold Spring Tragedy: Trial and Conviction of Mrs. Nancy E. Clem for the Murder of Jacob Young and Wife . . .* (Indianapolis: A. C. Roach, 1869), 7, 9; "Appalling Double Murder," *Journal*, Sept. 14, 1868, 8; "The Cold Springs Murder," *Journal*, Sept. 15, 1868, 8.

3. "The Cold Springs Murder," *Journal*, Sept. 15, 1868, 8.

4. W. R. Holloway, *Indianapolis: A Historical and Statistical Sketch of the Railroad City* (Indianapolis: Indianapolis Journal Printers, 1870), 8–9, 45.

5. Dye, opening statement, *Journal*, Dec. 2, 1868, 5.

6. "The Young Murder: Verdict of the Coroner's Jury," *Journal*, Oct. 10, 1868, 8; "The Cold Springs Murder: Arrest of Silas A. Hartman Yesterday," *Journal*, Sept. 22, 1868, 4; testimony, Garrison W. Allred, *Journal*, Dec. 3, 1868, 4.

7. "The Cold Springs Murder," *Journal*, Sept. 15, 1868, 8.

8. "Appalling Double Murder," *Journal*, Sept. 14, 1868, 8; testimony, Seymour Locke, *Nancy E. Clem v. State of Indiana* (1869), Office of Supreme Court Records, Indianapolis,

Indiana, 327. According to Locke, "They did not take us in to see [the bodies]. I just saw them through the window." Testimony, Garrison W. Allred, *Journal*, Dec. 3, 1868, 4.

9. "The Cold Springs Murder," *Journal*, Sept. 15, 1868, 8.

10. Ibid.

11. H. Aubrey Husband, *The Student's Hand-Book of Forensic Medicine and Medical Police*, 4th ed. (Edinburgh: E & S Livingstone, 1882), 62; Katherine Ramsland, *Beating the Devil's Game: A History of Forensic Science and Criminal Investigation* (New York: Berkley Books, 2007), 29; Douglas Starr, *The Killer of Little Shepherds: A True Crime Story and the Birth of Forensic Science* (New York: Knopf, 2010), 103, 105; Clare V. McKenna Jr., *The Trial of "Indian Joe": Race and Justice in the Nineteenth-Century West* (Lincoln: University of Nebraska Press, 2003), 85–87; McKenna, *White Justice in Arizona: Apache Murder Trials in the Nineteenth Century* (Lubbock: Texas Tech University Press, 2005), 128–129. For another instance of measuring footprints with a stick, see Suzanne Lebsock, *A Murder in Virginia: Southern Justice on Trial* (New York: W. W. Norton, 2003), 249–250.

12. *Cold Spring Tragedy*, 8; testimony, John Buser, *Cold Spring Tragedy*, 23; John Hanna, closing argument, *Cold Spring Tragedy*, 82; testimony, Luther D. Waterman, *Clem v. Indiana* (1869), 369–370; "Other Arrests," *Journal*, Sept. 16, 1868, 8.

13. "The Cold Spring Murder: Arrest of William Abrams," *Indianapolis Sentinel*, Sept. 16, 1868, 4; "The Cold Spring Tragedy: Arrest of William J. Abrams for the Crime," *Journal*, Sept. 16, 1868, 8; Federal Manuscript Population Census (hereafter FMPC), 1870, Indianapolis (2nd enum.), roll M593-339, p. 435A. Wilson had two sons, Charles, who would have been sixteen at the time of the murders, and Horace, who would have been thirteen. Either might have been the "boy" for whom Wilson contemplated purchasing the gun. John H. B. Nowland, *Early Reminiscences of Indianapolis, with Short Biographical Sketches of Its Early Citizens, and of a Few of the Prominent Business Men of the Present Day* (Indianapolis: Sentinel Job & Printing House, 1870), 428–429; *Manufacturing and Mercantile Resources of Indianapolis, Indiana* (n.p.: n.p., 1883), 642.

14. "The Cold Spring Murder," *Sentinel*, Sept. 16, 1868, 4.

15. Testimony, Elisha Kise and William Coleman, *Journal*, Sept. 9, 1869, 2.

16. Testimony, E. F. Ritter, *Journal*, Sept. 8, 1869, 2.

17. "The Cold Spring Tragedy," *Journal*, Sept. 16, 1868, 8.

18. *A. C. Howard's Directory for the City of Indianapolis* (Indianapolis: A. C. Howard. 1857), 18, 259; Jacob Piatt Dunn, *Greater Indianapolis: The History, the Institutions, and the People of a City of Homes* (Chicago: Lewis Publishing, 1910), 1:59; "The Cold Springs Murder: The Trial of William J. Abrams Postponed," *Journal*, Sept. 17, 1868, 5.

19. "The Cold Springs Murder: The Trial of William J. Abrams Postponed," *Journal*, Sept. 17, 1868, 5; testimony, Aaron L. Hunt and Mrs. Marot, *Journal*, Dec. 3, 1868, 5; testimony, Josephine Stevens, *Journal*, Dec. 4, 1868, 4; testimony, David C. Duvall, *Journal*, Dec. 4, 1868, 4.

20. Testimony, John A. Drew, *Journal*, Dec. 4, 1868, 4.

21. Ibid.

22. "City News: The Cold Springs Murder: Arrest of Silas A. Hartman Yesterday," *Journal*, Sept. 22, 1868, 4.

23. Testimony, John G. Wiley and John H. Wiley, *Journal*, Dec. 9, 1868, 2. The younger John Wiley was variously identified as John G. Wiley, John T. Wiley, and John P. Wiley. In the text, I have chosen to follow the two official transcripts, which designate him as John P.

24. Ibid.

25. "The Cold Springs Murder: Arrest of Silas A Hartman Yesterday," *Journal*, Sept. 22, 1868, 4.

26. "Statement of Mrs. Clem," *Journal*, Dec. 17, 1868, 2; *Cold Spring Tragedy*, 53–54.

27. Dye, opening statement, *Journal*, Dec. 2, 1868, 5; testimony, Adeline (Madeline) Everson, *Clem v. Indiana* (1869), 1066–1067.

28. FMPC, 1870, Pike Township, Marion County, roll M593-337, p. 476B; testimony, Silas Pollard, *Journal*, Sept. 9, 1869, 2; testimony, Benjamin Abrams and Ann Hottle, *Journal*, Dec. 7, 1868, 2.

29. "The Cold Springs Tragedy: Another Arrest," *Journal*, Oct. 8, 1868, 8.

30. "The Cold Spring Tragedy," *Sentinel*, Dec. 1, 1868, 4.

31. Dunn, *Greater Indianapolis*, 1:60; *Journal*, Oct. 13, 1868, 8; "Old Alabama Street House Still Holds Mystery of Famous Clem Murder Case," *Indianapolis Star*, Aug. 30, 1930, 2.22; *Cold Spring Tragedy*, 10; *Sentinel*, Feb. 13, 1869, 4; Dye, closing argument, *Journal*, Dec. 18, 1868, 2; Benjamin Harrison, closing argument, *Cold Spring Tragedy*, 70.

32. *Journal*, Oct. 13, 1868, 2; FMPC, 1870, Pike Township, Marion County, roll: M593-337, p. 476A; "A Murder Recalled," *Indianapolis Sun*, Sept. 22, 1891, 1.

33. "The Young Murder," *Sentinel*, Oct. 12, 1868, 4; *Sentinel* Oct. 21, 1868, 4; "The Young Murder Trial," *Sentinel*, Oct. 24, 1868, 4.

34. See, for example, W. P. Fishback, closing argument, *Cold Spring Tragedy*, 99–105, 118, 121–122.

35. Dye, opening statement, *Journal*, Dec. 2, 1868, 5; *Cold Spring Tragedy*, 17.

36. Harrison, closing argument, *Cold Spring Tragedy*, 78.

Chapter 5 · Trial

1. See, for example, "The President's Message," *Daily Columbus (Ga.) Enquirer*, Dec. 1, 1868, 1; *New Hampshire Patriot*, Dec. 2, 1868, 1; *Pittsfield (Mass.) Sun*, Dec. 3, 1868, 2; "General Grant's Annual Report," *Philadelphia Inquirer*, Dec. 1, 1868, 4; "Troops in the Southern States," *New York Times*, Dec. 1, 1868, 4: "General Grant's Report," *Indianapolis Journal*, Dec. 1, 1868, 1; "Standing Armies," *Indianapolis Sentinel*, Dec. 1, 1868, 2; "What Grant Is in Favor Of," *Sentinel*, Dec. 2, 1868, 1.

2. "The Young Murder: First Day of the Trial," *Journal*, Dec. 2, 1868, 4; "The Cold Spring Murder: Trial of Mrs. Nancy E. Clem," *Sentinel*, Dec. 2, 1868, 4. For similar coverage of a very different case, see Michael A. Ross, *The Great New Orleans Kidnapping Case: Race, Law, and Justice in the Reconstruction Era* (New York: Oxford University Press, 2015), 114.

3. "The Young Murder," *Journal*, Dec. 2, 1868, 4; "The Cold Spring Murder," *Sentinel*, Dec. 2, 1868, 4; "The Young Murder: Fourth Day's Proceedings," *Journal*, Dec. 5, 1868, 5; "The Trial," *Sentinel*, Dec. 11, 1868, 4; "For the benefit of the crowd," *Sentinel*, Feb. 24, 1869, 4; Sarah Hill Fletcher, diary, Dec. 19, 1868, Indiana Historical Society, Indianapolis.

4. Karen Halttunen, *Murder Most Foul: The Killer and the American Gothic Imagination* (Cambridge, Mass.: Harvard University Press, 1998), 35–59; Daniel Ray Papke, *Framing the Criminal: Crime, Cultural Work, and the Loss of Critical Perspective* (Hamden, Conn.: Archon Books, 1987); Amy Gilman Srebnick, *The Mysterious Death of Mary Rogers: Sex and Culture in Nineteenth-Century New York* (New York: Oxford University Press, 1995); Patricia Cline Cohen, *The Murder of Helen Jewett: The Life and Death of a Prostitute in Nineteenth-Century New York* (New York: Knopf, 1998); Daniel A. Cohen, "The Murder of Maria Bickford: Fashion, Passion, and the Birth of a Consumer Culture," *American Studies* 31 (Fall 1990): 5–30; Daniel A. Cohen, *Pillars of Salt, Monuments of Grace: New England Crime Literature and the Origins of American Popular Culture, 1674–1860* (New York: Oxford University Press, 1993); Benjamin Feldman, *Butchery on Bond Street: Sexual Politics and The Burdell-Cunningham Case in Ante-bellum New York* (New York: New York Wanderer Press, 2007); Michael Ayers Trotti, *The Body in the Reservoir: Murder and Sensationalism in the South* (Chapel Hill: University of North Carolina Press, 2008); Carole Haber, *The Trials of Laura Fair: Sex, Murder, and Insanity in the Victorian West* (Chapel Hill: University of North Carolina Press, 2013).

5. Mary P. Ryan, *Women in Public: Between Banners and Ballots, 1825–1880* (Baltimore: Johns Hopkins University Press, 1990), 70–71; Ann Jones, *Women Who Kill* (New York: Holt, Rinehart, & Winston, 1980); Judith A. Allen, *Sex and Secrets: Crimes Involving Australian Women since 1880* (Melbourne: Oxford University Press Australia, 1990); Mary S. Hartman, *Victorian Murderesses: A True History of Thirteen Respectable French and English Women Accused of Unspeakable Crimes* (New York: Schocken Books, 1977); Edward Berenson, *The Trial of Madame Caillaux* (Berkeley: University of California Press, 1992); Susan Branson, *Dangerous to Know: Women, Crime, and Notoriety in the Early Republic* (Philadelphia: University of Pennsylvania Press, 2008); Randolph Roth, *American Homicide* (Cambridge, Mass.: Harvard University Press, 2009), 265–269, 288–290, 325.

6. "The Young Murder: First Day of the Trial," *Journal*, Dec. 2, 1868, 4; "The Cold Spring Murder: Trial of Mrs. Nancy E. Clem," *Sentinel*, Dec. 2, 1868.

7. *The Cold Spring Tragedy: Trial and Conviction of Mrs. Nancy E. Clem for the Murder of Jacob Young and Wife . . .* (Indianapolis: A. C. Roach, 1869), 16; "From Indianapolis," *Cincinnati Daily Gazette*, October 8, 1868, 3; "The Cold Springs Tragedy: Another Arrest," *Journal*, Oct. 8, 1868, 8; "The Young Murder: First Day of the Trial," *Journal*, Dec. 2, 1868, 4.

8. Leander John Monks, *Courts and Lawyers of Indiana* (Indianapolis: Federal Publishing Company, 1916), 2:859–860; Jacob Piatt Dunn, *Greater Indianapolis: The History, the Industries, the Institutions, and the People of a City of Homes* (Chicago: Lewis Publishing, 1910), 2:559.

9. Dunn, *Greater Indianapolis*, 1:391, 394; Mildred C. Stoler, "Insurgent Democrats of Indiana and Illinois in 1854," *Indiana Magazine of History* 33, no. 1 (Mar. 1937): 7; Charles E. Meyer, "Indianapolis Literary Club," in *The Encyclopedia of Indianapolis*, ed. David J. Bodenhamer and Robert G. Barrows (Bloomington: Indiana University Press, 1994), 788; James W. Fesler, "The Commemoration of Antietam and Gettysburg," *Indiana Magazine of History* 35, no. 3 (Sept. 1939): 247.

10. Cohen, *Pillars of Salt, Monuments of Grace*, 29–30.

11. Dunn, *Greater Indianapolis*, 1:60–61; *Logan's Annual Indianapolis City Directory, 1868–'9* (Indianapolis: n. p., [1869]), 37, 85; Robert M. Ireland, "Privately Funded Prosecution of Crime in the Nineteenth-Century United States," *American Journal of Legal History* 39, no. 1 (Jan. 1995): 43–58; "Minor Notices: John S. Duncan," *Indiana Magazine of History* 11, no. 1 (Mar. 1915): 85–86; Charles W. Calhoun, "Benjamin Harrison," in Bodenhamer and Barrows, *Encyclopedia of Indianapolis*, 660–661; B. R. Sulgrove, *History of Indianapolis and Marion County, Indiana* (Philadelphia: L. H. Everts & Co., 1884), 214E; *Edwards' Indianapolis Directory, Municipal Record, and City Register* (n.p.: n.p., [1869]), 83, 150; *Journal*, Sept. 16, 1868, 4; *Commemorative Biographical Record of Prominent and Representative Men of Indianapolis and Vicinity* (Chicago: J. H. Beers & Co., 1908), 148; "Proceedings of the Indianapolis Bar Association in Memory of William Pinkney Fishback" (unpaginated typescript), Indiana Historical Society.

12. "The Young Murder: Fourth Day of the Trial," *Sentinel*, Dec. 5, 1868, 4; Sulgrove, *History of Indianapolis and Marion County*, 180–181, 214E–214F; *Cold Spring Tragedy*, 83; *Sentinel*, Dec. 5, 1868; John Hanna, closing argument, *Journal*, Dec. 21, 1868, 3; Tony L. Trimble, "Frederick Knefler," in Bodenhamer and Barrows, *Encyclopedia of Indianapolis*, 873; Dunn, *Greater Indianapolis*, 1:60.

13. "Criminal Court," *Sentinel*, Dec. 18, 1868, 4.

14. John T. Dye, closing argument, *Journal*, Dec. 18, 1868, 2; W. P. Fishback, closing argument, *Journal*, Dec. 21, 1868, 1; Fishback, closing argument, *Cold Spring Tragedy*, 95–98; Hanna, closing argument, *Journal*, Dec. 21, 1868, 3; in Clem's second trial, see W. W. Leathers, opening argument, *Cold Spring Tragedy*, 60.

15. Official transcripts are available only for the two trials (1869 and 1872) for which Clem appealed her convictions to the Indiana Supreme Court. Testimony, Thomas Mansfield, *Sen-*

tinel, Dec. 5, 1868, 4; testimony, John Patterson, David Cady, W. S. Armstrong, and Joseph D. Vinnedge, *Sentinel*, Dec. 9, 1868, 2; testimony, John Hitchings, John J. Gates, and George Knodle, *Sentinel*, Dec. 10, 1868, 4; testimony, Abraham Bond and William Wirt, *Sentinel*, Dec. 12, 1868, 2; testimony, John J. Gates and David Cady, *Sentinel*, Dec. 15, 1868, 2.

16. Jones, *Women Who Kill*, 86.

17. Testimony, Perry Todd and John G. Wiley, *Journal*, Dec. 9, 1868, 2; *Journal*, Dec. 12, 1868, 2–3; *Sentinel*, Dec. 12, 1868, 2; June 21, 1869, 4; Fishback, closing argument, *Cold Spring Tragedy*, 104–105; testimony, John Harbert, *Nancy E. Clem v. State of Indiana* (1872), 3647, Office of Supreme Court Records, Indianapolis, Indiana; John T. Dye, opening statement, *Journal*, Dec. 2, 1868, 4.

18. Stacy Pratt McDermott, *The Jury in Lincoln's America* (Athens: Ohio University Press, 2012), 86, 100; "The Young Murder: First Day of the Trial," *Journal*, Dec. 2, 1868, 4. The *Sentinel*, Dec. 2, 1868, 4, listed the jurors as follows. Information concerning age, property, marital status, household composition, and place of birth can be gleaned from the Federal Manuscript Population Census (hereafter FMPC), 1870, roll M593-337. The exception is William K. Richardson, of Franklin Township, who does not appear in either the 1860 or 1870 census. Given that his place of residence was overwhelmingly rural, he probably was a farmer as were the other jurors: George B. Richardson, Franklin Township (p. 389B); John McColley, Franklin township (p. 390A); Anthony Wiese, Warren township (p. 511A); Joshua Vandeman, Warren township (p. 496B); John Buchanan, Warren township (p. 512B); John E. Griffith, Perry township (p. 451B); James Wishard, Perry township (p. 438B); William J. Colley, Franklin township (p. 374A); Stephen Anderson, Franklin township (p. 379A); Lewis J. Toon, Franklin township (p. 385B); Uriah L. Thompson, Franklin township (p. 386A).

19. Dunn, *Greater Indianapolis*, 2:391.

20. "The Trial," *Sentinel*, Dec. 11, 1868, 4; "The Cold Spring Murder: Trial of Mrs. Nancy E. Clem," *Sentinel*, Dec. 2, 1868, 4. The *Journal*, Dec. 19, 1868, 8, explained Colley's predicament, identifying him only as "a highly respectable middle aged widower." Colley, age fifty-six, was the only juror to marry within a year of the trial; "Marriage," Wm. J. Colley to Mrs. Ally Ann Wheeler, *Journal*, July 15, 1869, 8. None of the jurors listed in the 1870 census had one-year-old twins, although one, Stephen Anderson, had a one-year-old singleton. Either the twins belonged to William K. Richardson, the one juror who evaded census takers, or one or both died before the 1870 census was taken. "The Trial," *Sentinel*, Dec. 11, 1868, 4.

21. *Memorial Meeting of the Bench and Bar of Marion County upon the Occasion of the Death of John T. Dye* (Indianapolis: Indianapolis Bar Association, [1913?]), 4–6, 18.

22. Dye, opening statement; Henry Ward Beecher, *Seven Lectures to Young Men, on Various Important Subjects* (Indianapolis: Thomas B. Cutler, 1844), 143–166.

23. Dye, opening statement, *Journal*, Dec. 2, 1868, 4.

24. "The Judicial Coup 'd Etat," *Journal*, Dec. 4, 1868, 4; "Suppressing Publishers," *Journal*, Dec. 4, 1868, 4; *Journal*, Dec. 7, 1868, 4; "The Intense Feeling," *Journal*, Dec. 4, 1868, 8; "The Murder Trial: Order of the Court Prohibiting Publication of the Testimony," *Sentinel*, Dec. 3, 1868, 2; "The Cold Spring Murder: Second Day's Proceedings," *Sentinel*, Dec. 3, 1868, 4; "The Murder Trial," *Sentinel*, Dec. 4, 1868, 1; "Spirit of the Morning Press, *Daily Evening Mirror*, Dec. 2, 1868, 2.

25. *Journal*, Dec. 4, 1868, 8.

26. "The Contest between the Press and the Criminal Court Ended," *Sentinel*, Dec. 5, 1868, 2; "Suppressing Publishers," *Journal*, Dec. 4, 1868, 8.

27. "Publication of the Testimony," *Journal*, Dec. 4, 1868, 5; "Letter from Indianapolis: The Cold Spring Tragedy," *Cincinnati Daily Gazette*, Dec. 4, 1868, 1.

28. "Letter from Indianapolis: The Young Murder Case," *Cincinnati Daily Gazette*, Dec. 7, 1868, 3.

29. Testimony, Luther D. Waterman, *Journal*, Dec. 2, 1868, 5; testimony, Millie Locke and Seymour Locke, *Journal*, Dec. 3, 1868, 5; *Sentinel*, Dec. 3, 1868, 4.

30. Testimony, Erie Locke, *Journal*, Dec. 4, 1868, 4; *Sentinel*, Dec. 4, 1868, 4.

31. *Journal*, Dec. 4, 1868, 8; testimony, Aaron Hunt, Rebecca Marot, and Isaac Sweede, *Journal*, Dec. 3, 1868, 5; "The Young Murder: Third Day's Proceedings" and testimony, Joseph Solomon, Josephine Stevens, and David C. Duvall, *Journal*, Dec. 4, 1868, 4; *Sentinel*, Dec. 4, 1868, 4.

32. Testimony, John A. Drew and John Culp, *Journal*, Dec. 4, 1868, 4–5; *Sentinel*, Dec. 4, 1868, 4.

33. Testimony, Mary M. Server and Mary Belle Young, *Journal*, Dec. 5, 1868, 5; *Sentinel*, Dec. 5, 1868, 4; testimony, Madeline Everson, *Journal*, Dec. 8, 1868, 2; *Sentinel*, Dec. 8, 1868, 2.

34. Testimony, Ann Hottle, *Journal*, Dec. 7, 1868, 2–3; "The Cold Spring Murder: Fifth Day's Proceedings," *Sentinel*, Dec. 7, 1868, 2; "Letter from Indianapolis: The Young Murder Case," *Cincinnati Daily Gazette*, Dec. 7, 1868, 3.

35. Testimony, Perry Todd and John G. Wiley, *Journal*, Dec. 9, 1868, 2.

36. Testimony, Louisa Merchant and Viola Pierson, *Journal*, Dec. 8, 1868, 2; *Sentinel*, Dec. 8, 1868, 2; "From Indianapolis: The Trial of Mrs. Clem for Murder," *Cincinnati Daily Gazette*, Dec. 8, 1868, 3; Dye, opening statement, *Journal*, Dec. 2, 1868, 4.

37. "The Young Murder: Fourth Day's Proceedings," *Journal*, Dec. 5, 1868, 5; "The Trial," *Sentinel*, Dec. 11, 1868, 4; "The Trial," *Sentinel*, Dec. 8, 1868, 4.

38. Testimony, Rebecca Hartman, *Journal*, Dec. 10, 1868, 2; *Sentinel*, Dec. 10, 1868, 4.

39. "Letter from Indianapolis: The Young Murder Case," *Cincinnati Daily Gazette*, Dec. 7, 1868, 3; testimony, Captain Benjamin Abrams, *Journal*, Dec. 7, 1868, 2; *Sentinel*, Dec. 7, 1868, 2.

40. Testimony, Benjamin Abrams, *Journal*, Dec. 7, 1868, 2; *Sentinel*, Dec. 7, 1868, 2.

41. FMPC, 1860, Indianapolis, Ward 7, roll M653-279, p. 620; testimony, Julia McCarty, *Journal*, Dec. 8, 1868, 2, and Dec. 10, 1868, 2; *Sentinel*, Dec. 8, 1868, 2, and Dec. 10, 1868, 4; "From Indianapolis: The Trial of Mrs. Clem for Murder," *Cincinnati Daily Gazette*, Dec. 8, 1868, 3.

42. Testimony, Julia McCarty, *Journal*, Dec. 8, 1868, 2, and Dec. 10, 1868, 2; *Sentinel*, Dec. 8, 1868, 2, and Dec. 10, 1868, 4.

43. Nicole Etcheson, *A Generation at War: The Civil War Era in a Northern Community* (Lawrence: University Press of Kansas, 2011), 231; testimony, Jane Sizemore, *Journal*, Dec. 10, 1868, 2; *Sentinel*, Dec. 10, 1868, 4; John Hanna, closing argument, *Journal*, Dec. 21, 1868, 6. See, for example, the records of slave owners William Sizemore (Baldwin County, Alabama, p. 69); Alexander, Charles, Virginia, Mary, and Frederick Sizemore (Baldwin County, Alabama, p. 73); Susan and George Sizemore (Monroe County, Alabama, p. 107); and F. M. Sizemore (Clarke County, Alabama, p. 474); Daniel Sizemore (Mecklenburg County, Virginia, p. 11), 1860 U.S. Federal Census—Slave Schedules (online database, Ancestry.com, 2010), http://search.ancestry.com/search/db.aspx?dbid=7668. William Sizemore's record suggests an additional possibility; in 1860 he was the owner of a sixteen-year-old female fugitive slave.

44. "The Trial," *Sentinel*, Dec. 11, 1868, 4.

45. Testimony, William N. Duzan, *Journal*, Dec. 10, 1868, 2; *Sentinel*, Dec. 10, 1868, 4.

46. W. W. Leathers, closing argument, *Journal*, Dec. 19, 1868, 2; testimony, Matthew Hartman, *Journal*, Dec. 12, 1868, 2; *Sentinel*, Dec. 12, 1868, 2.

47. Testimony, William Dowden, *Journal*, Dec. 12, 1868, 2.

48. "Letter from Indianapolis. The Clem Murder Case—The Mystery Increases," *Cincinnati Daily Gazette*, Dec. 14, 1868, 1.

49. "The Young Murder—Another Arrest," *Sentinel*, Sept. 22, 1868, 4; testimony, Silas Hartman, *Journal*, Dec. 14, 1868, 2; *Sentinel*, Dec. 14, 1868, 2; John T. Dye, closing argument, *Journal*, Dec. 18, 1868, 2.

50. Testimony, Aaron Fee and Mary Ann Fee, *Journal*, Dec. 14, 1868, 2; *Sentinel*, Dec. 14, 1868, 2; FMPC, 1870, Warren Township, Marion County, Indiana, roll M593-337, p. 508A.

51. Testimony, Aaron Fee, *Journal*, Dec. 14, 1868, 2; *Sentinel*, Dec. 14, 1868, 2.

52. Testimony, Noah Mock, *Journal*, Dec. 14, 1868, 3; *Sentinel*, Dec. 14, 1868, 2.

53. Testimony, Hampton Clark, *Journal*, Dec. 14, 1868, 3; *Sentinel*, Dec. 14, 1868, 2.

54. Testimony, Flora Ellerhardt, *Journal*, Dec. 14, 1868, 3; *Sentinel*, Dec. 14, 1868, 2; testimony, Benjamin Wert and Aaron Clem, *Journal*, Dec. 15, 1868, 2.

55. Testimony, Albert McLain, *Journal*, Dec. 15, 1868, 2.

56. Testimony, Charles Donnelan, Henry Reed, and Levi Pierson, *Journal*, Dec. 15, 1868, 2, 3; *Sentinel*, Dec. 15, 1868, 2.

57. Testimony, Charlotte Eva Bright, Mrs. Gunther, Marion C. Wilson, and Chris Lout, *Journal*, Dec. 16, 1868, 2; *Sentinel*, Dec. 16, 1868, 2. Newspapers used "Gunther" and "Ginther" interchangeably.

58. Testimony, John J. Gates and David Cady, *Journal*, Dec. 15, 1868, 2; *Sentinel*, Dec. 15, 1868, 2.

59. Testimony, Albert Patton, *Journal*, Dec. 15, 1868, 2; *Sentinel*, Dec. 15, 1868, 2; "Crime: The Clem Murder Case at Indianapolis," *Chicago Tribune*, Dec. 15, 1868, 1.

60. Leathers, closing argument, *Journal*, Dec. 19, 1868, 2; testimony, Marion C. Wilson, *Journal*, Dec. 16, 1868, 2.

61. Testimony, John M. Deem and B. F. Johnson, *Journal*, Dec. 16, 1868, 2, 3; *Sentinel*, Dec. 16, 1868, 2; "Statement of Mrs. Clem," *Journal*, Dec. 17, 1868, 2; testimony, Lucy Brouse and Jane Sizemore, *Journal*, Dec. 17, 1868, 2, and *Sentinel*, Dec. 17, 1868, 2.

62. Testimony, Jane Sizemore, *Journal*, Dec. 17, 1868, 2, and *Sentinel*, Dec. 17, 1868, 2.

63. Testimony, William Pray, *Journal*, Dec. 17, 1868, 2, and *Sentinel*, Dec. 17, 1868, 2.

64. Testimony, Corporal Patrick O'Keefe and Pet Hartman, *Journal*, Dec. 17, 1868, 2, and *Sentinel*, Dec. 17, 1868, 2; Dye, opening statement, *Journal*, Dec. 2, 1868, 4.

65. Dye, closing argument, *Journal*, Dec. 18, 1868, 2; *Sentinel*, Feb. 24, 1869, 4.

66. *Cincinnati Daily Gazette*, Dec. 14, 1868, 1.

Chapter 6 · *Self-Reliant and God Defiant!*

1. W. Lance Bennett and Martha S. Feldman, *Reconstructing Reality in the Courtroom: Justice and Judgment in American Culture* (New Brunswick, N.J.: Rutgers University Press, 1981), esp. ix–10. See also Kathryn Holmes Snedaker, "Storytelling in Opening Statements: Framing the Argumentation of the Trial," in *Narrative and the Legal Discourse: A Reader in Storytelling and the Law*, ed. David Ray Papke (Liverpool: Deborah Charles Publications, 1991), 132–157; Bernard S. Jackson, "Narrative Theories and Legal Discourse," in *Narrative in Culture: The Uses of Storytelling in the Sciences, Philosophy, and Literature*, ed. Cristopher Nash (London: Routledge, 1990), 23–50; Karen Halttunen, *Murder Most Foul: The Killer and the American Gothic Imagination* (Cambridge, Mass.: Harvard University Press, 1998), 98–107; Laura Hanft Korobkin, "The Maintenance of Mutual Confidence: Sentimental Strategies at the Adultery Trial of Henry Ward Beecher," *Yale Journal of Law & the Humanities* 7 (Winter 1995): 1–48, esp. 10–16; Lawrence M. Friedman, *Crime and Punishment in American History* (New York: Basic Books, 1993), esp. 254; Michael Grossberg, *A Judgment for Solomon: The D'Hauteville Case and Legal Experience in Antebellum America* (Cambridge: Cambridge University Press, 1996); and Richard Wightman Fox, *Trials of Intimacy: Love and Loss in the Beecher-Tilton Scandal* (Chicago: University of Chicago Press, 1999).

2. John T. Dye, closing argument, *Indianapolis Journal*, Dec. 18, 1868, 2.

3. Ibid.; testimony, Matthew Hartman, *Indianapolis Sentinel*, Dec. 12, 1868, 2.

4. Dye, closing argument, *Journal*, Dec. 18, 1868, 2.

5. Jacob Piatt Dunn, *Greater Indianapolis: The History, the Institutions, and the People of a City of Homes* (Chicago: Lewis Publishing, 1910), 1:60; "The Young Murder: Fifteenth Day of the Trial," *Journal*, Dec. 18, 1868, 2.

6. William P. Fishback, closing argument, *Journal*, Dec. 21, 1868, 1; John Hanna, closing argument, *Journal*, Dec. 21, 1868, 6.

7. "Death of William W. Leathers," *Cincinnati Gazette*, Dec. 17, 1875, 5; "The Last Honors to the Late W. W. Leathers," *Sentinel*, Dec. 18, 1875, 3; Dunn, *Greater Indianapolis*, 1:60; Leander John Monks, *Courts and Lawyers of Indiana* (Indianapolis: Federal Publishing Company, 1916), 3:1374–1375.

8. "Death of William W. Leathers," *Cincinnati Gazette*, Dec. 17, 1875, 5.

9. William W. Leathers, closing argument, *Journal*, Dec. 19, 1868, 2; "A Card," *Journal*, Dec. 22, 1868, 4. This was the second of two letters to the editor authored by Dorsey. The first accused the *Journal* of inaccurately transcribing his testimony: "To the Editor," *Journal*, Dec. 12, 1868, 3.

10. William W. Leathers, closing argument, *Journal*, Dec. 19, 1868, 2.

11. "The Young Murder. Seventeenth Day," *Journal*, Dec. 21, 1868, 1; "Another Large and Enthusiastic Fizzle at Masonic Hall," *Sentinel*, Oct. 9, 1868, 4; "The Young Murder Trial," *Sentinel*, Dec. 21, 1868, 2; *The Cold Spring Tragedy: Trial and Conviction of Mrs. Nancy E. Clem for the Murder of Jacob Young and Wife . . .* (Indianapolis: A. C. Roach, 1869), 92.

12. Fishback, closing argument, *Cold Spring Tragedy*, 96–97, 100; Gerald Linderman, *Embattled Courage: The Experience of Combat in the American Civil War* (New York: Free Press, 1987), 196–197. The *Sentinel* disclosed Hartman's Civil War experience in March 1869; see "The Young Murder: Another Bloody Chapter," *Sentinel*, Mar. 11, 1869, 4.

13. Dye, closing argument, *Journal*, Dec. 18, 1868, 2; Fishback, closing argument, *Cold Spring Tragedy*, 100.

14. Fishback, closing argument, *Cold Spring Tragedy*, 100. The *Journal* and *The Cold Spring Tragedy*, which reprinted his statement, offered slightly different versions of Fishback's closing argument.

15. Fishback, closing argument, *Journal*, Dec. 21, 1868, 1.

16. Fishback, closing argument, *Cold Spring Tragedy*, 101.

17. Ibid., 96.

18. Ibid., 122. For examples of the voluminous popular literature on the Thugs, see "The Thugs of India," *Harper's Weekly*, Dec. 12, 1857, 796–798; "The Kalee-Poojah of the Thugs," *Harper's Weekly*, June 5, 1858, 364–366; "The Thugs of India," *Harper's Weekly*, Jan. 29, 1870, 69; "The Thugs of India," *Missionary Herald* 68, no. 6 (June 1872): frontispiece–1; "The Thugs, Their Origin, Character, Tenets, Religious Observances, and Modes of Life," *Southern Literary Messenger* 28 (Feb. 1859): 100–116; Harriette B. Cotes, "Life in India: Heathen Cruelties," *Oliver Optic's Magazine* 2, no. 46 (Nov. 16, 1867): 618–619; and "The Indian Thug," *Missionary Magazine* 47, no. 3 (Mar. 1867): 93. For scholarly accounts, see Martine van Woerkens, *The Strangled Traveler: Colonial Imaginings and the Thugs of India* (Chicago: University of Chicago Press, 2002); Mike Dash, *Thug: The True Story of India's Murderous Cult* (London: Granta Books, 2006); and Kim A. Wagner, *Thuggee: Banditry and the British in Early Nineteenth-Century India* (London: Palgrave Macmillan, 2007).

19. Fishback, closing argument, *Cold Spring Tragedy*, 101.

20. *Journal*, Dec. 21, 1868, 7; John H. B. Nowland, *Sketches of Prominent Citizens of 1876: With a Few of the Pioneers of the City and County Who Have Passed Away* (Indianapolis: Tilford & Carlson, 1877), 287; "John Hanna in the House," *Martinsville Republican*, Mar. 7, 1878, 4.

21. Nowland, *Sketches of Prominent Citizens of 1876*, 284–288; Nicole Etcheson, *A Generation at War: The Civil War Era in a Northern Community* (Lawrence: University Press of Kansas, 2011), 22, 40–41.

22. *History of Hendricks County, Indiana* (Chicago: Inter-State Publishing, 1885), 619–622; Judge David McDonald, diary, June 14, 1862, repr. in *Indiana Magazine of History* 28, no. 4 (Dec. 1932): 296–297.

23. Hanna, closing argument, *Journal*, Dec. 21, 1868, 3.

24. Ibid., 6.

25. Nowland, *Sketches of Prominent Citizens of 1876*, 287.

26. Hanna, closing argument, *Journal*, Dec. 21, 1868, 3.

27. Ibid.; Leathers, closing argument, *Journal*, Dec. 19, 1868.

28. Fishback, closing argument, *Journal*, Dec. 21, 1868, 1; Leathers, closing argument, *Journal*, Dec. 19, 1868, 2.

29. Leathers, closing argument, *Journal*, Dec. 19, 1868, 2; Hanna, closing argument, *Journal*, Dec. 21, 1868, 6; Fishback, closing argument, *Cold Spring Tragedy*, 99–100.

30. Leathers, closing argument, *Journal*, Dec. 19, 1868, 2.

31. Michael D. Pierson, *Free Hearts and Free Homes: Gender and American Antislavery Politics* (Chapel Hill: University of North Carolina Press, 2003), 97–114, 165–190; Rebecca Edwards, *Angels in the Machinery: Gender in American Party Politics from the Civil War to the Progressive Era* (New York: Oxford University Press, 1997).

32. *Cold Spring Tragedy*, 38–40; *Indianapolis News*, June 7, 1872. On women's active involvement in commercial life, see Susan Ingalls Lewis, *Unexceptional Women: Female Proprietors in Mid-Nineteenth-Century Albany, New York, 1830–1885* (Columbus: Ohio State University Press, 2009); Susan M. Yohn, "Crippled Capitalists: Gender Ideology, the Inscription of Economic Dependence, and the Challenge of Female Entrepreneurship in Nineteenth-Century America," *Feminist Economics* 12 (2006): 85–109; Edith Sparks, *Capital Intentions: Female Proprietors in San Francisco, 1850–1920* (Chapel Hill: University of North Carolina Press, 2006); Angel Kwolek-Folland, *Incorporating Women: A History of Women and Business in the United States* (New York: Palgrave Macmillan, 2002); Wendy Gamber, *The Female Economy: The Millinery and Dressmaking Trades, 1860–1930* (Urbana: University of Illinois Press, 1997); and Gamber, *The Boardinghouse in Nineteenth-Century America* (Baltimore: Johns Hopkins University Press, 2007).

33. Dorothea Kline McCullough, "'By Cash and Eggs': Gender in Washington County during Indiana's Pioneer Period" (PhD diss., Indiana University, 2001), 142–165; Edwards, *Angels in the Machinery*, 24, 61, 68–74; *History of Hendricks County*, 619; Eric Foner, *Free Soil, Free Labor, Free Men: The Ideology of the Republican Party Before the Civil War* (Oxford: Oxford University Press, 1970), 15–39, 171–176; Eric Foner, *Reconstruction: America's Unfinished Revolution, 1863–1877* (New York: Harper & Row, 1988), 20–21, 233–235, 315–316, 488–493.

34. Hanna, closing argument, *Journal*, Dec. 21, 1868, 6.

35. William Stuart, diary, Mar. 15, 1869, Indiana Historical Society; Federal Manuscript Population Census (hereafter FMPC), 1870, Hensley, Johnson County, Indiana, roll M593 330, p. 358A. Stuart was born in Indiana and died sometime before the next census; therefore his parents' birthplace cannot be determined. The 1880 census record for his widow, Melinda, indicates that his in-laws had been born in Kentucky: FMPC, 1880, Jeffersonville, Clark County, Indiana, roll 269, Enumeration District 27, p. 137C.

36. Etcheson, *Generation at War*, 22, 40–41, 162.

37. Foner, *Free Soil, Free Labor, Free Men*, 15–17, 29–39; David Montgomery, *Beyond Equality: Labor and the Radical Republicans, 1863–1872* (New York: Knopf, 1967), 25–32.

38. Hanna, closing argument, *Journal*, Dec. 21, 1868, 6.

39. Ibid., 6, 3; "From Indianapolis," *New Albany Daily Commercial*, Jan. 1, 1869, 1.

40. "Charge of the Court," *Journal*, Dec. 21, 1868, 6–7; "The Young Murder Trial: The Charge of the Judge," *Sentinel*, Dec. 21, 1868, 2.

41. "From Indianapolis. Disagreement of the Jury Regarding Mrs. Clem's Guilt," *Cincinnati Daily Gazette*, Dec. 22, 1868, 3; "Disagreement of the Jury and Their Discharge," *Journal*, Dec. 22, 1868, 7; "The Young Murder Trial: The Jury Fail to Agree," *Sentinel*, Dec. 22, 1868, 2; *Journal*, Mar. 2, 1869, quoted in Harry J. Sievers, *Benjamin Harrison*, vol. 2: *Hoosier Statesman: From the Civil War to the White House, 1865–1888* (New York: University Publishers, 1959), 28–29. For Anthony/Antone Wiese/Weise/Weiss, see FMPC, 1870, Warren Township, Marion County, roll M593-337, p. 511A; for Christian Lout/Louts, see p. 508B. For their political affiliations (as of 1874), see *The People's Guide: A Business, Political and Religious Directory of Marion Co., Ind.* (Indianapolis: Indianapolis Printing & Publishing House, 1874), 504, 515. The *People's Guide* gave Wiese's first name as "Andrew." Given that his birthplace, birthdate, and place of residence are identical to information the census provides for Antone Wiese, odds are the two were one and the same.

Chapter 7 · Knowed It Was Them

1. See, for example, *Troy Weekly Times*, Jan. 2, 1869, [3]; "From Indianapolis," *New Albany Daily Commercial*, Jan. 1, 1869, 1; *Cincinnati Daily Enquirer*, Mar. 17, 1869, 2; "A Warning," *Indianapolis Journal*, Mar. 11, 1869, 8.

2. "The Police Board Investigation," *Indianapolis Sentinel*, Jan. 6, 1869, 4; *Sentinel*, Jan. 9, 1869, 4, Jan. 11, 1869, 4, and Jan. 13, 1869, 5; "Police Board Investigating Court," *Sentinel*, Jan. 14, 1869, 4; "Police Investigation," *Sentinel*, Jan. 15, 1869, 2; "Indianapolis Letter," *Cincinnati Commercial Tribune*, Feb. 5, 1869, 2.

3. John H. B. Nowland, *Sketches of Prominent Citizens of 1876: With a Few of the Pioneers of the City and County Who Have Passed Away* (Indianapolis: Tilford & Carlon, 1877), 521–522; James Sutherland, *Biographical Sketches of the Members of the Forty-First General Assembly of the State of Indiana* (Indianapolis: Indianapolis Journal Company, 1861), 203–204; Francis Marion Trissal, *Public Men of Indiana: A Political History from 1860 to 1890* (Hammond, Ind.: W. B. Conkey, 1922), 1:13–14; *Quarterly Bulletin of the Ripley County, Indiana Historical Society* 30, no. 3 (July 2009): 4; Suzanne M. Shultz, *Body Snatching: The Robbing of Graves for the Education of Physicians* (Jefferson, N.C.: McFarland, 1992), 31–45, Benjamin S. Parker and Enos B. Heiney, comp. and eds., *Poets and Poetry of Indiana: A Representative Collection of the Poetry of Indiana during the First Hundred Years of Its History as Territory and State, 1800 to 1900* (New York: Silver, Burdett, 1900), 115–116, 169–170, 315, 433; B. R. Sulgrove, *History of Indianapolis and Marion County, Indiana* (Philadelphia: L. H. Everts, 1884), 180–181; William Turner Coggeshall, ed., *The Poets and Poetry of the West: With Biographical and Critical Notes* (Columbus, Ohio: Follet, Foster, 1860), 424–427; Roger H. Van Bolt, "The Rise of the Republican Party in Indiana, 1855–1856," *Indiana Magazine of History* 51, no. 3 (Sept. 1955): 209; Benjamin F. Babcock, *The Presidential Favorites: A Political Hand-Book* (Chicago: Babcock, Fort, 1884), 74; James D. Richardson, *A Compilation of the Messages and Papers of the Presidents*, vol. 7 (Washington, D.C.: Government Printing Office, 1897), 5438; Charles W. Taylor, *Biographical Sketches and Review of the Bench and Bar of Indiana* (Indianapolis: Bench & Bar, 1895), 250–252; Mayo Fesler, "Secret Political Societies in the North during the Civil War," *Indiana Magazine of History* 24, no. 3 (Sept. 1918): 264; Jonathan W. Gordon, *An Argument against the Jurisdiction of the Military Commissions to Try Citizens of a Loyal State Delivered in the Case of William Bowles and Others* (Indianapolis: Hall & Hutchinson, 1865); Harry J. Sievers, *Benjamin Harrison*, vol. 1: *Hoosier Warrior: Through the Civil War Years, 1833–1865* (New York: University Publishers, 1952), 95–97; *Sentinel*, Feb. 10, 1869, 4.

4. Charles W. Calhoun, *Benjamin Harrison* (New York: Henry Holt, 2005), 2, 17; John B. Elam, "Benjamin Harrison the Lawyer. Read before the Students of the Law School of Indi-

ana University, May 18, 1908" [typescript], Volwiler MSS, Box 8 folder L-9, Lilly Library, Indiana University; *Sentinel*, Feb. 10, 1869, 4; *Journal*, Feb. 10, 1869, 5.

5. Census entries for real and personal property varied widely between the two enumerations taken in 1870. In the first, Harrison's real estate was valued at $21,200 and his personal estate at $6,000; in the second, $8,000 and $1,000, respectively. The value of Frank Clem's real estate was recorded as $12,000 and personal estate as $300 in the first enumeration and as $10,000/$2,000 in the second. Federal Manuscript Population Census (hereafter FMPC), 1870, Indianapolis, roll M593-340, pp. 17A and 9B; FMPC, 1870, Indianapolis (2nd enum.), roll M593-338, pp. 16A and 20A; Calhoun, *Benjamin Harrison*, 4–5, 17, 21; Sievers, *Benjamin Harrison: Hoosier Warrior*, 112–113, 135–161, 173–174; Harry J. Sievers, *Benjamin Harrison*, vol. 2: *Hoosier Statesman: From the Civil War to the White House, 1865–1888* (New York: University Publishers, 1959), 14–16, 20–21; Lew Wallace and Murat Halstead, *Life and Public Services of Honorable Benjamin Harrison, President of the U.S.* (n.p.: Edgewood, 1892), 449, 457–458.

6. "The Young Murder: Trial of Mrs. Clem: Second Day's Proceedings," *Sentinel*, Feb. 11, 1869, 4; "The Young Murder: Trial of Mrs. Clem: First Day's Proceedings," *Journal*, Feb. 10, 1869, 4. See, for example, "The Clem Case," *Daily Memphis Avalanche*, Mar. 4, 1869, [2]; "Brandy and Bitters as a Solace in a Murder Case," *New York Herald*, Mar. 9, 1869, 6; and *Critic* (Washington, D.C.), Mar. 12, 1869, 6.

7. "Mrs. Clem," *Vincennes Gazette*, Feb. 6, 1869.

8. "Mrs. Clem," *Cincinnati Commercial Tribune*, Feb. 1, 1869, 2. The author of the *Tribune* article, who described Clem as leading "the active, industrial life," was almost certainly the "lady reporter" Laura Ream; see " 'L R' A Hoosier Celebrity. A Sketch of a Notable Home Personage—Miss Ream," *Sentinel*, June 8, 1874, 5. Walter S. Smith, "The Uncalled Witness," *Indianapolis Star*, Aug. 18, 1907, SM1; "Musty Pages of History Opened," *Jeffersonville National Democrat*, Dec. 6, 1899, 4; see also *Fort Wayne Daily Gazette*, Apr. 27, 1869, 1.

9. *Sentinel*, Feb. 4, 1869.

10. *Sentinel*, Dec. 2, 1868, 4; Nicole Etcheson, *The Emerging Midwest: Upland Southerners and the Political Culture of the Old Northwest, 1787–1861* (Bloomington: Indiana University Press, 1996), 28–29; "Indianapolis Letter," *Cincinnati Commercial Tribune*, Mar. 16, 1869, 4.

11. "The Clem Case," *Journal*, Jan. 5, 1869, 2; "The Young Murder," *Journal*, Jan. 9, 1869, 8; "Clem Case," *Journal*, Jan. 18, 1869, 8; "Criminal Court," *Sentinel*, Jan. 18, 1869, 4; *Nancy E. Clem v. State of Indiana* (1869), Office of Supreme Court Records, Indianapolis, Indiana, 21–81.

12. "The Young Murder: Trial of Mrs. Clem: Second Day's Proceedings," *Sentinel*, Feb. 11, 1869, 4; "The Young Murder: Trial of Mrs. Clem: First Day's Proceedings," *Journal*, Feb. 10, 1869, 4; "The Young Murder Trial: Second Hearing of the Case of Mrs. Clem: Second Day's Proceedings," *Journal*, Feb. 11, 1869, 5; "The Clem Murder Trial," *Cincinnati Daily Enquirer*, Feb. 11, 1869, 4; *New York Daily Tribune*, Mar. 3, 1869, 2; "Indianapolis Letter," *Cincinnati Commercial Tribune*, Mar. 16, 1869, 4. Of the twelve jurors, ten appeared in the 1870 census. One had been born in Virginia, one in New Jersey, one in Pennsylvania, two in Ohio, one in Prussia, and four in Indiana. One Ohioan and one Hoosier had at least one southern parent. The remaining Indiana-born jurors could not be located in the 1880 census, which included parents' birthplace. Charles. G. Wilson, Sr. (FMPC, 1870, Indianapolis, roll M593-341, p. 291B), was a carriage painter; Benjamin Stokely (Indianapolis, 2nd enum., roll M593-338, p. 31B), an engine maker. The 1870 manuscript population censuses for Franklin, Washington, and Warren Townships are on roll M593-337: Charles F Hartman (Warren, p. 497B); Levi Conwell (Warren, p. 493A; 1880, Warren, roll 294, p. 504D); William Vance (Washington p. 545B); John Moore (Washington, p. 550A); Malcomb A Lowes (Franklin, p. 373A); Nathaniel Smith (Franklin, p. 385B; 1880, Perry, roll 294, p. 575D); Isaac Golden (Franklin, p. 380B);

John S. Smith (Franklin, p. 373A). The *Sentinel* was not entirely correct: William Vance was only about twenty-one, Nathaniel Smith, about twenty-seven, and John Moore, about thirty-two years old.

13. "The Young Murder: Trial of Mrs. Clem: Third Day's Proceedings," *Sentinel*, Feb. 12, 1869, 4; on treatment of suspects see, for example, Timothy R. Mahoney, "The Great Sheedy Murder Case and the Booster Ethos of the Gilded Age in Lincoln, Nebraska," *Nebraska History* 82 (Winter 2001): 164–165.

14. *Cincinnati Commercial Tribune*, Feb. 9, 1869. 8; see also *Boston Daily Journal*, Feb. 12, 1869, and *Journal*, Feb. 9, 1869, 5.

15. *Clem v. Indiana* (1869), 170, 304–338, 392–396, 397–446, 452–565; "The Young Murder: Trial of Mrs. Clem: Third Day's Proceedings," *Sentinel*, Feb. 12, 1869, 4; "The Young Murder: Trial of Mrs. Clem: Fourth Day's Proceedings," *Sentinel*, Feb. 13, 1869, 4; "The Young Murder: Trial of Mrs. Clem: Fifth Day's Proceedings," *Sentinel*, Feb. 15, 1869, 4; "The Young Murder Trial: Second Hearing of the Case of Mrs. Clem: Third Day's Proceedings," *Journal*, Feb. 12, 1869, 8; "The Young Murder Trial: Second Hearing of the Case of Mrs. Clem: Fourth Day's Proceedings," *Journal*, Feb. 13, 1869, 4; "The Young Murder Trial: Second Hearing of the Case of Mrs. Clem: Fifth Day's Proceedings," *Journal*, Feb. 15, 1869, 2.

16. Testimony, John Culp and Elijah Cooper, *Sentinel*, Feb. 16, 1869, 4, and *Clem v. Indiana* (1869), 636–640; "Sixth Day's Proceedings, *Journal*, Feb. 16, 1869, 2.

17. "The Young Murder: Trial of Mrs. Clem: Third Day's Proceedings," *Sentinel*, Feb. 13, 1869, 4.

18. "Seventh Day's Proceedings," *Journal*, Feb. 17, 1869, 3; "The Young Murder Trial: New and Important Testimony," *Journal*, Feb. 18, 1869, 6; "Eighth Day's Proceedings," *Sentinel*, Feb. 18, 1869, 4; *Clem v. Indiana* (1869), 928–929, 950–951, 976.

19. Testimony, John H. Wiley, "Eighth Day's Proceedings," *Sentinel*, Feb. 18, 1869, 4; *Clem v. Indiana* (1869), 978, 985, 1000; "The Young Murder Trial: New and Important Testimony," *Journal*, Feb. 18, 1869," 6.

20. Testimony, Charles Chenoworth, *Sentinel*, Feb. 18, 1869, 4, and *Clem v. Indiana* (1869), 1010–1012, 1016. See also "The Young Murder Trial: New and Important Testimony," *Journal*, Feb. 18, 1869, 6.

21. Testimony, Nancy Chenoworth, *Clem v. Indiana* (1869), 1031–1036; *Sentinel*, Feb. 18, 1869, 4; and *Journal*, Feb. 18, 1869, 6.

22. *Cincinnati Daily Enquirer*, Feb. 18, 1869, 4; *Cincinnati Daily Gazette*, Feb. 18, 1869, 3.

23. Testimony, Nancy Chenoworth, *Clem v. Indiana* (1869), 1047, and *Sentinel*, Feb. 18, 1869, 4.

24. FMPC, 1870, Indianapolis (2nd enum.), roll M593-338, p. 142B; testimony, Levi Pierson, *Journal*, Dec. 15, 1868, 3; testimony, John Pierson, *Clem v. Indiana* (1869), 1019, 1022.

25. Testimony, John Pierson, *Clem v. Indiana* (1869), 1022.

26. Testimony, John Pierson, *Clem v. Indiana* (1869), 1019, 1024, 1028, and *Sentinel*, Feb. 18, 1869, 4; *Cincinnati Commercial Tribune*, Feb. 20, 1869, 3. The official transcript had Pierson using the grammatically correct "Knew it was them," while the *Sentinel* recorded his words as "Knowed it was them."

27. *Journal*, Feb. 18, 1869, 8.

28. See, for example, *Cincinnati Daily Gazette*, Feb. 19, 1869, 3; *Cincinnati Commercial Tribune*, Feb. 20, 1869, 3; "Murder Trial," *Saint Paul Daily Press*, Feb. 25, 1869, [1]; for further commentary after the defense rested its case, see *Sentinel*, Feb. 26, 1869, 4; "The Young Murder Trial in Indiana: Probable Conviction of Mrs. Clem," *New York Herald*, Feb. 26, 1869, 4.

29. Testimony, John J. Gates, Matthew Walls, and David Cady, *Clem v. Indiana* (1869), 1233–1249, 1265.

30. Testimony, Aaron Clem, *Clem v. Indiana* (1869), 1258.

31. Testimony, Silas Hartman, *Sentinel*, Feb. 20, 1869, 4; *Journal*, Feb. 20, 1869, 3; and *Clem v. Indiana* (1869), 1368–1372, 1382–1382, 1421; John Hanna, closing argument, in *The Cold Spring Tragedy: Trial and Conviction of Mrs. Nancy E. Clem for the Murder of Jacob Young and Wife . . .* (Indianapolis: A. C. Roach, 1869), 81; *Journal*, Feb. 20, 1869, 8; *Sentinel*, Feb. 20, 1869, 4.

32. "Gen. Harrison Conducts the Cross-Examination for the State," *Sentinel*, Feb. 20, 1869, 4; testimony, Silas White, *Sentinel*, Feb. 22, 1869, 4, and *Clem v. Indiana* (1869), 1550–1554.

33. Testimony, Albert Patton, *Clem v. Indiana* (1869), 1557, 1559.

34. *Sentinel*, Feb. 22, 1869, 4; *Clem v. Indiana* (1869), 1651–1653.

35. Testimony, John Pierson, and Viola Pierson, *Clem v. Indiana* (1869), 1654–1655, 1631–1632.

36. Testimony, John Pierson, *Sentinel*, Feb. 22, 1869, 4, and *Clem v. Indiana* (1869), 1651–1658; see also *Journal*, Feb. 22, 1869, 3.

37. Testimony, Rebecca Hartman, *Clem v. Indiana* (1869), 1701–1702.

38. *Sentinel*, Feb. 23, 1869, 4. The *Journal*, Feb. 23, 1869, 6, reported that Hartman testified that Clem wore a "dark calico dress." The official transcript is more ambiguous. It records Hartman's statement as "She had on a calico dress and a dark hat." *Clem v. Indiana* (1869), 1702.

39. Testimony, Rebecca Hartman, *Clem v. Indiana* (1869), 1701–1702, 1705–1708, 1710, 1714; *Sentinel*, Feb. 23, 1869, 4; and *Journal*, Feb. 23, 1869, 6.

40. Testimony, Frederica Ginther, *Clem v. Indiana* (1869), 1744–1746, 1748–1750, and *Sentinel*, Feb. 23, 1869, 4.

41. Testimony, William J. O'Flaherty, *Clem v. Indiana* (1869), 1763–1771; *Sentinel*, Feb. 23, 1869, 4, and *Journal*, Feb. 23, 1869, 6.

42. Testimony, Christina Kellamyer, William S. Elliot, J. N. Cotton, Thomas E. Watts, Isaac Voorhees, John Jennings, Leander Gladwell, James C. Myers, and Joseph Loftis, *Clem v. Indiana* (1869), 1819–1822, 1859–1864.

43. Testimony, Peter Wilkins, *Clem v. Indiana* (1869), 1817, *Sentinel*, Feb. 24, 1869, 4; "Mrs. Clem and Peter Wilkins," *People* (Indianapolis), Apr. 23, 1880, 1; "Site of Young Murder," *Journal*, June 11, 1897, 8; "Chapters in the Life of Peter Wilkins," *People*, Jan. 15, 1871, and Feb. 5, 1871, 2. The nature of Wilkins's employment, both during and after the Civil War, is not entirely clear. Most often described as a "detective," he presumably acted as one of the Union army's "special agents," although his official military records identify him as an artificer for the Seventeenth Independent Battery Indiana Light Artillery. National Park Service, U.S. Civil War Soldiers, 1861–1865 (online database, Ancestry.com, 2007), http://search .ancestry.com/search/db.aspx?dbid=1138; U.S., Civil War Pension Index: General Index to Pension Files, 1861–1934 (online database, Ancestry.com, 2000), http://search.ancestry.com /search/db.aspx?dbid=4654; Stephen E. Towne, *Surveillance and Spies in the Civil War: Exposing Confederate Conspiracies in America's Heartland* (Athens: Ohio University Press, 2015), 92–96. Wilkins's relationship to the Indianapolis Police Department is similarly murky. The *Journal* identified him as a city policeman on May 19, 1863, 3. *Logan's Indianapolis Directory . . . for the Year Commencing July 1, 1868* (Indianapolis: Logan & Co., 1868), 223, listed him as a carpenter; Wilkins concurred in his testimony in *Clem v. Indiana* (1872), 3160–3161. The 1870 FMPC (Indianapolis, 2nd enum., roll M593-338, p. 149B), however, described him as a "Detective Police Officer," and city directories for the same period list him as a "U.S. Detective." *Bailey's Indianapolis Directory 1871–1872* (Indianapolis: Bailey, 1871), 515; *Swartz & Tedrowe's Indianap-*

olis Directory, 1872–73 (Indianapolis: Indianapolis Sentinel Printers, 1872), 266. Most likely his tenure with the department waxed and waned with local elections, and he combined carpentry with private detective work when not employed in an official capacity. Whether he was actually employed by the federal government after the Civil War is unclear: "U.S. Detective" may have been an embellishment.

44. *Sentinel*, Feb. 24, 1869, 4; John T. Dye, closing argument, *Sentinel*, Feb. 24, 1869, 4, and *Sentinel*, Feb. 25, 1869, 4; Dye, closing argument, *Journal*, Feb. 24, 1869, 5. The *Journal* and *Sentinel* reproduced different portions of Dye's argument, and recorded slightly different phrasing in cases where their coverage overlapped.

45. Dye, closing argument, *Journal*, Feb. 24, 1869, 5, and *Journal*, Feb. 25, 1869, 7.

46. Ibid.; Leathers, closing argument, *Cold Spring Tragedy*, 60, 61.

47. Leathers, closing argument, *Cold Spring Tragedy*, 66, 67, 61, 65, 60.

48. *Sentinel*, Feb. 26, 1869, 4; *Journal*, Feb. 26, 1869, 5. The *Sentinel* published a briefer summary of Duncan's argument; see Feb. 26, 1869, 4.

49. Taylor, *Biographical Sketches and Review of the Bench and Bar of Indiana*, 252; Sievers, *Benjamin Harrison: Hoosier Warrior*, 253.

50. Gordon, closing argument, *Journal*, Feb. 27, 1869, 7. The *Sentinel*, Feb. 27, 1869, 4, recorded slightly different phrasing: "Dorsey was more connected with Young than any other person."

51. Gordon, closing argument, *Sentinel*, Feb. 26, 1869, 4.

52. Gordon, closing argument, *Journal*, Feb. 26, 1869, 5, and *Journal*, Feb. 27, 1869, 7.

53. Gordon, closing argument, *Sentinel*, Feb. 26, 1869, 4, and *Journal*, Feb. 26, 1869, 5. On the prevalence of economic failure and its consequences, see Scott Sandage, *Born Losers: A History of Failure in America* (Cambridge, Mass.: Harvard University Press, 2005), and Edward J. Belleisen, *Navigating Failure: Bankruptcy and Commercial Society in Antebellum America* (Chapel Hill: University of North Carolina Press, 2001).

54. Gordon, closing argument, *Journal*, Feb. 26, 1869, 5; Alva C. Roach's *Cold Spring Tragedy* noted the "absurdity of such an explanation" (19).

55. Newspapers did not record this portion of Gordon's speech. Benjamin Harrison attempted to refute Gordon's claim in his own closing argument. Harrison, closing argument, *Cold Spring Tragedy*, 74. See, for example, Francis Wharton, *A Treatise on the Law of Homicide in the United States* (Philadelphia: Kay & Brother, 1875), 606–607, 732–735; "Photography in the Detection of Crime," *Criminal Law Magazine and Reporter* 18 (1896): 725; Frank S. Rice, *The General Principles of the Law of Evidence in Their Application to the Trial of Criminal Cases* (Rochester: N.Y.: Lawyers' Co-Operative Publishing Co., 1894), 150–154.

56. *Sentinel*, Feb. 26, 1869, 4. The *Journal* recorded a slightly different version: "When I look at that woman, the son and husband by her side, am I asking too much when I request that each of you cast aside all preconceptions as to her guilt or innocence?" The *Journal* made no mention of Grandmother Hartman's presence. Gordon, closing argument, *Journal*, Feb. 26, 1869, 5.

57. *Journal*, Mar. 2, 1869, 4; Sievers, *Benjamin Harrison: Hoosier Statesman*, 26–29; *Cold Spring Tragedy*, 19.

58. Harrison, closing argument, *Cold Spring Tragedy*, 68–76; Leathers, closing argument, *Cold Spring Tragedy*, 62.

59. Harrison, closing argument, *Cold Spring Tragedy*, 69, 76.

60. Sievers, *Benjamin Harrison: Hoosier Warrior*, 167–168; Harrison, closing argument, *Cold Spring Tragedy*, 76.

61. Harrison, closing argument, *Cold Spring Tragedy*, 74, 71.

62. Ibid., 79. John S. Duncan did note that Clem "has deprived a woman and a mother of her life" but made no mention of the child. *Journal*, Feb. 26, 1869, 5.

63. Hanna, closing argument, *Cold Spring Tragedy*, 79; *Journal*, Mar. 2, 1869, 8.

64. Hanna, closing argument, *Cold Spring Tragedy*, 79–83.

65. Ibid., 83–84; *Journal*, Mar. 1, 1869, 2; "From Indianapolis," *New Albany Daily Commercial*, Jan. 1, 1869, 1.

66. *Cold Spring Tragedy*, 85–87, 89; *Albany (N.Y.) Journal*, Mar. 5, 1869, 2; *Journal*, Mar. 1, 1869, 2–3; *Journal*, Mar. 2, 1869, 4.

67. *Cincinnati Daily Gazette*, Feb. 26, 1869, 1; *Saint Paul Daily Press*, Feb. 25, 1869, 1; *New York Herald*, Feb. 26, 1869, 4.

68. *Sentinel*, Mar. 2, 1869, 4.

69. *Sentinel*, Mar. 2, 1869, 4; *Journal*, Mar. 2, 1869, 8; *Cincinnati Daily Gazette*, Mar. 2, 1869, 3.

Chapter 8 · *I Wish I Was an Angel*

1. "The Young Murder Trial," *Indianapolis Journal*, Mar. 2, 1869, 4, 8; Sarah Hill Fletcher, diary, Mar. 1, 1869, Indiana Historical Society, Indianapolis.

2. "Mrs. Clem Convicted," *Journal*, reprinted in *Des Moines Daily State Register*, Mar. 9, 1860, 2; *The Cold Spring Tragedy: Trial and Conviction of Mrs. Nancy E. Clem for the Murder of Jacob Young and Wife . . .* (Indianapolis: A. C. Roach, 1869), 84, 85.

3. "Another Bloody Chapter," *Indianapolis Sentinel*, Mar. 11, 1869, 4; "Hartman Suicide," *Journal*, Mar. 11, 1869, 2; testimony, William J. Abrams, Samuel G. Thomas, and A. M. Penfield, *Journal*, Mar. 11, 1869, 2.

4. *Sentinel*, Mar. 3, 1869, 4; Emma Lou Thornbrough, *The Negro in Indiana before 1900: A Study of a Minority*, 2nd ed. (Bloomington: Indiana University Press, 1993), 244–248; "The Democratic Meeting," *Journal*, Mar. 6, 1896, 4; "Social Equality," *Journal*, Mar. 10, 1869, 4; "The Fire King," *Sentinel*, Mar. 8, 1869, 4; *Journal*, Mar. 8, 1869, 5; "The Lebanon Tragedy," *Journal*, Mar. 8, 1869, 8.

5. "Marion Criminal Court," *Journal*, Mar. 9, 1869, 8.

6. "Marion Criminal Court," *Journal*, Mar. 10, 1869, 8; *Sentinel*, Mar. 8, 1869, 4; "Sike Hartman's 'Confession,'" *Journal*, Mar. 10, 1869, 4; "The Rumored Confession of Syke Hartman," *Sentinel*, Mar. 10, 1869, 4; "The Case of Mrs. Clem: The Suppressed Testimony," *New Albany Daily Commercial*, June 23, 1869, 2.

7. "Sike Hartman's 'Confession,'" *Journal*, Mar. 10. 1869, 4; *Cincinnati Daily Gazette*, Mar. 10, 1869, 3; see also "Crime," *Cleveland Plain Dealer*, Mar. 10, 1869, 2.

8. *Chicago Tribune*, Mar. 10, 1869, 4.

9. "A Short Talk with Wm. J. Abrams," *Sentinel*, Sept. 22, 1869, 4; "The Rumored Confession of Syke Hartman," *Sentinel*, Mar. 10, 1869, 4; "From Indianapolis: Another Event of the Great Tragedy," *Cincinnati Daily Gazette*, Mar. 11, 1868, 3; "Spiritual Convention: Jacob Young Appears," *Sentinel*, June 19, 1869, 4; Aug. 30, 1869, 4; Henry Ward Beecher, *Seven Lectures to Young Men, on Various Important Subjects* (Indianapolis: Thomas B. Cutler, 1844), 134, 142–143, 147, 150–155, 158–160.

10. *Sentinel*, Mar. 10, 1869, 4; "Sike Hartman's 'Confession,'" *Journal*, Mar. 10, 1869, 4; "Hartman Suicide!" *Journal*, Mar. 12, 1869, 5; *Sentinel*, Mar. 30, 1869, 4; B. R. Sulgrove, *History of Indianapolis and Marion County, Indiana* (Philadelphia: L. H. Everts, 1884), 487 (Sulgrove's list of city marshals did not include Fiscus).

11. The Mar. 9, 1869, issue of the *Indianapolis Daily Evening Mirror*, the first publication in which Hartman's confession appeared, has not survived. Testimony, William J. Abrams, "Hartman Suicide!" *Journal*, Mar. 12, 1869, 4; "Mrs. Clem: An Hour's Talk with Her," *Sentinel*, Mar. 29, 1869, 4.

12. Testimony, A. M. Penfield and Samuel G. Thomas, "Hartman Suicide!" *Journal*, Mar.11, 1869, 2; "Another Bloody Chapter," *Sentinel*, Mar. 11, 1869, 4.

13. "Hartman Suicide!" *Journal*, Mar. 11, 1869, 2; testimony, William J. Abrams and Frank Brancamp, "Hartman Suicide!" *Journal*, Mar.11, 1869, 2; testimony, William J. Abrams, "Another Bloody Chapter," *Sentinel*, Mar. 11, 1869, 4.

14. "Hartman Suicide!" *Journal*, Mar. 12, 1869, 4; "The Young Murder: Another Chapter Written in Letters of Blood," *Daily Evening Mirror*, Mar. 10, 1869, 4.

15. "Indianapolis: Another Act in the Young Tragedy," *Cincinnati Commercial Tribune*, Mar. 11, 1869, 1; "Another Bloody Chapter," *Sentinel*, Mar. 11, 1869, 4; "Hartman Suicide!" *Journal*, Mar. 12, 1869, 4.

16. "Letter from Indianapolis: The Hartman Suicide—Was It Suicide?" *Cincinnati Daily Gazette*, Mar. 15, 1869, 1. See also "The Young Murder!! Suicide of Hartman. Was It Suicide or Murder?" *Daily Evening Mirror*, Mar. 12, 1869, 3.

17. "Hartman Suicide!" *Journal*, Mar. 12, 1869, 4; *Sentinel*, Mar. 13, 1869, 4; Gary Laderman, *The Sacred Remains: American Attitudes toward Death, 1799–1883* (New Haven: Yale University Press, 1996), 18–21; Stuart Banner, *The Death Penalty: An American History* (Cambridge, Mass.: Harvard University Press, 2002), 77–80; Suzanne M. Shultz, *Body Snatching: The Robbing of Graves for the Education of Physicians* (Jefferson, N.C.: McFarland, 1992), 31–45.

18. "Hartman Suicide!" *Journal*, Mar. 12, 1869, 4; "Syke Hartman's Funeral," *Sentinel*, Mar. 12, 1869, 4; *Sentinel*, Mar. 13, 1869, 4.

19. Patricia Cline Cohen, *The Murder of Helen Jewett: The Life and Death of a Prostitute in Nineteenth-Century New York* (New York: Knopf, 1998), 269–270; Daniel A. Cohen, "The Murder of Maria Bickford: Fashion, Passion, and the Birth of a Consumer Culture," *American Studies* 31 (Fall 1990): 13; John T. Dye, opening statement, *Journal*, December 2, 1868, 4.

20. "Appalling Double Murder," *Journal*, Sept. 14, 1868, 8.

21. *Cold Spring Tragedy*, 16; Jacob P. Dunn, *Greater Indianapolis: The History, the Institutions, and the People of a City of Homes* (Chicago: Lewis Publishing, 1910), 1:483–484.

22. "The Young Murder," *Journal*, June 9, 1869, 4; *Journal*, June 25, 1869, 8; *Journal*, Dec. 21, 1868, 7; *Cold Spring Tragedy*, back cover.

23. John Hanna, closing argument, *Cold Spring Tragedy*, 82.

24. "Interview with Mrs. Clem," *Journal*, Mar. 12, 1869, 4; Rebecca Edwards, *Angels in the Machinery: Gender in American Party Politics from the Civil War to the Progressive Era* (New York: Oxford University Press, 1997), esp. 5–7, 31–35, 76–81, quote at 77.

25. "Behind the Bars: Prison Life of Mrs. Clem: A Half-Hour with the Lady from Indianapolis," *Louisville Courier-Journal*, May 7, 1869, 4.

26. "Mrs. Clem: An Hour's Talk with Her," *Sentinel*, Mar. 29, 1869, 4; Edwards, *Angels in the Machinery*, 24, 61, 68–74.

27. "Woman Suffrage," *Journal*, June 10, 1869, 5; Amy Dru Stanley, *From Bondage to Contract: Wage Labor, Marriage, and the Market in the Age of Slave Emancipation* (Cambridge: Cambridge University Press, 1998), 197–209. "Woman's Rights," *Sentinel*, June 10, 1869, 4; Carolyn Strange, "'On no account of sex': Husband Killers and the Character of Gubernatorial Clemency in Gilded-Age New York," paper presented at the Sixteenth Berkshire Conference on the History of Women, Toronto, May 2014; Lee Chambers-Schiller, "Seduced, Betrayed, and Revenged: The Murder Trial of Mary Harris," in *Lethal Imagination: Violence and Brutality in American History* (New York: New York University Press, 1999): 185–209; Lisa Tetrault, *The Myth of Seneca Falls: Memory and the Women's Suffrage Movement, 1848–1898* (Chapel Hill: University of North Carolina Press, 2014), 19–37.

28. "Mrs. Clem Sentenced Yesterday," *Journal*, Mar. 30, 1869, 5.

29. "Mrs. Clem Sentenced Yesterday," *Cincinnati Daily Enquirer*, Mar. 31, 1869, 2.

Chapter 9 · A Good Soldier

1. *Indianapolis Sentinel*, Sept. 13, 1869, 4.

2. "Criminal Court," *Sentinel*, Apr. 7, 1869. 4; "Criminal Court," *Sentinel*, Apr. 8, 1869, 4; "Criminal Court," *Sentinel*, Apr. 15, 1869, 4.

3. *Sentinel*, Apr. 14, 1869, 4; "The Abrams Trial," *Sentinel*, Apr. 17, 1869, 4.

4. Andrew W. Young, *History of Wayne County, Indiana, From Its First Settlement to the Present Time* (Cincinnati: Robert Clarke, 1872), 269–270.

5. Federal Manuscript Population Census, 1870, Indianapolis, roll M593-338, p. 148B, and roll M593-340, p. 158B; B. R. Sulgrove, *History of Indianapolis and Marion County, Indiana* (Philadelphia: L. H. Everts, 1884), 496.

6. "An Interview with Abrams," *Sentinel*, Mar. 29, 1869, 4; *Indianapolis Journal*, Sept. 1, 1869, 4.

7. "Melancholy Death of Judge Johnson," *Sentinel*, Apr. 29, 1869, 4.

8. "The Abrams Trial: Second Day's Proceedings," *Journal*, Sept. 2, 1869, 4; "The Young Murder: Trial of William J. Abrams: First Day's Proceedings," *Sentinel*, Sept. 1, 1869, 4; "The Young Murder: Trial of William J. Abram [*sic*]: Second Day's Proceedings," *Sentinel*, Sept. 2, 1869, 4. "The Young Murder: Trial of William J. Abram [*sic*]: Third Day's Proceedings," *Sentinel*, Sept. 3, 1869, 4.

9. *Sentinel*, Sept. 8, 1869, 4; *Journal*, Sept. 4, 1869, 8.

10. *History of Fayette County, Indiana* (Chicago: Warner & Beers, 1885), 99; *Journal*, Sept. 4, 1869, 8; "Trial of Wm. J. Abrams: Third Day's Proceedings," *Journal*, Sept. 3, 1869, 4; "The Young Murder: Trial of William J. Abram [*sic*]: Third Day's Proceedings," *Sentinel*, Sept. 3, 1869, 4.

11. *Sentinel*, Sept. 4, 1869, 4.

12. "Trial of Wm. J. Abrams: Fourth Day's Proceedings," *Journal*, Sept. 4, 1869, 4; "Trial of Wm. J. Abrams: Fifth Day's Proceedings," *Journal*, Sept. 6, 1869, 4; "Trial of Wm. J. Abrams: Sixth Day's Proceedings," *Journal*, Sept. 8, 1869, 2; "Trial of Wm. J. Abrams: Seventh Day's Proceedings," *Journal*, Sept. 9, 1869, 2; "The Young Murder: Trial of William J. Abrams: Seventh Day's Proceedings," *Sentinel*, Sept. 8, 1869, 4.

13. "The Young Murder: Trial of Wm. J. Abrams," *Journal*, Sept. 4, 1869, 4; "Trial of Wm. J. Abrams: Sixth Day's Proceedings," *Journal*, Sept. 8, 1869, 2; "Trial of Wm. J. Abrams: Seventh Day's Proceedings," *Journal*, Sept. 9, 1869, 2.

14. W. W. Leathers, opening statement, *Journal*, Sept. 3, 1869, 4, and *Sentinel*, Sept. 3, 1869, 4.

15. Testimony, Aaron L. Hunt and Josephine Stevens, *Journal*, Sept. 6, 1869, 5; testimony, W. F. Clem, *Journal*, Sept. 10, 1869, 8.

16. *Journal*, Mar. 31, 1869, 8; "The Young Murder: A Short Talk with Wm. J. Abrams," *Sentinel*, Sept. 22, 1869, 4; "Another Suit against Abrams," *Sentinel*, Apr. 14, 1869, 4.

17. *Journal*, Sept. 10, 1869, 8; "The Young Murder: Trial of William J. Abrams: Ninth Day's Proceedings," *Sentinel*, Sept. 10, 1869, 4.

18. William P. Fishback, closing argument, *Journal*, Sept. 11, 1869, 2, and *Sentinel*, Sept. 11, 1869, 4. On the lynching of various members of the Reno Gang, see "Letter from Seymour," *Journal*, July 28, 1868, 5; "Saturday's Tragedy," *New Albany Daily Commercial*, Dec. 14, 1868, 4.

19. Fishback, closing argument, *Journal*, Sept. 11, 1869, 2.

20. Ibid.; see also John T. Dye, closing argument, *Journal*, Sept. 14, 1869, 2.

21. Tony L. Trimble, "Frederick Knefler," in *The Encyclopedia of Indianapolis*, ed. David J. Bodenhamer and Robert G. Barrows (Bloomington: Indiana University Press, 1994), 873; Robert Perlman, *Bridging Three Worlds: Hungarian-Jewish Americans, 1848–1914* (Amherst: University of Massachusetts Press, 2009), 87; Leander John Monks, *Courts and Lawyers of Indiana* (Indianapolis: Federal Pub. Co., 1916), 3:1301–1302.

22. Frederick Knefler, closing argument, *Journal*, Sept. 11, 1869, 2, and *Sentinel*, Sept. 11, 1869, 4; Fishback, closing argument, *Journal*, Sept. 11, 1869, 2, and *Sentinel*, Sept. 11, 1869, 4.

23. Common names and limited information available for most Civil War soldiers make it impossible to state definitively how many jurors were veterans. There's a good chance that at least five, Jacob S. Brown, John Horton, Franklin Hall, Jacob Horner, and A. P. Carr, served in the Union Army. "The Young Murder: Trial of William J. Abram [*sic*]: Third Day's Proceedings," *Sentinel*, Sept. 3, 1869, 4; U.S., Civil War Soldier Records and Profiles, 1861–1865 (online database, Ancestry.com, 2009), http://search.ancestry.com/search /db.aspx?dbid=1555.

24. John Stauffer, "Embattled Manhood and New England Writers, 1860–1870," in *Battle Scars: Gender and Sexuality in the American Civil War*, ed. Catherine Clinton and Nina Silber (New York: Oxford University Press, 2006), 120–139; James M. McPherson, *For Cause and Comrades: Why Men Fought in the Civil War* (New York: Oxford University Press, 1997), 78; Nicole Etcheson, *A Generation at War: The Civil War Era in a Northern Community* (Lawrence: University Press of Kansas, 2011), 146–147; Michael E. McGerr, *The Decline of Popular Politics: The American North, 1865–1928* (New York: Oxford University Press, 1986), 24–30; Morton Keller, *Affairs of State: Public Life in Late Nineteenth Century America* (Cambridge, Mass.: Harvard University Press, 1977), 251; Rebecca Edwards, *Angels in the Machinery: Gender in American Party Politics from the Civil War to the Progressive Era* (New York: Oxford University Press, 1997), 76; Trimble, "Frederick Knefler."

25. Drew Gilpin Faust, *This Republic of Suffering: Death and the American Civil War* (New York: Knopf, 2008); James H. Madison, "Civil War Memories and 'Pardnership Forgittin',' 1865–1913," *Indiana Magazine of History* 99, no. 3 (Sept. 2003): 198–230; Eric T. Dean Jr., "'A Scene of Surpassing Terror and Awful Grandeur': The Paradoxes of Military Service in the American Civil War," *Michigan Historical Review* 21, no. 2 (Fall 1995): 37–61; James Alan Marten, *Sing Not War: The Lives of Union and Confederate Veterans in Gilded Age America* (Chapel Hill: University of North Carolina Press, 2011), 89–90, 103–108; Knefler, closing argument, *Journal*, Sept. 11, 1869, 2, and *Sentinel*, Sept. 11, 1869, 4.

26. John Duncan, closing argument, *Journal*, Sept. 11, 1869, 2. The *Sentinel* did not include Duncan's remark about Abrams "blasting" Young's reputation: "The Young Murder: Trial of William J. Abrams: Tenth Day's Proceedings," *Sentinel*, Sept. 11, 1869, 4.

27. John Hanna, closing argument, *Journal*, Sept. 11, 1869, 2, and Sept. 13, 1869, 2; *Sentinel*, Sept. 11, 1869, 4, and Sept. 13, 1869, 4.

28. Hanna, closing argument, *Journal*, Sept. 13, 1869, 2. The *Sentinel* offered only brief summaries of Hanna's remarks.

29. Ibid.

30. Dye, closing argument, *Journal*, Sept. 14, 1869, 2–3, quotation, 3; *Sentinel*, Sept. 13, 1869, 4.

31. See, for example, "Joseph E. McDonald," *Cleveland Plain Dealer*, June 16, 1891; "'Old Saddle Bags' Dying," *Idaho Statesman*, June 18, 1891, 1; "Ex-Senator McDonald," *New Haven Register*, June 22, 1891, 2; *Journal*, Sept. 14, 1869, 3.

32. *Journal*, Sept. 14, 1869, 3.

33. "William J. Abrams," *Louisville Courier-Journal*, Sept. 17, 1869, 3.

34. "The Abrams Case: The Verdict of the Jury," *Journal*, Sept. 16, 1869, 5; "Verdict and Petition of the Jury," *Sentinel*, Sept. 16, 1869, 4.

35. "End of the Abrams Trial," *Journal*, Sept. 20, 1869, 4; "The Clem Business," *Cincinnati Daily Enquirer*, Oct. 5, 1869, 3.

36. [J. H. Banka], *An Illustrated History and Description of State Prison Life by One Who Has Been There* (Toledo, Ohio: O. A. Browning, 1871), 300–314; "The Clem Business," *Cincinnati Daily Enquirer*, Oct., 5, 1869, 3.

37. *Sentinel*, Oct. 26, 1868, 4; "The Clem Business," *Cincinnati Daily Enquirer*, Oct. 5, 1869, 3.

38. *Sentinel*, Oct. 26, 1869, 4.

Chapter 10 · Lebanon

1. "The Northern Prison: Sketches of the Condemned: William J. Abrams," *People* (Indianapolis), Mar. 24, 1872, 4.

2. *Indianapolis Journal*, Jan. 6, 1871, 8; *Indianapolis Sentinel*, Jan. 6, 1871, 4; *San Francisco Daily Evening Bulletin*, Mar. 4, 1871; *People*, Jan. 8, 1871, 1.

3. "The Young Murder Trial," *Journal*, Mar. 2, 1869.

4. James B. Black, *Reports of Cases Argued and Determined in the Supreme Court of Judicature of the State of Indiana*, vol. 33 (Indianapolis: Journal Company, 1871), 430–433; "Mrs. Clem," *Sentinel*, repr. in *Goshen Democrat*, Dec. 7, 1870, 2; "Indiana's Great Tragedy," *Daviess County Democrat*, Dec. 31, 1870, 2; "Indiana Southern Prison," *New Albany Daily Ledger*, Dec. 10, 1870; "Behind the Bars: Prison Life of Mrs. Clem," *Louisville Courier-Journal*, May 7, 1869, 4.

5. "Indianapolis: Change of Venue in Mrs. Clem's Case Granted," *Cincinnati Commercial*, July 11, 1871, 5.

6. "Mrs. Clem's Trial," *Sentinel*, June 7, 1872, 8.

7. "The Clem Case," *Journal*, Sept. 28, 1871, 4.

8. Richard F. Nation, *At Home in the Hoosier Hills: Agriculture, Politics, and Religion in Southern Indiana, 1810–1870* (Bloomington: Indiana University Press, 2005), 15; Gregory S. Rose, "Upland Southerners: The County Origins of Southern Migrants to Indiana by 1850," *Indiana Magazine of History* 82, no. 3 (Sept. 1986): 245.

9. *Lebanon Pioneer*, June 7, 1872, 3; "The Clem Trial," *Lebanon Weekly Patriot*, July 4, 1872, 4.

10. Cline & McHaffie, *The People's Guide: A Business, Political, and Religious Directory of Boone Co., Ind.* (Indianapolis: Indianapolis Printing & Publishing House, 1874), 120–121. On p. 133, however, Cline & McHaffie claimed that Lebanon had three thousand inhabitants.

11. "Lebanon: A Pencil Sketch of the City and Its Attractions," *Lebanon Weekly Patriot*, Sept. 28, 1871, 4.

12. "The Young Murder Case," *Lebanon Weekly Patriot*, Sept. 28, 1871, 2; *Lebanon Weekly Patriot*, Sept. 28, 1871, 3; *Boone County Pioneer*, Sept. 29, 1871, 3.

13. *Boone County Pioneer*, [likely Oct. 13, 1871, 3; date and pagination missing].

14. "Lebanon," *Lebanon Weekly Patriot*, Sept. 28, 1871, 4; Samuel Harden, *Early Life and Times in Boone County, Indiana: Giving an Account of the Early Settlement of Each Locality, Church Histories, County and Township Officers from the First Down to 1886* (Lebanon, Ind.: Harden & Spahr, 1887), 169.

15. "Lebanon: A Pencil Sketch," Sept. 28, 1871, 4; "Town and Country," *Lebanon Weekly Patriot*, Oct. 26, 1871, 3; "We are pained to hear," *Lebanon Weekly Patriot*, Oct. 26, 1871, 3; "The Young Murder," *Sentinel*, Sept. 27, 1871, 4; Harden, *Early Life and Times in Boone County*, 452.

16. "The Young Murder," *Sentinel*, Sept. 28, 1871, 5; "Mrs. Clem at Lebanon: She Is Treated the Same as Other Prisoners," *Sentinel*, Oct. 10, 1871, 4. According to the *Sentinel*, Lee supplied Clem's meals: "The Young Murder," *Sentinel*, Oct. 9, 1871, 3.

17. "The Young Murder," *Sentinel*, Sept. 27, 1871, 4; "Great Flood of Strangers in the City," *Lebanon Weekly Patriot*, Sept. 28, 1871, 2; "The Clem Trial," *Boone County Pioneer*, Sept. 26, 1871, 2.

18. "Minor Notices: John S. Duncan," *Indiana Magazine of History* 11, no. 1 (Mar. 1915): 85–86; John H. B. Nowland, *Sketches of Prominent Citizens of 1876* (Indianapolis: Tilford & Carlon, 1877), 393–394; "The Trial of Mrs. Clem," *Journal*, Sept. 26, 1871; "The Clem Case," *Journal*, Sept. 28, 1871, 4.

19. "The Young Murder," *Sentinel*, Sept. 28, 1871, 5; "The Clem Case," *Journal*, Sept. 29, 1871, 2; "The Clem Case," *Journal*, Sept. 30, 1871, 2; "The Young Murder," *Sentinel*, Sept. 30, 1871, 2.

20. Testimony, Erastus Everson, *Sentinel*, Oct. 6, 1871, 3; "The Young Murder," *Sentinel*, Oct. 7, 1871, 3; "Notes on the Clem Trial," *Lebanon Weekly Patriot*, Oct. 5, 1871, 3; testimony, John T. Wiley, *Sentinel*, Oct. 5, 1871, 3.

21. *Boone County Pioneer*, Oct. 6, 1871, 3.

22. *Journal*, Sept. 29, 1871, 4; "William J. Abrams," *Indianapolis Evening Journal*, Sept. 29, 1871, 4; "From Indianapolis," *Cincinnati Daily Gazette*, Sept. 28, 1871, 1; "The Cold Spring Tragedy," *People*, Oct. 1, 1871, 1.

23. "The Young Murder," *Sentinel*, Oct. 2, 1871, 1; *Lebanon Weekly Patriot*, Oct. 5, 1871, 3.

24. "The Clem Case," *Journal*, Sept. 30, 1871, 2; "The Clem Case," *Journal*, Oct. 2, 1871, 4; "The Clem Case," *Journal*, Oct. 3, 1871, 1; "The Young Murder," *Sentinel*, Oct. 2, 1871, 1, 5.

25. "The Cold Spring Tragedy," *People*, Oct. 1, 1871, 1; *Journal*, Oct. 2, 1871, 4.

26. "The Cold Spring Tragedy," *People*, Oct. 1, 1871; "The Clem Case," *Journal*, Oct. 3, 1871, 1; "The Young Murder," *Sentinel*, Oct. 3, 1871, 2.

27. *Journal*, Sept. 26, 1871, 5.

28. "The Trial of Mrs. Clem," *Journal*, Sept. 26, 1871, 5, and Sept. 30, 1871, 2; "The Young Murder," *Sentinel*, Oct. 5, 1871, 3; "The Clem Case," *Evening Journal*, Oct. 4, 1871, 4; *Lebanon Weekly Patriot*, Oct. 5, 1871, 3; "Trial of Mrs. Nancy E. Clem" *People*, Oct. 8, 1871. See also "The Clem Case: New and Highly Important Evidence for the State," *Journal*, Oct. 5, 1871, 1.

29. *Sentinel*, Oct. 3, 1871, 2.

30. "The Young Murder," *Sentinel*, Oct. 5, 1871, 3.

31. *People*, Oct. 8, 1871, 1; *Sentinel* Oct. 6, 1871, 3; "The Clem Case," *Journal*, Oct. 6, 1871, 2.

32. "The Clem Case," *Journal*, Oct. 7, 1871, 1; "The Young Murder," *Sentinel*, Oct. 5, 1871, 3; *Sentinel*, Oct. 6, 1871, 3.

33. *Bailey's Indianapolis Directory, 1871–1872* (Indianapolis: Bailey, 1871), 520; Oliver Morris Wilson, *A Digest of Parliamentary Law: Also, the Rules of the Senate, and House of Representatives of Congress: with the Constitution of the United States . . .* , 2nd ed. (Philadelphia: Kay & Brother, 1869); Oliver M. Wilson, *Reports of Cases Argued and Determined in the Superior Court at Indianapolis* (Indianapolis: Journal Co., 1875); Major Oliver M. Wilson, *The Grand Army of the Republic under Its First Constitution and Ritual* (Kansas City, Mo.: F. Hudson, 1905).

34. Jonathan W. Gordon, opening statement, *Sentinel*, Oct. 6, 1871, 3; testimony, Major O. M. Wilson, *Sentinel*, Oct. 7, 1871, 3.

35. "The Clem Case," *Journal*, Oct. 7, 1871, 1; testimony, Major O. M. Wilson, *Sentinel*, Oct. 7, 1871, 3; testimony Hon. John Coburn, *Sentinel*, Oct. 7, 1871, 3; O. M. Wilson to Hon. J. W. Gordon and Benjamin Harrison, repr. in "The Young Murder," *Sentinel*, Oct. 9, 1871, 3.

36. Karen Sawislak, *Smoldering City: Chicagoans and the Great Fire, 1871–1871* (Chicago: University of Chicago Press, 1995), 21–22, 29, 36–37; "Latest from Chicago," *Evening Journal*, Oct. 10, 1871, 2; "The Chicago Fire," *Evening Journal*, Oct. 8, 1871, 2; "The Fire Panic," *Evening Journal*, Oct. 10, 1871, 2.

37. "The Clem Case," *Journal*, Oct. 11, 1871, 2.

38. The defense called Fiscus in order to cast doubt on John Wiley's credibility. Fiscus testified that he was nowhere near Cold Spring on the day of the murder, but the judge ruled him an incompetent witness because his testimony potentially conflicted with his previous alibi, and hence his testimony inadmissible. "The Young Murder," *Sentinel*, Oct. 7, 1871, 3; "The Clem Case," *Journal*, Oct. 7, 1871, 1; "The Young Murder," *People*, Oct. 8, 1871, 1.

39. *Evening Journal*, Oct. 13, 1871, 2; *Bailey's Indianapolis Directory, 1871–1872* (Indianapolis: Bailey, 1871), 78; "The Clem Case," *Sentinel*, Oct. 13, 1871, 4.

40. Eric Foner, *Reconstruction: America's Unfinished Revolution, 1863–1877* (New York: Harper & Row, 1988), 454–459; "The Election of 1872," *Sentinel*, Oct. 14, 1871, 3; *Fort Wayne Weekly Sentinel*, May 10, 1871, 6. See, for example, "Political Notes," *Sentinel*, July 15, 1872, 4; "North Carolina," *Sentinel*, July 29, 1872, 3.

41. Foner, *Reconstruction*, 469–472; James C. Mohr, *The Radical Republicans and Reform in New York during Reconstruction* (Ithaca, N.Y.: Cornell University Press, 1973); *Sentinel*, Oct. 13, 1871, 4.

42. Emma Lou Thornbrough, *Indiana in the Civil War Era, 1850–1880* (Indianapolis: Indiana Historical Bureau & Indiana Historical Society, 1965), 575; "Our New Two Million Dolly Varden Court House," *People*, Sept. 22, 1872, 2. See also *People*, Nov. 10, 1872, 2; Dec. 8, 1872, 2; Dec. 29, 1872, 4; and "Take a Common Sense View of It," *People*, Dec. 8, 1872, 2.

43. "Our New Two Million Dolly Varden Court House," *People*, Sept. 22, 1872, 2, repr. in *Sentinel*, Sept. 23, 1872; "Something More about Our New Two Million Dolly Varden Court House," *People*, Sept. 29, 1872, 9; Thornbrough, *Indiana in the Civil War Era*, 575.

44. Morton Keller, *Affairs of State: Public Life in Late Nineteenth Century America* (Cambridge, Mass.: Harvard University Press, 1977), 239–240; *Daily Arkansas Gazette*, June 12, 1872; Thornbrough, *Indiana in the Civil War Era*, 575; Emma Lou Thornbrough, *The Negro in Indiana before 1900: A Study of a Minority*, 2nd ed. (Bloomington: Indiana University Press, 1993), 229–230.

Chapter 11 · The Indiana Murderess

1. *Indianapolis Sentinel*, June 4, 1872, 8; "The Clem Case: A Card," *Sentinel*, June 8, 1872, 4; "An Effort Being Made to Secure Mrs. Clem's Acquittal," *People* (Indianapolis), Mar. 24, 1872, 1.

2. Leonard S. Kenworthy, *The Tall Sycamore of the Wabash: Daniel Wolsey Voorhees* (Boston: Bruce Humphries, 1936), 36–40, 54–87; W. W. Thornton, "Daniel W. Voorhees as Lawyer and Orator," *The Green Bag: A Useless but Entertaining Magazine for Lawyers* 14, no. 8 (Aug. 1902): 361; Thomas B. Long, "Daniel W. Voorhees," in Harriet Cecilia Voorhees, *Forty Years of Oratory: Daniel Woolsey Voorhees, Lectures, Addresses, and Speeches* (Indianapolis: Bowen-Merrill, 1897), 4–7; *Pictorial and Biographical Memoirs of Elkhart and St. Joseph Counties, Indiana* (Chicago: Goodspeed Brothers, 1893), 495; Frank Smith Bogardus, "Daniel W. Voorhees," *Indiana Magazine of History* 27, no. 2 (June 1931): 91–108; Thomas E. Rodgers, "Liberty, Will, and Violence: The Political Ideology of the Democrats of West-Central Indiana during the Civil War," *Indiana Magazine of History* 92, no. 2 (June 1996): 133–159; Harry J. Sievers, *Benjamin Harrison*, vol. 1: *Hoosier Warrior: Through the Civil War Years, 1833–1865* (New York: University Publishers, 1952), 151–152.

3. A. Cheree Carlson, *The Crimes of Womanhood: Defining Femininity in a Court of Law* (Urbana: University of Illinois Press, 2009), 61–62; Lee Chambers-Schiller, "Seduced, Betrayed, and Revenged: The Murder Trial of Mary Harris," in *Lethal Imagination: Violence and Brutality in American History*, ed. Michael A. Bellesiles (New York: New York University Press, 1999): 185–209; David W. Blight, *Race and Reunion: The Civil War in American Memory* (Cambridge, Mass.: Harvard University Press, 2001), 122–129; Harry J. Sievers, *Benjamin Harrison*, vol. 2: *Hoosier Statesman: From the Civil War to the White House, 1865–1888* (New York: University Publishers, 1959), 56, 59–60; Heather Cox Richardson, *West from Appomattox: The Reconstruction of America after the Civil War* (New Haven: Yale University Press, 2007), 53–57, 121–142.

4. "Grant Meeting in Columbus—Speech of Major Jonathan W. Gordon," *Sentinel*, July 25, 1872, 3.

5. "A Bit of Evidence That Was Never Brought Out," *Indianapolis Star*, Aug. 18, 1907, SM1; "An Effort Being Made to Secure Mrs. Clem's Acquittal," *People*, Mar. 24, 1872, 1.

6. See, for example, "Indiana: Mrs. Clem," *Kalamazoo Gazette*, Aug. 3, 1872, 1; *Pomeroy's Democrat* (Chicago), Mar. 1, 1873, 5; *Patriot* (Harrisburg, Penn.), June 18, 1873, 1; *Stoughton (Mass.) Sentinel*, Sept. 13, 1873, 4; "Final Release of Mrs. Clem, the Alleged Indiana Murderess," *Chicago Daily Tribune*, Apr. 30, 1874.

7. [J. Harrie Banka], *State Prison Life: By One Who Has Been There* (Cincinnati: C. F. Vent, 1871). Advertisements for *State Prison Life* appeared in numerous newspapers in late September; see, for example, *Cincinnati Daily Gazette*, Sept. 27, 1871, 2; for a review, see "Prison Barbarities: Life in the Indiana State Prison," *New York Commercial Advertiser*, Nov. 2, 1871, 1.

8. David Ray Papke, "Legitimate Illegitimacy: The Memoirs of Nineteenth-Century Professional Criminals," *Legal Studies Forum* 9 (1985): 165–77; Banka, *State Prison Life*, 379.

9. "The Northern Prison: Sketches of the Condemned: William J. Abrams," *People*, Mar. 24, 1872, 4.

10. "Death of William J. Abrams' Daughter," *People*, Mar. 24, 1872, 4; *Chicago Tribune*, Mar. 22, 1872, 4.

11. "The Cold Spring Tragedy: Mrs. Clem on Her Trials," *Sentinel*, June 5, 1872, 2; *Sentinel*, Oct. 10, 1871, 4; "The Trial of Mrs. Clem," *People*, June 9, 1872, 1; *Lebanon Pioneer*, June 7, 1872, 3; "The Cold Spring Horror: Nancy W. Clem and Her Fourth Trial," *People*, June 16, 1872, 1.

12. "The Clem Trial," *Lebanon Weekly Patriot*, June 6, 1872, 3.

13. "The Young Murder," *Indianapolis Journal*, June 10, 1872, 5.

14. *Lebanon Weekly Patriot*, June 27, 1872, 2; "'L R' A Hoosier Celebrity. A Sketch of a Notable Home Personage—Miss Ream," *Sentinel*, June 8, 1874, 5; "Home Gossip," *Sentinel*, Nov. 16, 1872, 3; "Indianapolis Letter," *Cincinnati Commercial Tribune*, Mar. 16, 1869, 4; "Mrs. Clem," *Cincinnati Commercial Tribune*, Feb. 1, 1869, 2.

15. "A Pioneer Newspaper Woman," *Star*, Mar. 31, 1913, 6; "Gossip from Indianapolis—A Breach of Promise Case," *San Francisco Daily Evening Bulletin*, Apr. 19, 1867; "Home Gossip," *Sentinel*, Nov. 16, 1872, 3.

16. *Sentinel*, Jan. 12, 1869, 4; *Lebanon Weekly Patriot*, June 27, 1872, 2; *Journal*, Jan. 12, 1871, 8; *People*, Jan. 15, 1871, 2; *People*, Jan. 15, 1871, 4; "Additional Local," *Lebanon Weekly Patriot*, June 27, 1872, 2; *Journal*, Sept. 15, 1871, 4; "Literary Club Pays Tribute to Mrs. Fairbanks's Memory," *Star*, Nov. 5, 1913, 7; "Will Sell Cut Flowers," *Star*, Apr. 15, 1911, 9; "Home Gossip," *Sentinel*, Nov. 16, 1872, 3. See "Democratic Party" in *Encyclopedia of Women in American Politics*, ed. Jeffrey D. Schultz and Laura Van Assendelft (Phoenix: Oryx Press, 1999), 52–53; Thomas E. Rodgers, "Liberty, Will, and Violence: The Political Ideology of the Democrats of West-Central Indiana during the Civil War," *Indiana Magazine of History* 92, no. 2 (June 1996): 156–157; and Rebecca Edwards, *Angels in the Machinery: Gender in American Party Politics from the Civil War to the Progressive Era* (New York: Oxford University Press, 1997), 18–27.

17. "At Liberty Mrs. Clem, after Being Tried Five Times for Murder, Is Released," *Inter Ocean* (Chicago), Apr. 30, 1874, 4; *Journal*, June 12, 1872, 4.

18. "The Cold Spring Horror," *People*, June 16, 1872, 1; *Nancy E. Clem v. State of Indiana* (1872), Office of Supreme Court Records, Indianapolis, Indiana, 3150; *People*, June 2, 1872, 8.

19. Testimony, Mary E. C. Brown, in *Clem v. Indiana* (1872), 3129, 3136.

20. Federal Manuscript Population Census, 1870, Pike Township, Marion County, Indiana, roll M593-337, p. 65A; "The Young Murder," *Journal*, June 10, 1872, 5. Harbert's initial testimony is not included in the surviving transcript. "Evidence in chief not furnished & if it is needed in addition to his *recall* it will be inserted here," read the clerk's notation; see *Clem v. Indiana* (1872), 2663.

21. "The Young Murder," *Journal*, June 10, 1872, 5; "Mrs. Clem's Trial," *Sentinel*, June 10, 1872, 2.

22. Testimony, John Harbert, *Clem v. Indiana* (1872), 3642–3652.

23. Ibid., 3643.

24. Testimony, George Hollingsworth, *Journal*, Dec. 15, 1868, 3, and *Clem v. Indiana* (1872), 3179–3180, 3182.

25. Testimony, Peter Wilkins, *Clem v. Indiana* (1872), 3171–3175; *Journal*, June 15, 1872, 5; "Nancy E. Clem Dead," *Journal*, Jun. 9, 1897, 5; "Death of Nancy E. Clem," *News*, June 9, 1897, 8; and June 10, 1897, 8; "Chapters in the Life of Peter Wilkins: Peter among the Deserters: Takes Eight at One Haul," *People*, Jan. 1, 1871, 1. Neither the *Journal* nor the *News* identified the "Indianapolis man" who went to Missouri in search of Cravens Hartman, but Wilkins's testimony indicates that he was that man.

26. "Mrs. Clem Free," *Logansport (Ind.) Chronicle*, Sept.15, 1883, 1; "Mrs. Clem Free Again," *New York Times*, Sept. 13, 1883, 5; "Nancy E. Clem Dead," *Journal*, June 9, 1897, 5; "Site of Young Murder," *Journal*, June 10, 1897, 8.

27. "Wm. J. Abrams Dies at the Soldiers' Home," *News*, June 2, 1910, 3; "Neighborhood Gossip," *Lebanon Weekly Patriot*, June 13, 1872, 4.

28. Testimony, Silas M. Gist, *Clem v. Indiana* (1872), 3253; "The Clem Murder Trial," *Indianapolis News*, June 15, 1872, 3.

29. Testimony, William J. Abrams, *Clem v. Indiana* (1872), 3262–3263.

30. "Disappeared," *Sentinel*, June 17, 1872, 8.

31. "The Clem Case," *Indianapolis Evening Journal*, June 19, 1872, 3; *People*, June 23, 1872, 1; "The Clem Trial," *Lebanon Pioneer*, June 14, 1872, 3.

32. *Cincinnati Enquirer*, June 27, 1872, 4; *Lebanon Weekly Patriot*, July 4, 1872, 2 and 3; "The Clem Trial," *Lebanon Pioneer*, July 5, 1872, 2; Harriet Cecilia Voorhees *Forty Years of Oratory: Daniel Wolsey Voorhees Lectures, Addresses and Speeches, Compiled and Edited by His Three Sons and His Daughter, Harriet Cecilia Voorhees* (Indianapolis: Bowen-Merrill, 1898), 404.

33. "The Clem Trial," *Lebanon Pioneer*, July 5, 1872, 2.

34. *People*, June 30, 1872, 8; *Lebanon Weekly Patriot*, July 4, 1872, 3.

35. Voorhees, *Forty Years of Oratory*, 2:404.

36. *Sentinel*, June 27, 1872, 1; *Journal*, June 28, 1872, 4.

37. "The Cold Spring Tragedy," *People*, June 23, 1872, 1; *Journal*, June 28, 1872, 4; *Lebanon Weekly Patriot*, July 4, 1872, 4.

38. "The Clem Case," *Journal*, June 29, 1872, 4; "The Clem Case: The Jury Agreed—Verdict of Guilty," *Sentinel*, June 29, 1872, 8; "Mrs. Clem Convicted," *Lebanon Weekly Patriot*, July 4, 1872, 4.

39. "A Sold Out Editor: The Market Price of B. Angel Smith" *Lebanon Weekly Patriot*, July 4, 1872, 4; *Journal*, July 10, 1872, 4.

40. "The Clem Case," *Journal*, June 29, 1872, 4.

41. "Mrs. Clem Convicted," *Lebanon Weekly Patriot*, July 4, 1872; "The Clem Case: The Jury Agreed—Verdict of Guilty," *Sentinel*, June 29, 1872, 8; "He Has a Soft Heart," *Denver Evening Post*, Jan. 28, 1896; "Won't Prosecute a Woman," *Bismarck Daily Tribune*, Jan. 31, 1896; "Quite a Lady's Man," *Emporia Daily Gazette*, Feb. 5, 1896.

42. Charles W. Calhoun, *Benjamin Harrison* (New York: Henry Holt, 2005), 155–156, 159–161.

43. "The Lesson," *Journal*, July 1, 1872, 4.

44. Eric Foner, *Reconstruction: America's Unfinished Revolution, 1863–1877* (New York: Harper & Row, 1988), 488–511; Blight, *Race and Reunion*, 122–129; "The Fighting on Tuesday Night," *People*, Aug. 18, 1872, 1; "The Lesson," *Journal*, July 1, 1872, 4.

45. *Brooklyn Eagle*, July 17, 1872, 2.

46. The same story appeared under two different titles, "Circumstantial Evidence" and "A Remarkable Case." Most of the various versions attributed the piece to the *St. Louis Democrat,* also known as the *Missouri Democrat.* See, for example, "Circumstantial Evidence: History of a Remarkable Murder Case," *Chicago Tribune,* July 3, 1872, 2; "Circumstantial Evidence: History of a Remarkable Murder Case," *Detroit Free Press,* July 13, 1872, 3; "A Remarkable Case: The History of a Great Crime in Indiana," *Daily Albany Argus,* July 6, 1872, 2; "Circumstantial Evidence: History of a Remarkable Murder Case," *Daily Picayune,* July 7, 1827, 9; "A Remarkable Case," *Cincinnati Daily Gazette;* July 3, 1872, 1.

47. "Conviction of Mrs. Clem of Murder in the Second Degree," *Chicago Tribune,* June 29, 1872, 1.

Chapter 12 · Indiana Justice

1. *Lebanon Weekly Patriot,* July 11, 1872, 3; "The Clem Case: Motion for a New Trial Overruled," *Indianapolis Sentinel,* Aug. 2, 1872, 5; "Will Mrs. Clem Get a New Trial?" *People* (Indianapolis), July 14, 1872, 1; "State Items," *Sentinel,* July 20, 1872, 5.

2. Jacob Piatt Dunn, *Indiana and Indianans: A History of Aboriginal and Territorial Indiana and the Century of Statehood,* vol. 5 (Chicago: American Historical Society, 1919), 1043; Roger H. Van Bolt, "The Rise of the Republican Party in Indiana, 1855–1856," *Indiana Magazine of History* 51, no. 3 (Sept. 1955): 209.

3. Van Bolt, "Rise of the Republican Party," 187.

4. *People,* July 14, 1872, 1; "State Items," *Sentinel,* July 20, 1872, 5; "People and Things," *People,* Sept. 15, 1872, 7; "The Clem Case—Mrs. Clem Convicted of Murder in the Second Degree," *Daily Memphis Avalanche,* Mar. 4, 1869, [2].

5. "City Gleanings," *Sentinel,* July 12, 1872, 2; "Glittering Generalities," *People,* July 14, 1872, 1.

6. *Chicago Tribune,* Sept. 29, 1872, 8; *Daily Democrat* (Sedalia, Mo.), Oct. 30. 1872; *Cincinnati Enquirer,* Oct. 1, 1872, 2; *San Francisco Evening Bulletin,* Oct. 7, 1872, 4.

7. "Criminal Law," *Sentinel,* Dec. 3, 1872, 7.

8. "General City News," *Sentinel,* Dec. 11, 1872, 2; "Try, Try, Try Again," *Sentinel,* Dec. 13, 1872, 8; "The Clem Case," *Sentinel,* Mar. 3, 1873, 8.

9. "Visit to the State Prison in Jeffersonville," *Sentinel,* June 23, 1873, 2; "Inside the Grating: The Jeffersonville Inspection," *Sentinel,* Feb. 18, 1873, 4.

10. "Clem v. The State," in James B. Black, *Reports of Cases Argued and Determined in the Supreme Court of Judicature of the State of Indiana,* vol. 42 (Indianapolis: Journal Company, 1874), 420–449.

11. "How the Murderess Heard the News," *Sentinel,* June, 18, 1873, 2.

12. "Crime and Criminals: The Drift of Public Opinion," *Sentinel,* July 22, 1873, 7.

13. "The Clem Murder Case—Newspaper Comments," *New York Times,* June 19, 1873, 1; "How the Murderess Heard the News," *Sentinel,* June, 18, 1873, 2; "Murderers' Loopholes," *Sentinel,* June 16, 1873, 1; *Sentinel,* June 19, 1873, 4.

14. "How the Murderess Heard the News," *Sentinel,* June, 18, 1873, 2; "The Removal of Mrs. Clem," *Sentinel,* June 23, 1873, 5.

15. *Sentinel,* June 27, 1872, 4.

16. *Rochester Democrat,* quoted in *Sentinel,* July 10, 1873, 3.

17. *Sentinel,* Sept. 24, 1873, and June 27, 1873; John Steele Gordon, "To a Speculator Dying Young," *American Heritage* 43 (Nov. 1992): 18–19; Hendrik Hartog, "Lawyering, Husbands' Rights, and 'the Unwritten Law' in Nineteenth- Century America," *Journal of American History* 84 (June 1997): 67–96; Robert M. Ireland, "Insanity and the Unwritten Law," *American Journal of Legal History* 32 (Apr. 1988): 157–172; Robert M. Ireland, "The Libertine Must Die:

Sexual Dishonor and the Unwritten Law in the Nineteenth-Century United States," *Journal of Social History* 231 (Autumn 1989): 27–44; Melissa J. Ganz, "Wicked Women and Veiled Ladies: Gendered Narratives of the McFarland-Richardson Tragedy," *Yale Journal of Law and Feminism* 9 (1997): 255–304. See also Carole Haber, *The Trials of Laura Fair: Sex, Murder, and Insanity in the Victorian West* (Chapel Hill: University of North Carolina Press, 2013), 117–118, 161–162.

18. [J. Harrie Banka], *State Prison Life: By One Who Has Been There* (Cincinnati: C. F. Vent, 1871), 378.

19. The quintessential example would be H. H. Holmes, the Chicago serial killer; see Erik Larson, *The Devil in the White City: Murder, Magic, and Madness at the Fair That Changed America* (New York: Vintage, 2004). Again, though, Clem hardly fits his modus operandi. On respectability and crime, see Michael A. Ross, *The Great New Orleans Kidnapping Case: Race, Law, and Justice in the Reconstruction Era* (New York: Oxford University Press, 2015), 99–100, 209–210.

20. "The Mystery: A Dark Page from Hoosier History," *Chicago Times*, quoted in *Sentinel*, May 9, 1874, 3; Lee Chambers-Schiller, "Seduced, Betrayed, and Revenged: The Murder Trial of Mary Harris," in *Lethal Imagination: Violence and Brutality in American History*, ed. Michael A. Bellesiles (New York: New York University Press, 1999): 185–209; A. Cheree Carlson, *The Crimes of Womanhood: Defining Femininity in a Court of Law* (Urbana: University of Illinois Press, 2008), 39–68. At least one newspaper compared Clem to Laura D. Fair, who was tried and convicted for murdering her lover but was acquitted after a second trial; see "Personal," *Milwaukee Sentinel*, Oct. 10, 1872. See also Haber, *The Trials of Laura Fair*.

21. "How the Murderess Heard the News," *Sentinel*, June 18, 1838; "The Nancy Clem Case," *Chicago Inter Ocean*, Apr. 27, 1874.

22. Karen Halttunen, *Confidence Men and Painted Women: A Study of Middle-Class Culture in America, 1830–1870* (New Haven: Yale University Press, 1982), 198.

23. *Sentinel*, Feb. 4, 1869.

24. "The Nancy Clem Case," *Chicago Inter Ocean*, Apr. 27, 1874.

25. Nicole Hahn Rafter, *Partial Justice: Women, Prisons, and Social Control*, 2nd. ed. (New Brunswick, N.J.: Rutgers University Press, 1990), 32.

26. "How the Murderess Heard the News," *Sentinel*, June 18, 1873.

27. "Indiana's Romancer," *Indianapolis News*, Mar. 30, 1880; B. R. Sulgrove, *History of Indianapolis and Marion County, Indiana* (Philadelphia: L. H. Everts, 1884), 45; "What Mrs. Clem Thinks," *Sentinel*, Feb. 18, 1873.

28. "City News: Home Notes," *Sentinel*, Feb. 27, 1874, 8.

29. Jacob Piatt Dunn, *Greater Indianapolis: The History, the Industries, the Institutions, and the People of a City of Homes* (Chicago: Lewis Publishing Company, 1910), 1:259; Edward A. Leary, *Indianapolis: The Story of a City* (Indianapolis: Bobbs-Merrill, 1971), 129–130; "The Strike," *Indianapolis Journal*, Feb. 5, 1874, 4; Nathaniel Deutsch, *Inventing America's "Worst" Family: Eugenics, Islam, and the Fall and Rise of the Tribe of Ishmael* (Berkeley: University of California Press, 2009), 21–22, 26.

30. William T. Holmes, "Pasadena History: Early Days in the Indiana Colony," *Los Angeles Times*, Nov. 26, 1889; *An Illustrated History of Los Angeles County, California* (Chicago: Lewis Publishing, 1889), 315; obituary, Mrs. R. C. Locke, *Los Angeles Times*, Nov. 24, 1890; *Sentinel*, Feb. 11, 1874, 3; "Rather Wrathful: Another Note on the Clem Story—Hard Names and Explicit Denials," *Sentinel*, Apr. 23, 1874, 8; "The Clem Trial," *San Francisco Daily Evening Bulletin*, Apr. 30, 1874; "Indiana Justice Hard Up," *Sentinel*, Oct. 24, 1873, 3.

31. *Sentinel*, Mar. 19, 1874, 8; *Sentinel*, Apr. 28, 1874, 4.

32. *Sentinel*, Apr. 24, 1874, 4.

33. *San Francisco Daily Evening Bulletin*, Apr. 30, 1874; "Indiana Justice Hard Up," *Sentinel*, Oct. 24, 1873, 3; "The Clem Case Uncared For—Public Opinion in Regard to It," *Cincinnati Daily Gazette*, Mar. 24, 1874, 2; "A Woman's Trial: Mrs. Clem, After Four Trials for Murder, Set at Liberty—A Specimen of Indiana Justice," *Cleveland Plain Dealer*, May 4, 1874, 2.

34. *Sentinel*, Apr. 23, 1874, 8; "The Clem Trial," *Sentinel*, Apr. 24, 1874, 4; "Clem's Acquittal," *Sentinel*, May 5, 1874, 3.

35. *Daily Republican* (Decatur, Ill.), Apr. 29, 1874.

36. "Free. Nancy Clem at Large: The Last of the Law's Delay," *Sentinel*, Apr. 30, 1874, 4–5.

37. Leander John Monks, *Courts and Lawyers of Indiana* (Indianapolis: Federal Publishing Company, 1916), 2:608–609; *News*, Apr. 29, 1874, 1.

38. "Mrs. Clem," *New York Times*, May 4, 1874, 4.

39. "Free. Nancy Clem at Large: The Last of the Law's Delay," *Sentinel*, Apr. 30, 1874, 4–5.

40. "Town Topics," *Sentinel*, May 2, 1874, 4.

41. "A Midnight Whiz: A Mile a Minute to Lebanon," *Sentinel*, May 4, 1874, 3.

42. *News*, Apr. 29, 1874, 2; *Sentinel*, Apr. 30, 1874, 4. See also "Nancy E. Clem," *Journal*, Apr. 30, 1874, 4–5, and "Mrs. Clem," *News*, Apr. 30, 1874, 2.

43. "Indiana Justice," *New York Times*, Mar. 6, 1874, 4; "Mrs. Clem," *New York Times*, May 4, 1874, 4.

44. "Indiana Justice Hard Up," *San Francisco Daily Evening Bulletin*, Apr. 30, 1874; "A Woman's Trials: Mrs. Clem, after Four Trials for Murder, Set at Liberty—A Specimen of Indiana Justice," *Chicago Inter Ocean*, May 1, 1874, 2; "Indiana Justice—Pair of Fiends Escape the Gallows," *New York Times*, May 23, 1874, 1.

45. "Mrs. Clem Enjoys Street Promenades after Release from Prison," *Chicago Inter Ocean*, May 11, 1874, 2.

46. *News*, Apr. 30, 1874, 2; "Other Important Murder Trials," *Sentinel*, July 12, 1875, 8; "It Serves Him Right," *National Police Gazette*, May 15, 1880, 5.

47. "Death of William W. Leathers," *Cincinnati Daily Gazette*, Dec. 17, 1873, 5; *Sentinel*, Dec. 17, 1875, 4; "The Sequel to a Murder Trial," *Sentinel*, Apr. 18, 1875, 8, and May 6, 1875, 3.

Chapter 13 · I Kept It Rolling

1. "Mrs. Clem at Home Again," *Indianapolis Sentinel* Aug. 8, 1874, 8; "Gleanings by Late Mails," *Philadelphia Enquirer*, Aug. 4, 1874, 4; "Mrs. Clem's Residence," *Indianapolis Saturday Herald*, June 7, 1879, 8; "Mrs. Nancy E. Clem at Home," *People* (Indianapolis, Ind.), May 3, 1874, 1; *S. E. Tilford & Co.'s Indianapolis City Directory, 1877* (Indianapolis: Publishing House, 1877), 320; *R. L. Polk & Co.'s Indianapolis Directory for 1878* (Indianapolis: R. L. Polk, 1878), 412; marriage, William A. Patton and Beulah J. Wilcox, Indiana Marriage Index, 1800-1941 (online database, Ancestry.com, 2005), http://search.ancestry.com/search/db.aspx?dbid =5059; Federal Manuscript Population Census (hereafter FMPC), 1870, Indianapolis, roll M593-339, p. 505B; "More Trouble for Mrs. Clem," *Sentinel*, Dec. 25, 1876, 3; "The Notorious Mrs. Clem in Court," Dec. 20, 1877, 1; "A Tale of Gambling and Murder: Mrs. Nancy Clem the Heroine of Four Murder Trials," *New York World*, quoted in *San Francisco Daily Evening Bulletin*, May 8, 1877.

2. "Mrs. Clem," *Chicago Daily Tribune*, Nov. 27, 1876, 8; "A Remarkable Woman. A Strange Murder and the Peculiar Circumstances Surrounding It—Mrs. Clem's Escape from Justice—New Developments," *San Francisco Daily Evening Bulletin*, Dec. 15, 1876; "A Tale of Gambling and Murder: Mrs. Nancy Clem the Heroine of Four Murder Trials," *San Francisco Daily Evening Bulletin*, May 8, 1877.

3. FMPC, 1880, Perry Township, Marion County, Indiana, roll 294, p. 538B; *News*, July 1, 1878, 1; "Nancy's Nippers," *Cincinnati Enquirer*, Nov. 27, 1876, 4; "A Chat with Mrs. Clem," *Sentinel*, Apr. 2, 1877, 3.

4. "A Remarkable Woman," *New York World*, quoted in *San Francisco Daily Evening Bulletin*, Dec. 15, 1876. See, for example, "That Dreadful Woman" and other comments published in the *Saturday Herald*, June 15, 1878, 4–5. See also *Saturday Herald*, June 22, 1878, 4, and "Home Notes," *Sentinel*, June 25, 1878, 8.

5. "Indiana's Romancer: Mrs. Clem's Later Financial Operations with Hinkston, Miller, et al. Her Story, as Told in the Deposition That Wrecked Her—Remarkable Credulity of the People with Whom She Dealt," *News*, Mar. 30, 1880, 2.

6. Florence Evans, "Feeding of the Hungry by Mayor Caven," *People*, June 30, 1877, 2; "Indianapolis: Events of Interest at Indiana's Capital," *Cincinnati Gazette*, June 7, 1877, 5; B. R. Sulgrove, *History of Indianapolis and Marion County, Indiana* (Philadelphia: L. H. Everts, 1884), 211–213; "Life and Public Services of General Benjamin Harrison," in *The Republican Party: Its History, Principles, and Policies*, ed. John D. Long (Boston: William E. Smyth, 1881), 374–376; Charles W. Calhoun, *Benjamin Harrison* (New York: Henry Holt, 2005), 33–36.

7. "Indiana's Romancer," *News*, Mar. 30, 1880, 2; "Nancy E. Clem! On Trial for Perjury and Found Guilty," *People*, Mar. 20, 1880, 1; "Mrs. Clem: An Unwritten Chapter by Peter Wilkins.—He Tells Where the Money Comes From—The Secret of Her Financial Operations," *News*, Mar. 31, 1880, 4; "Elbow Shots," *Saturday Herald*, Apr. 3, 1880, 1.

8. "Indiana's Romancer," *News*, Mar. 30, 1880, 2; FMPC, 1870, Perry Township, Marion County, Indiana, roll M593-337, p. 438B; FMPC, 1880, Perry Township, Marion County, Indiana, roll 294, p. 543C. Newspapers described Wishard as Hinkson's nephew, but genealogies indicate Wishard was his son-in-law. Lomax family tree, Ancestry.com, http://trees.ancestry.com/tree/10028591/person/25792177711; sjg_2010-04-01 family tree, Ancestry.com, http://trees.ancestry.com/tree/41075973/person/20485524567.

9. Ibid.; "The Clem Reunion, Some Suggestions from One of the 'Little Woman's' Victims," *Saturday Herald*, July 27, 1878, 8; "Mrs. Clem's Trial," *News*, Mar. 16, 1880, 4; "Mrs. Clem Convicted," *Saturday Herald*, Mar. 20, 1880, 8.

10. "Indiana's Romancer," *News*, Mar. 30, 1880, 2; "Criminal News. The Long List of Rogue Bugbee's Forgeries at Indianapolis," *Chicago Tribune*, Apr. 6, 1878, 2; "A Tale of Gambling and Murder," *San Francisco Daily Evening Bulletin*, May 8, 1877; "Mrs. Clem: An Unwritten Chapter by Peter Wilkins," *News*, Mar. 31, 1880, 4.

11. "A Tale of Gambling and Murder," *New York World*, quoted in *San Francisco Daily Evening Bulletin*, May 8, 1877.

12. "Mrs. Clem and Miss Miller," *News*, Mar. 2, 1880, 3; "A Tale of Gambling and Murder," *San Francisco Daily Evening Bulletin*, May 8, 1877.

13. Wendy Gamber, *The Boardinghouse in Nineteenth-Century America* (Baltimore: John Hopkins University Press, 2007), 97–102; "Mrs. Clem and Miss Miller," *News*, Mar. 2, 1880, 3; *Manufacturing and Mercantile Resources of Indianapolis, Indiana* (n. p.: n. p., 1883), 543.

14. "Indiana's Romancer," *News*, Mar. 30, 1880, 2.

15. Ibid.

16. "The Clem Reunion," *Saturday Herald*, July 27, 1878, 8; "The Clem Coterie," *Saturday Herald*, Aug. 17, 1878, 3; "Free: Nancy Clem at Large," *Sentinel*, Apr. 30, 1874, 5.

17. Evidence from city directories suggests that Frank Clem sold his share of the business to his brother in 1870, resumed his status as partner in 1876, and was once again demoted to clerk in 1880, at a time when he again had significant legal expenses. This time he may have sold his share of the firm to a third partner, Luther R. Easterday, who appears as a member of the firm beginning in 1876. The 1870 directory listed Frank Clem as a bookkeeper; 1871, 1872, and 1873 as a clerk, and 1874, as having no occupation. In 1875 he seems to have formed a partnership with another man, J. E. Robertson, but by 1876 he was once again listed as a partner in A. Clem & Co. By 1880, he was a clerk once more. *Hutchinson's Indianapolis City Directory* (Indianapolis: Sentinel Steam Printing, 1870), 48, listed Frank twice, once as a

grocer, and once as a bookkeeper for A. Clem—a cataloguing that is consistent with the two enumerations of the 1870 census. *Bailey's Directory Series: Indianapolis Directory 1871–72* (Indianapolis: Bailey, 1871), 121; *Swartz & Tedrowe's Indianapolis Directory, 1872–73* (Indianapolis: Indianapolis Sentinel Printers, 1872), 69; *Indianapolis City Directory, 1873* (Indianapolis: Sentinel Company, 1873), 95; *Swartz & Tedrowe's Annual Indianapolis City Directory, 1874* (Indianapolis: Sentinel Company, 1874), 104 (listed Frank as having no occupation); *Swartz & Tedrowe's Indianapolis City Directory, 1875* (Indianapolis: Sentinel Company, 1875), 96 (lists Frank as being in the grocery business with J. E. Robertson); *Swartz & Tedrowe's Indianapolis City Directory, 1876* (Indianapolis: Sentinel Company, 1876), 29; *S. E. Tilford & Co.'s Indianapolis City Directory, 1877* (Indianapolis: Indianapolis Publishing House, 1877), 96; *R. L. Polk & Co.'s Indianapolis Directory for 1878* (Indianapolis: R. L. Polk, 1878), 170; *R. L. Polk & Co.'s Indianapolis Directory for 1879* (Indianapolis: R. L. Polk, 1879), 159; *R. L. Polk & Co.'s Indianapolis Directory for 1880* (Indianapolis: Indianapolis Publishing House, 1880), 165. Enumerators for the 1870 census visited the Clem family—and most of Indianapolis—twice. The first enumeration, dated June 13, 1870, listed Frank Clem as a retail grocer with $12,000 of real property and $300 of personal property; the second, dated February 10, 1871, as a "grocer clerk," albeit one who still possessed a substantial amount of property ($10,000 worth of real estate and $2,000 in personal estate). Clem appears as a grocery clerk in the 1880 census, which unfortunately did not ask respondents to enumerate their property. FMPC, 1870, Indianapolis, Ward 1, roll M593-340, p. 9B, and 2nd enum., roll M593-338, p 20A; FMPC, 1880, Indianapolis, roll 295, p.332C. None of these sources is entirely reliable, but Frank Clem's changing status is certainly in keeping with the economic havoc mounting legal expenses must have wrought. "The Clem Coterie," *Saturday Herald*, Aug. 17, 1878, 3.

18. *Saturday Herald*, Sept. 28, 1878, 5; "That Dreadful Woman," *Saturday Herald*, June 15, 1878, 5. I can find no evidence that the *Journal* actually published such a statement.

19. "A Remarkable Woman.," New York World quoted in *San Francisco Daily Evening Bulletin*, Dec. 15, 1876; *Saturday Herald*, June 29, 1878, 4; "Measuring Worth: Seven Ways to Compute the Relative Value of a U.S. Dollar Amount, 1774 to Present," www.measuringworth .com/uscompare.

20. "Clem: An Ex-Prosecuting-Attorney's 'Quickened Conscience,'" *Journal*, quoted in *Chicago Tribune*, May 17, 1878, 5; *Report of the Senate Committee on Privileges and Elections with the Testimony and Documentary Evidence on the Election in the State of Florida in 1876* (Washington, D.C.: Government Printing Office, 1877), 8–20; Roy Morris Jr., *Fraud of the Century: Rutherford B. Hayes, Samuel Tilden, and the Stolen Election of 1876* (New York: Simon & Schuster, 2003); Tracy Campbell, *Deliver the Vote: A History of Election Fraud, an American Political Tradition, 1742–2004* (New York: Carroll & Graf, 2005), 79–81; Richard Wightman Fox, *Trials of Intimacy: Love and Loss in the Beecher-Tilton Scandal* (Chicago: University of Chicago Press, 1999), 39–44; Altina L. Waller, *Reverend Beecher and Mrs. Tilton: Sex and Class in Victorian America* (Amherst: University of Massachusetts Press, 1982); "Crime," *Milwaukee Daily Sentinel*, Mar. 17, 1878, 8.

21. "Clem: An Ex-Prosecuting Attorney's 'Quickened Conscience,'" *Chicago Tribune*, May 17, 1878, 5.

22. "Alleged Bribery on the Bench," *Chicago Inter Ocean*, May 17, 1878, 5.

23. "Nancy E. Clem," *Saturday Herald*, June 8, 1878, 4; "The Clem Case: Feasibility of Continuing the Prosecution—Interview with General Ben Harrison," *News*, July 2, 1878, 4; "Nancy E. Clem," *Saturday Herald*, June 1, 1878, 4.

24. "The Clem Case," *News*, July 2, 1878, 4; *Saturday Herald*, June 15, 1878, 5.

25. "The Notorious Mrs. Clem Arrested for Larceny," *Cincinnati Gazette*, June 14, 1878, 1; "Minor Topics," *Louisville Courier-Journal*, June 17, 1878, 2; "Elbow Shots," *Saturday Herald*, June 22, 1878, 1; "Mrs. Clem," *Chicago Tribune*, June 14, 1878, 5; "Indianapolis Letter,"

Cincinnati Enquirer, June 22, 1878, 5; *Saturday Herald*, June 15, 1878, 4; Abrams Pardoned," *People*, July 6, 1878; "Nancy E. Clem!" *People*, Mar. 20, 1880, 1.

26. *Saturday Herald*, June 22, 1878, 4; *Kokomo Tribune*, quoted in *Saturday Herald*, June 22, 1878, 1.

27. "Mrs. Clem," *Chicago Tribune*, June 14, 1878, 5; "Executive Clemency: Reasons Why Certain Pardons Have Been Granted. The Governor's Course Will Receive the Approval of All Fair-Minded Men." *Sentinel*, July 30, 1878, 3.

28. Howard R. Burnett, "The Last Pioneer Governor of Indiana: 'Blue Jeans' Williams," *Indiana Magazine of History* 22, no. 2 (June 1926): 101–130; "Indiana: Sketch of a Republican Meeting, *New York Herald*, Oct. 5, 1876, 3; Harry J. Sievers, *Benjamin Harrison*, vol. 2: *Hoosier Statesman: From the Civil War to the White House, 1865–1888* (New York: University Publishers, 1959), 108–124; Charles Joseph Oval, *Governors of Indiana, Illustrated* (Indianapolis: Oval & Koster, 1916), 84.

29. "Executive Clemency," *Sentinel*, July 30, 1878, 3.

30. "The Abrams Release: The Tragedy of September 12, 1868, Again—the Man Who Bought the Gun—Governor Williams Pardons William J. Abrams," *News*, July 5, 1878, 4; "What Shall Be Done?" *News*, July 17, 1878, 3; *Saturday Herald*, July 20, 1878, 1; "The Clem Reunion," *Saturday Herald*, July 27, 1878, 8.

31. *Saturday Herald*, July 6, 1878, 1; *News*, July 6, 1878, 4; "At Liberty Mrs. Clem, after Being Tried Five Times for Murder, Is Released," *Chicago Inter Ocean*, Apr. 30, 1874, 4; " 'L R' A Hoosier Celebrity: A Sketch of a Notable Home Personage—Miss Ream," *Sentinel*, June 8, 1874, 5; "A Pioneer Newspaper Woman," *Indianapolis Star*, Mar. 31, 1913, 6.

32. "What Shall Be Done?" *News*, July 17, 1878, 3; *North Vernon Plain Dealer*, July 11, 1878, 5; *Winchester Journal*, July 10, 1878, 2; *Journal*, July 6, 1878, 8; "Executive Clemency," *Sentinel*, July 30, 1878, 3.

33. *Saturday Herald*, July 20, 1878, 1; "Return of W. J. Abrams from the Penitentiary," *Sentinel*, July 18, 1878, 8; "The Abrams Release," July 5, 1878, 4; "Additional City News: Return of William J. Abrams," *News*, July 18, 1878, 1; "The Return of Abrams," *Journal*, July 18, 1878, 8. The man who introduced himself as an old friend of Abrams's family was actually a reporter for the *Journal*.

34. "Death of Nancy E. Clem," *News*, June 8, 1897, 8; "Another Squeal," *Saturday Herald*, Aug. 31, 1878, 6; "Indianapolis Letter: Some Unwritten History Concerning Mrs. Clem," *Cincinnati Enquirer*, Dec. 29, 1876, 4.

35. "The Clem Litigation Again—The Law's Delay," *Saturday Herald*, Feb. 1, 1879, 3. The author of this ostensibly disinterested commentary was H. W. Cook. "A Scene from a Modern Celebrated Case," *Saturday Herald*, Jan. 1, 1879, 5.

36. "Elbow Shots," *Saturday Herald*, Feb. 8, 1879, 1; "Mrs. Clem Again in Court," *Sentinel*, Apr. 23, 1879, 8.

37. "The Guetig Case: The Murderer of Mary McGlew to Be Tried Tomorrow: A Review of the Tragedy," *Sentinel*, Nov. 18, 1878, 3; *Saturday Herald*, June 14, 1879, 2.

38. "Elbow Shots," *Saturday Herald,* June 22, 1878; "Once More to the Front," *Sentinel*, June 14, 1878; "That Dreadful Woman," *Saturday Herald*, June 15, 1878; "A Tale of Gambling and Murder," *San Francisco Daily Evening Bulletin*, May 8, 1877.

39. *Saturday Herald*, July 20, 1878, 1; "The Return of Abrams," *Journal*, July 18, 1878, 8.

40. Burnett, "Last Pioneer Governor of Indiana," 127–128.

41. *Manufacturing and Mercantile Resources of Indianapolis*, 396, 496, 549, 633; Joan Hostetler, "Indianapolis Then & Now: Vance Block/Zipper Building/Broadbent Building," *Historic Indianapolis*, May 10, 2012, http://historicindianapolis.com/indianapolis-then-now-vance-blockzipper-buildingbroadbent-building/; William Robeson Holloway, *Indianapolis: A Historical and Statistical Sketch of the Railroad City* (Indianapolis: Indianapolis Journal Printers,

1870), 99; Cathleen F. Donnelly, "Denison Hotel," in *The Encyclopedia of Indianapolis*, ed. David J. Bodenhamer and Robert G. Barrows (Bloomington: Indiana University Press, 1994), 501; Dunn, *Greater Indianapolis*, 918; Francis H. Insley, *Indianapolis Literary Club: Summarized Record, 1877–1976* (Indianapolis: n.p., 1977), 1, 8, 9, 174, Indiana Historical Society.

42. Robert V. Robinson and Carl M. Briggs, "The Rise of Factories in Nineteenth-Century Indianapolis," *American Journal of Sociology* 97, no. 3 (Nov. 1991): 629–630; James H. Madison, "Economy," in Bodenhamer and Barrows, *Encyclopedia of Indianapolis*, 61–65; *Manufacturing and Mercantile Resources of Indianapolis, Indiana* (n. p.: n. p., 1883), 407, 528, 441, 466, 411–412, 530.

43. Emma Lou Thornbrough, *The Negro in Indiana before 1900*, 2nd ed. (Bloomington: Indiana University Press, 1993), 211, 229; Emma Lou Thornbrough, "African Americans," in Bodenhamer and Barrows, *Encyclopedia of Indianapolis*, 5–6; Hester Anne Hale, *Indianapolis: The First Century* (Indianapolis: Marion County Historical Society, 1987), 94–95, 106–107; Paul R. Mullins, "African-American Heritage in a Multicultural Community: An Archaeology of Race, Culture, and Consumption," in *Places in Mind: Public Archaeology as Applied Anthropology*, ed. Paul A. Shackel and Erve J. Chambers (New York: Routledge, 2004), 57–69.

44. Sievers, *Benjamin Harrison: Hoosier Statesman*, 67–68, 362; Calhoun, *Benjamin Harrison*, 54; "America's New President: Why and How He Was Elected," *Westminster Review* 121 (1889): 445–446.

45. "Fun House Facts," Benjamin Harrison Presidential Site, http://www.president benjaminharrison.org/learn/discover-the-house-that-ben-built/fun-house-facts; Timothy J. Sehr, "Three Gilded Age Suburbs of Indianapolis: Irvington, Brightwood, and Woodruff Place," *Indiana Magazine of History* 77, no. 4 (Dec. 1981): 305–332; Frederick D. Kershner Jr., "From Country Town to Industrial City The Urban Pattern in Indianapolis," *Indiana Magazine of History* 45, no. 4 (Dec. 1949): 327–338; George S. Cottman, "A Hoosier Arcadia," *Indiana Magazine of History* 28, no. 2 (June 1932): 96–113; Thornbrough, *Negro in Indiana before 1900*, 211, 229; Thornbrough, "African Americans," 6–7; Dunn, *Greater Indianapolis*, 434; Edward A. Leary, *Indianapolis: The Story of a City* (Indianapolis: Bobbs-Merrill, 1971), 136; Robert G. Barrows, "Beyond the Tenement: Patterns of American Urban Housing, 1870–1930," *Journal of Urban History* 9, no. 4 (Aug. 1982): 395–420.

46. "Nancy E. Clem! On Trial for Perjury and Found Guilty," *People*, Mar. 20, 1880, 1.

47. Clem's defense included three additional lawyers: James Cropsey, Henry Spaan, and F. M. Wright. "Mrs. Clem's Trial: A Jury Empannelled This Afternoon—The First Witness," *News*, Mar. 16, 1880, 4; *Annual Reports of the President, the Deans, and Other Officers of Miami University for 1915–1916* (Oxford, Ohio: Miami University, 1916); *Men and Women of America: A Biographical Dictionary of Contemporaries* (New York: L. Hamersly, 1910), 560; "John S. Duncan," *Indiana Magazine of History* 11, no. 1 (Mar. 1915): 85–86. The official records of Clem's 1880 trial for perjury have been lost.

48. *Saturday Herald*, Sept. 13, 1879, 7; Leander John Monks, *Courts and Lawyers of Indiana* (Indianapolis: Federal Publishing Company, 1916), 1:318, 3:1160, 1360; "Mrs. Clem's Trial," *News*, Mar. 16, 1880, 4; "Lizzie and Rachael Gohl," *News*, Mar. 12, 1880, 4.

49. "The Clem Case," *News*, Mar. 19, 1880, 1.

50. "City News," *News*, Mar. 19, 1880, 4; "Mrs. Clem Convicted: The Result of an Exciting Trial," *Saturday Herald*, Mar. 20, 1880.

51. "Elbow Shots" and "What the Herald Wants to See," *Saturday Herald*, Mar. 20, 1880, 1; "Effects of Destructive Cyclone in Indianapolis," *Daily Graphic*, Mar. 12, 1880, 107; *Saturday Herald*, Mar. 7, 1880, 1.

52. Mrs. Clem Convicted: The Result of an Exciting Trial," *Saturday Herald*, Mar. 20, 1880.

53. "Mrs. Clem Found Guilty," *News*, Mar. 20, 1880, 4.

Chapter 14 · Aunty Smith

1. Nicole Hahn Rafter, *Partial Justice: Women, Prisons, and Social Control*, 2nd. ed. (New Brunswick, N.J.: Rutgers University Press,1990), 31; "Indiana Female Reformatory. Unreliable Witnesses, but a Bad State of Affairs at Best," *Cincinnati Commercial*, Jan. 29, 1881, 1; *Cincinnati Commercial Tribune*, Jan. 29, 1881, 4. In 1877, after lobbying by Smith and other prison reformers, the state legislation decreed that all members of the board of managers be women. The only exception to the women-only rule was that the board of managers might assign the husband of a married superintendent to an administrative position. Smith's husband, James, served as the reformatory's steward. See "Indianapolis Letter," *Cincinnati Enquirer*, Feb. 7, 1877, 2, and Rafter, *Partial Justice*, 31. For a corrective to the standard narrative, see Michelle Jones, Lori Record, and Kelsey Kauffman, "Were Magdalene Laundries the First Women's Prisons in the US?" paper presented at the Indiana Association of Historians, Mar. 8, 2014.

2. "The Prison at Jeffersonville," *Cincinnati Daily Enquirer*, Mar. 1, 1869, 4; [J. Harrie Banka], *State Prison Life: By One Who Has Been There* (Cincinnati: C. F. Vent, 1871), 179–180, 254; Estelle B. Freedman, *Their Sisters' Keepers: Women's Prison Reform in America, 1830–1930* (Ann Arbor: University of Michigan Press, 1984), 16.

3. Rafter, *Partial Justice*, 30.

4. *Report of the Board of Managers of the Indiana Reformatory Institution for Women and Girls* (Indianapolis: R. J. Bright, 1871), 6.

5. Wendy Gamber, *The Boardinghouse in Nineteenth-Century America* (Baltimore: John Hopkins University Press, 2007), 140–157; Ellen Dwyer, *Homes for the Mad: Life inside Two Nineteenth-Century Asylums* (New Brunswick, N.J.: Rutgers University Press, 1987), esp. 1–5, 57–75; Peggy Pascoe, *Relations of Rescue: The Search for Female Moral Authority in the American West, 1874–1939* (New York: Oxford University Press, 1990); Anne M. Boylan, *The Origins of Women's Activism: New York and Boston, 1797–1840* (Chapel Hill: University of North Carolina Press, 2002); Rafter, *Partial Justice*, 32.

6. Rafter, *Partial Justice*. 30–32; *Annual Report of the Board of Managers of the Indiana Reformatory Institution for Women and Girls* (Indianapolis: Wm. B. Burford, 1882), 16.

7. "Indiana," *Chicago Daily Inter Ocean*, Jan. 27, 1881, 3; "Investigation," *Indiana State Sentinel*, Feb. 2, 1881, 4.

8. *Annual Report of the Board of Managers of the Indiana Reformatory Institution for Women and Girls* (Indianapolis: Wm. B. Burford, 1881), 13; *Cincinnati Commercial*, Jan. 29, 1881, 4.

9. *Annual Report of the Board of Managers of the Indiana Reformatory* (1881), 13–14.

10. Michelle Jones, "Women's Prison History: The Undiscovered Country," *Perspectives on History* (Feb. 2015): 42–43; Leslie Hauk, Kim Baldwin, Lori Fussner, and Kelsey Kauffman, "Controversial Heroes," and Anastazia Schmid, Shelley Dillman, Cynthia Long, and Kelsey Kauffman, "Captive Patients: Dr. Theophilus Parvin and the Indiana Women's Prison," papers presented at the Indiana Association of Historians, Mar. 8, 2014; "Investigation," *Indiana State Sentinel*, Feb. 2, 1881, 4; "Hoosier Reform, as Seen in an Indiana Institution: Inhuman Cruelty Practiced Upon Women and Girls," *Cincinnati Enquirer*, Jan. 14, 1881, 2; "The Reformatory Investigation," *Cincinnati Daily Gazette*, Jan. 28, 1881, 1; "Indianapolis: Investigation of the State Female Reformatory," *Cincinnati Commercial*, Feb. 2, 1881, 4; "Again the Talk of the Investigating Committee Is Heard in the Land: Proceedings of The Investigation," *Sentinel*, Jan. 25, 1881, 5; "Indianapolis, Indiana: Legislative Acts/Legal Proceedings," *Cincinnati Commercial*, Jan. 27, 1881, 2; "The Indiana Female Reformatory," *Kansas City Evening Star*, Jan. 28, 1881, 1; *Cincinnati Commercial*, Jan. 29, 1881, 4; "Another Andersonville: Investigation of the Indiana Female Reformatory," *Cincinnati Commercial*, Jan. 28, 1881, 1.

11. "Indiana," *Chicago Inter Ocean*, Jan. 27, 1881, 3; "The Reformatory Investigation," *Cincinnati Daily Gazette*, Jan. 27, 1881, 2; "The Reformatory," *Journal*, Jan. 27, 1881, 8.

12. "Again the Talk of the Investigating Committee is Heard in the Land," *Sentinel*, Jan. 25, 1881, 5; "The Female Prison," *Cincinnati Daily Gazette*, Feb. 4, 1881, 2; "Indiana Investigations," *Cincinnati Enquirer* Feb 14, 1881, 5; *Cincinnati Commercial*, Jan. 29, 1881, 4; "The Reformatory," *Journal*, Feb. 3, 1881, 5.

13. "Indiana Affairs: The State Reformatory Investigation—How Female Prisoners Are Treated," *Cincinnati Daily Gazette*, Feb. 8, 1881, 2; "Indianapolis: Female Reformatory Investigation," *Cincinnati Commercial*, Feb. 7, 1881, 4; "The Other Side of the Story about the Alleged Cruel Treatment toward the Reformatory Inmates," *Sentinel*, Feb. 5, 1881, 5; "Indiana Female Reformatory," *Chicago Inter Ocean*, Feb. 5, 1881, 2; "The Reformatory Investigation," *Cincinnati Daily Gazette*, Feb. 5, 1881, 4.

14. *Annual Report of the Board of Managers of the Indiana Reformatory* (1881), 13–14; "Indianapolis Female Reformatory Investigation," *Cincinnati Commercial*; Feb. 7, 1881, 4; "Local Brevities," *Sentinel* Apr. 5, 1881, 8; "The Other Side of the Story," *Sentinel*, Feb. 5, 1881, 5; "The Female Reformatory: Newspaper Comment upon Mrs. Rhoda M. Coffin's Resignation," *Sentinel*, Apr. 7, 1881, 8.

15. *Annual Report of the Board of Managers of the Indiana Reformatory Institution for Women and Girls* (Indianapolis: Wm. B. Burford, 1884), 21.

16. *Annual Report of the Board of Managers of the Indiana Reformatory* (1881), 14.

17. Federal Manuscript Population Census, 1880, Indianapolis, roll 295, pp. 273B, 274A, 274B, 275C, 275D.

18. Rev. John Dudley, "Harvest of the Great Revival," *Congregationalist* (Boston), Aug. 3, 1881, 2; "The Evangelist: A Red Letter Day in the Mission Work of Rev. George O. Barnes," *Sentinel*, Sept. 3, 1882, 4.

19. "Indiana: Insubordination in the Female Reformatory," *Cincinnati Commercial*, Jan. 2, 1883, 2; "Rebellious Prisoners: Insubordination in an Indiana Female Reformatory," *Daily American* (Nashville), Jan. 3, 1883, 1.

20. Virginia Dill McCarty, "From Petticoat Slavery to Equality: Women's Rights in Indiana Law," in *The History of Indiana Law*, ed. David J. Bodenhamer and Randall T. Shepard (Athens: Ohio University Press, 2006), 177–192, esp. 181–182; "Frank Clem Asks a Divorce," *News*, Mar. 23, 1883, 4; "Indiana. Nancy Clem's Husband Seeks a Divorce," *Chicago Daily Tribune*, Mar. 24, 1883, 7; *News*, Apr. 4, 1883, 4; "Items from Indianapolis," *St. Louis Globe-Democrat*, Apr. 9, 1883, 4; "The Notorious Nancy F. Clem Defendant in Divorce Proceedings," *Cincinnati Enquirer*, Mar. 24, 1883, 5; "The Notorious Mrs. Clem Again a Single Woman," *Cincinnati Enquirer* Apr. 8, 1883, 2.

21. "Mrs. Nancy E. Clem: What She Has to Say of the New Complications in the Affairs of the Clems—Developments about to Be Made," *News*, May 10, 1883, 4.

22. "The Notorious Mrs. Clem and the Young Murder," *St. Louis Globe-Democrat*, May 8, 1883, 2; "Mrs. Albert Patton's Dowery Interest," *News*, May 8, 1883, 1; "Mrs. Nancy E. Clem: What She Has to Say," *News*, May 10, 1883, 4; "Mrs. Nancy E. Clem: She Corroborates the Statements of Her Daughter-in-Law, Mrs. Patton," *Chicago Daily Tribune*, May 11, 1883, 8; "Mrs. Clem Again," *Louisville Courier-Journal*, May 13, 1883, 15; "Fresh Outbreak in the Clem Family," *Cincinnati Enquirer*, May 8, 1883, 1; "The Irrepressible Claims," *Jeffersonville Daily Evening News*, May 11, 1883. Mrs. Beulah F. Patten, died June 29, 1889, Cook County, Illinois, Marriage and Death Indexes, 1833–1889 (online database, Ancestry.com, 2011), http://search.ancestry.com/search/db .aspx?dbid=2433. No records survive to indicate whether the Pattons actually divorced.

Chapter 15 · Mrs. Dr. Patterson

1. "Release of Mrs. Clem," *Indianapolis News*, Sept. 11, 1883, 1; "Indiana: Mrs. Clem," *Chicago Tribune*, Sept. 12, 1883, 9; "Mrs. Clem's Release from Prison," *St. Louis Globe-Democrat*, Sept. 12, 1883, 6.

2. "Western," *Postville (Iowa) Post*, Sept. 21, 1883, 4; "City News," *News*, Sept. 13, 1883, 3; *R. L. Polk & Co.'s Indianapolis City Directory for 1889* (Indianapolis: R. L. Polk, 1889), 239; *R. L. Polk & Co.'s Indianapolis City Directory for 1890* (Indianapolis: R. L. Polk, 1890), 243; *R. L. Polk & Co.'s Indianapolis City Directory for 1891* (Indianapolis: R. L. Polk, 1891), 243; *R. L. Polk & Co.'s Indianapolis City Directory for 1892* (Indianapolis: R. L. Polk, 1892), 252; *Indianapolis Sanborn Map, 1887*, Plate 51, Indianapolis Sanborn Map and Baist Atlas Collection, Center for Digital Scholarship, Indiana University–Purdue University, Indianapolis Library, http://indiamond6.ulib.iupui.edu/cdm/singleitem/collection/SanbornJP2/id/370/rec/55.

3. "Western," *Postville (Iowa) Post*, Sept. 21, 1883, 4; "Nancy Raises Objections," *Chicago Daily Inter Ocean*, June 24, 1887; "A Singular Divorce Suit," *New York Times*, June 24, 1887, 5; "An Old Case Revived," *Chicago Tribune*, June 24, 1887, 3; *Caron's Directory of the City of Louisville for 1884* (Louisville: C. K. Caron, 1884), 190; *Caron's Directory of the City of Louisville for 1888* (Louisville: C. K. Caron, 1888), 1287; *Caron's Directory of the City of Louisville for 1891* (Louisville: C. K. Caron, 1891), 263, 1884; *Caron's Directory of the City of Louisville for 1893* (Louisville: C. K. Caron, 1893), 264; "Musty Pages of History Opened," *Jeffersonville National Democrat*, Dec. 6, 1899, 4; "Clem's Chest Was Opened," *Brownstown Banner*, Jan. 19, 1899, 3; marriage, Frank Clem and Jennie Rich, Indiana Marriage Index, 1800–1941 (online database, Ancestry.com, 2005), http://search.ancestry.com/search/db.aspx?dbid=5059; "The Money of Mrs. Clem," *Indianapolis Journal*, June 10, 1897, 8.

4. "City News," *News*, Mar. 31, 1883, 3; *Polk & Co.'s Indianapolis City Directory for 1884* (Indianapolis: R. L. Polk & Co, 1884), 292; *News*, June 10, 1897, 8.

5. Marriage, William Patton and Carrie Booth, Indiana Marriage Index.

6. U.S. House of Representatives, *Annual Report of the Commissioner of Patents for the Year 1888* (Washington, D.C.: Government Printing Office, 1889), 666; *The Druggists' Circular and Chemical Gazette* 33, no. 1 (Jan. 1889): 24; "Fire Force Veteran Victim of Paralysis," *Indianapolis Star*, Nov. 8, 1915, 15.

7. Sarah Stage, *Female Complaints: Lydia Pinkham and the Business of Women's Medicine* (New York: W. W. Norton, 1979), esp. 64–92, 102; Kyle J. Fernandez, "'No Lady Need Despair': Abortion, Pharmaceuticals, and the Regulation of Birth Control Commerce" (PhD diss. in progress, Indiana University); for various advertisements, see *Logansport (Ind.) Journal*, June 14, 1888, 3; *Indianapolis Freeman*, Aug. 17, 1889, 6; and *Star*, Sept. 16, 1915, 12. "Mrs. Clem Tells Her Tale," *News*, Dec. 15, 1892, 2.

8. Andrea Tone, *Devices and Desires: A History of Contraceptives in America* (New York: Hill & Wang, 2001), 13–16, 25–42, 47–66, 82–86; *Indianapolis Freeman*, Aug. 17, 1889, 6.

9. "Fire Force Veteran Victim of Paralysis," *Star*, Nov. 8, 1915, 15; "Funeral of Mrs. Clem," *News*, June 10, 1897, 8. Early-twentieth-century advertisements for Slavin's Infallible Female Tonic advised potential customers to contact Mrs. Vogt; see, for example *Star*, Sept. 8. 1915, 12. Federal Manuscript Population Census (hereafter FMPC), 1900, Indianapolis, roll 338, p. 8A; *Annual Message of Joseph E. Bell, Mayor of Indianapolis, with Annual Reports of Heads of Departments of the City of Indianapolis for the Year Ending December 31, 1915* (Indianapolis: Sentinel Printing Co., 1916), 277.

10. "Funeral of Mrs. Clem," *News*, June 9, 1897, 8; United States Bureau of the Census, *Historical Statistics of the United States: Colonial Times to 1957* (Washington, D.C.: U.S. Government Printing Office, 1960), Series D589, 91.

11. "Funeral of Mrs. Clem," *News*, June 10, 1897, 8.

12. "Site of Young Murder," *Journal*, June 11, 1897, 8; "The Money of Mrs. Clem," *Journal*, June 10, 1897, 8. See, for example, *Indianapolis Freeman*, Aug. 17, 1889, 6; Aug. 24, 1889, 6; and Sept. 14, 1889, 7.

13. The Money of Mrs. Clem," *Journal*, June 10, 1897, 8.

14. "Biographical Sketch," Cassius M. C. Willis Collection, Indiana Historical Society, Indianapolis; Wilma L. Gibbs, "African American Business," in *Encyclopedia of Indianapolis*, ed. David Jo. Bodenhamer, Robert G. Barrows, and David Gordon Vanderstel (Bloomington: Indiana University Press, 1994), 234.

15. Indiana Deaths, 1882–1920 (online database, Ancestry.com, 2004), http://search.ancestry.com/search/db.aspx?dbid=7834; "Medication by Mrs. Clem," *News*, Dec. 14, 1892, 2.

16. "Police Searching for Mrs. Nancy Clem," *Chicago Tribune*, Dec. 15, 1892, 2; "Crimes and Casualties: A Search for a Female Doctor," *New Orleans Daily Picayune*, Dec. 15, 1892, 2; "News Notes by Wire," *New York Herald*, Dec. 15, 1892, 8; "The Clem Case Recalled," *Sandusky Daily Register*, Dec. 15, 1892, 1; "Alleged Doctress Wanted," *Connersville Daily News*, Dec. 15, 1892, 4.

17. "Mrs. Clem Testifies," *Journal*, Dec. 16, 1892, 8; "Mrs. Clem Tells Her Tale," *News*, Dec. 15, 1892, 2.

18. *Journal*, Dec. 15, 1892, 2.

19. "Mrs. Clem Tells Her Tale," *News*, Dec. 15, 1892, 2.

20. Ibid.

21. "Mrs. Clem Testifies," *Journal*, Dec. 16, 1892, 8; "Mrs. Clem Tells Her Tale," *News*, Dec. 15, 1892, 2. The *News* noted the coroner's plans to subject the formula to chemical analysis but failed to report the results.

22. "Mrs. Clem Tells Her Tale," *News*, Dec. 15, 1892, 2; "Very Mysterious Death," *Journal*, Dec. 15, 1892, 8; "Sore Feet: Novel Cure Prescribed for Them Kills the Patient," *Cincinnati Enquirer*, Dec. 15, 1892, 1.

23. See Stage, *Female Complaints*. According to the 1880 manuscript census, John Martin could neither read nor write, and Amanda Martin could read but not write. FMPC, 1880, Indianapolis, roll 295, p. 166C.

24. George Bacon Wood, *A Treatise on the Practice of Medicine*, 5th ed. (Philadelphia: George Lippincott, 1858), 2:224–226; "Death of Matthew Hartman," *Journal*, Aug. 7, 1892, 1.6; *News*, Aug. 8, 1892, 8; *Journal*, Aug. 8, 1892, 5.

25. Edward A. Leary, *Indianapolis: The Story of a City* (Indianapolis: Bobbs-Merrill, 1971), 136; "The Lesson of the Indianapolis Street Car Strike," *New Nation*, Mar. 5, 1892, 148; "The Lessons of the Strike," *Clay-Worker*, Mar. 15, 1892, 359.

26. "Death of Nancy E. Clem," *News*, June 9, 1897, 8; "Funeral of Mrs. Clem," *News*, June 10, 1897, 8; "The Money of Mrs. Clem," *Journal*, June 10, 1897, 8; "Nancy E. Clem Dead," *Journal*, June 9, 1897, 5; Nancy Clem burial permit, Crown Hill Cemetery, Indianapolis.

27. "Nancy E. Clem Dead," *Journal*, June 9, 1897, 5; "The Money of Mrs. Clem," *Journal*, June 10, 1897, 8. It is, of course, possible that the Slavins were Protestants; relevant obituaries do not mention religious affiliation.

28. *Journal*, June 10, 1897, 8. Minelda Slavin married in April 1897. Lillie May did not marry until 1899, so she must have been the "Miss Slavin" to whom the *Journal* referred. Marriages, Minelda L. Slavin and Charles H. Lindstrom, Lillie M. Slavin and Henry G. Vogt, Indiana Marriage Index; "Death of Nancy E. Clem," *News*, June 9, 1897, 8.

29. "Funeral of Mrs. Clem," *News*, June 10, 1897, 8; "The Money of Mrs. Clem," *Journal*, June 10, 1897, 8.

30. "Funeral of Mrs. Clem," *News*, June 10, 1897, 8; "Relics of Barbarism," *News*, Mar. 13, 1883; Newman Ivey White, ed., *The Frank C. Brown Collection of North Carolina Folklore*, vol. 7 (Durham, N.C.: Duke University Press, 1977), 92; lot book, Crown Hill Cemetery.

31. "Mrs. Clem Had No Money in Bank," *Journal*, June 11, 1897, 8.

Epilogue

1. Charles W. Calhoun, *Benjamin Harrison* (New York: Henry Holt, 2005), 66, 73, 92; Nicole Etcheson, *A Generation at War: The Civil War Era in a Northern Community* (Lawrence: University Press of Kansas, 2011), 211–212.

2. Patrick R. Pearsey, *A History of Our Neighborhood* ([Indianapolis]: [P. R. Pearsey], 1987), 5, Indiana Historical Society; "Home Notes," *Indianapolis Sentinel*, Jan. 13, 1879, 8; "Wm. J. Abrams Dies at the Soldiers' Home," *Indianapolis News*, June 2, 1910, 3. The *News* article contains the only mention of Abrams's janitorial career; it's possible that the story is apocryphal.

3. John H. Dundas, *Nehama County* (Auburn, Neb.: n.p., 1902), 10; Federal Manuscript Population Census (hereafter FMPC), 1880, Peru, Nemaha County, Nebraska, roll 752, p. 100B. Newspaper accounts claimed that Margaret Abrams remarried, reportedly to an Indianapolis man, and lived "in the southern part of the city." See, for example, *Indianapolis Journal*, July 18, 1878, 8, and *People* (Indianapolis), July 20, 1878, 5. No evidence survives to tell us to whom. She might have died before the state of Indiana began keeping death records in 1882—part of the same bureaucratic apparatus that exposed Mrs. Dr. Patterson's true identity. Or the former Margaret Abrams might have lived for decades, shielded from publicity and historians' scrutiny by her new name.

4. Rolston-master-dec-2014 family tree, Ancestry.com, http://trees.ancestry.com/tree /75792433/person/3633305648.

5. Dundas, *Nehama County*, 213.

6. William J. Abrams, in U.S., Civil War Pension Index: General Index to Pension Files, 1861–1934 (online database, Ancestry.com, 2000), http://search.ancestry.com/search/db.aspx ?dbid=4654.

7. William J. Abrams, application for admission to Indiana State Soldiers' Home, Indiana State Archives, Indianapolis; "The State Soldiers' Home," *Journal*, June 7, 1897, 6; Marion Registers, 5292, Leavenworth Registers, 10884, Sawtelle Registers, 5003, Danville Registers, 7093, in U.S. National Homes for Disabled Volunteer Soldiers, 1866–1938 (online database, Ancestry.com, 2007), http://search.ancestry.com/search/db.aspx?dbid=1200; Patrick J. Kelly, *Creating a National Home: Building the Veterans' Welfare State, 1860–1900* (Cambridge, Mass.: Harvard University Press, 1997), esp. 4–5, 99–102.

8. Abrams, application for admission to Indiana State Soldiers' Home.

9. *News*, June 2, 1910, 3; "Figured in Murder Case," *Fort Wayne Sentinel*, June 2, 1910.

10. Jacob Piatt Dunn, *Greater Indianapolis: The History, the Industries, the Institutions, and the People of a City of Homes* (Chicago: Lewis Publishing, 1910), 1:434; Indianapolis Baist Atlas Plan #5 (1908), Indianapolis Sanborn Map and Baist Atlas Collection, Center for Digital Scholarship, Indiana University–Purdue University, Indianapolis Libraries, http://indiamond6 .ulib.iupui.edu/cdm/singleitem/collection/SanbornJP2/id/2275.

11. Max R. Hyman, ed., *Hyman's Handbook of Indianapolis: An Outline History* (Indianapolis: M. R. Hyman Company, 1907), 64; Connie J. Zeigler, "Indianapolis Amusement Parks, 1903–1911: Landscapes on the Edge" (MA thesis, Indiana University, 2007), esp. 30–37.

12. "The Return of Abrams," *Journal*, July 18, 1878, 8; "A Pump with a History," *News*, June 30, 1906, 16; "In Order to Encourage the 'Water-Wagon' Movement, the City Is Restoring Pumps in Many Downtown Wells," *News*, July 14, 1906, 12; "Old Town Pump Passes," *News*, May 19, 1914, 20; "Long Arm John," *News*, June 24, 1922, 19; Timothy J. Sehr, "Three Gilded Age Suburbs of Indianapolis: Irvington, Brightwood, and Woodruff Place," *Indiana Magazine of History* 77, no. 4 (Dec. 1981): 305–332.

13. James H. Madison, "Economy," in *The Encyclopedia of Indianapolis*, ed. David J. Bodenhamer and Robert G. Barrows (Bloomington: Indiana University Press, 1994), 63–54; Robert V. Robinson and Carl M. Briggs, "The Rise of Factories in Nineteenth-Century

Indianapolis," *American Journal of Sociology,* 97, no. 3 (Nov. 1991): 632; "Hon. John Hanna," *News,* Oct. 24, 1882, 4.; Oscar Carleton McCulloch, *The Tribe of Ishmael: A Study in Social Degradation,* 4th ed. (Indianapolis: Charity Organization Society, 1891), 4–5; Brian Siegel, "Tales of the Tribe of Ishmael: A Research Note," *Indiana Magazine of History* 106, no. 2 (June 2010): 189–196; Nathaniel Deutsch, *Inventing America's "Worst" Family: Eugenics, Islam, and the Fall and Rise of the Tribe of Ishmael* (Berkeley: University of California Press, 2009). My thanks to Anastazia Schmid.

14. "Aaron Clem Dead," *News,* Oct. 14, 1901, 10; "Clem Grocery Corner," *News,* May 3, 1897, 5; Frederick D. Kershner Jr., "From Country Town to Industrial City: The Urban Pattern in Indianapolis," *Indiana Magazine of History* 45, no. 4 (Dec. 1949): 329.

15. For a small sampling of newspaper reports on confidence games, see "A Neat Confidence Game," *Journal,* Feb. 11, 1880, 8; "Louis Grafflin," *Journal,* June 18, 1881, 8; "The Gigantic Confidence Game," *Indianapolis Evening Minute,* Oct. 15, 1885, 2; "Edward Delaney," *Journal,* Aug. 5, 1881, 8; "Charles S. Thompson," *Indianapolis Sun,* Jan. 23, 1889, 1; "An Old Confidence Game," *Sentinel,* May 8, 1889, 1; "Eli's Confidence Game," *Sentinel,* Aug. 21, 1889, 7; "City Life," *Sun,* Sept. 24, 1889, 1; "Joe Trince," *Sun,* Aug. 31, 1893, 1; "Held on Swindling Charge," *News,* Nov. 28, 1909, 5; and "Pays $200 for Some Imitation Diamonds," *News,* June 4, 1910, 3. "Newcastle's Rise in Business World," *News,* Apr. 20, 1907, 2; "An Eccentric Bachelor," *Indianapolis Patriot Phalanx,* Nov. 4, 1897, 5; "The Real Captains of Industry," *Sun,* Apr. 16, 1902, 4; "Just the Story of a Man," *Sun,* May 10, 1904, 4; "Far from It," *News,* Dec. 30, 1907, 6; "Financial," *Indianapolis Star,* Sept. 11, 1908; "Money to Loan," *Sun,* Sept. 13, 1897, 7; "How the Professional Money Lenders Conduct Their Business," *Indianapolis Monroe's Iron Clad Age,* Apr. 16, 1887, 3. See Suzanne Lebsock, *A Murder in Virginia: Southern Justice on Trial* (New York: W. W. Norton, 2003), 13,130.

16. Mary Ashton Rice Livermore, *What Shall We Do with Our Daughters? Superfluous Women, and Other Lectures* (Boston: Lee & Shepard, 1883), 111, 60.

17. Martha Louise Rayne, *What Can a Woman Do?* (1893; repr., New York: Arno Press, 1974).

18. Rebecca Edwards, *Angels in the Machinery: Gender in American Party Politics from the Civil War to the Progressive Era* (New York: Oxford University Press, 1997), esp. 59–61.

19. Mark Wahlgren Summers, *A Dangerous Stir: Fear, Paranoia, and the Making of Reconstruction* (Chapel Hill: University of North Carolina Press, 2009), 83; Kenneth M. Stampp, *Indiana Politics during the Civil War* (1949; rpnt., Bloomington: Indiana University Press, 1978), 211; Etcheson, *Generation at War,* 175,191; Gordon speech, *People,* Nov. 16, 1878, 5; "Fishback on Grant," *News,* May 13, 1872, 1.

20. Hyman, *Hyman's Handbook of Indianapolis,* 64; Paul R. Mullins, "African-American Heritage in a Multicultural Community: An Archaeology of Race, Culture, and Consumption," in *Places in Mind: Public Archaeology as Applied Anthropology,* ed. Paul A. Shackel and Erve J. Chambers (New York: Routledge, 2004), 64; Zeigler, "Indianapolis Amusement Parks, 1903–1911," 2, 84–85, 98.

21. "Found Dead in Bathroom," *Star,* Sept. 22, 1915, 1; "Found Dead in Bathroom," *News,* Sept. 22, 1915, 1.

22. "Found Dead in Bathroom," *News,* Sept. 22, 1915, 1; "Fight against Notoriety," *News,* Sept. 24, 1915.

23. Albert's will, dated December 18, 1912, named his "daughter, Daisy F. Patton," as his sole heir. A "Daisey Patten," who worked as a servant for a German family in Indianapolis, surfaces in the 1900 census but does not appear in the 1910 census. A "Miss Daisy Patton," age twenty-three, married James F. Logan on June 18, 1908, in Chicago, a likely location given that city was Beulah Patton's last known residence. Of course Albert's will specified Daisy Patton not Daisy Logan, but if he and his daughter were estranged, it is possible he had

not learned of her marriage at the time he made his will. The only subsequent census records for Daisy and James Logan, however, are for a different couple who married at later ages; the wife's maiden name was Collett, not Patton. William Albert Patton, Last Will and Testament, Dec. 18, 1912, Marion County Wills, Box 195, Indiana State Archives; FMPC, 1900, Indianapolis, roll 390, p. 3A; Cook County, Illinois, Marriages Index, 1871–1920 (online database, Ancestry.com, 2011), http://search.ancestry.com/search/db.aspx?dbid=2556; FMPC, 1920, Brookville, Franklin County, Indiana, roll T625-430, p. 4B; burial locator, Crown Hill Cemetery, Indianapolis, Indiana, http://www.crownhill.org/locate/. Thanks to Tom Davis, Crown Hill Cemetery tour developer, for this observation. Davis, email message to author, Nov. 16, 2006.

24. Geoffrey C. Ward, *A Disposition to Be Rich: How a Small-Town Pastor's Son Ruined an American President, Brought on a Wall Street Crash, and Made Himself the Best-Hated Man in the United States* (New York: Knopf, 2012), 119, 146–271. "Stealing by Wholesale," appeared in several Indiana newspapers, including the *Newport Hoosier State*, July 8, 1885, 4; the *Brazil Clay County Enterprise*, July 8, 1885, 4, and the *Critic* (Logansport, Ind.), July 12, 1885, 2. "Nancy E. Clem Dead," *Journal*, June 9, 1897, 5; "Many Memories Stirred by Robert Underwood Johnson," *News*, Nov. 21, 1923, 22; "Old Alabama Street House Still Holds Mystery of Famous Clem Murder Case," *Star*, Sec. 2, Aug. 30, 1930, 22; "Counterpart Here for Mrs. Chadwick," *Indianapolis Morning Star*, Dec. 25, 1904, 8; "Old Reporter's Reminiscences," *News*, June 9, 1906, 14. It is possible but highly unlikely that Clem and Ward ever met. Clem was incarcerated in the Marion County Jail during Ward's two weeks as an Indianapolis bank clerk.

25. "Death of Nancy E. Clem," *News*, June 9, 1897, 8; *Star*, Nov. 7, 1971, A5, B3; James Trofatter, *Cold-Blooded* (performed Oct. 2014) and *Cold-Blooded at Cold Spring: The Third Trial* (performed Oct. 2008).

26. *News*, June 9, 1897; Catherine Ross Nickerson, " 'The Deftness of Her Sex': Innocence, Guilt, and Gender in the Trial of Lizzie Borden," in *Lethal Imagination: Violence and Brutality in American History*, ed. Michael A. Bellesiles (New York: New York University Press, 1999): 260–281; A. Cheree Carlson, *The Crimes of Womanhood: Defining Femininity in a Court of Law* (Urbana: University of Illinois Press, 2008), 85–110.

27. Timothy R Mahoney, "The Great Sheedy Murder Trial and the Booster Ethos of the Gilded Age in Lincoln," *Nebraska History* 82 (Winter 2001): 163–79; Janet L. Langlois, *Belle Gunness: The Lady Bluebeard* (Bloomington: Indiana University Press, 1985).

28. "Mrs. Clem," *New York Times*, Jan. 2, 1869, 2; *News*, June 10, 1897.

Page numbers in *italics* refer to illustrations.